Cape Breton Lives

Cape Breton
LIVES

A BOOK FROM **CAPE BRETON'S MAGAZINE**
EDITED BY RONALD CAPLAN

Unless otherwise noted, all photographs are by Ronald Caplan. The photograph on page 83 is by Clara Dennis. It first appeared in her *Cape Breton Over*, and is taken from the collection of the Public Archives of Nova Scotia. The photographs of dory-fishing are by William Frederick Wallace, from the collection of the Nova Scotia Museum of the Atlantic. The photograph of soldiers, page 150, is courtesy the Beaton Institute, University College of Cape Breton.

For help in preparation of this book, thanks to Bonnie Thompson (Indian Brook), Eleanor Vokey (Coxheath), Weldon Bona (Sydney), and Mary Ann Wilson (Tarbot Vale). The darkroom work is by Carol Kennedy, Murray Road, Cape Breton Island.

Canadian Cataloguing in Publication Data
Main Entry under title:
Cape Breton Lives
(Canada's Atlantic Folklore-Folklife Series, ISSN 0708-4226
ISBN 0-920911-47-1 (bound)
ISBN 0-920911-49-8 (paper)
1. Nova Scotia — interviews. 2. Cape Breton Island (Nova Scotia) — Biography. I. Caplan, Ronald. II. Series: Canada's Atlantic Folklore and Folklife Series.
FC2343.3.A1C3 1988   971.6'9'00992   C89-098502-2
F1039.C2C3 1988

Breakwater gratefully acknowledges the support of The Canada Council.

Contents

Editor's Introduction

The last, long visit I had with Red Dan and Mary Smith, Red Dan stretched out on the couch, a cigarette in the corner of his mouth, and he worked on remembering. It was a conversation, with a stop for tea and questions about our neighbours, Red Dan talking about other people's rumrunning, work with his father, and a time aboard a schooner in a terrific storm out of Gloucester. "By God, now this is something," he said, pulling me in—striking on that story after hours of what might be considered just talk. And it *was* something. It was not part of his usual repertoire. The fact of our being together, and his wanting to come up with a unit called "story," encouraged him to dig this out.

Red Dan Smith shook my hand as I left and said to me, "You made a good visit." And all the way home I thought about that. Not that I had "paid" a visit, or that we had "shared" a visit—but that I had "made" one, *we* had, we had created one together, talking and letting the other talk, reaching for more and giving the stories shape. I thought of the poet Robert Duncan's definition of responsibility, as maintaining the ability to respond. And I realized that conversation wasn't simply a reservoir to be tapped but an active creation, an act of creation. And I thought of conversation as one more way we encourage life in one another. And I had a clearer understanding of the role of the other, myself, in these engagements.

Oh, arguably it is not a "natural" situation. I am not rooted in this place, Cape Breton Island, and in some random but serious way I travel the island with a tape recorder and camera, my eye focused on the person I'm with but also on the next issue of *Cape Breton's Magazine*. But it is my life, and theirs—and after 16 years of it, it is as natural a relationship as it's going to be. And one in which I am continually grateful to be involved.

To get back to Red Dan and the visit we made—one that doesn't happen to be included in this book—I realized once again that conversations do not just happen. They take effort, theirs and mine. Some stories are told for the first time—because I asked or because something in our being together called them up—and some are stories they've worked on for years. I am sure that it is the process of storytelling, that we are watching what may be traditional tale in the making—if only we keep talking, hearing old lines re-used and the events re-created slightly differently each time, each time, just that much more finely honed. And I'm there to tape one more step in the process, otherwise known as living together, talking, passing the time. I want to apply no less and no more to the conversations offered in this book.

There is no particular purity in these conversations. Most of the people knew they might appear in *Cape Breton's Magazine*. And as for myself, I knew I'd eventually transcribe the tape, develop the photos, look for collateral materials in archives or a family album—and then I'd go out and sell the ads. I'd stop for a period of editing, ideas and final layout with Bonnie Thompson, send it off to the printer—and turn back to search for more stories, further conversation.

Conversation. It is as informal and as rigorous as it sounds. It's a word I like very much. It's very much at the heart of *Cape Breton's Magazine*, and I think it's the reason the magazine has survived for 16 years.

I had the idea—that of letting Cape Bretoners speak directly—while driving out that obdurate spit of land from Jersey Cove toward the Englishtown Ferry in 1972. I designed *Cape Breton's Magazine* as I drove. To be seen, it had to be the biggest thing on the newsstand. So I made it 10 by 14 inches—something like a tabloid newspaper but bound as a magazine. Black-and-white was both sound economics and another way of standing out against multi-coloured magazines. I used newsprint for economy and put my money on high-quality coated cover stock to both protect it and print the photos extremely well. I wanted big photos and plenty of them. I put in the "apostrophe s" as a kind of prayer, that it eventually would become Cape Breton's magazine. And I decided I would not write about Cape Bretoners but instead would offer their stories in the words in which I found them.

Oral testimony. Oral history. Conversation became the heart of the work.

The chapters in this book, *Cape Breton Lives*, do not fairly represent the mix of an issue of the magazine. These chapters would normally be found among traditional tales, natural history, scholarly work, music, diaries and travel descriptions reprinted from various sources. But they do represent, as I say, not only the central idea of the magazine, but what I suspect most sustains the publication and most sustains me—the conversations and the life stories out of which these chapters were born.

For me, I still see the chapters as separate units. I see them as Katie Margaret Gillis and Dan Alex MacLeod, Mike Oleschuk, Clarence and Mary Lashley, Archie Neil Chisholm and Bill Daye—every one of them a person who troubled to talk to me directly and in detail. I am still honoured and amazed by the seriousness with which this continuing work is taken. That people continue to take their time, and give their time, and at length.

It comes down to a book I have put together. *Cape Breton Lives*. I like the order, but these conversations can be read in any order. It can justifiably be seen as part of a growing portrait of Cape Breton. Or simply as something to read. A chapter. A life. A night. Passing the time.

·   ·   ·

A few words regarding the editing. I have edited toward a readable format. I have omitted my part in the conversation except where it seemed necessary for clarity. These chapters are edited down from texts in the magazine, themselves edited from tapes of from one to several visits with each speaker. They are not to be considered accurate transcriptions of raw tape. Language has often been regularized, especially in cases where that was specifically requested. Whole paragraphs and single sentences have been omitted or moved to where I thought they reasonably linked up. In conversation, subjects would be dropped and later returned to. And while it would be specious to argue that "This is exactly what the speaker meant"—I do consider these true to my own experience with the speaker. Complete, unedited tapes are deposited in the collection of the Public Archives of Nova Scotia.

.   .   .

This book belongs to Cape Bretoners. Counting advertisers, storekeepers and their staffs who display it, people who have contributed with suggestions, taped conversations, writing and photographs, staffs of public and insitutional libraries—it would not be hard to make a list of five or six hundred people who have contributed directly to *Cape Breton's Magazine*. Perhaps it is many more. And that does not include the thousands who've subscribed to it over the years, or who buy it over the counter. I am grateful to all of them.

I dedicate my own work in this book to the people who especially make that work possible, Bonnie Thompson and Sharon Hope Irwin.

Ronald Caplan
Cape Breton's Magazine
Wreck Cove
Cape Breton Island
1988

With Katie Margaret Gillis, Mabou Coal Mines

My name is Katie Margaret Rankin (Gillis). I was born in Mabou Coal Mines, and went away at the age of 17 to New York, my sister and I. We worked there. I was there 15 years.

I worked since I was 12 years old. We were of a family of 8. My father was a fisherman. Mother was not very well. I was the oldest of them. And there were 5 dead besides those 8, died young. So I went out to work for $5 a month, for a merchant in town, to take care of a little baby—the mother was sick. And got very little school. I went to school (later) in New York, winters, for 3 nights a week—so that's where I picked up most of my school. Mom was sick. And then, I suppose maybe I didn't like the school myself. But oh, it wasn't that I was staying away from it. But I had to, because we weren't that well-off that we could have some.

And then I worked in the lobster factory for 10¢ an hour in the Coal Mines one year, and two years at Mabou Harbour. Walked 3 miles (to the Harbour). Got up at 5:30 in the morning to be there on time. I was only about 13 and 14 then. They put me in cleaning claws and arm meat, for the first time. And then when I was there for a little short time, they put me in

1

the sink cleaning tails, taking that thing that's in the tail of the lobster out and opening it. I was washing them in the first water, and then putting them in the next water, and seeing that those little black things were off them. And then putting them in the collander and bringing them over to the packing table. We had the rotten job—cold hands in May. It wasn't nice. Just cold water coming from the sea in your sinks. So I got kind of sick. Dr. Kennedy told them to take me out of the sink. They put me in the claws and in the arm meat again.

Ten cents an hour. Ten hours a day. We'd like the day we had to scrub cans—a stormy day; a day that there was no fishing—because that was an easy day. We'd all sit in the back together and we'd polish the cans. I got to the packing table the following year.

But then, from that on, I went to work in Mabou Asylum. (*What was that?*) Mabou Asylum, where those people were kept up here—you know, those that were not well. (*Do you mean, in their heads?*) Yes. There were about—oh, I suppose there were about 80 in all—maybe 40 men, 40 women. And they had two women on the two floors. And I was on the upstairs floor with them. Mabou Asylum, that went on fire. They haven't got any more here. The odd poor person that didn't have a home was put there. But it wasn't a hospital; it was asylum. (*Did it serve more than Mabou?*) Oh yes, they were there from Cheticamp and Margaree and this side of Port Hawkesbury, and West Bay.

(*How old were you, going to work at the asylum?*) I was 15 and 16. That was in the 1920s, early '20s. (*What kind of work would you do there?*) I was where they were very, very poor, and bad, and no medicine in those days, and very hard to keep clean. And I was on the upper floor, on the bad ward. You had to watch your P's and Q's, or they'll knock you down. They did knock me. I had long curls those days. And one morning, one of them knocked me down and tried to choke me. Only for the other patients, I was finished. They came and screamed for the help, in the kitchen, for the others to help me. She was, like, going on those turns, you know what I mean. She was to go to the strong room.

(*What was a strong room?*) Strong room is a place where you go, and there's not a bed, not a thing at all. It's one of those swinging windows up above, to give them air. But not a thing on them, because they're liable to choke. Oh, you know, it's like a prison. If you give them a sheet, they're liable to choke. Oh, when they go on a turn, they're right bad. We called it the strong room in those days. The walls were made very strong and the window was all barred. And when you gave them the meal, you had to look—sneak in—and if you saw they were cooping in one little corner, and not paying any attention to you, you'd just open the door quick. It had to be just so—the soup would come all over your head in a minute. Sometimes we'd have to go and get one of the men from over, that was taking care of the men there, to stay behind us. But if she saw that, she would get mad then—she'd probably kill me.

Oh, they were very poor. It was a poor place, too. They didn't have the things they have in tablets, like today. See, there was nothing to calm them down. If they had these epileptic fits, there was nothing to cool them. The doctor would come in, maybe once or twice a month, and just check a little bit. But there wasn't a thing like medicine, unless castor oil. Oh, I know the score.

(*You were only 15 years old?*) 15 and 16. I left, well, I was going on 17, and that fall I went to New York. (*How many other women worked with you on that?*) My cousin worked with me on the lower ward, and my other cousin was in the kitchen. The woman over us—she was the supervisor— she liked the girls from the Coal Mines. We were, I suppose, stupid, and starting out. Well, we weren't afraid of anything. I wouldn't do it today, if you want to know something. I wouldn't go to that ward today. But those days, my mother went once, visiting up there, and, "Oh, my gosh," she said to the doctor, "that Katie—she's not going to live through that! That's an awful place." And she said, "Let me out, let me out of this place. I don't want to visit them at all." We used to take them out—those that had friends—and put them in a room. And if a priest came in, or a minister, we had to stay while they were there. Sometimes they'd just grab them. Oh, it was a lot of care. Nobody knows it but the one that was there.

And then I had a cousin working in the kitchen. She was the cook there. The patients were doing mostly all the laundry in the basement. Those that were good were mostly all doing the work on the asylum. It was very few help we had, but those that had to be on the wards. The women were doing the laundry in the cellar, and the women sometimes helped to cook in the kitchen. And the men were always at the horses and in the barn and the cows. We had nothing to do but supervise. We had enough to watch them coming down the stairs to the meals. And see that they got their meals. (*So the asylum was taking care of itself to a certain extent.*) Very much. And running very cheaply, too. (*Your pay wasn't high.*) Yes, and besides, the food was quite, at times, scant enough, I guess. Not with us. I don't know if that comes out, but they were fed the 3 meals, and fish was quite a bit. You know what I mean.

(*Did the people at the asylum ever get well and go back home?*) I never—no. It was a place, too, in that day, dear, where they put people in that had no homes. It was an awful lot of people in those days—no pension, no nothing—that used to beg and come from home to home. You know what I mean. And people those days were very, very nice and kind to people that didn't have much in the world. When if they themselves didn't

3

have much of the world, they were so good to the poor, that they'd keep them overnight sometimes. (*But you feel the sick ones were not getting well?*) I don't know of many that ever.

(*What happened to older people? Who took care of them, usually?*) Nobody, dear, those days. Those days, those poor poeple were probably as well as you and I, but they were in their 70s or 80s, and there was no home. There was no pension. Indeed, indeed, as I say, the people were awful good to keep them if they could at all, at all. But there was an awful lot of people that had nobody to take care of them, like sisters or brothers or man or wife. (Relatives) were gone, and they were old, and they were just led from house to house. And people used to feed them from house to house. But they were put there. Then when they died, if they couldn't find some relatives away back, or they were gone to Ontario—well, then they'd go and call the parish, and the parish would go and get somebody to dig their grave, and they'd put it behind the asylum in a blessed little spot there. A little cemetery. If there was somebody—anybody—friend at all, they'd put them in Mabou, in the regular cemetery. But if there was nobody going about it, they were just buried in the back there. I've seen the cemetery, I was up at it. It's behind the asylum.

(*What did they pay you for work like this?*) When we went there first, we got just $10 a month. We thought that was beautiful here, then, in the '20s. And then, the supervisor was good enough, she let us have our free uniforms. And she put us up to $15. It was a government thing.

(*I was reading a little about the Nova Scotia Asylum. And there were some people there because they were involved in sex.*) Yes, there were some in that. Oh, I suppose that in those days we were too young to understand it. We were brought up those days so different, we hardly knew anything about that. These little country places, we were brought up very, very—I don't know—modest-like. Well, we were taught, "Watch this...." There wasn't such a thing as that brought up to us before we went away. The doctor in New York that we worked for—my sister Ann and I worked 9 years—he was an old, old doctor. Many's the good advice and things he told us. He was really the first to explain most of everything to us. We were young, leaving. My sister was only 16, and I was only 17.

(*Were you afraid at the asylum?*) Not me—I was too young! I got many a slap, and I got my hair pulled. I had curls, and knocked down and put her foot right on my throat. I can swear to it. Other people saw me. Mom wanted me to come out. But what could you do? There was nothing to do. No work here.

There were 28 of us went to New York. There were 17 went on one drive—mostly all cousins. And we all got work in New York, mostly all of us, through one friend. We didn't need a reference because there were a few of them up before—and one lady'd tell the other. We all got jobs. And green—as green—we didn't know a cabbage from a lettuce.

My sister Katherine, she wasn't working, and I went home one day from my day off—she said, "I'm going to New York. I'm going to Uncle Angus." Angus was a cop in New York. Donald Beaton's uncle. And he was a cop in New York, and a relative of ours. Mom thought the world of him, 'cause they grew up and knew each other very well. He was on Wall Street for 27 years. And a big article was in the *Times* about him. He was a beautiful man. We called him "Daddy," because he was a daddy of all the 28. And his word would go anywhere there.

Oh, Mom didn't want Katherine to go, and she didn't want me to go. So she told Fr. Beaton in Port Hawkesbury. He was a relative. Oh, Fr. Beaton didn't approve of us going, so young, at all. He said, "It's no place for young girls, a big city." For me, I don't know, it was the way you were brought up. When you did domestic work, you were amongst very beautiful people, you know what I mean. Real Yankees. Oh, there were all kinds.

But anyway, we went away. We went to pay our head tax in Sydney. We had to pay a taxi $5, where it's $50 today. Earl Hawley, God love him, he took us over for $5, waited until we had paid our head tax and got our papers to go, $8 head tax each. We had to borrow the money. And I don't think we borrowed more than—what?—$50. It was cheap. We had that little money we had made in Mabou.

And everybody was vaccinated. Anybody that wasn't vaccinated had to pay $5 more and stay for the night. And I hadn't been vaccinated. Luckily, I got a cut when I was small, from a dog. I had a slash here. The girls were saying, "Oh, just push your sleeves up, and don't say anything." Well, see, I'd be very poor off, if I didn't get on with them to New York. I was lost. I was a greenhorn. One of the older girls said to me. "Just leave your hand out." Everybody's hand was out. He said, "Okay." And here, the dog passed! They had a joke on this.

We went by train. September. About 17 of us went. It was the time of the year it was muddy roads, no cars on this road. And everybody had a wagon with whatever little bit of clothes he had. My mum—very, very sad goodbye. But for us, it wasn't, because we were all nerved up and excited, and we were amongst—some we worked in the factory with, and school chums—it was just like that.

(*So you went to New York. And what did you do for work?*) Housework. Housework. My sister was a helper in housework, and she learned it, and then she got to be a good cook. Then I cooked for a doctor there for 9 years, and my sister was the waitress. And I used to go up nursing with the doctor in the evening. When his nurse was gone at 5 o'clock, I'd put my white uniform on. I'd give them the lamp, the sunray lamp. He taught me how to do those things. And patients that had cancer, or big cuts—I had to boil the instruments, and maybe hold their hand, and give him a hand with the bathing. And I'd get a little money. Which I was not cut down, when the bad time came, in the Dirty Thirties. Oh, a lot of the girls that were on jobs for 20 years and so on were cut down. Instead of that, I was *getting* a little more.

Another thing, when times were hard up there, you were like a bunch of sheep when you'd go to the employment office. You had to walk the row, when the ladies came in to see you. I remember that. You had to walk on the floor, around in the employment office, see how you looked and what was your shape and how neat you were and how do you walk. When they didn't need so much help, they could get their pick. Oh, it was tough. I didn't have to, but a lot did. Girls from Margaree told me so.

I only got two places in my life that treated me very mean, before I came to the doctor. Oh, it wasn't easy in a place when you went away. You had to really have a backbone, and have somebody like Angus Beaton, God love him. As we called him, "Daddy." He was the man. Once I told him, "I have a great job, Angus, coming up. A woman asked me the other day, a young woman, and she said, "You just make a beautiful size 8 or 9. You'd better come in and do some modelling. And you'll see the money you'll make evenings." Oh, Angus wouldn't hear of it. He said, "No, no way!" He said, "That's filth. You don't know who's going to have their hands around, or what's going on. You're not going to go that." Well, I said, "This is extra work in the evenings, and I feel that I can do it." "No way." Well, there you are. There's where the points came where you learned.

My sister was very bright, Katherine. She went when she was 16 to New York. She had a hard life, she had a hard time. She wasn't getting the jobs that were suitable. She'd get in a place where they'd demand too much of you, where some of the other girls said, "She's not supposed to do this or that." They'd pile on you, say, wash. Well, naturally, we had linens to do, and we were very careful and ironing them, in my day, too, not too much. But they seemed to take advantage of her, and give her more work than she should for her age. And you know, too many things at one time. She hit one or two bad places like that. But then she stayed a few weeks with Angus and the wife—she wasn't very well. That helped her an awful lot—Angus Beaton, the cop—that gave her a good idea of what was to be done, in housework.

(*But there were girls who were just being taken advantage of.*) Well, I suppose they didn't understand that we could be so far back. After all, even if we were born on farms here, all we had was grain and wheat and potatoes and barley, and we had plenty of that. We'd put that in the barn. We'd put it to the mill and get flour out of it, and oatmeal out of the oats. All those things. But when it came to vegetables, there was nothing to speak of at all. Maybe a few cabbage. But of all, potatoes, feeds of potato. And you see where we were on the stupid side, and it was pretty hard to learn things the new way. It was just like going to another country.

And even meats, in the fresh meat, because we usually had salty codfish and salty pork—we'd have our own pork—kill her. And we'd have a cow, we'd kill that cow. And Papa'd have lots and lots of this hard, nice fish, codfish, on flakes, you know, that we'd have all winter. He'd have some of it pickled in another barrel, and another couple of barrels of mackerel and herring. That was our winter's supply.

(*And in New York they weren't eating that.*) Well, now, there was no such thing as salt there. Very little. And there was broccoli, and there was spinach. (*Had you ever eaten a tomato before?*) No. I didn't know what a tomato nor a banana was. No, that's very true. Oh, we didn't know the stove from the table.

The doctor's wife was a very hard person to get along with, although she was nice in other words, but she was hard of hearing. When she was young, she lost her hearing. No family. And the doctor, oh, he had a heck of a time. He was a maternity doctor and he'd come in all hours. And she'd be out all day with her car. As deaf as she was. But anyway, by gosh, he'd start. And you know, they'd have everything so beautiful, butter plates—they had everything beautiful. Only themselves at the table, it had to be just so. No drinking in that place. It was just cocktails of tomatoes or something; doctor had no use for liquor. But she'd say, "Hon, put that out of your mouth while you're talking to me." And him so hungry, going to eat. "Hon, put that out of your mouth while you're talking to me." He'd just do like this and put it on the butter plate, to please her. So that tells how strict she was.

7

You'd think she was deaf—she had an instrument in her ear. But she could hear the hay growing! She was that strict that if we were washing the dishes without a towel in the bottom of the sink, she'd ring the bell at the table. (*Why did you have to have a towel in the bottom of the sink?*) So the noise of the dishes wouldn't disturb her when she was in the next room, dining room, eating.

I saw her one time—the nurse that was with the doctor—she said (to her), "There's tacks in the bottom of your shoes. You're ruining the house, the flooring." And she said, "I see a mark." One day she just lifted her foot like this and looked at the bottom. The nurse gave her a kick, she landed over on the carpet. And so the nurse came down, she told us, "I guess I'm fired. I'm here for 3 years. I'm fired. Do you know what I did?" And we knew what she did—we heard the thump and the row. So she said, "I might as well pack my things." So Doctor came in the front door at the same time, and he wondered what the commotion—we gave her a cup of tea—she was upset. Doctor said, "No way am I firing her. You had not the right to go and lift her foot and look." But she let her have a kick. She did darn good. She deserved it. Oh, she said it on Ann, often. In the dining room. She said, "I think—look at those little marks there now, Mary Ann." She said, "I believe, to my soul, that your shoes—let me see them." And she'd look, and she wouldn't find a nail in them. She'd just pick her foot like that up, like a horse, and make you show it.

A lot of times the doctor came to the kitchen, often, and said to us, "Oh, now, girls, don't mind her. She gets awful contrary." We had our suitcases packed 2 or 3 times, going. And he said, "Oh, now, listen here girls, don't you mind. I'm married 30 years. I've put up with it."

We were there 9 years. We worked 9 years with that woman. But, as I say, there were beautiful principles in her. When we'd go to the country, she'd get 3 or 4 dozen eggs. And she'd bring them down from the country. And she'd say, "Bring those up to your sister that's married." But the doctor put up with hell on earth. However, that was the best 9 years we ever had together, Ann and I. You'd put up with heck, being you were together.

And my first wages in New York—not at the doctor's—the first wages I had when I landed first as a greenhorn, was $50 a month. It was a good money. So that means we could send home. And they were nice to give us clothes and things there, too, what they didn't want. If they had anything left over, which would be very good, if they matched at all, many times I'd send it home. Oh yes, they were beautiful people. Oh, I can never say anything else but "Dear America." It was really—it helped my parents. And it helped me. I had my good days there. And we sent the money, paid our fare. Then we had to put the rest of the money home for our parents, 'cause

8

they had a hard time. Papa was a fisherman. And there was no farming. Lost all the animals that year with some poison in the woods. They were really out of—we had to buy a horse, buy a calf.

They were very beautiful people (the doctor and his wife). There were 4 of us in help. They had a furnace man and a garden man. And my sister was a chambermaid and waitress. That's the one that's in the picture—we were together all those years.

(*And would you see other Cape Bretoners, too?*) Oh, yes. Visiting, and going to the Cape Breton Club. Oh, I loved dancing. We weren't allowed to have any males in, but all the girls could come, and we could have them a tea and cookie, and whatever we

Katie Margaret and her sister, dressed for a costume dance in New York City

wanted to. Have our own little music in the kitchen. It was a very strict place, but a beautiful, beautiful place. And a good place for young people. Gosh knows, they were strict about your company, very strict. (*Were they sort of like parents?*) Oh, yeah. The doctor was a real man, yes, he certainly was. I'll never forget him. My sister even—her first child, she called him after him. He sent her a beautiful gift, a couple of hundred dollars.

(*Did most of the 17—and later it became 28—who were from Mabou, did they all stay up there?*) No, not too many. They skitter-skattered—a lot of them came home and got married. Not very many stayed at all. Except my sister and a couple of the MacEachern girls, and one Beaton girl—they got married up there. (*But you didn't?*) No, I don't know how—I've been asked that question so often. (*What question is that?*) How is it that I ever came home, and how I loved being there. I met Angus. I came home here (for a visit). And Angus was born in that house up there, just above me. That's the old home.

I was in the Coal Mines, and there was a little dance, a little house dance. So Angus was only 16, a little better than 16, when I met him. I

9

was older. I'm 4 years older. So I went to the dance this night—no intentions—walking with high heels from the Coal Mines, and gravel road. After coming from New York, you know. We didn't go with anybody—Katherine, my neighbour, and I. We thought, well, we'll go up and see what it's like. And there was a lot of moonshine and things. And of course, I wasn't very fond of this. So, oh, we danced anyway. If there was a dance in blazes, I'd get it—oh, I loved dancing. And going home—this uncle of Angus came and he said, "I'm going to walk you home." And I said, "Oh, we're fine"—Katherine and I—it was coming 5 o'clock in the morning. Danced all the time! So this young fellow comes out, and he comes over, and he says, "Are you going to walk down in the dark through here?" I said, "Katherine is with me, and we're not afraid of anything." So Angus took my arm, and off we went. He was only that young, and shy. Oh, they all teased him home about the New Yorker!

Well, then I went (back to New York) that fall, and he sent me a Christmas card, never thinking anything of it. 'Cause I didn't bother—I had a good time, the way I was. By gosh, after that, wrote for 13 long years. And I only saw him about twice in all that time. Oh, no thoughts I'd ever be home, no. Only just crazy letters about fishing. He was fishing in the Coal Mines. He gave me all the news about the Coal Mines gang that I chummed with, and where I was born.

Then on, in 1936, Mom died. She died with cancer; she was 56. I came home from New York. He was home fishing that year. Only saw him once or something, home. I had no desire for anyone when Momma was gone. We were so sad for her, you know. First in the family.

He sent me a diamond on Christmas Day; it came to New York. In the mail. But for all, we had no intentions, or never said too much—you know, when you don't see anybody for 13 years, only just once or twice. I didn't know what to say, when the registered letter came to the door. I had no intentions I was going to get such a gift. I had sent just a card or something, down to him. It was from Noranda, Quebec. Then I wrote back and said I got it, I was very happy.

Angus, then, always said, "Well, why don't you come to Quebec?" "Oh," I said, "I wouldn't go to that part, you hear so much about it." But when I went, I found out what it was. (*So, did you go?*) Finally, in June in '39. (*You were in no hurry to get married, that's for sure.*) Well, I was having just a good time, and lovely jobs, see, and I wasn't really interested in it. I was seeing a lot of failures in some. Ones that got married young—had a hard life—married a fellow that was heavy on the liquor, and kids were coming, and times were hard. You see, I really watched. My sister Ann and I just saw a little of that, and it put us right to the test, that what's going to happen, anybody. Mom was forever writing, hoping for the best, and be sure: "Don't have anything to do with people up there."

But anyway, from then on, I came to Quebec. Oh yeah, he wrote me in March, "I'm not going home fishing this year." He went home every year, fishing. And he said, "How about, please call me on the phone and let me know what your intentions are." So, I was on a good job then, an awful good job. He sent me beautiful things, and messages, and everything. So, of course it was a long time, and I knew that he wrote what he meant, that he meant it. He wrote several letters all the following year, '38, and so on. Oh, we broke up for a year, almost, between. We didn't bother writing, hardly at all. I don't know why. But I was contented and happy and working. So, final-

Angus and Katie Margaret Gillis

ly, I came down to Quebec, and Angus's brother Neil stood for us, and a French girl, no English—there were no other girls. She'd have a catalogue, show me the pictures, and I had to go by that.

So, they stood for us. And oh, from then on, Angus was awful good to me. Never left me, in my life. If he had to carry me on his back, he would just carry me through muskeg on his back. I never saw the like. I was married, and then we went out on a job. And I had no jeans, little thin clothes, New York clothes. The flies were taking the piece out of me and going up into the trees, the big mosquitoes! Oh, me crying away, Angus trying to carry me, and a packsack, and I had diddle-daddles from New York, things that should be thrown out, instead of dragging them to a camp. I was to a camp, I lived with my husband there. He was foreman on the drill there. For 4 months, saw no woman. Not a thing. Not even a call. We were going out on a plane, and we'd meet the mail down in the boat once a month. But oh, what a life!

Those men had to carry machines on their back, and the packsacks. Oh, what they went through, you'll never know. It did me the world's good to see what people had to go through. They carried the machine through muskeg on their backs. Drilling for zinc or gold or iron—mostly gold.

11

(*Did you have a house of your own?*) No, no. I camped out where there's bears and wolves—40, 45 below zero. They were pretty good; they gave us a good camp. I cooked there. They gave me something to do so I wouldn't be lonesome in there at all.

I was cooking. I got good, good, good money. In fact, we built the barn out here with that, Angus and I, with the money of that year. With the wages. We had a hard winter, though. It wasn't easy. But my cooking was very plain—just pies, and meats, and so on. Homemade bread. I had to make my bread. They'd send out a pig on the plane. And they put it in a place where it was freezing. There was no freezer. Oh, it was tough. We used to cover it with soda and things, so the flies wouldn't (get it) in the spring. The pork. (*Did you ever have a home, the two of you?*) Oh, not in Quebec. But in Rockingham (Halifax) we lived for 21 years. Angus and his brother Neil were drillers there. (*Were they looking for water mostly?*) Yeah. He drilled in Canso. And then we drilled in New Brunswick for water, too, in Yorkton. And then we drilled for zinc and gold in that new mine in Bathurst. We stayed in camps there. We stayed together. That was in the '40s. Oh, Angus would never see me behind. That's one thing I say. And he did have a hard time, taking me all around. Because I was only a nuisance to him, a lot. But never did he leave me behind. Well, it was beautiful. We were very happy together. As I say, it's something to look back on.

We had this house (in Cape Breton) built the year we got married. Papa made us build it—Angus's father. And we never lived in it, only one winter in our life. My brother and the children lived here for 17 years. So we were only in here two years in our life. Angus loved it. Well, we always came home from Quebec in the summer to fish. He had his gear all put away. But we never spent a winter here until the last two winters. That's all the fun he had here. He was coming home, he was retired, he was going to have a ball, and that's what happened, dear. And he was looking forward to smelts. And he was looking forward to so many nice things when we'd come home. We both took all the walls down. And we put the insulation all through, as sick as he was, and the following year, Angus went.

.   .   .

(*Katie Margaret, you have no regrets at all about going to the States?*) No. They put me on my feet. They put most all of us that left that year on our feet. What would we do down here—there was nothing here—10¢ an hour in a factory, and go out to work, maybe $5 a month. Well, of course, we were very young, no experience. But still and all. Oh, only for the States, people would have starved here.

(*Were you able to keep up your Catholic religion?*) More so than home. I agree with that. I'll lift my hand and ask any of the girls. We were just talking about that—Katherine was in the other night. And Katherine said,

"When I think of what they were saying." And it wasn't the church. It's just how you live. It's the way you live and how you go about it. My God, I didn't think the devil was there, at all, at all. Beautiful people. More so than probably some of my own. I'll say that. (*You didn't feel that you had lost from your religion at all.*) No, no. It did me better. Where I'd be far away—what?—7 miles from the Coal Mines (to church). Where I was there was only two blocks. Well, it's my own fault if I can't make my own little time when I was off to go—well, goodbye, that's my own trouble. I wasn't pushed to go there. I didn't have to, but I loved it. And the people I worked for showed that to me.

But you see, they called us "girls." We weren't maids, we were girls. We weren't maids at all. (*And they themselves were not Catholic.*) No, no. She was in the English church, and I worked over there as waitress for her. And I'd go over and make the cookies when they had those big events there in the late '20s—we'd go over, serve the meal. To us, they were the same as our own. When we were in the Children of Mary, she'd go to see us in our white, making the parade—she'd love to go. And, you see, the doctor was a minister's son. And he—"My girls, oh, my girls have got to get to church today. Honey, which one of us will go with her? Are you tired? And it'll only be half an hour—there'll be lots of time for golf." They saw us there. Oh, they were beautiful people.

(*You were saying when your mother got sick and you took her up to New York....*) And he wouldn't let her stay up at my sister's that got married—the babies were small. He said, "You just put another cot in your room. Keep your mother with us." It cost her not one thing. And she had all the best doctors in the world. He did it, and it cost her nothing. Took Mama for a month up with us. He went himself with her to the highest building, where I wasn't in, after all my 17 years in New York. He took Mama up. He loved Mama. Mama was very broken English—a lot of Gaelic—we'd speak Gaelic. And he saw Mum's painting—Mum was a beautiful painter—he went out and got her stuff to paint.

My father was a fisherman. He was a very, very patient man. Mother was cross—she was like me. No flies would stand on Mum. She was strict, boy—you got it if you did something bad. But Papa, maybe you'd get the ear, but that was it—he was a very patient man, to his wife. Because I was an awful tomboy. Because I used to be up with Grandpa. I got the knack of it. I was the oldest. And I did the mowing when I was only 10 and 11 years old. Papa was a fisherman. So I did all the mowing when I was young, with the two horses and the machine. And the raking. And Mum just let me stay out because she knew Papa wasn't used to farming. Grandpa died, her father, so he said, "Move up on the place." And Papa was no—God love him—no farmer whatsoever. For horses and things, you see. But I was the little tomgirl all the time—horseback riding—I couldn't fast enough drive the horse for me. Ooo, I was really bad. Milked cows. Got kicked from a colt, and got kicked from an anything. Got knocked out from the colt. I was on something all the time.

And mowing and raking was my work. I did make many a load. Pitch it, too. Pitch it in the wagon. And I'd come home and I'd have to get the pitchfork and put it up in the barn. The horses knew me, see, and I knew their nature. I came home many a time with my thin dress and my petticoat and my underwear and a little skirt I had on—there was no such a thing as jeans those days—a hole coming from where I was sitting—you know, the iron seat on the mower. On the 3 pieces of cloth. I saw myself often, and I'd be watching nobody was coming, so I'd get in to change my clothes. I saw it. I saw it all.

Oh, I milked and I sheared sheep for 10¢ a sheep, and I made more holes in her shearing than there was wool. There'd be holes. And I'd throw the creoline in the cut with the warm water over her, and she'd cure. But I know there was more holes than wool! And I used to mark the sheep. Oh, I had a hard heart. Papa couldn't. You know, everybody had a sign—there was a V put in one ear. Then the other one, a little bit under. And I cut the tail off. I'd just do like that with the knife, very sharp. The little she-sheeps, I'd cut the tail off—so that when they'd be snubbed, they're much cleaner. But the he-sheeps, we'd leave the tail on so they'd be easy to mark when we were chasing them, and they were heavier. (*When you went to sell them?*) You'd have a little tail left—that'd weigh half a pound. And then, they were easier to get in the field. And they're wild—jump up on your head! Oh, I tied them—I know. I know what it is.

And the churning and the butter. (*If a cow were going to deliver....*) Well, I'd have to sit near her and explain to them if there was nobody older around, in case I'd have to go for a neighbour. Once or twice I had to go and help a cow with my small hand. When the man came up, he said, "Your hand is smaller—try and turn that calf." The man was near us was a

Katie Margaret Gillis at Mabou Coal Mines

very kind old soul, and he knew a lot about veterinary work. And when we'd see the cow having a hard time—maybe Papa was working in the woods, and it'd come all of a sudden, spring of the year. The calves were coming. And Mom was not too much for that. She never was too much for that, although she was for everything else.

All kinds of excitement. Especially when Papa wasn't a real farmer. Although he was beautiful to work with the small scythe. Oh, he would be around me all the time. He never left me alone, because he was afraid that anything would happen to me on the machine, cutting. And oh, I'd take a little wrench they had, and I'd turn the guards, and I'd see if they were loose, try them. And then you'd jump out and put it out of gear. I'd turn them up, and he'd call me. So Papa would be mowing—oh, he was a beautiful mower—so fast. Grandpa used to say, "I wish I had strength"— he was a strong man. (*He'd be mowing with a hand scythe.*) Yes. And he'd do just as much in a day as two people. He had to go in the corners (of the field). Oh, you'd be on the side like that on the machine—we had mountains down Mabou Mines—you want to see where I'd be sitting on the machine! Just slipping right off it, on the side. But Papa—he wouldn't allow me up without being in a place that I could call to him. He was very careful.

(*Were other girls doing this work?*) No. They were talking to me the other day, they said, "My gosh, do you ever think of it?" I said, "No, I don't. I don't think it was anything. I enjoyed it so much—I could sleep with the horses." Just loved the horses.

I sawed wood with Dad, on the other end of the saw, those crosscut saws. Oh yes, I sawed, and I "tootched" it from the hills with a horse. Very bad mountains to work, too, down there. It was very hard. You have to have an easy-going horse. Of course, I was more used to horses than Papa was, 'cause I lived up with Grandpa a lot, when I could sneak up with Grandpa. He was all alone, and only an old uncle there that wasn't doing much. And I knew what sheep and horses were, and I fell for the horses, and from then on, I knew more about horses than Papa. Papa was fishing all his life.

(*Did you ever do any fishing with your father?*) No, but I used to go down with him early mornings and pick up squid. And we'd have a little fork, like, and push, and put it in the bag for him, to help him get them. No, I never went out fishing when I was with Papa. With Angus I went fishing. I went fishing in the ice here, smelts. Every day he went out, I dressed them, when he was fishing smelts. We'd send them to New York. Sometimes, maybe if there was a good run, there'd be $45, $50. Smelts, going to New York, Fulton Street in New York. You were just putting them up to the train. We put ice with them. The only thing is, they

15

were awful cold on your hands. Gill nets, taking them out. Oh, they'd be so cold before you'd get them all out. We had a few gill nets, because we had little spots where you couldn't put the trap nets. You had the little corners where the gill nets were good. We'd have big wool mitts on. Angus could work with the mitts on, but I couldn't. I had to have my hands bare. But his mother always said, "By God, that one takes more cold than any woman I ever saw!" Angus'd be freezing, thinking, "We won't stay any longer." "Oh, we'll finish this!" He'd be thinking of me, you see, that I'd be cold. I know what he was thinking of.

I did it for years, if we ever were home in the winter, until we went back to Quebec. Oh, we made so many times to Quebec. Angus would be called all of a sudden, maybe that spring, that fall, especially in the fall—he'd go the winter drilling, and he'd come back in the spring to fish lobsters. He had his own gear. (*Did you fish lobster with him?*) No, but I baited the traps for him, and I made the nets. I can make the small and the big nets. I can lace the traps. I'd help him all that. He did the traps. And I tied them. And I'd put the herring on them when he'd come in from the sea—the herring would be on the stick—and he'd only have to put them on the boat. I'd help him with them. Go out again with a load, come in, and they were all baited for him again to go out. That's all I did as far as lobstering. (*That'd be when he'd be setting at the beginning of the season?*) Yeah. And when he took them in, we saw they'd be cleaned off and put away. Very often we stored them in the barn.

Then one year he decided that the perch were eating all the bait. And he said, "Katie, take the sewing machine and make me a couple of hundred bags of linen or of strong, strong cotton, just little bags, and put them in a way that you can put a string in them and tie them tight." He got more lobsters than the whole rest because the perch couldn't eat through this, and the juice was coming out. Oh, we used to get smelts or trout, and we'd stick that, make the smell of that draw them. One year he was the leader. He was a great fisherman.

.   .   .

I didn't think of this the last 30 years, until this man brought it up the other day. Didn't even tell anybody else. I wasn't bothering.

(This young fellow) I guess he was getting into little jimmy-jammies in the city of Halifax and, oh, (his) father was thinking it would be better—which it is, very good—to drive the kids to a country place. They learn a lot. He was about 17. Halifax was—well, kids didn't have anything to do but go and meet people and probably listen to things they shouldn't. You know yourself, they were too idle. So the man, the father, had a few boys, and he decided to send them there. He was getting along good, he was a handsome young boy. Working on the farm. And he was there for a

16

month, doing good. But he went on the (mowing) machine and moved a gear that he shouldn't. And then he stumbled, and down he goes in the scythe.

Whatever I was doing at the time. I was frying or something—doing something up for their lunch. When this panel truck came. And he said, "Where's Angus?" So I told him. Just as he was looking for some books in the truck—by God, I look down at the tractor. He couldn't see with the trees what happened. But I could, because I was in the open yard. My God, a leg went up in the air. I saw it going up.

And I ran down. But I had no idea what was going to be ahead of me. I figured, well, holy Moses, the other people, there's somebody going to come. So I just tore my apron, and it was a job, too. I know it was one of the big white aprons, wasn't a little stinking tea apron at all. And I twisted. And I got a piece of rock or a piece of a rough stick near, and I twisted and twisted. And I screamed and I screamed. I just took the apron off and put it around the foot of—this one was dangling.

And lucky there was cold water near by, that they were working and they had it for drinking. So I just grabbed the end of the apron and put it on his mouth. He wanted water, but I was afraid he wouldn't swallow it, because he was the colour of that. He was fainting on and off. And he said, "Light me a cigarette, Katherine, light me a cigarette." And I'd light a cigarette and put it to his mouth. All of a sudden, I'd hold the cigarette down and it would go. I took the apron and just made half of it and just rolled it around this one (leg). I didn't touch the other one at all. I was in too much excitement. Everything was going so fast. And I called and screamed.

And the man ran down with the truck—he heard the noise. He didn't know me—I'd only met him for a minute. So he ran down. "Oh," I said, "my God, this man has to get to the hospital." He said, "I'll take him there." And here was the man after taking me—and a cop ahead of us. There was a cop blowing the horn. And the blood was even coming out on the back of the panel truck. His head (in my lap)—I looked like if I was a murderer—and one of the nurses rolled my clothes up and, "Just put them in water when you come home." I wasn't very dressed, only in the kitchen. She said, "Take this, and put it around you going back, and then you can sit in the front." She gave me rubber, kind of sheeting. (*You held his head all the way in.*) All the way. And every time—I had this water, this wet rag, and a little bottle of water, and I put it on his lips. And oh, my God, he was passing out—I thought he wasn't there when I got there. But they rushed him in, and I don't know how many hours—he was hours. I took off then with the man, back, because he wanted to see Angus.

Angus came back to the trailer and asked, "Where in the name of God did Katie go? She's supposed to have this gentleman that's coming to look at the rock." And they told where I was and that I'd be back pretty soon, that he was making 100 miles an hour when they saw him, with the cop ahead of him. And that the man was bleeding. Angus buried the leg there in the field when he came home in the evening.

(*Did you ever see the man again?*) Well, I'll tell you what. In the '50s Angus was drilling a well down near Ketch Harbour—this new house that wanted a well, and wanted Angus's divining rods. And Angus got water. Angus said, "My wife is with me and we're going to have a bite of lunch." "Oh, your wife is with you?" He said, "Yeah." "Well, I want to see your wife." I went over. And he grabbed me and he said, "Boy! You saved my life!" And I said, "I don't know." "Yes," he said, "look at me today. Do you remember the day you took me in?" That's just the words he said. "Do you remember how far I was gone?" And I said, "Oh, is that *you*?"

Anyway, he'd built 3 houses. He'd throw his (artificial) leg off like this and run—that's the way he was doing the shingling—faster than you and I. He'd pull them off—and run—going over the shingles just like a little monkey. Quick! He built 3 houses, and he drove a taxi for 15 years. He's got a family of 8 and a lovely wife.

.   .   .

I'm an old-fashioned person. I had a lovely life. I had all kinds of friends. Very, very lovely life. And I felt that, as I said before, marriage was—for me, like—a scared thing, at the time, because I saw so many broken marriages in my day. A big lesson. Worse today. It's a shame, it's a darn shame. I feel sorry for the young ones of today, growing up. Don't you? It's another way today. It's a big worry. I mean, there's too much dope and stuff around today. And you think you're smart. You have to be really brave to avoid this smoking and dope and drinking, because you're not smart today—I know it—in fact, in Halifax there—go out to a party— you're not smart if you don't take drinks. And, you know, the dear souls, the young ones, are going to listen to a lot of this dope stuff. (*It's hard to say, "No."*) Well, you think you're odd. Just put it that way. Because I know it. Oh, I've seen the world, and I've seen a lot of the world, and I was in danger, too, and often. As I said, I lived in camps where there were only men. The 4 men, being married to Angus there, none of them ever showed dirt to me in my life. Often I was asked—that was in Quebec, out in the big woods. That the little young fellow was going to get married to a girl, and he used to read the letters, and sit and talk to me for hours. Well, Angus wasn't the type that was jealous. He'd go and lay down. Here the two of us would be at the table. Now, that's a lot. As I say, they were beautiful people. And they were wild men, too, wild drillers. Because I can say—miners, they're very hard to find but wild. You know what I mean. I mean, they're good and bad. I probably shouldn't say, but you know what I mean, there's many men out in the wild woods, and nothing but drink—poor fellows away from their people and their homes, their wives. I know what I'm talking about, out in those places. But I never was afraid.

(*When you were younger, were you more interested in the older people?*) More or less, I think. Because, in one way, we had to respect them so much. Our parents, when the people came, "Oh, you've got to be quiet—no word out of your mouth. If I hear a word, you're going to get it when they're gone. Just listen." Well, that listening was a beautiful listening. It's some of it that comes back today.

But today there's no time. There's too much TVs and radios and cars, go, go. I don't mean to say, but they're lovely, the young ones, yes they are, they're priceless. But it's not—and it's not like—they don't—the old ones—they don't really care too, too much, you know, to be amongst them. Oh, probably if they were interesting or something. Oh, I don't know, maybe I'm wrong. I don't know. Do you find it that way?

How Mike Oleschuk Got His Farm

I was born in Austria. Then after the war, it became occupied and called the Ukraine. And then in 1918-19 the Polish occupied it. And with the Polish passport I came to Canada. But my nationality is Ukrainian.

I came to Canada in 1929—May 31st —I landed in Quebec. I came there to be on a farm. See, in the Old Country I had two sisters, and we had there only 12 acres of land. And I didn't want to work like a slave. I could see what would happen. I'd get married and my father would split up the piece of land—a piece for one sister, a piece for another sister, piece of land for me—and after, I'll have nothing to give my children. In the Old Country, some people ended up working for landlords all their lives. That's all they had. But I did not want to work like a slave. And that's what made me decide to sell my land and pay my fare and come away to Canada.

Okay. I came to Canada. I brought all my money—$1200. That time that was quite a lot of money. I didn't know one word of English. And those agents get you, you don't know—took me to where there were bushes and bushes everywhere. I got a homestead and nobody there. I was by myself. Lots of Ukrainians came to that area, but everybody was around, living far away from one another. I found a farm—80 acres cleared land, a

20

house was built up with logs. It was nice, three rooms—$3000. I was satisfied. I gave down $1000. Now I've got to work and pay it up—$2000, that's the mortgage. All those neighbours there said, "Don't worry." They said, "In a couple more years there you'll be cleared up. Don't worry."... But my grain stays there. I can't sell it. What's the good? Mortgage combined with interest, interest. I went working for 50¢ a day, cleaning up their land, other people's land—what's the 50¢ a day? How am I going to make the payments?

Well, I started looking around every place there to find a better job—no job. And I had a brother-in-law living here in Sydney. And before I left the Old Country, he was sending money to his wife in the Old Country. She bought land, built a nice home. He was in Sydney. He worked in the steel plant. I wrote him a letter. I said, "Look, I would like to come to Sydney." He wrote, "Don't come, because there's nothing here." He said, "I'm working only one shift in a month, one furnace going—that's all. Only one furnace."

I don't want to believe it. Because how did that happen there in two years—so quick? Well, I said, "There's something fishy. He doesn't want me there." I decided to go. I met a fellow—a Ukrainian guy, but he was born in Ontario and he talked Ukrainian and he had good English. That's good for me, you know. Anything I'd want to know, I could find out in my language. He was my buddy.

Well, we became hobos right through to Sydney on the train. Sometimes the police chased me out but, well, you catch another one. That's the way I landed in Sydney. One morning, the boxcar landed in the yard there in Sydney. We woke up to the stink from the steel plant. We got up, opened the door—I looked and, by jeez, there's *lots* of stacks. I said, "Oh, we'll get a job here. A big factory. Oh by gosh."

Well, we get up, go and wash ourselves with the stinky water there by the brook, and we go to Number 1 gate. Nobody stopped us. We landed in the bar mill. By gosh, I could see lots of butts there, cigarette butts. We saw nobody there, so we picked up those butts, made a smoke. Then we walked. Didn't see anybody. We came back and I go back to the gate and I asked the fellows there, "Where's the Whitney Pier?" And they told me where to go.

Well, we came to the Pier. I asked, "Where's my brother-in-law, anybody know?" Well, they sent me to another fellow with the same name. I found him and I see that's not my brother-in-law. But he called me into the house, gave us something to eat. And he gave us each a package of tobacco. And he told me to go to Edel Hirsh on Lingan Road, that all the foreigners deal there. Ukraine, Polish, Hungarian, Italian deal there. It's a grocery store. He speaks Ukraine, Polish, all kind of languages—he's an

Old Country Jew. So, "Yeah," he said, "he deals here in my store. He lives on Henry Street."

I go there and a lady hollers up, There's somebody to see him. Right away I'm recognized. We shake hands and everything. He asks me questions: how I landed, how did everything go there. Sat down and talked. I told him all the history. He asked me about his wife and children in the Old Country and how are things there.

"Well," he said, "Mike, there's nothing here in Sydney." He's saved a few dollars, and he had to pay the board for me. I saw, by gosh, I've got to go looking for something. A fellow had a farm at Blackett's Lake. He wanted someone to clear up the land. Well, I went there with my buddy, the Canadian-born fellow I came with to Sydney.

"Yeah, I could take you both." We've got a job. I don't ask him how much he pays because I am glad to have some place to sleep and something to eat. Well, he paid us 25¢ a day, and board. And we slept in the barn. That was summer. That was okay. And I was a good worker. And every Saturday he goes with the eggs and everything to town—and every Saturday he bought me tobacco, half a pound—but none for my buddy. I think that's because he'd go away and his wife would watch what I do. And when I work, I work. If I want to smoke, that's the only time I stop.

We worked there for pretty near 4 months—25¢ a day. And it was in September, a hot day, and my buddy sat down by a tree and took a snooze. And the farmer's wife watched. He came home in the evening and his wife told him—says, "Mike is working, and that fellow sat down and was asleep." He told my buddy to go. "If you want to stay, Mike, you can stay. And I'll give you 50¢ a day." I worked one more week. Then one day my buddy walked out to Blackett's Lake, 8 miles. He said, "Mike, a boat came to load pulp. I put your name there. Thirty dollars a month and board." I had just got 50¢ a day. By gosh, now I had a dollar a day. I'll be a millionaire. And we went there and we loaded pulp. We worked there 3 months before it froze and we quit. Well, I made 90 dollars. I was a rich man.

After that, relief was open to us. And we had to go to City Hall and "carry the bag." We had to go from Whitney Pier to Sydney and register for the relief, and we had to go there every Wednesday, go pick up our groceries . Give you the codfish, turnips, two loaves of bread—a dollar's worth. That was relief at that time. This was not only Ukrainians. English people were doing this, too. Didn't make any difference what you were— it's the 'thirties and nobody's working.

In 1933 I got married to a Canadian-born girl, and jobs started to pick up, the steel plant started to pick up a little bit. Open hearth got 4 furnaces and blast furnace got one furnace—and I tried to get a job. My wife was working with Mrs. Melnick in the store, and Mrs. Melnick told her there's going to be an opening at the coal bank, a job dumping coal. "Only thing," my wife told me, "you've got to give the foreman a bottle of rum." And I said, "Where would I get the money to buy the bottle?" And I had to give him the bottle to *get* the job. *And* you had to be lucky. You had to have, beside the rum, that Mrs. Melnick *knows* him. If she didn't know him, I wouldn't get the job even if I had the rum.

My wife went to Mrs. Melnick, and Mrs. Melnick bought a bottle of rum and gave it to her. And I took the rum and got a job. Only thing, to actually work, it has to be a stormy day—because the boss had lots of friends. He gave the work first to his friends. There was no such a thing as you go there in the morning and go to work. He says, "Okay, go pick up the shovel there—you, you, you, you, you, go pick up." I've got to stay back. If he takes me, okay. If he doesn't take me, I'll have to go back home.

(Even though now you have a job?) Yeah, I have a job. I gave him the rum and he gave me a job. But each day I've got to go there. If he wants me to work that day, he picks me. If he doesn't want me, he doesn't pick me. *(And do you get paid if you don't get picked?)* No. *(And that's the job you have.)* That's the job I have. And if the weather is bad, some of the

Aerial view of the steel plant in Sydney, Cape Breton Island

fellows don't come out. Lots of times, I prayed that they'd have bad weather so I could get a shift.

(And what was the job you were lucky enough to get?) A loaded train comes out on the bank of coal, and you've got to take the coal off. The last cars, maybe the last 10 cars, you had it easy—you open the door and the coal falls down the bank by itself. They could be dumped. But if you're by the engine, you've got to shovel every piece of coal, because you're far away from the edge of the bank. *(And which cars did you get?)* I'd have the cars by the engine. I had to shovel the coal out of the car and over the bank, every time.

Hard work. And dirty work. And those times, for us there was no such a thing as a bathtub, sink—you had to bring a bucket inside to wash yourself. And coal is dirty. You had to clean up. Only the work clothes that I used, I put aside, and in the morning I'd put them on—so I'd get dirty again, before I'd go. If I worked or didn't work—when I came back, I'd be dirty and have to wash again. I'd be dirty anyhow. And lots of times I had to come back without working. I'd only get to work in the worst weather—snowing, blowing, rain—that's the day I'd get a job.

(And your pay?) Twenty-eight cents an hour. That was good money, that time. I made $2.80 a day. And if I'd work a whole day there, I'd come home and get something to eat, and wash myself, and you could say there was music, there was dancing—I didn't care. I was beat. And I was young. I was young and I was beat.

(How much would you shovel in a shift?) Oh, the small cars, two men could shovel 10 cars in a day—that's 15 tons in a car. That's in a shift when an engine was always there, you could shovel up to 10 cars, that's 10 trips. But if you had two engines going, you could get 10 cars—you were supposed to be working 10 hours, but sometimes it would get dark and you'd only get 8 hours. *(So even into the 'thirties, you were working those long days.)* Oh yeah. And some days you'd work 24 hours—when you changed your shift (going from night shift to day shift or day shift to night). You stayed 24 hours in the steel plant. They'd give you an hour to go home, take your lunch, and go back. Only you never worked on the coal bank at nighttime.

(That sounds like a rough job.) People do it. I did it. *(Was this the kind of job you'd only give to people from the Old Country?)* Oh no, no such a thing there. Canadian-born people too. They were fair on that. Only generally, the foreign peoples had to *buy* the job, like I told you. *(A bottle of rum to get the job.)* Well, if you wanted to work steady in Sydney, you had to give the boss a bottle every week. He forgets that first bottle. There even was an agent in the open hearth and the mixer, he collected two dollars from each one there and gave it to the boss, so those fellows could

stay on the job. The bosses had the power that time. No union. What place could you go? The foremen controlled the whole thing. If you're in good with the foreman, okay, you could be working. In 1933, my father-in-law was working in the big plant. And he told the foreman to take me there in the spring, take me to make brick. So I got that job.

You have a tank there and a chute and molds, and you have to beat mud, and beat it good so you don't have a rock—so that it will be solid and smooth. You work with another man who picks up the bricks and puts them onto a car to go to the kiln. After the fellows there took them out, the bricks went to the open hearth and the blast furnaces and other places they used it in the plant. *(Was it easier than working on the coal bank?)* Didn't make any difference at the steel plant what you did—it was a hard job. Making brick, you've got to work like a son-of-a-gun—4" by 9", you've got to make 2000 bricks, and slab brick, 9" by 10", you've got to make about 1200 to 1400 for each car. You made 4, 5, 6 cars a day—there was no contract on that. And they paid you by the hour. Stripper had 28¢ an hour, and mold man working at the beater there, he had 30¢ an hour.

(You must have been tired all the time.) I was young. You get a little bit of rest, and you forget. And no such a thing as a union. You talk about union, and you're out. *(So you didn't talk about unions?)* Well, I talked. But you've got to know to whom you talk. You watch for the progressive people who know what is what. If you figure there is danger, you don't talk about those things. I was two years, and all summers I made the brick. And in the wintertime we'd go there in the general yard. I worked with the bricklayers. I carried the brick with the wheelbarrow. *(What were bricks used for?)* Used it for the furnace, used it for what the gas goes through, it's called the checkers. Gas goes through the checkers to the furnace to melt the steel, coming from the gas producers. The clay bricks from Scotland and other countries, they go in the checkers. The bricks that I made here in Sydney, they went to line the furnaces—in the roof and the sides of the furnace. I helped line the furnace.

And if the furnace is hot—that's a hard job there again. If the furnace has got to go through a repair, put the new brick there, you've got to go in there with bars and break the old brick out. Then you go into the furnace and you line it. *(Did they turn the furnace off, let it cool down before you go in?)* Oh no, no. Not too cool. Sometimes hot, by jeez. But the boss said go, and there was no union that time—if he told you to go, you put a wet bag over your head and go in there. The wet bag is so you don't burn yourself. Your shoes—you're working two shifts there, you don't have shoes.

You climb into the furnace. You can't stay in too long. The heat chokes you. You go in for as long as you can stand. Pick up the bricks and throw them away outside. Pick up the bricks and throw them away—pick up as much as you can there. After they see you choking and your back steaming where you put the wet bag over your head—you get out and another fellow's got to go. *(Terrible job.)* I know that. And no union to protect you. The boss said, you go in. And you'd have to come early to get a shift—wait maybe an hour and a half—the boss would check you in—and sometimes not. And if you don't get a shift that day, you go home, no pay. No such thing as a guarantee that you have a shift. No sir. *(And when you had the old brick out?)* The bricklayers and helpers go in there and line the furnace again.

And after 1935 I changed my number to the open hearth. There were slag pockets, and you have to take that slag out. Sometimes it was so hard, you're jigging and jigging with the air hammer and you only get a little piece. I go with the air hammer, and the other fellows shovel up into the boxes, and I go again with the air hammer. You've got to break it, and they shovel it into boxes and the train picks it up and takes it away.

After that, I was millwright for awhile. And when I retired I was in the brick—lining the ladles for the steel. I retired in 1970. I worked 39 years

Men working in "cooled-down" open hearth furnace

at the steel plant. And I was always active. In 1936 we went for a union. We made a start. We called a mass meeting and people were scared. Only 7 of us landed there in the C.C.F. hall in the pier. But we finally got organized and got the legislation, and we got the check-off. And the union bargained from 10 hours to the 8-hour day.

And I was active in 1948, I was involved. The Seamen's Union came out on strike, tied up the ore boat. And Corbett was president of 1064, called me up. I was on the grievance committee, represented all the workers there on the open hearth. We went to a meeting in Glace Bay. Jenkins was there. He represented the miners. And we decided, What are we going to do with the Seamen's Union? And it was solid—miners and steelworkers would support them. And we discussed that we needed a place to put them up. We had a Labour Temple Hall on Mount Pleasant Street, and Jenkins and Corbett asked me if I would give the Labour Temple Hall for the Seamen's Union to stay. I can't give it because we had at that time 90 members, and the members own that hall. Next day I called the meeting of our members, Ukrainian Benefit Society. I explained what the struggle was, and our members, nearly every one, were for the union—it was a progressive organization, you know what I mean. The motion was agreed, give the hall for the seamen to stay there, cook there, go on the picket line. And we supported them—oh, over 3 months. Miners supported them. They even came from New Waterford and Glace Bay for the picket line. And the steelworkers went and helped them there on the picket line.

But then propaganda was started that this Seamen's Union was a communist union, all kinds of stuff that put the bogeyman to the people. And next Sunday priests and ministers said, if those people stay out and we don't have the ore, the plant would be closed down. And the trouble started. And local boys were in the Seamen's Union.

The steelworkers had a mass meeting. One fellow stepped up and told all the steelworkers there that we've got to look after ourselves, it's a communist union—if the plant goes down, where will we go? There was a meeting, and some said, "Go out and beat them." Anyhow, they went down and broke up the Seamen's Union picket line. And at that time, even miners from Glace Bay and New Waterford were on the picket line. Chased them away. And that broke the Seamen's Union strike.

And because I supported the Seamen's Union and my wife made sandwiches for the picket line and everything—some even said, "Go burn Mike Oleschuk's house." The committee stopped them, said if I wanted to support them, it was my idea.

Well, Jack Moraff, the Jew, he was my good friend. He didn't work at the plant but he was a good progressive man, and he knew me well. He came the next day. He said, "Mike, you have small children. By jeez, if

27

you get kicked out of that plant, what are you going to do?" I said I didn't know. He said, "You saw what happened to Forlett—he had to go to the Old Country. He got blacklisted and he can't get citizen papers and he can't get a damned thing—this'll be happening to you." He said, "Quit that. Let the Canadian people do it. You're a foreigner."

I said, "Jack, I can't do it. It's too late for me." I said, "What the hell am I going to do?" He said, "Buy a piece of land and go there and farm there. If you get a kick in the ass, at least you can make a living." "How can I buy a piece of land?" "Don't worry. You're my good friend, and if you'd like to go on the farm—I'll buy it."

And that's the way I landed on the farm. He took the mortgage. The farm cost $10,000 and I paid $10,000. I paid only for the bank administration, 2 dollars a year for 18 years—so I paid $36 interest for $10,000. You could say that was a good friend? He didn't make anything. An Old Country Jew.

I'd come home from the plant and work the farm. We had cows—10 cows at that time—and horses, pigs, chickens, garden—everything there. I'm coming on 74. I fought, and I'm still fighting. And you could say the Seamen's Union and Jack Moraff finally put me there on the farm.

Rev. Charlie MacDonald Shoes Bad Horses

When I was young my father used to work away from home and we had a cross mare and my mother and I used to have to go to the forge. I think we went one time to 3 forges and we came back without getting the mare shod. And I said to myself, I'm going to shoe her myself. Anyway, it worked on me. And the first money I ever got I made at the Oxford Paper Company—90¢ a day and my board, handling pulp. I made enough money to buy our first mower and to buy this course in the newspaper—a correspondence course, and the whole equipment—kneepads, surcingle (a kind of belly band), rope, instructions, and everything—was going for $35.

It was a complete course for all the different habits of the horse. It started out with showing the different types of heads and judging by their heads whether they'll have a tendency to be balky or a runaway. Now a horse with a round forehead and the eyes sunk kind of in the head—that's a horse that's very easily made into a balker or a kicker or a runaway. But a horse that had a dished forehead and the eyes are set out far in the head means that the nervous organization is so highly developed in the horse, he's much easier to train. If you have a good horse and you study the lines in his face, you see a horse with a round forehead and the eyes sort of set in a little scary—watch out.

Anyway, I took the complete course and I got my diploma and I used to boast about it. A school teacher at Lake Ainslie had a grey horse and he heard that I could handle bad horses, so he came to the manse this morning and left the horse for me to shoe. Now he did a dirty trick because he was the kind of a guy would love to get something over you. Because this horse, nobody could shoe his hind legs. Or he might have been shod a couple of times. But he never told me. A terrible thing to do. I went up to the barn. An old woman could shoe his front feet. No trouble at all. And I went to catch his hind leg and the first thing, boy, he almost broke my leg with a kick. And I was all alone. But I had the pitching machine rope. I tied his foot to that. I got the two hind shoes on. At 3:30 here comes the owner with a grin on up the road. I told him that was a bad thing. I could have broken a leg. But I did shoe him. And then I had all kinds of trouble. Wherever there was a bad horse, they'd get me to go and shoe him.

There weren't that many horses that were beyond what the blackmiths could handle. People worked them without shoes or they didn't care or put up a fight with them—but there was only an occasional one that would be that bad that they'd come to me. I didn't make a business of it. Or a regular practice. It's just that I delighted in doing it. Because I was determined. I proved it to them.

The first shoeing I did was a little red Kenny Carmichael had. A lot of people would say, "Aw, Charlie can't do that"—but Kenny respected me. He had faith in me. And this horse was full of life. And when we got the strap on him he was kicking and kicking and kicking. I said, "We've got to get some way to knock him down." Do you know that I was strong enough in those days to knock a horse down. I'll tell you how I did it. It's not exactly the strength. You get a horse and tie one foot up and get a hold of his bridle and his tail. You pull his head and his tail together. The stronger you are, the closer the head and tail comes. And he'll whirl around and it's a matter of who will get dizzy first. When the horse gets dizzy he falls over on his side. Well, didn't Kenny laugh. I sat on the horse and we got a strap on him. Oh, I wish we had a bad horse some-wheres and get a movie of that—I'd make money on that. You have to do it on the side that the foot is up. Whirl around till he gets right dizzy. And you run with him. And he goes right down—flop. That's a way of getting a horse to say his prayers.

Some people are of the opinion that some horses cannot be shod. For instance, a horse at Lake Ainslie. Over 20 years without shoes. Never shod. Could never shoe him. I was preaching at Lake Ainslie and they got to know that I had been handling bad horses, so they got all the bad horses they could get hold of—they doubted that I could do it. And the blacksmith that tried to shoe this one told the boy that brought the horse, "The devil can't shoe him." "Well," I said, "what would you say if a Presbyterian minister would shoe him?"

I got in that barn. And that horse showed no signs of being vicious until you'd go to catch his foot. And then he'd give you a kick and wouldn't let you touch his feet. That horse broke plank on the barn floor, and the boy's mother came down horrified and she started hollering, "Leave the horse alone, Mr. MacDonald, leave the horse alone! He's going to kill you." "No," I said, "your son is strong, and we'll go it if he does everything the way I want it." I said to the boy, "I'm supposed to know. I took the course and I have my diploma—will you do what I tell you?" He was strong and I was strong then too. The horse fought and fought and fought. But I could tell the minute he started giving in. We put a new plank in the floor. And we had quite an audience, saying, "Give it up, give it up."

To do the forefeet we put the surcingle on him. (The surcingle is a kind of belly band with two rings underneath.) We took a rope and pulled his foot up and tied it with a short strap to the belly band. That horse was so bad we had to make a lasso and make him walk into it. We got it on his ankle and we threw the rope over his back and pulled and the foot came up. Then we put a strap with a ring on. Then the hame strap went between that ring and the ring on the belly band—and that held his foot up. Then we took the rope off and walked him around on 3 legs until he got tired. Tied him to a post—the rope around his neck because a bad horse will break the halter every time. Take a hammer and start hitting the hoof. Till he feels it. Or use the rasp. The horse in Lake Ainslie was terrible. He'd jump and come down and that's when he broke the plank. But when they'll give in you'll open the rope and walk him around some more and bring him back. Hit his hoof with the hammer. You may have to do this 2 or 3 times until he relaxes and gets used to it. And before very long you can just catch his foot. You get him subdued so you can use your rasp on the hoof.

If they are really bad to jump, you put a big rope with a slip noose around his middle just in front of his hind legs and run that to a post—and you hit him on the nose with a little switch. And he jumps back. And when this tightens right around his middle, that hurts and he jumps ahead—and that'll stop him from backing. And when you've got these two things done the rest is simple. He'll stand there and you'll rasp the hoof and put the shoe on a nail at a time.

That's the front feet. But when the hind ones came the mother said, "Leave the hind ones, leave the hind ones!" But we took the big rope from the hayfork and took his foot up and held it. (Rev. MacDonald took the foot up in the same way as shown in the photographs. It should be pointed out that the horse shown here is not a bad horse at all. Rev. Charlie: "She had a stiff foot and didn't want to give it, and I couldn't hold it up—she

31

was so heavy. But I used the same method as I would for a bad horse.") First, you have to braid the horse's tail. Then you put a knot on the horse's tail and then you tie a rope to the tail. You put a strap with a ring on the fetlock. You have one end of the rope fastened on the horse's tail and you run the other end down through the ring on the fetlock and up through a pulley or over a brace in the barn— something high enough so that when you take the horse ahead and your assistant holds the rope, you'll take the horse's foot up. You mustn't be too severe. Just make it convenient for yourself.

With that horse in Lake Ainslie, when we took his foot up and held it, he jumped and jumped and jumped—until you could wipe the white foam off him. We never beat him. And after I had all 4 feet shod, an old fellow came down and I thought he was going to commend me. He knew the horse—he was an elder in the church and I knew him well—a real dry wit about him. And when the horse was shod he came up, and I thought he was going to give me a medal—because I thought I had accomplished a feat that nobody else could do. And he saw the horse shod and he turned around and he said, "Aw, well," he said, "the horse was 20 years without shoes, you could have let it go the rest of its time without them."

(*Did you ever have a horse you couldn't shoe?*) Never. Even today I'd launch a challenge to anybody. If I had a good assistant, I know how to do it. Most of the blacksmiths wouldn't come to me—they were too jealous that I could do something that they couldn't do—but the guys that owned the horse would come. I did it wherever I went. I delighted in doing it.

And you know, my brethren in the church thought it was disgraceful for a minister to do that. I was into everything. I could not only shoe horses but I had experience in carpentry and painting and bricklaying—just do everything. I wouldn't want anybody to think I am a professor or anything, but I have a wide range of experience—and I love horses. When I was young, before I went into the ministry, I did this. I enjoyed doing it. I was strong.

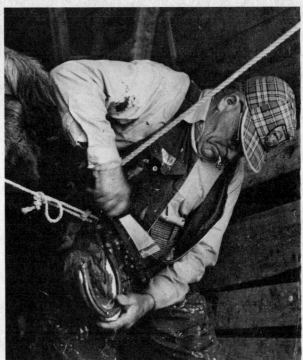

People said it wasn't becoming of me to shoe horses. It wasn't becoming of me to go out with a rifle and shoot a deer, or go up on the roof of a barn or a house and paint and shingle and do the like of that. Christ ministered to the physical needs of the people when he was on the earth, and I won the confidence of people. I built more than one barn for people who couldn't afford to build a barn. I was ambitious and strong and conscientious, and nothing was too hard for me to tackle. And when I got in the ministry I couldn't give it up. I like to trap. I like to hunt. I like to shoe horses. I can put up a bluff at painting and carpentry work. And I'm a first-class barber. Some condemned me. Some commended me for it and even named their children after me.

There's a minister from Scotland came to Canada. He was a great minister and he loved deer and I loved to hunt. So I was at Middle River at the time. "Charlie," he said with his Scottish accent, "where can I get a deer?" He knew I was pretty good at shooting deer. And there was a Presbytery meeting the next day at Sydney. I said, "You're not giving me much time. I have to go to the meeting tomorrow. But I'll get up early and I'll go at daybreak to an orchard." I said, "You do the praying and I'll do the hunting."

33

Well, boy, I came out of the house early in the morning. I had the rifle in one hand and a Bible in the other. Two cars went by and it was all over creation that Charlie MacDonald came out of the manse with a Bible in one hand and a rifle in the other. So I went down to the orchard. It was just after daybreak. I was looking at my watch, so I could get to Sydney to the Presbytery meeting on time. And boy, didn't I see this big buck coming down into the field. At the edge of the woods. I said, "Hallelujah. He's coming." Sat still, and I believe he sensed me. I just sat as still as death. And here he came down and I took aim and, bang, he tumbled down to the

apple tree. And I said, "Praise the Lord!"—and I went and I almost killed myself getting that deer in the car. I threw him in the garage for the minister and I made it to the Presbytery meeting in Sydney on time.

I'll tell you, I couldn't sit down and fold my hands and put my feet out and do nothing. I'd have to get out and help the people. The other ministers didn't approve of the things I was doing, but usually the people themselves thought it was wonderful to help them shoe their horses and help with painting and carpentry—but some of them will condemn me for it. But anyway, I wanted to be myself. And I'd just as soon be myself as some of the guys that are condemning me.

Margaret MacDonald, Glace Bay:
One Miner's Family

My husband is buried at Black Brook Cemetery. And all his people are. It's an old old cemetery. The starting of the cemetery—it was a dark, stormy night and this ship came in, and they knew it was a stranger. That ship was there a couple of days. Finally, the ship sailed away. And after the ship sailed away, they got curious and they went to this place off from where the ship was anchored, and they found a big grave and a small grave. So that was all right. They never knew who it was. But a year—just one year from that—this ship came back. It laid to for a couple of days, and then it left. And after it left, they went to find out what was going on. And there was a headstone there. The captain's wife had died, giving birth to a baby, and the baby's grave was there. They sailed away—where, it's never been known. A year from that again, they went to see the grave again and there was an iron fence around it and a huge headstone. So this was the starting of the Black Brook Cemetery.

After that, people started to use it. It's a Protestant cemetery. And my husband—Dan W. MacDonald—is buried there and all his people are. It's a beautiful spot. It's Black Brook—it's black water and it's coming around a kind of high bank, not terribly high. And there's a drive right around, and as you come towards the water, this grave is there. It's a pleasant place to go. When I go in that cemetery, something happens. It's not just that I'm imagining this. I get a feeling that I'm in a good place. Maybe it's my nonsense, but I love to visit there perhaps once a year. And a lot of people say the same thing.

I was born in Big Lorraine, about three miles from Louisbourg. I was a Fiander. All fishermen out there then. Small village—English and Scotch mainly. I met my husband in Louisbourg; he was from Broughton. They owned a farm out there. We moved to Broughton after we were married. Then, when Broughton closed, we moved to Glace Bay and I have been here ever since. Broughton today is nothing. When I went there to visit it was working, but when I went there to live, it was already closed down. Well, we had a farm—his father's farm—I've picked berries in around the mines. But he was still a miner. He used to walk across the woods to mine Birch Grove. He mined Broughton before that. Birch Grove closed down and we had to come to Glace Bay. Then he worked till he was killed in 24 Colliery.

He lived six hours after he was hurt. He was hurt around 10 o'clock in the morning and he died in the evening. Just one person in that accident. And he was a man who was never hurt in the pit, till that one.

(*How did you find out about the accident?*)

I happened to be in town that day. I was in the doctor's surgery and apparently they were looking all over for me. The first thing I knew was when I came home. We had a black dog. And the dog was lying on the ground with the paws stretched out like that and her nose flat on the ground. And otherwise, that dog would run to meet me. But she never looked up. When I looked at her, I thought to myself, What's the matter with her? Till I walked in the house and found that he was in the hospital, just about gone. He lived 5 or 6 hours after. That's the way it goes. You have to face up to those things.

(*All those years of having a man in the mine, did you worry?*) Well, no. You get used to it. You know, it's your living. You don't worry about things like that. Anymore than you worry about a fisherman. My father was a fisherman. He went out fishing, and he could have an accident out fishing same as he could have an accident in the mine. I didn't fear for him. I never gave it a thought. He was supposed to go and that's the way he went. That's my belief.

Anna, what year did your father die?

Anna Lamb: 1952

(*Of course, by 1952, I suppose there was help for widows of miners.*)

Anna Lamb: Yeah. She got $50 a month, that's the help she got. $50 a month for a woman of fifty-five years old that had worked hard all her life.

$50 a month in 1952. (*That's a knockout.*) That's a knockout is right. April the 28th, 1952, $50 a month was what my father's life was worth. Not another cent.

When Dad was killed, we got his two paycheques. He worked Friday, Monday, Tuesday, Wednesday, and Thursday—well, that was the pay he would get the next week. And then he worked Friday and the day he was killed. 1952, mind you. Got the two paycheques together. One full week, 50 dollars and some cents—and off of that was hospital and doctor and coal and church and all this stuff, till it came down to 30-some dollars. And the two days was about $22—they didn't take the off-tax off those two days.

That's what a man is worth after working from the time he was 13 years old till he was 62—which is 49 years in the pit. They put a price on him. Exactly $50 a month. And this was 1952. The war was over and times were good. This was prosperity.

Margaret: I promptly went to the sewing machine and I started sewing and dressmaking, doing alterations for the stores—I just went to work.

Anna: Of course, we kids were all married when Dad died. (*But as a child, did you think of accidents?*) The only life my father knew was the pit. That's where he was happy. You take him out of there and he'd be dead. It was his life. He loved it. He had all his friends and all his buddies and he wouldn't miss a day, by God, he could drag himself there at all. He loved it. He was never unhappy in the pit, was he? **Margaret:** No, he loved it.

Anna: Leave here at 4 o'clock in the morning and walk from here out to 24, which is out near the Glace Bay Lake. You know where the heavy water plant is—well, across the bay from there. There's where he walked, every day. He went underground—probably walked a couple of miles underground. Then walked back at the end of the day, came up, showered and changed and walked from 24 home. Later on, there were buses. He'd get off the bus in town and he'd bring my kids something in his pit can from the pit man. Gum or candy or pop. Said, this is what the pit man put in his can for them. But he'd be the pit man, really.

But we never lived with death as a possiblity. We loved our father dearly, and we never thought he'd go down there and be killed. We never thought of that. He was out and he was grubbing a living as best he could for us. We were good to him. We thought the world of him. But we never dwelt on the fact that he might be killed. Because you can be killed walking along the street.

(*It's interesting when someone not involved tries to imagine how you'll feel, how wrong I can be.*)

37

You are wrong. My father loved the pit. If he wasn't working, he was talking about it. He was either working or sleeping or talking about the pit. It was their life.

Margaret: I wasn't that fond of the coal mines. I mean, I wasn't afraid of the coal mines. But I didn't like the coal mines. I would rather he would have stayed on the farm and worked, but he was a coal miner—that was it. He had no use for the farm. I couldn't tell you why. It's just one of those things. I would have rather my husband had been fishing instead of working on the mines— but I don't know why. But I never had use for the mines. Although I wasn't a worrier. I never worried. Everything came day by day, and I took

Margaret Fiander MacDonald with three of her six daughters—Dorothy Margaret, Ann, and Annice —standing behind Margaret's mother, Ann MacLean Fiander, at Broughton. The child is Myrna, Annice's daughter.

what came. And I think we women were all very much alike. It's what we were used to. We didn't meet trouble halfway. If we had to sit down and darn and mend and sew to keep the kids covered and keep things going, we did it.

I never found it hard to keep the house clean. You learn how to do those things. When I moved to Glace Bay, there was no such thing as a washing machine. Take the wash behind the house and scrub the clothes all day. And the miners' clothes—perhaps twice or three times a year— brought their pit clothes home. You shook the coal out of them and you went out to the tub and washed them. They never came really clean. You got the coal out and some of the perspiration off them—but the rest, it never came really clean. But you put it out. Everybody did. It was just my hand and a washboard. I have the washboard yet.

We worked hard. Yes. But we had a lot of fun. We had house parties, for an evening's fun. You danced, you heard music, you played cards— maybe a birthday party. We had pie socials for the school. Everybody took a decorated pie and it was auctioned off and sold, and the money was turned over to the school. That's the way we lived in those days.

We had a big old-fashioned glass pitcher up on top of the cupboard. When he came home, he put his pay envelope in that pitcher. If he wanted to take money for something—he didn't drink and he didn't smoke—he took it. To go play cards, he took some. But we knew just how much we could spend or we never wasted. And I don't waste anything today.

Now I've been sewing, doing alternations for the stores, ever since he was killed. I didn't own this house when he was killed. But altogether I've had a good life. I can't complain. I've never envied anybody else what they had.

Anna: You know the part of the mine that bothered me more than anything else? To open my father's pit can when we'd be doing the dishes. And to smell it. That's what killed me. (*What did it smell like?*) I don't know. **Margaret:** But there is, there is an odor out of the pit can. **Anna:** Smelled like death, maybe. Horrible. **Margaret:** It smells like the pit. If you go down in the mouth of the pit, you get the same smell that you get out of a miner's pit can.

Anna: That's the only thing that ever bothered me. I had to wash that can every night. My father was a fussy man, and that pit can was his lunch can. You had to wash his pit can and his water bottle—scour them—and that to me was the most horrible thing to have to do, was to open that can and get the smell out of it. Now why, I don't know. And that's what I remember more than anything else.

Margaret: Sometimes he'd come home at night 3 o'clock, 4 o'clock, even 5 o'clock. When they had so many boxes of coal filled. And he was a greedy man. He wanted to make a good day's work. Like he often said, "If I have to go down in the mine to earn a living, I'm going to stay there until I make a good day's work."

Anna: He used to come home, have a sleep till supper was ready. He was either working or sleeping or going to a funeral or going to church or going to a local union meeting or a relief workers' association meeting. Right, Mother?

(*And how much time did he have left for the children?*) **Margaret:** He was awful good to the children. **Anna:** He was a good father. **Margaret:** If there had to be anybody chastised, I had to do it. **Anna:** He wasn't a playing kind of man. **Margaret:** He was either sleeping or working.

Anna: That's the one thing for fathers today, they seem to play more with their kids than fathers did in those days. But these poor old buggers getting up at 4 o'clock and walking out to 24 and walking back—they were pretty tired when they got home. In that pit bent double all day. It was a hard life, but I would say that Dad was a very happy man.

Margaret: They had a lot of friends, they had a lot of jokes.

Anna: We never had very much style, but we always had loads to eat. Dad used to take us, the three little ones, down to Commercial Street on Saturday morning to Eaton's Groceteria—cash and carry. Always have to show you off to everyone. Bacon then was 19¢ a pound and it was cut in pound squares. And we'd count down 10—and that was our bacon for the week. And we'd get up in the morning—there were 6 of us girls—and whoever'd hit the kitchen first, that was first fry. We would fill that frying pan—however many slices it would take—that was our breakfast, plus an egg. We'd have that every morning.

Margaret: We didn't have a garden. You couldn't get him to work in a garden. He didn't like it. The mine was his life.

Anna: By the time Friday would come, things would be a little bit slim. But we were allowed to eat. Daddy brought it home, and Mom cooked it—and we ate it. And we weren't told, "No, you can't have that, that's for tomorrow." Eat what you want. People always said, "What you don't put in your kid's stomach, you put on doctor's bills." Today, kids don't have what we had to eat.

Margaret: I remember once a week I baked an eating pan, a mixing pan—great big—pan full of cookies, oatmeal, ginger, sometimes a corn cake, sometimes a ginger cake—and bread galore. Twice a week, great big batches of bread. You can't be a loafer and get along. When you see a miner's wife or a miner's family that haven't got the things they need, you know there's a loafer somewhere—because if they both have their health and willing to work, they're going to make a living. It was a tough life. But it was a healthy life.

Anna: You don't know the meaning of toughness, boy. **Margaret:** We never were hungry. **Anna:** But this is everybody. You went to school and you wore your rubbers till you were so damned ashamed—it was a dead giveaway. You know, when you were a kid, you want to skip and you want to play hopscotch—and your pride because you've got holes in the soles of your shoes, so you've got to wear your rubbers to keep your feet off the ground. But my mother would be having a card game every Sunday night, making a little lunch and making an apron or something for a prize. And she'd have all her friends in and they'd play cards, and whatever she made over the cost of it, she would put it in the teapot. And when there was enough in the teapot is the time the 3 little ones got their shoes. I'm not telling any lies. The pride, the pride you had.

Margaret: Talk about pride. She was going to school and had holes in her shoes, and the teacher wanted her to take a pair of shoes—"No," she said, "I'll get shoes Saturday."

Anna: "My mother is trying to earn the money for our shoes and we don't need them. We're not poor." And another thing. They used to have free milk in school, in the little half-pint bottles—glass ones. And the cream was at the top. And we were so proud, no way would we take that milk. They had milk lunch and milk. Our tongues would be hanging out on the desk for the want of milk. You know what we would pray? For a stormy day and half the kids would be home from school, and the milk would go bad if we didn't drink it. So then we'd drink it, just so they wouldn't be stuck with all this milk going bad.

And in the winter, it wasn't refrigerated, but it was cold, and the little bits of frost would be in the milk, from off the truck—and oh my God,

wouldn't that be good! But the only time we'd take it was because the teacher would tell us it was going to go bad. And wouldn't we be happy! That's pride.

Margaret: We were never down and out. When he was sick on time away, I papered walls and worked at the dry-cleaner—I did everything I could to get along. And that's where the kids got their pride.

Anna: We had a good life. We didn't have fancy clothes. We had what Mom was able to make over from somebody else—and they were very nice clothes—but what it took out of her to try and do it!

Margaret: I'm still alive.

Anna: I mean, after she finished her day's work, then she used to start the sewing.

Margaret: I made flour-bag panties. In those days you got the flour, the eighth bags were not duck but a heavier grade of cotton. Those were the panties. The thin ones were slips. I knit their over-stockings. I knit their mitts. Their caps and their scarfs, I crocheted.

Anna: We were so much better off because Ma was so handy with her hands. Now, a lot of kids would wear the flour bags with "Robin Hood" on them. But Mom knew how to take it out. She used to wet them and rub bar soap on them and roll them up tight for a couple of days.

Margaret: Yes, I'd rub the soap on and scrub them out, and then I'd put them on to boil and that generally took it out. And if not, you put them out on the grass in the sunlight—and the sun would bleach them. I was careful. But people you read about, their lives were hard because the parents were careless. Didn't bother. (*So you feel anybody could have had as good a life as you had?*) Definitely.

Anna: Unless there was liquor or illness involved—then you didn't have too much of a chance. But I remember—we had a beautiful life. I look back on it and think that I'm a better woman for the life we did have. I can sew and I can make do. Not that we have to—but I can.

You know, you should have been in Glace Bay the day my father was buried. He was a plain old miner, and St. Paul's Church—they couldn't seat them all. And in those days you waked people in the houses, and the undertaker had to stand by the front door and let so many people in at a time because they were scared something might happen to the floor.

Margaret: But the explosion we had 2, 3 weeks ago—it brought everything right back. The next night I couldn't sleep, thinking of my husband and the other soul. And in your afterlife, those things will come back to you. But I'm not a sentimental woman. I'm as hard as nails.

After my husband was killed, I was younger, I was busy with the kids, I had lots of things to do—and I didn't think so much. But the explosion in 1-B, it made me think of everything. I realized what those people were going through, and how they'll fare out. These things don't end. When you bury your husband or bury your son, it doesn't end. Because when you hear of something, it comes back and you go through all of that again.

You wake up. Many's the night I've sat in the window and thought of those miners—when they faced death, what was it like?

We raised 6 daughters. No sons. It didn't make any difference to me. I had healthy children, I had good children. A lot of people said it would be no time at all before I'd be married again. Well, I never go outside the door, never bother my head. I'm contented in the house, I read a lot, do the housework, work in my garden—and I'm very happy. I have no regrets. I'm satisfied with my life.

Theodore Rideout: "I Went Sealing"

There were 9 of us from Neil's Harbour. The rest were from Newfoundland, all parts of Newfoundland.

We had to walk to North Sydney. Took us 8 hours to go to Ingonish the first day. With a pack on our back, 25 or 30 pound. Next day we walked up D. B. MacLeod's North Shore. We walked in the sleigh track.

I'll always remember, when we got up to D. B. MacLeod's our feet were wet, and an old woman gave us dry socks to put on. And the next day we got our feet wet walking across Englishtown. Across the ice.

(That) day we ended up in Bras d'Or. And the next day went to North Sydney. Took us 4 days. We stayed while an old ship came from Halifax. We met her in Louisbourg. Another day or two, the Newfoundlanders came aboard. Came over and came aboard. We started out the 4th of March. And we went to the ice.

I'll always remember it. We got up 10 or 15 miles north by St. Paul's, we struck the ice. That night—it was a moonlight fine night. The first ice we struck, she started to go like this. Rocking. And we were at seals that night. So he stopped and he stayed there all night. And next morning we got 90.

Come on a storm from the southeast, thick-a-snow. And old Capt. Marley from Trinity Bay, Newfoundland, was the captain of the ship. He blew the whistle and all hands went on board. He started up the Gulf. Went for 4 days and 4 nights—the vessel—through the ice. We went up, I guess up around Anticosti, the other side of—you couldn't see any land, anyway. And we got stuck. And there we lay in one spot for 6 weeks and 3 days. Couldn't move. If you'd get out and look at the ship, look back at it, there was no sign of her, it was like a snowbank.

But we never got any seals, and we stuck in the ice too long. And we had nothing to eat. Lots of food aboard. All we had to eat was hardtack and molasses. She had lots of grub aboard. She had everything. For the sailors, captains, and doctors—they had all kinds of fresh meat, ham and eggs, and porridge and bacon. Sealers never got any of that. There were 175 sealers. And 25 of a crew. The crew didn't go sealing. They stayed on the ship all the time. They got all kinds of grub. We got nothing. That's what we got—old hardtack and old fish with the skin and all on it.

I don't know how to tell you this. There's a long story. I'd be four days trying to tell you.

We got no seals. But I used to go out on the ice with some old fellows from St. John's, Newfoundland. And we left one morning at 7 o'clock. And we walked till 7 that night. All day on that ice. We got one seal. They were just out looking, see if they could find any. They came back with one seal. Well, you'd sooner do that than lay around the ship all day.

We did nothing while we were jammed in the ice, only roaming around the ship, go out and try to kill a few sea-birds and pick them and eat them. Bake them. Edgar Lillington (of Neil's Harbour) used to bake some buns for us. We never got any bread, only hardtack—so he used to bake buns. Molasses buns. So we used to enjoy them. It's that bad of a story, I don't know if I should be telling it to you.

44

Well, it's starvation. We had starvation on the ship. And all kinds of meat aboard of her. Twenty-five quarters of meat going spoiling—big western quarters of meat—we didn't get any. Not a crumb. Only the captain was getting that, and officers and doctors. They got all kinds of steaks. We got a roast beef Sunday—a bone. And through the week we got a pot of pea soup. And for breakfast in the morning, there's a big barrel of hardtack in the corner there, and a bucket of molasses over there. And you go and take a hardtack out of the barrel, if you had good teeth, and had some molasses, and put it in your cup. And tea—they used to call that "switchel"—because that was boiled over and over and over and over. And that was our breakfast, every morning.

Well, come dinner-time we'd have potatoes with hake, old hake—I don't know if you know what hake is—skin and all on, just like they come out of the water. You eat that, if you had a good stomach. They would boil it up. We had different cooks from what the officers had. We had 3 old cooks that had never cooked before. Well, they had real chefs, the captains and officers and doctors. There were two doctors on it. When they'd pass through in the morning, you could smell the bacon and eggs. We never got one bit.

And come a mild day, and we had to get up on deck. About 25 quarters of western beef was getting mouldy; we had to wash the slime off of it. Fresh water with baking soda in it. To wash the slime off the meat—it was spoiling. (*So you knew the meat was there.*) We knew the meat was there. What we should have done was raided the ship! You couldn't believe it unless you saw it!

If we'd have got some seals, I guess we'd have got some good grub. If we didn't get any seals, we got no grub. And we had no tobacco. But the Newfoundlanders that were out the year before had their tobacco. They knew what was going to happen. If we didn't get seals, we wouldn't get any tobacco. And no grub, either.

I was thinking about it in bed the other night—up there, stuck in the ice. And I was telling my wife yesterday—that's where you used to see the rough days out there on the ice fields. The winds were blowing nor'west. You couldn't see anything. There was no woods, there was no nothing — only ice and snow and wind.

Then we got lousy—I'm telling you everything! We all got lousy. And that wasn't too good. You get out on the ice and try to pick your shirt. This is a beautiful story to go in a magazine, I guess! I guess it's going to go, but I don't give a damn. This is right. It's all true, what I'm telling you.

And our old cooks used to cook puddings. And you couldn't eat it— there was no way you could eat it. And when we got out of the ice, you'd look back and there was a big pile of puddings, big as this house! About

5000 gulls trying to eat it. It was made out of hardtack! I guess they couldn't do that today with a bunch of people, eh?

I was only young, right young. I was the youngest one aboard perhaps. Fifteen, I suppose I was. Perhaps 16.(*Where did you sleep?*) Well, they had bunks, all around the wall, like that. About 3 high, 3 or 4 in a bunk—there were 4 in ours—right around like that. It was on the deck. But down, right there (below us), she was full of coal down there. And when the bunkers got empty, we had to hoist that coal out of there. So you know what kind of a mess there was—there was ice and coal everywhere we slept.

We had to hoist it back, carry it back to the bunker in wheelbarrows. (*Through the place where you slept?*) Through the place where we slept. (*And the place you slept, was it cold or warm?*) Fair. (*Fair. Nothing was good.*) No, there was nothing good about it. (*And where did you eat then?*) Eat right there. And no table, we never had a table. Just stood up wherever you could, and eat. Just sitting up like I and you, and eat away.

So, after the 6 weeks was up, there was another big storm come. And a swell got under the ice, and opened it up, opened it up. And we got back. When we got to St. Paul's, we came out of the ice. He landed us in North Sydney. There was nothing running then, no roads. You had to walk it. Or run it? We got down by an old boat from Ingonish. An old fellow was up after freight. He brought us back here, landed us in Neil's Harbour, Jimmy Brewer from Ingonish.

So we landed. We made 2 dollars and 40 cents each. We ended up with a dollar and 8 cents. Anybody had oil-clothes, and stuff like that—they took that off of him. (*From the $2.40?*) Yeah, that's right. Well, they'd pay for a few suits of oil-clothes, out of everybody. A dollar and 9 cents, that's what we got, when we were cleared up. Well, 240 seals among that many men. And the spring before, she got 12,000. They made $400 apiece, the spring before that.

(*Did you ever go back again?*) No, I never went back again. But I would have. 'Cause I know that times changed after that. I'd have gone back next year, yeah. (*Why didn't you go?*) Well, I never got a chance to go. That old boat was seized in New York, with a load of rum.

It was a good experience in a way. We never had any tobacco, and we never had any grub. And I'm telling you. The holes in hardtack? Some of them had maggots in them. (*Couldn't have been worse.*) No, couldn't have been any worse. We all gained weight! All the young fellows gained a lot of weight—it must have been the fresh air out in the Gulf of St. Lawrence! It wasn't grub, eh?

46

Joseph D. Sampson
of Petit-de-Grat

I can tell you the way we were brought up, kind of a job we had, and things like that. I wasn't quite born in this house—I was born the same time the house was built, 78 years ago. I can tell you the way it went. I was brought up as a fisherman. Boy, we didn't have much then. We had to do something—fishing—in order to live. And plant potatoes and things like that. I didn't go to school too much. I had to stop school in order to help my father try and make a living. It was a hard time then.

I was pretty near all kinds of trade all right. I was a boatbuilder for quite awhile. I used to fix up engines in big boats, building houses, or anything at all, farming. We used to have 8 cattle here. We had 3 or 4 different fields, you know, and we used to buy hay. (*This area is not an easy place to farm.*) You can't do it. If you've got to farm, farm for yourself— it's all you can do. I had a good place way back there, by the lake. It was only an acre of land. It was just enough for your winter grubs.

(*Your father was a fisherman.*) Yeah. Father, grandfather, and myself. I don't really remember the first time I went out—I was awful young— 12 years old, I guess. And then at the time, they had a fish trap, catch all

47

kinds of fish. They were fishing in the trap, and we were trying to help them, fishing around, with the small boat, a dory—tried to help them. My brother was a little older than me, so I was fishing with him. I was fishing hook and line outside the trap. While they were fishing in the trap.

We fished that way for 3 or 4 years, I guess. And after that I had to take over my father's place in the trap, at 14 years. We were 8 men. I was among them, helping them.

(That's heavy work.) We had all big handfuls: 400, 1200, 600 pounds. Twice a day. We used to go in the morning around 6 o'clock, 7 o'clock in the morning, pursing, getting the fish in. One time I had 40, 50 thousand pound of fish. Then you had to take it in, dress them. You had to do it among 8—you had to do all your work, forking your fish on the wharf, and then weighing with the bar, those times, not the way they are now. Had to weigh them, dress them, and get them ready for shipping. Didn't salt it though—it was fresh. And then in the afternoon, we used to go back around 3 o'clock or 4 o'clock, and sometimes I had just as much or more. Well, you had to do the same thing over again: dress them, clean them, weigh them. Sometimes it would be about 11 or 12 o'clock before you would be home again. Before you got through.

So we were fishing long hours, and at small pay. At the trap, you were paid in money. But you didn't get too much for your fish. I think when we first started, we were getting $1.50 a hundredweight—a cent and a half a pound. Then it came up to two cents a pound. It stood there for a little while, and it dropped after that. It dropped low enough that we had to sell for 50¢ a hundred—half a cent a pound. Came pretty near when people had to stop fishing altogether.

(How could you buy your goods with that kind of money?) I'm going to tell you the way we used to do it. We use to fish all summertime, getting all the odd dollars you could get. And then try to pay what you had bought the winter before, to pass your winter. And then the next winter you were just as bad off—you had to go back on credit for your next spring coming. So that's the only way we could do it.

After that was over, it came up a little better. The fish were coming up a little more. For 3¢, 4¢ a pound, things like that. So we were doing a little better. But you couldn't make enough to put money in the bank. Just enough to keep you up, and that's all.

I wasn't more than 16, 17, 18 when I took over the trap. I was boss of the trap then, boss over all the crew. But I'll say one thing, when I took over the trap, my mother was alive. And my mother used to have a little education—not too, too much, but a little. In order to look after the trap, I had to get a book. Mark every fish that was selling—for bait, haddock or cod or mackerel, whatever it was. So, I didn't know how to mark the name, and mark the kind of a fish. We tried that for about a month—she tried to show me how to do it. Every night, every night. So, at last I got it, anyway. I got it that way.

I started from there. I tried to get the kind of fish—haddock, cod, and herring—whatever kind of fish we had, to put that down. And then I tried on the names that used to come around the trap for bait, for fish. The men. All kinds of different men. So I did learn it pretty well. So I ordered one of those books that used to tell the amounts of fish, and price, and things like that. If it was two cents a pound, or one cent a pound, things like that, I had a special book. You could find anything at all you wanted to find in it—wood, or lumber, or whatever it was. Even the dividends in the bank. Well, it was a clear book for that. I had that to depend on. So, all that I was selling through the trap, I had to put it in my book. And when I'd go to settle on Saturday, I had to take that over, what I had sold during the week, how much money I had made.

So I got along Number One on that. I never made a mistake on that. *(You were probably extremely careful.)* I had to be, because if I was losing money, it was off my pocket. So I had to be careful. But I never made any mistake with it. When I took over captain in the trap, I was between 17 and 19. I was good and strong, though. They trusted me. I never tried to cheat anybody. That's something I never did try. Tried to do my best to keep everything nice and clean, and no more.

This trap that we bought was between 8 men—8 shareholders. We were fishing, and paying according to what we were fishing. Those traps were costing that time around $12,000. But we were paying according to were we making the money. But you used to make good money in it. Oh, cripes almighty! We got all kinds of fish inside here. You could make good money. It was nothing for you to pay 3 or 4 thousand dollars during the year, on the trap. So when the trap was paid, this was yours. *(How long did it take?)* Oh well, you could have paid in 3 or 4 years, as far as paying straight. But every year you had to order new stuff, something that was bad.

It was all kinds of fish then. You could make a living off of the trap. But you only had two months to fish. You had to make all that you could in two months. 'Cause at the end of two months you had to take your gear ashore.

(You told me about a time that each man only got $18.) Oh, yeah. That's a year when the fish was so low—the price was so low—they couldn't sell haddock and fish of any kind. What we were selling, you called it "selling it," but you were giving it away fresh, anyway! A cent a pound, cent and a half, two cents a pound. And we put in our mind to salt the haddock. Well, we used to go and purse, and then come ashore, dress

those fish, split it, and salted them. We used to work from 5, 6 o'clock in the morning until 2, 3 o'clock the next day. Right through days and night. We were pursing in the afternoon, and then we used to salt it at night. And we did that for two months and a half. We salted over 200 puncheons of haddock. When we got a sale for it, the best sale we could get, I think, was 4¢ a pound. And we had to pay all the expenses—puncheons, salt, and the few men we had hired to help us. When we settled after the season was over, we had $18 a man, clear, for two months and a half work. That was some cheque!

(It would seem it would take years and years to see $12,000.) Yes, but you'd be surprised there. We used to make 3 or 4 thousand dollars a man, in two months. I'd say it's about 45 years ago.

That's gone a long time ago. The fish is gone, the trap is gone, and everything is gone. You can't get a fish now—the same place—you can't get a fish there to eat. At that time, you didn't have to go too far out. Five minutes outside of here was good enough. Now you have to go 2 or 3 hours in order to get some. And in the same place where we used to get the haddock, at that time, now you can't get enough for a meal. You can't get one. Some people claim it's the dragger, or they say it's the causeway. I feel the draggers didn't help any. But I've got a different story on that. I think myself—at that time, all the people around here had their trawl outside. And they used to bait the trawl all day long. There were thousands and thousands of pounds of bait going down to the bottom, to feed the fish. So, after awhile, they stopped setting trawl, after we had those traps. Well, they fished around here for quite awhile. But I think that's what it is that does it: the fish that feed around here, you can't expect that he's going to come back year after year for nothing. We used to bait up outside, and throw the bait outside. It was keeping the fish around.

(It interests me how much you did learn and how much you were able to do, even though you say you didn't have a lot of formal education.) Oh, none at all. And it's the same as a good many people, they can't understand how I could come and build boats, with no education or anything. *(How did you do it?)* Well, it just passed in my mind that I could do it. I saw a few guys building boats around here. And I thought to myself that if a man could do it, I could do it. It seems to me when a man does something, and you want to put it in your head, you can do it. It doesn't matter what it is. You can do it. But you have to have it in your head.

(Did you earn a living building boats?) Well, that was a help from all kinds of different ways I was trying. I was trying planting, farming, doing something for myself. And what little money I could get from different places where I could build boats and sell boats. You know, it kind of helped me from all kinds of ways. But I used to work till 10, 12 o'clock at

night every night, in order to make a living, keep up the family. I had long hours, right through my life. Now it's the same thing: I'm getting up at 5 o'clock in the morning. I don't have to. But I've still got to do it; I can't stop it. I'm getting up at 5 o'clock in the morning. I'm getting up at 5 o'clock in the morning, and I'm up all day.

.   .   .

(A place like this, I should think that when a storm came up, it would come up pretty fast.) Oh yes, coming pretty fast. *(Have you ever been caught out there in a bad storm?)* Oh, I got caught in a bad storm. I got caught when there were two guys from here got drowned. Oh, that's quite awhile ago.

We were trawl fishing in the fall of the year. So that morning, (the fellow) I was fishing with wanted to go fishing. Of course, all the boats were going out. But I knew there was a kind of a breeze or a storm coming in. So I said to him, "I think it would be just as good for us to stay in, the way it's looking." "Oh," he said, "okay, we're going to go out and we'll set 3 or 4 tubs of trawl, anyway."

So, we used to go way down outside L'Ardoise, fishing. So we started, anyway. And we met all the other boats that were coming in. It was too rough then to go out.

All the other boats had turned back, were coming in. All right, we went towards there and started setting trawl. We set the trawl. And when we got the last tub, ready to draw the last handful, one of those guys that got drowned was just passing us, coming in. But it was too rough for him to stand. He had only a Swampscot dory. It was a gasoline boat, you know; it was a flat-bottom boat.

Anyhow, he was coming in, and the sea was too hard for him to control it. I don't think he went more than 5 or 6 hundred yards from where we were before he swamped. The sea was hard enough that he passed the bow under, and he never came back. He sank there. And another fellow that was there with a big boat—he had a 40-, 45-foot boat, I guess—he went to try and help them. But when he came there, he couldn't see anything—everything was under. All he could see, it was a man tied in a bow of the boat, or something—so he tried to go and help him.

He could see the head of a man—he was tied there—he was supposed to be tied there. He had tied himself—they claimed it was, anyway. And when he went to get him, that boat came (up) and he passed right through the other fellow's boat—you know, the one that went to give him the help. (*The bow came up.*) It came up, and he passed right through. He split it right through.

So they were caught right there themselves, outside there. And all that they had to save their lives was a dory. And there was one of them that was used to the dory, so he said to the other guy, "All you can do now, take a barrel aboard, and we're going to try to make ashore somewheres. I don't know where we're going to take it, but we're going to try it."

(*Take a barrel aboard the dory?*) They took it aboard, and he started for shore then, rowing ashore. They were quite a distance from the shore, but the wind was so heavy that it was going fast, just the same. It was too rough for the dory, but they put the barrel in tow of the dory, so the sea could break on the barrel before it could get to the dory. So they had a chance. So he landed in Gros Nez, I think. In a mound of rocks and everything, but they saved their lives, anyway. But the two other guys got drowned.

(*So where were you when all this happened?*) We were outside. That's where I'm coming up now. We were outside, still fishing. And it was too rough for us, that was for sure. We only had a small boat. So anyhow, we hauled pretty near all the trawl. We were in the last tub. We were almost in the end of her. Came a breaker. And the one that was hauling trawl in the bow just got it—it broke right aboard—he got it. He came right across where I was, and I grabbed him across the waist, and I threw him down in the bottom of the boat. And the boat was halfways full of water. The motor stopped. There he was under water, and everything was under. So, I had no choice. The only thing I could do was to go in the bow and take a bowline, make two knots into the bow, and try to bail her out with a bucket.

So I bailed out, I bailed out—when the other guy came (to). So he said, "Where am I?" I said, "Never mind where you are—you're aboard. Try and get your courage—help me to pump all the rest out." He did the best he could, took the pump, and he helped me out. I went to start the engine. And everything was full of water, badly—motor, carburetor, the whole works was full of water. But the boat was light, anyway. The battery those times was a dry cell, not a car battery. We had to take the battery and dump the water out. And then I drained out the carburetor, drained out the engine. And I tried it. First kick, it went.

It was in a rough sea. And from there, to get inside Little Anse there—you couldn't see if it was a breaker, or the tide from the wind—everything was a solid breaker. All solid breaker—the comber was coming about the height of the house here. There was no chance you could make it, (unless) you would take it easy. So, when I was ready to leave, I put that guy on the steering gear, at the rudder. I said, "Now, don't take the sea right in the stern, because if you do, we're not going to go too far." So anyway, he took it, and the first one he took, he took it from the stern. Lord, we went about that far from going underneath. *(An inch?)* Yeah. So I said, "That's enough now. I'm going to stop that. I've got to do something else."

So, I was running the engine, and I headed towards a comber when the comber was too big. I had to slow her down, in order to let them pass ahead. And when I thought I couldn't make it, well, I was speeding the engine, in order to pass ahead. Anyhow, I said to him, "Next time you take one, try and take it in the quarter, so the motor will have a chance to raise the whole works."

So, all right. You weren't going too far before we were getting one. So, the next one he took, he didn't take it on quarter, he took it on the side. So she went side on the other way. We got about 3 or 4 barrels of water. And then we turned back. I said, "That's enough now. You go and run the engine and I'll take the rudder." He didn't want to. He didn't want me to take the rudder. I said, "I'll try and do my best, anyway. I'm going to get it." So I was watching, I was watching. And the third one came, I jumped over the box and I went behind and I grabbed the rudder from his hands and I hauled it over. So I held it now. We were coming in Number One.

So we made ashore, anyway. Before we got ashore, at about 3/4 of a mile or a mile for Little Anse buoy, they saw us once outside the buoy. And from there they couldn't see us until we got inside the harbour. It was too rough to see us. They didn't know if we had sunk or not. *(You never thought you were going to sink.)* No. I got a few more hairy ones, but I never thought I was going to drown or anything.

But I've got a son that was drowned here. Right here alongside of the shore. A storm, that big gale we had, 115 miles an hour. October storm. *(Is that the one that took the roof off the school?)* Yeah, that's the same. Stripped the whole works around here, all right.

We were fixing up a wharf down here. And we had all kinds of logs on the beach. It was on Sunday morning. He had gone to church, came back.

And he was just getting ready to go across, at the beach, with this friend. They were going to pick up the logs that were going adrift.

So they left the shore, and he had an outboard motor on her—it was working Number One. He went and he got a couple of logs. I didn't want him to go and get it, because it was too dirty, too windy. So he went, and they got it. And he threw it about, oh, about 10 or 15 feet ahead. And then his motor broke down. I think, myself, he had run out of gas. 'Cause the motor was working Number One. And we had a big boat anchored there. So he cut the rest of the log, left it adrift, and he tried to catch up with that boat, in order to hold himself. And it was blowing so hard, he couldn't make it. They couldn't make it. He just was far enough he couldn't reach the boat, and that's all. It was something that had to be done, as far as I can understand. He couldn't fetch the boat, so he went. And when he went, I said, "Goodbye. I'll never see him again."

So, sure enough, we never saw them after that. He reached for the boat, but he couldn't get ahold of it. Couldn't reach far enough to hold it. He was in a skiff. But he was trying to get ahold of the big boat. *(And he fell over?)* No, he didn't fall over. He just missed—to get ahold of it, see—he just missed. And then he went adrift. He couldn't go close enough in order to get ahold of it. He couldn't go close enough. He tried his best.

He was drowned off here, from here to the island here. There was no boat that could go out that day in order to get them. Both drowned. I was looking at them until I couldn't see them in the fog, in the water, that was splashing. I was watching them going, but I knew it was the end of it.

(After your own good fortune in a storm...) Yeah...well, not so much wind, but just as hard as that, and I saved myself. But this one, I think it's something that had to happen....

I was in quite a few breezes, things like that. But not enough to hurt too much. The only one when it was too rough for us to be out is one time I left from here to cross to Canso—it's not too far. And we had an old sailboat, but we had a motor aboard her. My uncle (was) in Canso. And we had sold 8 barrels of herring to him. So, it had been blowing for 3 or 4 days, northeast wind, with a regular gale. So, we were watching for the wind to cut down in order to go across with it. The both of us were loaded with herring, so we wanted to go across.

It was this kind of a morning, it was half decent calm. And poor Joe Richard, he was the only boat that was outside of here. And he wasn't scared of the wind. So I said to Johnny, "We better try and take that fish across." So we left from here, and we put the 3 sail on her, and the motor. She was going good. Poor Joe Richard was (out) there. He got up in his boat and he tried to make us turn back. And at that time, I think it was too rough for us to turn back. So I stopped the engine, and I said, "There go

54

the sails. We're going to try our best with the sails." I'm telling you, she was going. I didn't put any sails down, though, I put the full sail on her. And she was going some.

And sometimes the water was coming over the boat. She wasn't coming in, but she was splashing both sides. So, I kept it up with all the sails on her and everything, and we went right through into Canso. I thought for sure she was going to sink before she would have gone three-quarters across. We had no dory or anything; I couldn't turn back. Said, "We'll have to try, anyway."

So when we got in the wharf in Canso, oh, there were about 50 men there. Came and looked at the boat, and looked at the kind of men that were aboard—how crazy they were. They had gone out of that with big boats there, 50- and 60-foot boats. We only had about a 25-, 27-foot boat. And we went across. Well, you know, a racket on the wharf! How could I have made it! But still, we made it. It was the only trouble I had too much in a boat.

You know, I've been caught quite a few times, but I never was scared I was going to get drowned, or anything. Even in a fog, or things like that.

One time in a fog, I was fishing off Canso, trawls. We were fishing outside the buoy there. And it was thick-a-fog—you could hardly see from the bow to the stern of the boat. So, we were hauling trawl, and we heard a horn blowing once in a while. He wasn't blowing too often, but he was blowing once in awhile. And I had the motor on. When you have the motor on, you can't hear too much. We had the motor on, and were keeping on hauling. So, (the fellow with me) told me a couple of times, "You'd better cut your trawl, put a buoy line on her, be-

cause that boat's coming for us. I'm pretty gol-darned sure it's coming for us." So I didn't bother too much. I said to myself, if she happened to come just for the sake of shifting one side or the other of the boat, I can do it.

But when I saw that ship—Christ Almighty, it was the size of the house here, in height! So I cut the trawl and I pressed on the gas. Then the motor stopped right still, boys. Stopped right still! Just the same as if I had cut the wire off altogether. And the captain was good enough that he reversed his boat to stern. He hauled his astern. And I got a chance, and went on one side.

That was luck, though. You can call that luck. Oh, Christ, I was some white! But it was my fault. Because he had told me a couple of times, you know. I should have cut it before and just looked around. But I didn't do that; I kept on hauling. Because I was depending on the motor. When I pressed on the gas, I gave it too much gas at one time, and (it) stopped. Right still, boy. Didn't make a cake. Sometimes you can take awful chances.

Travels with
Johnny "Butch" MacDonald

*About half of this interview was made riding in Johnny MacDonald's
truck, visiting farms in Cape Breton County.*

I wasn't the first fellow to carry a cow in a truck but I'm sure I was the
second. I think Jack Munro was a little ahead of me. He was a competitor
from Whycocomagh. Before 1929, I had a Model T truck. You can call it
a truck. The box on the back of it was no bigger than the inside of this
cab. You couldn't haul anything in it. You might take one calf in it if you
tied his legs, you know. Take one or two calves. But at that time, you
know, all the boats are running up the Lakes. And you'd go up with this
Model T, you travelled around the country everywhere. You were in everybody's gate. "Anything you're parting with? Any cattle or calves to put
out?" Maybe they'd have something, and maybe they wouldn't. If they
wouldn't, they'd tell you they'd have something next week or next month.
Maybe they made a little, maybe I made a little. It was no gold mine, by
any means. And whatever you would buy, the farmer'd put it onto the

lakeboat. And the boat would come into Sydney. Oh yeah, you were going around then just buying the stuff. You didn't have to fight with it and wrestle it.

You'd be travelling around now like up in Middle River there, in the fall of the year, you'd be buying two-year-old heifers and steers right off of the mountain. And they'd be as wild as deer. The going price was 25 dollars a head. You'd tell the farmer to put it on the boat, either Wednesday's boat or Friday's boat, whichever. And, boy, those old farmers, they'd deliver them, they'd get them there. They'd get them in, they'd have their legs tied, their heads tied, boards on their eyes, so that they couldn't see. Those things were wild, and they had to try to drive them. But they'd land them there, you know. They'd get them to the boat, 5 or 6 or 7 miles away.

Then the competition was getting keener. The farmer says, "Well, I'll sell it to you, but I can't take it to the boat." "Well, I'll pick it up myself." I got a bigger truck then, one that would carry an animal. I'd pick it up. This is how you were getting ahead of the competition, you know. Oh, she was dog eat dog, then.

(*Were the farmers loyal to you?*) Well, I got along pretty good with them. Farmers then, they were used to getting gyped a lot. There were a lot of gangsters going through the country buying stuff. They had a habit of buying, and, "I'll pay you when I come back, I'll pay you when I sell it"—and all this stuff. Some of them would never come back with the money.

But when I started, I promised myself that I would never take 5 cents worth from the gate without leaving the money. Not that money was that plentiful with me, either. Because, when we started out, we had nothing. We had to sell one to buy another one. So the drovers, they were called— they had a mark against them, you know. But after the farmers got to know me, they weren't suspicious, no. I always paid them right on the spot.

Then when the boat would land in Sydney, I'd go down and I'd herd everything up the Esplanade to the slaughterhouse there, and kill them. Sometimes there'd be a bunch of sheep, sometimes there'd be cattle. Sometimes you'd bring in carloads of sheep. They'd come into the C.N.R. You'd unload them down there, drive them through the city, right up to the slaughterhouse. It was rugged work, hard work, hard, holy God, it was hard.

But it was an interesting life. By God, I had quite a career. Worked at that all my life, travelling around. Then, there were farms everywhere, not like it is today. You only have a few fellows to do business with today. Just a few fellows that are shipping milk, that's all. There's no other farm-

ers. At that time, it was farms everywhere. Everybody was farming.
There's places I used to buy cattle, there's not even a house or nothing,
it's all grown up in woods now. You take River Denys—it was all farmers through there. No trouble to load a car of lambs up there—that's 100,
110 lambs. No trouble. Now you couldn't load a wheelbarrow up there.
Or they'd have a cow or a bull there—something that wasn't giving any
milk—they couldn't get it with calf or something. And maybe there's
some other fault to find with it. And they'd sell it. It provided them with a
little bit of money. The sheep used to pay the taxes in the fall of the year.

(*Your father was a butcher before you.*) Oh yes, he was an old-timer.
He was one of the best. I had two other brothers, and I was the oldest. So
as soon as we were 8 or 9 or 10 years old, he had you out in the slaughterhouse working, you know. He worked hard himself and he made you
work hard, too. Long hours. You'd go out after supper and kill a hundred
lambs. Fifty or 60 or 100 lambs after supper. You'd do the whole bit.
You'd dress them. Make them ready for the market. The old man and myself, and have another fellow there. Do a hundred. Two fellows could do
10 an hour. We used to do that, no problem.

See, there was no refrigeration then. So you couldn't kill in the heat of
the day, like in the afternoon, like you can now. That time you'd kill them
after supper. In the morning you would spread them around, sell them
out. Deliver. You had your regular customers every week, then. Sold
everything to the stores.

Then when the brother next to me, when he got old enough, he had to
get out and work. The same as I used to work. I was the oldest, so I was
the first. (*Was your father easy to work for?*) Oh, he was tough, he was

59

tough. All you ever heard was, "Hurry up! Hurry up!" So, that's tough enough, isn't it? He was a slave himself.

My father used to send me out—13 and 14—yes. He sent me to Iona. He said, "They'll be bringing the lambs into Iona a certain day. You go and weigh them and load them." See, the merchants up through the country then, they used to do the business with the farmer. The storekeepers. So, he would contact this storekeeper, and say, "Make a day. Could you get 70 or 80 lambs for next week, a certain day?" Well, the storekeeper notifies all the farmers to bring their lambs in on this certain day. And you have a car there. Well, you weigh them and you pay them for them.

(*Does the merchant get anything for this?*) No. It may seem unusual. But it was also a benefit to him. It was bringing money into the country. And that money was needed. Lots of the times, these farmers would owe the merchant money. And the merchant would be there with his hand out, I suppose, when I'd pay the farmer. So that's the way it was done then, you know.

(*If there was a big snowstorm, would you still go that day?*) Well, practically, practically, yes. It would take quite a storm if I wouldn't make it. If I told the fellow I'd be there on a certain day, I was there on a certain day. Especially if you're dealing in lambs. Cattle is not so bad. But when you're dealing with lambs, if you tell a man you're going to be there on a certain day, you want to be there. That man goes through that trouble of catching those lambs.

See, if you disappoint that farmer, that news would travel all around that neighbourhood. And the next fellow you said, "I'll be up there Wednesday," he would just say, "Well, maybe he will and maybe he won't." It was building a reputation, of course it was. They know you're going to be there. And you have to do that to stay in business. You're dealing with farmers. You've got to trust them, and they trust you. If they don't, you don't do business with them. (*You certainly have to trust them. I see you put animals onto their farms, and you don't take money back.*) That's right, yes. I wasn't always like that. When I started out, I had to sell a calf to buy another calf.

But in buying beef cattle, you don't make too many mistakes. Sometimes you'll be off. You'll figure they should dress so much, and they won't do that. You'll probably be 10, 40, or 50 pounds short. And there you are, boy, that's serious, you know. But in handling dairy cattle, that's tricky business, that's tricky business. There's so many problems that a cow can have. And the only person knows it is the fellow that raised it. And you buy his problem then. And you don't know till after you bought it. And then they're just garbage. They're for beef. Only worth half as much as a milk cow.

(*Do you buy milk cows?*) Yes, and sell them to the farmers. (*From one to another?*) Right. (*Like used cars.*) Right. The same thing, the same thing. (*So it's not just a matter of butchering?*) No, no. Selling dairy cattle is half the battle too, you know, dairy cows. Oh yes. You take a farmer, she had a cow, and she's going down in her milk. And you come along: "I've got a nice fresh cow. Are you interested in her? How much will you give me for this one? What do you want for yours?" So you make a trade, eh? Hoping that she's satisfied and you're satisfied. (*You take the cow that doesn't milk so well, and you butcher that.*) That's right. Yeah.

It takes time, but they all work themselves out, you know. Bound to. (*How do you mean?*) Well now, there's this cow I left with this woman. She condemned this cow. Well, you'd think it was the end of the world, that I'd have to take the damn thing and kill it. She was saying, "You can't get much beef off of that." That's not a beef animal, that's a milk cow. This other fellow will take it, and he'll like her, too. I know it. (*And what'll make the difference?*) Well, just the difference between him and her. He'll give the cow a chance. He knows, he's been around cattle all his life, he knows. She's there, she was scared to death. "The cow's kicky , the cow's this." The cow's not. I know it.

(*And even though this other fellow owed you money, you'll still give him more animals.*) Yes, yes. Oh yeah. Sure. These fellows are as honest as the sun. It'll take time, but you'll be taking cattle from him. He'll call up when he has a cow to sell, or a couple of cows to sell. (*So you may never actually see money from him.*) From him, no. I'll never see money like that, no. (*But you'll see it in the form of another cow.*) That's right, that's right, yes. (*Your banker must be delighted.*) Johnny laughs: Well, let him worry about it. (The same cow is taken off at another farm.)

(*Now here, there was no dickering, no nothing. They're happy to take the animal.*) That's right. Well now, this cow (one we've just taken on the truck), I left it there some time ago. I had no place for it, and I just left it there. I said, "Here, I've got a cow." Sometimes you leave a cow in a place. I said, "Milk her." And I said, "When I get a sale for her, I'll come and take her." And he said, "All right. If she's good, I'll keep her." I said, "All right." So I was talking to him, and he's not going to keep her. So I left him another one, and I'm sure he'll buy the other one. (*Now what will you do with the cow you've just taken from him?*) This one? Oh, there's another fellow waiting for it. Somebody'll take her. (*Does the other fellow know he's waiting yet?*) Oh yes, he knows he's waiting. He's expecting me this evening. I told him I'd be there.

(*So now, this cow has been at one farm, but they weren't completely happy.*) That's right. She was only there for about, oh, a week. (*And this fellow wasn't pleased with her.*) That's right. (*Now, you've just given this fellow a new cow that didn't work out somewhere else.*) That's right. (*But he may end up happy with it.*) That's correct. I know it's going to happen this time. I'm sure of it. (*And you're taking away a cow that he wasn't completely satisfied with.*) That's right.

In the first place, he's against the colour. (*He likes black and white.*) He should have kept a cow like this, because it would bring up the quality of his milk. One Guernsey cow would bring up the butterfat in his milk. Holstein's just a little better than water. (*All the milk goes in the same place?*) That's right. In the same tank. And even her milk, from one Guernsey cow, would improve the whole tankful. (*But he didn't like the colour.*) He didn't like the colour, no. And he said she wasn't giving enough milk. Well, that could be, too. (*But you'll take her to someone else, and it's just possible....*) That he'll be satisfied with her.

I put them on trial. It's just as well to do that. If I sold the cow and the cow was no good, I'd take the cow back anyway. I wouldn't leave anyone stuck with the cow. Understand?

(Johnny took a bull calf on the truck.)

Oh, this calf in here, that little thing, nobody wants them. No, no, no, no. Take too long to feed them; it's a losing battle. Nobody wants them. But if it was a year old, there'd be people looking for it. A lot of people would take a bull for breeding, you know. I have a lot of bulls out, I just lend them, put them there, let them use them. That brown bull you saw (on a farm we stopped at) , that belonged to me. He was looking for a bull, and I dropped that one off there. (*You'll let him use it for breeding. Do you*

charge for that?) No. (*Then what's the good to you?*) Well, hopefully, that it will put on 100 pounds while he has it. (*And you'll take it back and butcher it.*) Not necessarily. If it's a quiet bull, I might give it to somebody else. It may live for a couple of years. Growing all the time. (*So you have a lot of breeding bulls out there.*) Yes, a lot, kicking around the country everywhere.

(*So what kind of a hand do you really have in the creation of the herds that we have in Cape Breton?*) I don't play too important a part in that. The bulls I give them, they're not looking for stock. Just to get her milking again. It costs 12 dollars to breed them artificial. So, this way, they'll have a bull of their own. And it's a cow that they're not fussy if they raise a calf off or not, you know. Sometimes, breeding artifical, they don't catch, and they get caught with a bull. There's all these things enter into it.

(*Today we've made three stops. What would a normal day be for you, years ago?*) Oh, to put it like that, I don't know. I'd stay up in the country for 2 or 3 days, going around. Buying, and shipping it down on the boat. And then it would come into Sydney. Then you would have to take it up, and you'd work all night butchering it. Then you're out trying to sell it the next day to these little stores. And the price was low—7 and 8 cents a pound—that was the going price. So you were working for very little, but so was everybody else. There was nobody had any money. I can't get over it. I see everybody you look at now has got a pocketful of money. And I can't get over the whole years when nobody had any money. Nobody had folding money. God almighty.

I used to be travelling the country, walking in the wintertime. You'd get off the train, say now, at Alba. And I'd walk down as far as South Cove. Maybe that's 7 or 8 or 10 miles. And go down the South Side 5 or 6 miles, and this way 5 or 6 miles. (*Looking for what?*) Cattle. (*What would happen if you found one?*) The farmer would deliver it to Alba, put it on the train. There'd be snowbanks, you know. Put them in the sleigh or something. I'm telling you, it was out of this world, you know, what was going on then, what you'd do. And the price of the cow wasn't much, either. Twenty-five, 30 dollars. These would mostly be milk cows, you know. You'd trade them around. Everybody around Sydney kept milk cows then. Everybody, up around Alexandra Street there. Not farmers. There were farmers, too. But everybody around kept cows. There were cows kept right down here on Crescent Street, you know. Down at the north end of George Street. Some fellow would have 3 or 4 cows. There were a lot of cows kept in the city at that time. And outside the city, just out a mile or two, a lot (of) people kept cows.

The farmers, one time, were the best-off people, because money was scarce. Nobody had any money. Time of the Second World War—before the war, and after the war—well, that's when everybody started to leave the farms. They went in the army, and they went to the cities and got work. The farmers just sold off all their stock. And the farms gradually went to nothing.

I bought up, I don't know how many farms, bought the last hoof off of them, you know. Then they'd ask me, "Do you know anybody'd want to buy a farm?" No, no, I didn't know anybody. You could have bought the farm for a couple of thousand dollars. Everybody left the farms, all the farms closed up. You know, yourself, even down where you are, Wreck Cove, there's nothing now. Down North River, there used to be good farms down through there. I used to buy a lot of stuff down there. And Inverness County, yes. Around Mabou.

I had some of the best cups of tea anybody ever had, and I drank the worst that anybody ever had. A lot of both. And wherever you'd get in the nighttime, they'd say, "Well now, may as well put up for the night." So I'd stay for the night. There was no paying. Everything was free. I had more free meals than any man in Canada. They seemed to like to put you up for the night. And talk, kind of talking, see.

And suffered with the cold, too. You got to, those old houses. There was no heat in them. There was a kitchen stove. And that had to be put out when everybody went to bed. And God almighty—you'd see the oilcloth on the floor would just be waving with the drafts coming through. It's different today. You go to a farmhouse today, they're better off than the city. They've got everything. But then, there was nothing. They'd put you up in

64

a house. Everybody, they all had a spare room, eh? Well, maybe that bed wasn't slept in for two or three months. And everything is damp, and this and that. It'd be cold, freezing, and you get into that. But you wouldn't be in there long before it'd start to warm up, and you'd go to sleep, and then in the morning—you'd hate to get up. Because you'd have to go outside to get warm. No matter how cold it was outside, it was colder inside.

Sometimes, you'd be on the road all night, trying to find a breakthrough, trying to shovel through. Say, if you were coming from Baddeck just to Sydney, and there was snow. There were no plows. By the time you'd get to Boularderie, everything would be blocked up. So if you'd get stuck, you'd just have to start shovelling. And it wouldn't be long before another truck would come along, or another car, and the first thing you know, there's half a dozen lined up together, and you'd be all working together. Finally, you'd get through. Shovelling, and pushing, breaking through. That was common then, too. No snowplows. No salt.

Barachois Mountain, there, lots and lots of times, I'd be coming home with a load of cattle, 12 o'clock at night or 1 o'clock in the morning. All alone, you know. And you'd be trying to make the Barachois Mountain. Just the other side of Leitches Creek, before you get to Boisdale. This is a long hill, a mile or two miles long. And you'd be going, and praying that she'd make it. Be slipping, ice, you know. And you'd get pretty near the top, and there, that's it, she's stopped. The wheels'd be going, and that's as far as you'd get. Then you'd have to get out, get underneath that thing, put the chains on—all alone. Didn't matter if it was raining or snowing. Put the chains on—nothing to it—get up the hill. Then you take the chains off. A set of chains wouldn't last any time.

I was on a drive from Margaree to Nyanza. Went to Margaree by truck, with the little Model T. I used to be buying cattle in Middle River, you know. I used to take down 7 or 8 a week. The farmers would deliver them to Nyanza. But they were all cleaned up in Middle River. This was getting late in the season. Pretty near December or something. Just about the last trip of the lakeboat. There was nothing around Middle River, so I went down to Margaree. I hadn't been down there; I wasn't known down there. Anyway, I went around and I bargained 24 head of cattle. They were to deliver them, I think it was at Ross's Hill; they had a field there. They were to deliver them there Monday morning.

So, Sunday it started to snow. And I thought, by geez, I'd better take off for Margaree. It was rough going; I just made Hunter's Mountain. I got up there, then I got to Lake o' Law. And that was it, that was as far as she was going. She was in the snow. And it was dark, you know. So, there was a house —you could see a light up there. So I walked up to the house, told them my troubles. Truck in the road, and I was going to try to get to

65

Margaree. "Well," they said, "there's a wake here tonight, and there's not much we can do for you. But," they said, "you go to such a place down here, you cross over here, and you go this way—there's two or three men there, they'd be only too glad to go down with you. They've got a horse."

So I walked there, told them. Oh yes, yes, they'd go. So much apiece. Anyway, I slept on a little bench that night, about 6 inches wide. Waiting for the morning to come. And finally, we had to get going, up around 4 or 5 o'clock. So we got the horse hitched up and we got down to Margaree, down to the place. And there were some of the cattle there. Finally, they all came in. There was a young fellow there, very young. He said, "Mister, if I help you out with the cattle, will you pay my way on the boat?" I said, "Yes."

So, we started off with the cattle. Well, everything was going all right. But it was taking quite awhile. There were the two hired fellows, and myself, and then this young fellow. (*Did you have the cattle all tied together?*) No, no, no—loose. Just a bunch of cattle, and you drove them. That's where the name "drover" came from. Same as out west, they herd them with horses. We were on foot. We drove them. They stayed together. It seems that's their nature, when you're driving them. It has to be that way, or nobody could drive them. Whoever set up the system set it up that way. Same with sheep, they stick. Just walk behind them. And then if you see one turning off the side, you'd run up the side and put it back on the road.

Anyway, we got up around Lake o' Law there sometime in the afternoon. Drove them in the yard, and got the farmer to put some hay out, give them some feed. I think the old farmer gave us something, too. And we started off again. (*Had you planned that stop in advance?*) No, no. (*Just picked a farm.*) Well, yes. Asked him. You'd give him something. A dollar would go a long way then.

Anyway, we got to Middle River that night. And these two fellows, they were bellyaching and growling all day about how hard it was, and they weren't getting enough money, and all this kind of stuff. We put the cattle in the yard there and fed them, and I went in and went to bed. The young fellow, they put him up, too. I paid those two fellows and I told them that I'd get the cattle there myself.

So the next morning, this young fellow and I, we borrowed a lantern from the fellow, and we started off driving to Nyanza. Pitch dark. So, the young fellow took his suitcase and the lantern. And he went ahead. And I was behind. With 24 cattle. We drove them down. We got them turned into the Yankee Line. Pretty near every gate was open. And they'd go in the gate. He'd sit down on the suitcase with the lantern. And I'd have to get over the fence, or through the fence, round them out, get them out on the road again.

So anyway, there were fellows came along, going to catch the boat, you know, with horses and sleigh. I told them to tell the captain that I was coming with these cattle, and to wait for me. So, I suppose he waited an hour. But by God, you talk about hardship. You know, there was a lot of snow down then, pretty near a foot of snow—we were plowing through that. But we finally landed them there, got them down, got them aboard the boat. And the truck was still stuck up in the Lake o' Law.

The worst experience I ever had was out on the ice. I was to Arichat. I was buying hides. This was in the winter. And I had a load of hides in the truck. Coming back, at St. Peters, it started to snow, and I was tired, so I put up for the night. And the next morning, everything was bright with snow. I said to the people in the hotel there, "Looks like I'm in trouble. I guess I'll be here for the winter!" "Oh, now," they said, "I don't know. You may get through. The doctor had a call last night to Soldiers Cove, and he was down on the ice." "Well, there's his track. You can follow his track." And I said, "Where'd he get on the ice?" And they said, "Down at the canal." And I was scared of the ice. Because I was after losing a truck in the ice. I just went through the ice, off of North Sydney there. I had gone out on the ice, and down she went. I had the Model T Ford.

The Caribou—that was the Newfoundland ferry—she had backed out, you know, she made a path for herself. Sunday night she broke it. And this ice had just frozen over. I was there Monday morning. I had this little Ford, but the wind was blowing me out. I had her steering this way, and she seemed to be going out that way. Anyway, she just hit the end of the ice, where the boat had opened it—there was just a scum of ice over it. I hit that, and down she went. Oh, just a second. I got wet up to here. See, there was no top on her. That time, cars, they had little canvas tops. Well, through the time and rough usage, this top was gone. It was just an old wreck of a thing, you know. If there had been a top on her, I'd have never got out of her. But when she went down, I just jumped away from the wheel, and I put my foot on that door there, and then the ice caught me here. Across the waist. The hands were out on the ice. She was underwater that much then. I had a big pair of woolen mitts, and the mitts were out on the ice like that, you know. I went to put a little pressure on them, and I could see where they were freezing to the ice, and I thought, "By God, this is not so bad after all. So I didn't panic. I just took my time, gave my arse a little twist, and I was on the ice. (*Did you ever get that car back?*) No.

But I was scared of the ice after that. And they were telling me at Arichat, "Oh, you've got nothing to worry about. His track is there ahead of you." So I went down, and sure enough, there was his track. Oh, a great track, great travelling on the ice. And I was going along, sailing along. Geez, this is too good to be true! My God, this is great travelling. Then all of a sudden, it was as bare as that pavement there—there was nothing—no track at all. I said, "Geez, what happened to the track? I'm going back. To hell with this." And I went to go back, and there was no track behind.

And there I was, out there. The wind started to blow, and it just cleaned off the ice. And I was away to hell out on the Bras d'Or Lakes. I didn't know whether to go this way, this way, this way, or this way. I didn't know what to do.

I was driving along. And I saw a fellow coming out from the shore. He had a spear; he was going spearing eels. Well, I made for him. And I got up to him. I said, "Can you tell me where to get off of this ice?" "Well, you might get off there"—and he started pointing. But he pointed back. He said, "Look, do you see that point that you just came through there?" I said, "Yes." He said, "There was never, never as much as a horse crossed there." "Well," I said, "I made it."

(*Why did you buy hides?*) That's part of the business. And I used to buy wool, too, in May or June or July—after they'd shear the sheep. The big kill was in the fall, but there'd be hides and skins the year round. There's not very much of that done now. But at that time there was a lot of local butchers around, all through the country everywhere. They would buy from their neighbours. They used to come into Sydney every week. Some would go to Glace Bay, some would go to Waterford. They had their regular customers. and they'd have produce. They'd kill a cow, they'd be killing lambs. And they'd have eggs, they'd have butter, they'd have socks. They'd have everything like that. Homemade socks. They would buy from the country people. They'd come in every week with a load. Regardless of the weather, winter or summer. and they'd all have some hides and skins. (*You'd buy some of these.*) Yes.

(*Would they be some of your competition?*) Well, in a way they would be, yes. Not that much, but to a certain extent. They sold at houses. We sold at stores, you know. But there were dozens of them, all through the country everywhere, that made a living, peddling. I'm the only one that survived out of —I'm the last one. I'm going to keep going for another 30 years! (*For 25, for sure.*) For sure, yes. I'll be awful disappointed if I don't make 25. Then I'll take 5 years off. I've got it figured out pretty good, haven't I? (*Why did you survive it? Why, of all your competitors, are you still at it?*) Well, I'll tell you. I worked harder at it than the rest of them. I was young and I was active and I was going. I was ahead of the other fellow when he was buying it, and I was ahead of him when he was trying to sell it. That's what it takes. But I worked at it. Holy God Almighty.

(*What about the animals themselves? Did you ever have any trouble with them?*) Certainly you have trouble with them. Sure you do. They're not always easy as these, you know. (*The ones we had on the truck today*) These are milkmen's cows, and they're kind of domesticated. But you get these other animals, you know, that are not handled. You put a rope on them, boy, you've got a tiger by the tail. Vicious. Your life is not worth 5 cents. But I've been very lucky all my life, that I never got hurt. Nothing worth speaking of. I got shook up a good many times. Well, you'd get tangled up in a rope, or they'd trip you and knock you up, kick you, and hook you, and all this. (*Lean on you.*) Oh, that's nothing. You don't mind that. But they'll kick you, they'll do everything.

There was a cow that—she was really rough. See, they go out of their mind, they go berserk. They're just like a crazy person. (*Any special reason?*) Well, any more than that it was tied, and it didn't want to be tied, and it was trying to get away. And it just went crazy. Jumping up this way, up that way, standing on its head. One case, we had to kill it on the truck. It got itself down, tangled up. Had to take the knife and cut its throat. They'll bite you, they'll hook you, they'll try to get at you with their feet, their front feet. They're really making for you, you know. They're trying to get you. (*And yet, on the farm, they wouldn't be like that?*) No, quiet as.... But you put a rope on them and try to handle them and they just get excited and that's it, you know.

I bought a cow in the country. I had a truckload of cows. And we were unloading them (in Sydney). And there was this cow and she was wild. And I was extra careful with her. I had a long rope on her, and I had the truck backed right up to the door, only about 6 or 7 inches to spare. And I had another fellow with me. He was untying the cow. And instead of untying the cow and letting it go, he held onto the rope just as the cow's head was facing this little opening. And that's all that cow needed. She made the rest of the way for herself. And off she goes, up the street—up Townsend Street. Then she decided to go up Charlotte Street. I was after her. She decided to go up Charlotte against the traffic. And then there were kids gathering everywhere. Hollering, yelling, one thing and another. And this cow stopped right at the Tip Top Tailors. And she was looking in the window. She saw her own reflection in there. I was watching her, and I was expecting to see her jump through the window. But no, she decided to go up Charlotte Street further. In her galloping through the streets, she sideswiped a car. At Townsend and Charlotte, she broke a railing going up the steps. We were trying to corner her there. She just went to jump the railing, and she only got half over it, and came down on it and broke it. So she went up the street, galloping around. Then she got onto George Street. Down near the corner of George and Townsend, some fellow got ahold of the end of the rope, tied it to a post. And they had her anchored. We took her from there. Got ahold of the rope, gradually got her into the truck.

But things always seem to work out. There always seems to be some way to catch them. They'll get into a corner somewhere. But some of them, now, they can give you a hard time. You wrote a story one time about an animal that got clear in Sydney. And it was me that caught her. This was off one of the lakeboats. Damn little things, wild as hell. I've had to butcher them on the truck. I was up West Bay Road one time, when a cow jumped over the side of the truck, and broke her neck. Right in the road. And I had to butcher her right there. Cut her throat, take the guts out of her, drag her up on the truck, head for home.

(*And would you do it all again?*) If I had to work like I did, killing those lambs, no, I wouldn't do, I wouldn't do it. Because, I'm telling you, it was terrible. Day and night. Lambs, in all kinds of weather. You had to have them shipped at a certain day. They had to be shipped Tuesday. I'd leave here Monday at noon. You'd go around Monday and you'd collect up enough money to go and buy the load, you know. And then I'd start off for the country. I wouldn't know where I was going to load them. Wouldn't know where I was going to get a carload. And I'd get up there. Well, I knew the country. I knew the people. Maybe this fellow couldn't catch them, maybe something else happened. And you'd keep going till you'd get a fellow with a bunch that, yes, he would have them. Well then, all right.

The nearest station to that fellow, that's where you would load. So you'd go to the station and you'd order a car. Then you'd start this, going around and around, and you'd tell them, "Have them in tomorrow, have them in tomorrow"—the handiest station. And it was always trouble. Maybe this one couldn't catch them: "Yes, I'll have them in. Look, they're down in the field, it'll only take a minute." The only minute is an hour, you know. And time is important.

You'd start Monday. And you'd go around Monday night and make the contacts, you know. And Tuesday you'd pick them up, eh? From the farmer, and haul them in to the station. The train was coming through Tuesday night. Well, that train would be in here Wednesday morning. And I would get home Tuesday night sometime, with a load of lambs on the truck. And a carload coming in. Instead of driving them up from the station then, we'd truck them up. Then we'd start butchering Wednesday. We had to have the lambs to deliver Thursday. Because the stores wanted them Thursday or Friday. And that's when you had to have them. The stores are doing business with you every week. This store would take 10, this one would take 15. But they wanted them every week. And you had to supply them every week.

So, they'd arrive Wednesday morning. Start butchering Wednesday afternoon. Maybe Wednesday after supper. Well, you didn't mind that, you didn't mind the butchering. That had to be done. You were working inside. But when you're picking them, getting them, and it raining—it's not a very pleasant job. It's mud to your knees. (*How late would you butcher?*) Maybe 12 o'clock, 1 o'clock, something like that. If we wouldn't do them all that night, we'd do the other half the next night. Gracious, the work.

When I think of it. You had to be crazy. I had to be crazy. I had to be.

But I worked like a slave at it. I had the best career of anybody, clear of the slavery, you know. It's a picnic now: good roads, good truck, heater. I used to like to kill lambs. I could kill a lamb in 4 minutes. I've done it. That doesn't mean to say that I could do 15 an hour. But I tried it one time. And it was just 4 minutes from the time I started it till it was hanging up, ready for the store. But we worked at it, holy God, all night, driving it, killing those things, lifting them around, throwing them around. And I liked doing it. I had to be crazy, didn't I? (*I*

don't think "crazy" is the word.) All right, demented—you can call it demented. There's some word.

With Karoline Siepierski, Whitney Pier

I was born in Poland, in Rzeszow. I came to Canada in 1926, just New Year's Day. (*What were you doing in Poland before you came here?*) Well, I'm working in the village and in the farm, plant potatoes and work in the harvest and everything like that, working in the summertime in the hay and everything. (*For your family?*) No, I'm working for big, big farms—big shots, see—and the people go working. Lots of people go, and you get paid. My own home—small house, two rooms and a little pantry—that's all. I had 4 sisters and 2 brothers. One sister came to Canada—her husband came first. After that he took his wife and two children. And him, he worked in the steel plant. In Poland he worked same as I was working—on the farm. He had a sister, an older sister here. And the sister took in the brother. (*And the brother brought his wife and children.*) And after two years my sister took me; my sister and her husband sent me a ticket.

(*Did you really want to leave Poland?*) Yes. In Poland, well, there was no good life. Now I've got money and they're working all the time. You make enough money for your work. I wanted to go to Canada, look...for more life. I was married in Poland. After two months, I'm going—because I had the ticket already. I had the paper. I had a boy friend. "You want to marry? Before I'm going?" Then I'm married, and after two months I went. My husband came after. I came here in 1926 and he came 1927. And coming to Canada, he just went right to farm work, in Vancouver, some place. (*He didn't come right to you?*) No, no, no. Just go, well, you take it, go to Canada to work on some farm. (*He didn't come to Sydney.*) No, no, no. Just go on the farm, whatever place you're sent, the address. And he called me here, right away, and he said, "I'm short of money, send me $100, I'm coming to Sydney, to Cape Breton."

(*What did you say?*) Well, I'm working, I'm working for a family—they paid me $10 in a month. I'm staying there, I'm eating and sleeping in the same place—their place—and I'm working, and the month would come and he'd give me $10. But those $10 I'm giving my sister for my ticket. (*How much work did you do for $10 a month?*) Everything in the house. I'm washing clothes, I'm scrubbing floors, I'm washing windows, venetian blinds—everything. (*Was $10 pretty good pay?*) Well, $10, for a long time, that's good money. My work—it's worth more, but she's not paying me. For those jobs, I'm working, doing everything in the house—she should have paid me more than the $10.

(*Why did you take a job that doesn't pay you what you're worth?*) What place am I going? I could stay at my sister's place. My sister said, "You don't want to go, don't go—stay at my place." Just I'm thinking to myself, What for I'm sitting down? Better I go work and make a few dollars, for myself. (*I see. Was there any other job?*) No, I had no luck. This is all you could get, this time—1926—you can't get another job. What place? (*Especially, I guess, when you're a woman—there's even less work you could do.*) That's right. (*For instance, if you wanted to work in the steel plant....*) No, no, they wouldn't take a woman at that time. (*And certainly not the coal mines.*) That's right. There's lots of men. (*And was there any other kind of work that a young woman could do?*) No. Just, I had no luck. I was a stranger.

(*And what about your language? Did you speak English then?*) Oh no, nothing. I understood nothing. Just the woman where I was working—she spoke Polish and everything. And her husband. The children didn't speak Polish, just English.

. (*So you worked hard in this home. And you got $10 a month. And it was not high pay.*) No, no. (*But it was something.*) That's it. It was good for me. I had just come here, I had nothing—I'm glad I got $10. If I sat down at my sister's place, I'd have nothing. (*I understand. So, you heard* *from your husband. He wants $100 to come and be your husband.*) Yes. I gave the letter to my sister, she read it. She said, "Okay, okay, I'll give you back that money"—and her husband sent it right away. I was giving her money every month to pay for the ticket.

(*Your sister, did she have money?*) Well, her husband was working, in the plant. She's got a car—yeah. Her husband was here just 3 years before taking his wife to Canada. And saved money—him working, smart man. (*So a person coming here from Poland, in a short time, they could make a decent living?*) Yes. Oh, yes. You're working double time sometimes. Soon you send for wife and children. (*And was it hard for Polish people to get work at the plant?*) No. Everybody glad to get a job. And make dollars. In Poland you're working and working and you have small money. (*I mean, did Polish people have an easy time to get the jobs at the plant?*) I can't tell you for sure. Just, he said he liked it, he was working hard.

(*Did you send money for your husband to come?*) Yes. He came—it must be in two weeks. He stayed with my sister, with me. And after that I caught sick with my fingers, I got poisoned—from the wax and different stuff, working for this woman. After that, I quit that job. I said, "I'm sorry, my finger's sore." And my sister's husband found a job for my husband. And they hired him for the plant. He worked in the open hearth. (*I heard sometimes people had to buy their jobs.*) No, not my husband. Just the right time they wanted men for work. (*Did he make a good living right away?*) Oh, yes. He was working for 12 to 14 hours. Because he wanted to make money to pay my ticket and to pay his ticket—he'd borrowed money in Poland. He paid over $200.

And then he got sick after. (*Did he get sick because of his work?*) Yes. He was working all the time, overtime—sometimes, working day shift, he'd stay for another shift. Sometimes tired, you've got to, in your spare time, sit down, lay down on some steel—and he'd catch, here, awfully cold. (*In his back?*) That's right. And after, it went in his chest—and he was sick 5 years in the hospital. Five years sick—before dying.

Eighteen months he stayed in the TB hospital in Sydney. Eighteen months, one piece, steady. And after, you know, sometimes you think, it'd be better if I went far away, see a doctor who could maybe help me. And he went to Halifax. Stayed 3 months in a hospital in Halifax. They did something here—I can't explain to you. (*They did something to his neck?*) Yes, back here. And it didn't help. And after those months, he sent me a letter: "If you want to see me, you'd better take me home." Just awfully sick. He came home. He stayed more than a year home. And after awhile, he came a little bit better. And he went back to work some more. (*To the plant.*) Yeah. They took him back. He was working, some easy job. Maybe working one year, that's all.

74

He got sick again. Same sickness. And he went in the hospital some more. He stayed a couple of months, and after the doctor said, "You're not *really* sick—a little bit cured. Well, you'd better go home." And every week he'd just go for something they'd give him for the chest. Some gas, something—I don't know. I can't explain. And he went every week, once a week. And he stayed home, he didn't work, just kept in. The steel company gave him a benefit. They didn't give all the time, just 3 months they gave you benefit, and they finished. (*Not a great deal of money.*) No, no—but still good. At least then for one dollar you could buy *something*. Today you can't. When my man was sick, the city gave me $7 a week, every week. Called relief. (*How could a person survive?*) Well, just do it. The hard time. Just I'm glad the city gave me $7. And the boarders gave me money, that paid for my rent. I'm glad.

(*Did you have any children yet?*) I had 3 children. I kept 3 boarders. Rooming, see? I'm washing clothes. I make meals, not just my meals—those men bought meals I cooked. I give him a room, he paid me $5 in a month. I'm telling you: when I think of it, I nearly cry. I didn't have a machine like that today—just I'm washing their clothes by hand. Those men—they'd tell me in the morning when they went to work what they wanted for dinner. When they come from work. Well then, the fellow come from the store with what he wanted—pound of meat, bread and butter. That's all. And I'm cooking some soup and like that for supper. And I lived. I'm paying $15 in rent every month. What those boarders gave me I paid in rent. And the heavy clothes, the men come from work with heavy clothes, dirty clothes and everything. (*You worked hard for your rent.*) I was young. I didn't mind. I didn't mind those jobs. Just young, I'm strong and I'm working.

(*How does your husband take this? He's come to this country, he's tried to start a new life—and for 5 years he's sick.*) Well, he wasn't expecting to get sick. Well, sickness comes, that's all. I'm telling him, "What for are you working too many shifts?" And he said, "Well, you know what I'm doing—I'm working and I'll save money and go back to Poland." He must have been missing Poland too much. All the time saying, "Oh, well, I'm staying a couple of years, I'll make money, and after I'll go." But he got sick, he can't go. But the whole thing, in the 5 years— I'm counting him sick, that's all. After the doctor took him to the hospital the third time, he stayed a couple of months and he died. Now I had 3 children, I'm sending to school.

(*Was the church any help to you?*) No. The church came around collecting money. The man came every Monday, for the church, collecting. A couple of times, I gave. After, I'm saying, "You know that my husband's not working, how'm I to give you collection? I don't have money; I have 3 children." No help, nothing. For Christmas, my children had nothing; Salvation Army brought stockings for my children. Yes. And the Salvation Army, when they make a collection, they come to my door now and I'm giving them money all the time. I'm not forgetting them. (*And you were Catholic.*) Yes. (*And the Salvation Army is not Catholic.*) No. (*But they remembered you.*) Yes. And the Salvation Army went to the hospital all the time, sometimes shaved my husband, gave him a nice haircut, everything—for nothing. (*Good is good.*) Oh yes, that's beautiful. And I'm not forgetting the collection for Salvation Army when they'll be at my door. The priest didn't come, no.

After, I had one boarder that was a good one. Mike Oleschuk came. He said, "Mrs., I know you keep boarders. I've got a good boarder for you." I said, "I don't know, maybe my husband doesn't want him." Just that this man liked to drink a little bit. Mike went to the hospital, to see my husband, with this man. And he said, "Yes." Next day, I visited my husband, my husband said, "Just take him. Just you want to live, that's all. You want money. You've got two boarders, he's three—that's a good man, help you maybe"—and that's the way I'm taking that man. And he helped me. And this is the way I lived.

(*He was a Polish man?*) A Polish man, yeah. (*He must have been glad to get a chance to get Polish food.*) Yes. And he lived with the Polish people in the coke ovens. And Mike Oleschuk said, "That's no good for you, you stay all the time drinking—you're working and drinking, you've got lots of friends—and no money." That's why Mike wanted to find him a good place. So I told him, "You come, my husband said it's okay—but you know I've got 3 kids, I don't want you coming home too drunk." "Oh, don't worry, Mrs., no, no, no." I said, "You've got holes in the bottom of your shoes." I said, "Man, what's the matter, you're working for nothing, you've not got clothes." I want to wash his clothes. I said, "Where are your clothes?" "Oh," he said, "I left them at the place I was staying." I said, "Well, bring it, I'll wash. I don't want a dirty man here." He didn't bring anything. He went to the store and bought. He didn't have clothes. He didn't have a good suit. Just pants, no jacket, nothing. Well, after he listened to me a little bit, he said, "You're a smart woman," he told me. And he stopped a little bit drink. He didn't come home drunk, no. That's a good man. He said, "If I'd come a long time ago to board at your place, I'd have lots of money."

After my husband died, he stayed with me. He stayed at my place 22 years. (*Did you marry him?*) I'm not married, what for? I'll be married, he'll not listen to me what I'm telling him. He'd drink like he drank before. (*So you have more control on him when you didn't marry him.*) Oh yeah, some time I'm giving him this. (<u>Karoline held up her fist</u>. *But you made him into a better man?*) Yes. And bought a car after, got car, he got a good life. (*And you were together 22 years?*) Yes. (*And he helped raise your children?*) Yes. (**Karoline's son, Kazimir:** If it wasn't for him, God knows where we'd be today. He was supporting us.) And he went to visit my husband every second day, in the hospital. And my husband told him, "I know I don't think I'll live. You watch my children. Don't leave my wife with the children." And this is when he stayed with me. And that's all.

He wanted to marry. I said, "No, I don't want to marry, what for? When you're married, maybe you'll beat me and everything when you're drunk." Now, I'm not married. And I'm building a house myself. (*Did you actually do work on the house?*) Yes. I built my house in 1941. Just when my husband died, 1941, in June. After a couple of months, I bought a lot here and I started building a house. I looked for carpenters—some Ukrainian fellows. And I went and explained. And I went to Chappell's and bought wood, boards, and two-by-fours, and everything like that. And I'm going far and buying cheap and I brought it here. And the carpenters came.

And I dug the basement myself. Myself! I'd get up at 4, 5 o'clock in the morning, summertime, and I took a shovel and came here, and so much ground I'm taking every day. (*With a shovel?*) Yes. (*A pick?*) I had everything. (*A wheelbarrow?*) No. Just I'm throwing it. After, those men that stayed with me were hauling, two men. Then my man paid two men—"You no dig"—he paid two Italian men and they finished the basement. (*But first you were digging it.*) Myself, yeah. (*Did anyone ever tell you that wasn't women's work?*) Next door, the man said, "Woman, you'd better watch, just for old age, you'll feel that work, you're working too hard." I said, "Well, I can't help it. What I make with my hands, I'm not

77

paying money." Oh, the poor man, he'd stay here all the time and see the house I was digging. (*So you didn't shovel the whole basement.*) No, no, no. (*But a lot of it.*) Yes. Then carpenters took a contract with me. He told me how much it would cost me to make a frame, a roof, and inside— inside just two-by-four, the plaster I'm paying extra. I said, "Okay, I'll pay you cash money when you finish." I told him how much I want, how many rooms, and this and that. The whole downstairs finished; the whole upstairs just two-by-four. After I move here, my man with the boys—they put gyprock upstairs and fixed those two rooms. Oh, yeah.

1942 or 1943—I got a job in the steel plant. I'm happy they're taking a woman for work in the plant. My man came with word, "You say you're looking for a job"—because I talked all the time, if I'd find a job I'd take it—because I wanted some nice furnishing for the house. He said the company was taking women for work in the plant. And he told me one day— I'm dressed and I'm gone. They marked my name, they sent me to a doctor who said I'm healthy—and after, I went to work. (*Did you want to work in the steel plant?*) Yes. And I worked hard.

I'm working in the bar mill. Other women worked in the open hearth. Lots of women worked. In the bar mill I tied the rods, with wire, on tight. Bundles. One woman one side, and other one the other side—on a big bench. (*You have a scar on your arm....*) Yes, with wire. Right through. Sometimes they were short of men different places. Rod mill. I went behind the furnace, pushing billets into the furnace. (*Is this heavy work?*) Ho, ho—I'm sweating. and it's dangerous. When the billets come this side, you've got to hook something to stop them, not let too many go. When the fellow blows the whistle, some go in the furnace. Just sometimes they were short of men and they'd call me. The boss knew I was good, I'd watch. Same as a man. That's the way the boss got a surprise: in the arms, I'm strong. And short of men, they called me right away. They paid more money for those places, behind the furnace in the rod mill—little bit, a few cents more. Women used to say, "Why take Siepierski and not me?" Boss said, "Never mind, she's a good woman."

Sometimes I'm working bundle shack. Wire bundles go with hooks, and the women tied it twice with the small wire, both sides—and men took it out with the hooks. (*Did you ever have to lift anything?*) No, no, no, no. The war time, lots of women worked. Women worked in the open hearth, for the brick laying, just piled the bricks. I didn't work those jobs. I just worked in the bar mill. (*How long did you work?*) Nearly three years.

Men working in the plant were taken in wartime; this is the way they were short of men. After the war stopped, the men came back and they went to work in the place they worked before. (*What did they tell you?*) Well, the women were laid off. (*Was there a chance you'd be called back?*)

No, no. Just leave some women that worked in the office. (*Otherwise*....) Everybody home. (*How did you feel about that?*) Oh, I felt sorry. Because I wanted to work, I wanted to make money. I made money. I bought those chesterfields. I bought a furnace in the basement with money from work. But I think myself, it's better the women stay home and the men working—can't help it. (*You don't think women who want to work in the steel plant should?*) No. How? The women work and the men stay home—that's no good. Better men got jobs and women go home and stay. That's woman's job in the house. (*If you had had a husband to work for you, you'd have stayed home?*) Oh, never would be going to work, no sirree. Just a woman got job in a home, cook, clean house, wash clothes nice, watch children. (*And you would have been satisfied with that.*) Oh, yes.

(*How did you make a living after the war?*) I didn't keep boarders. I kept that man. He was like a stepfather for those children. One time I'm mad. I throw everything of his outside—the kids cry, for him, and he came back. My family grew. My man bought a Blackett's Lake place and made a cottage, nice bungalow for summer, and I went every summer, sometimes sleeping in the house. After 22 years, he died. He got diabetes, high blood pressure. I raised 3 children. Two boys and one girl. And everybody's married. And they all feel good.

Sometimes I sit down in the evening, I think of when I was working hard; why can't I work now?—nothing. I've lost everything, strength. (**Kazimir**: She's forgetting she's 77.) Sometimes I sit down and I'm thinking to myself how much has passed, that I'm crying. What do you do? Old people, they pass everything to young people: hard work, worrying, everything. That's all.

Wishie Rose:
From 50 Years at Sea

We had some good years—it wasn't all bad weather—but there was some rotten time, too.

I was born in Jersey Harbour, Newfoundland, but I lived in Harbour Breton most of my time there. It was just a little village, an outport, maybe 25 families. People all fishing, nothing else. Some shore-fished, some Bank-fished— some of them went to Lunenburg, some Bank-fished in Newfoundland—that's what they call dory fishing, in two-masted schooners, you know. That's actually the reason I came here to live. Because we used to come to Lunenburg every year, make a few hundred dollars; you'd go back to Newfoundland, spend it in the winter to the merchants down there. So, my mother was dead any-

way, and I figured if we had to come out of Newfoundland to make a living, why not stay out of it? Although in Newfoundland it's just as good now as any other place, maybe better, I don't know. The last time I went back, there were nothing but oil tankers back home, a busy place. But there's nobody in Jersey Harbour today.

(*What did your father do?*) He fished, too, in latter years. See, we had quite a little business there. I wasn't even born when we lost a Banks

80

schooner. She was only new, too—no insurance. All hands lost. The last man that saw her said she looked all right—they saw her in the evening. The breeze came up that night, and she never was heard tell of afterwards. (*Was your father aboard?*) No, no. But my mother had a brother on her at that time. It was my father's schooner. Brand new—newly repaired. She was an old schooner; he had her rebuilt new, you know. Her first year out, and no insurance on her. But that spring I heard poor old Dad say that there was a guy came up from St. John's, an insurance agent, insuring schooners' crews. And Dad took a thousand dollars out on each man — there were 19 men on her. But that's all the insurance. Just the men were insured, but the schooner wasn't. And that winter—the schooner was lost in August—that same winter our shop burned, the store, and no insurance. Just a little grocery and clothing store. Had 5 or 6 hundred dollars cash in it, too. In 1901, 1902.

So that kind of knocked us back. Poor old Father, he only had a small schooner anyway, he wasn't out in the big ones at all. So he continued on fishing. And when we got big enough, we went fishing with him for awhile. I was 13 when I started. She was a little schooner, carried two dories, two masts, sails, had a little power too—8- or 9-horsepower—just enough to move her along if it was calm. But we made a living at it. It was just what you call shore-fishing, 10 or 15 mile off was the farthest. Didn't go on The Banks at all. Trawl with the dories. I'd hold the gear, bring it back aboard the boat. Had to split the fish, too, salt it. But everybody was doing that; there was no particular job. Just making enough to get a bite. You hardly knew what a dollar was.

I was 16 when I made my first trip across in a 3-master—one of those foreign vessels taking fish across to Spain, Italy, those places. I wasn't quite 16—that was in July—they were loading fish home. And the captain wanted me to go with him. Poor old Mother, she didn't want it very bad— me to go. But I really wanted to go. She said, "Look, Steve"—he was the captain of the schooner; they were reared up together—"if you look after him, he can go." I wasn't long getting ready, I'm telling you. I wanted to get away so bad. But I got seasick, oh brother, seasick. Up on the masts of the schooner, stowing the topsails. If you were the last man to come aboard, you had the worst jobs. You had the foremast to look after—that's the forward one. And you had all the rigging to look after. You had somebody to tell you what to do, but you had to do it. And no use saying, "I'm not going to do it"—you had to do it. You had the jumbo, you had the jib, and you had the balloon, you had the gaff topsail, and you had a part of the staysail. You had to look after it, see it was in order. You had to stow it up at nighttime, take it in. You'd have to learn how to tie the knots and do everything that was supposed to be done. Then the mate and the bosun, they'd all tell you what to do. They would sometimes help you out when they were a good bunch. They'd show you what you had to do if you get with a bunch of strangers. So therefore, you could get along all right.

But I remember one night—I thought I was a big shot anyway, you know—I had that kind of a queer notion—I thought I knew what to do. We were crossing the Gulf Stream. It worked out bad weather, and the captain said, "I think we'll stow the topsails before dark—we're not going to use them tonight, anyway." So we clewed up the topsails. The captain said, "Rose, I'll go up and stow your topsail for you, tie them up, you never did much of that." I said, "No, captain, I'm gonna go up." I went up, you see, and I didn't know how to do it right. I did it, but I wasn't fast enough. Two o'clock in the morning, it was bad—thunder and lightning and rain, wind—not a hell of a lot of wind, but enough. And I heard a hullabaloo on deck. So I jumped out of bunk and put my knife sheath around me, and I went up on deck. The lashing'd come off the topsail, blowing right across the rigging. So I went for the rigging. The mate said, "No, no, I'm going to go up." I said, "No, if I can't do it, you can come up."

Well, I got up there, and I didn't mind when she rolled to leeward with the sea, but when she'd go back against the wind, almost take your breath. From the cross-tree up to the top of the masthead was 9 feet. That was all roped in—you couldn't fall off, hard job to fall off. But this goldarn topsail—I got up, got a couple of gantlines hooked, and then the wind would take it away from me. So then I got seasick. One time I was scared I was gonna die, and the next thing I was scared I wasn't going to die—I was that sick. But finally, you know, I had heard the men talking about it—if you couldn't get a topsail stowed good, just rip it with a knife and let the wind out of it. So I just took my knife and I stuck it in back behind me in the canvas. Well, what a screech of wind came out of that sail! Then I rolled them all in by the masthead, got them tied up, about half of them hanging down by the foresail. I got down. I never was so sick in my life as I was that night. Poor old captain, he was mad because I went up, he said, "You might have fallen out of that, and I told your mother I'd look after you." But I got out of it. Actuallly, I didn't mind. And I spent my 16th birthday about 200 mile outside the Gulf Stream on the way across.

You had watch-on watch-off; you had 4-hour watches. (*What would you do as a watch?*) Steer, keep watch, have to stick with her. One man would be to the wheel, the other'd be up forward, blowing the horn—you always had hand horns, you had no power at all—nothing, only sail. So in a fog, you had to stay up forward and blow the hand horn, so many blasts, whatever blasts were required for the course you were going, the direction you were in. And when the other man'd be through the wheel, he'd ring the bell and you'd go back and take the wheel from him and he'd go forward—you had 40-minute wheels. Then when your 4 hours were up, if there was no trouble at all, you'd have a snack and go on down and go to bed. There was nothing wrong with the 4 on and 4 off for watch. That's plenty of sleep for anybody to get—the whole day, the whole season, the whole trip. But if any trouble started when you were in bed, well, you were called out. Because there were only 7 men on the vessels, including the captain.

The cargo was fish—all salt and dried. What you'd usually do is fish in the summertime, and when the fish were dry, you'd take them across to Portugal and Spain and Italy sometimes. And then you'd bring back salt, for ballast. When you were fishing, when you'd go home—we call it "go home" to Lunenburg or any part of Newfoundland that the vessel belonged—you'd take the fish in a dory over to where they were going to wash it. You'd land so much to each person around that had flakes—you know, made of wood, sticks covered with dry boughs—what you dried fish on. They'd put the fish in a pound off in the water, and they'd wash it with brushes or mops or something—wash the slime off of it, you know—this is fish that had been salted and struck. It had to be in the salt so long before it was what was known as "struck"—the salt goes through it. And then they'd put it on their flakes in what you'd call a "water horse"—that's to press the water out if it, piles probably 50 or 100 quintals. A long pile of fish, probably 4 feet high, and the length of a big codfish wide.

And they'd leave it in the water horse for probably a week, see, or 4 or 5 days—depending on the weather—and had to press all the water out of it. Sometimes they put boards and rocks on top of it, make more weight, to press the water right out. Well then, when it would dry, it would be right smooth. Then you spread it.

Fish drying in a pile, in a faggot, and on flakes at North Ingonish

Well, when the fish was just newly spread on the flakes to dry, if the weather was very hot, you'd have to turn it over two or three times a day, back-up and then face-up and then back-up and so on. Then you put them in what's known as faggots. It's a small pile, probably 100 or 150 pound of fish. You make it up head and tail, head and tail—the big part one way, then the other way—till you get probably a little pile. All back-up clear of the bottom tier. The bottom tier would be face-up. You'd keep them in faggots—and every day you'd spread them in the morning, for 5 or 6 days, good days—take them up again in the evening, back into faggots.

And then you made up what they called "piles." Well, the fish were getting pretty dry then. They'd be I suppose 5 feet in diameter, round. They started from the bottom and they'd come out bigger, wider, as they got to the top. That would keep the rainwater off. They'd begin by making a circle, all napes out, big part out. When you'd get built up, you'd fire a few in the middle of the pile. And when you'd get up as high as you were going, you'd make what is known as the "roof." And the last, there'd be just one fish on the top. It would be sharp and that would run the water off of it. The backs are up on these. And some people had canvas covers, but a lot of people didn't—they'd just have this roof, one fish over the other, and it looked like shingles. All built of dried fish.

Well then when you'd get it so many days in piles, then the next thing was the "stores"—a building where you put your fish. Take it out in the morning and put it back in the night. And it was getting pretty dry then. And before the vessel would come to load it, you'd dry it all—just give it a day's sun on the beach or on the flakes again, whatever you'd have.

Usually women did the most of the drying. My mother dried thousands of quintals. She'd have 7 or 8 women working with her. Thousands of quintals, from the Bank schooners. We had a great big beach on our place. We could spread 900 quintals in one spread. She'd have as high as 11 women working with her, when the weather was good. A lot of fish on hand.

(*And if it started to rain?*) Everybody'd be there and just faggot the fish, or put it in piles if it was dry enough for piles.

All handwork. And then when you'd start to load those three-masters, handwork again. (*You'd fish the season on the two-masted schooner, and then you'd go to work on a three-masted schooner for the foreign trade?*) That's right. And the cargo you carried was what the women dried. All dried fish. Putting it aboard, it was all handwork—two quintals on a barrow—it was a handbarrow, no wheels on it, a fellow in the front and one in the back. It's just flat, with handles. You'd go out on the gangplank and you'd dump it in the hold of the schooner. Just dump it. And then there was a bunch, probably women or girls or men or something—whatever you could get—stowing it in the hold of the schooners. And the vessels were all limed in the hold. You put it into a burlap bag and then you slapped that all around the ceiling and the partitions of the schooner—get it right white. (*What was that for?*) Well, the fish wouldn't get damp. You'd be 15 or 20 days going across—the fish will be just as good when you get over as it was when you left. Dry lime picked up the dampness.

The people in the hold would put the fish in what you called "shingles." You don't pile it, you shingle it. Start along the bulkhead, we'll say, and you keep on going up—and come forward at the same time. And there's so many in the other part of the vessel, doing the same thing. You'd build up and build out at the same time, using the flat fish. The whole schooner was just filled solid full—3000 to 4000 quintals in the hold, some of them.

When we'd go over there with fish—Portugal or Spain or Italy or France—you weren't allowed to handle the cargo. They'd take the fish out. You'd be working at the schooner—painting or doing something, sewing sails. If you had warm weather, you'd have an awning over the spanker boom, a sail, and you'd be sewing sails under that. You always had sails torn up, always. From one trip to the other, you'd be sewing sails all the time. There's no sailors today. There's nobody can put a decent whipping on a piece of line, you know. They never learned it. They can't tie knots. In Lunenburg, yes, there's some seamen up there yet, sailing seamen. 'Cause you take all those powerboats—they don't know anything at all about seamanship, not a thing in the world. You ask someone to tie a square knot and they wouldn't be able to do it. Maybe a square knot, yes—but they couldn't tie a rose knot, a turk's-head, none of that stuff. You take when the boom's on the saddles, they had what they call gantlines around them. They were all braided with canvas right around, and they were all painted different colours. And on the ends, that'd be rose knots, you know. That's all you did—fancy work all the time. But you didn't use that stuff fishing at all. It was all just in what we call the "foreign trade." They were like yachts, those vessels. God Almighty, they were painted up to the nines. And they had nothing, only fish and salt, that's all. You'd take over a load of fish and you'd bring back a load of salt, fishery salt.

One time, from Gibraltar through to Louisbourg we were 84 days. That's a long time. In the wintertime, you know, too much ice. We sighted Cape Race, Newfoundland, three times, and had to go back out over the Grand Bank to get the ice off—sinking with ice. The frosty weather, making ice on the rigging, on the decks, top structure of the boat, the sails and everything else. Too heavy. So you'd go back out into the warm weather again and get the ice off it. Go south. You get out in the Gulf Stream and the ice'd start to go off again. You'd pound some off. Then you'd get straightened away and you'd come in again and strike the same damn things—ice, frosty weather. Sometimes snow, just plain frost, you know, northwest wind, freezing.

(*And would you be shovelling snow?*) No, no, the water'd keep the snow off, wash it off—sea water, any wind. There'd be maybe a little on the poop deck you'd have to shovel off, but not the main deck down below, that's always clean. (*You mean the ocean is coming aboard?*) Oh yes, when they're loaded—phew! Sometimes you've got a hard job getting forward on them. They put lifelines running the whole length of the schooner from spar to spar. If you're forward and you want to come aft, you hold the lifeline. You put the lifeline on you before you started pumping. And then when the schooner was pumped out, you'd watch if there was no sea coming to you off your lifeline—go for the cabin. They had no wheelhouse, you know. If you were to the wheel, you were out in the open air, didn't matter what the weather was. But you had plenty of warm clothes, you had your oilskins, you didn't mind it.

And if you had any work to do in the rigging, you'd go up. There'd be no ice very far up—the spray water wouldn't go very far up. The only time is, you may get a silver thaw—then the rigging would be full of ice, the masthead and all. You'd always have a little wooden mallet, and you'd take that and you'd pound the rigging as you'd go up, knock the ice off it.

But there was nothing to get frightened of, you know. You had a good vessel—my God, they were good sea boats. The only thing is your supplies, if you're too long. The time that we were 84 days, we took grub from steamers. The last one we took grub from was a ship from St. John's. We didn't really need it, but he said we'd better take some. So they sent aboard a lifeboat with a bunch of stuff, flour, butter, molasses. (*You had no idea how long you'd be out there.*) We didn't know, no. We had plenty of water—she had good water tanks. You weren't allowed to use any water for washing your face or clothes, you know. You had barrels on deck to catch rainwater for washing clothes. For making bread, the cook always used saltwater, ocean water. Made better bread, beautiful homemade bread. So it wasn't so tough.

You only had the trouble that you expect. Because you know what the ocean is like. It's no picnic, anyways, sometimes. There's a place out there, just this side of the Azores—that's called the "Stormy Region," the "Rolling 40s" they call it—up in the 40 latitude, you know. And we got too close to it, I guess, somehow or other, and there was no wind—we lost the wind altogether—but thunder and lightning, and sea—oh, my God—the sea. There was an awful tide out there. So we were three days there with everything tied up on the booms. And you couldn't get anything

on the table, you couldn't keep anything on the stove—rolling, you see—
no way to keep her steady at all. So finally a little southerly wind—we got
the jumbo up, and got her before the sea—in no time you were out of it—it
didn't last. Two days and a night we were there—couldn't move—no
sail—couldn't keep any sail on her, you'd smash it to pieces, flapping
around.

But I liked the foreign trade. You wouldn't be at it all seasons. You'd
probably be in the Bank fishing in the summer. In the winter you'd go
across with a load of fish. I went Bank-fishing for years—in 10-dory
schooners in Newfoundland. The Dutch schooners—the Lunenburgers—
we only had 7 dories. I went 9 years, 9 seasons, from March until the last
of September usually. Some winters, if you had a good chance, you'd
probably stay fishing. I did both. It was all two-masted schooners you
fished on. The French and the Spaniards, they used 3-masters and 4-
masted vessels—but our people didn't. Always fore and aft—2-masters.
(*When you say "our people"*....) I mean Newfoundlanders, Dutchmen—
that's the Lunenburgers—Americans—all were the same, they had only
two-masted schooners for fishing.

(*What would you have for a crew?*) Two men in each dory. Then you
had the captain. And you had what they call a "dress gang" on the Lunenburg schooners. When the first dory came alongside with fish, the captain
and the dress gang would start to split fish. You have the "header" and the
"throater" ("gutter"), and you had the "salter." The captain, he was the
"splitter"—that's all he did all day—the Lunenburg fellows. But the Newfoundland skippers didn't touch the fish. On the Newfoundland vessels
the crew split them themselves. And the Newfoundland vessels had the
"catchee." All he'd do was catch the dory's painter—it's a strong rope in
the front end—catch it when you came alongside. And he'd help when
they were splitting fish. He didn't go in a dory.

In the summertime—you only made 3 or 4 hauls in a day. You'd get
up. The cook would probably get what's known as a snack—warm the tea
and probably some bread and some soda crackers, some cheese or something. If you wanted something to eat before you went in the dory, you
could get it. Then you and your dory mate—you might be what's known
as a "dory skipper," boss of the dory—you had your own dory. They
were all numbered and you had to look after the dory, see. They're piled in
a nest on the deck, what they call a "cradle." If your trawls were anchored
right around your schooner—what's known as "handy buoys"—you put
the dories over in any order. But if you're what they call "flying setting"—
that's setting under sail—you put one off on one side, one off on the other, and put them off in order. You get in the dory and usually the cook on
one side and the catchee or somebody on the other—takes the dories back

to the long painter. You put all the dories on long painters astern of the schooner, tow them along. She's not going too fast—she's moving probably 4 or 5 knots, something like that. And the furthest dory away, that's the first one that would set—from the far end of the long painter.

But the last years, you dropped them right out of the sling, right out of the dory grips, the tackle joists. I'd throw my dory overboard and let out 100 fathom or 60 fathom or 70 fathom of buoy line. Well then, the very minute my buoy line would be almost out, they'd drop my dory onto the water. Then the other fellow on the other side of the schooner, he'd throw out his buoy, and he'd run 60 or 70 fathom, and they'd drop him. When the grips opened, she was away. You put your anchor overboard and your gear was tied fast to it and you'd flick it out, flick it out—until you'd get the whole works out. You set with a stick; it was something to toss the gear out of the tub. (*You don't reach in the tub and pull the line out?*) Oh my God, no. A little stick about a foot long, made for this purpose, sharp on the end—"gear stick"—and you just keep flicking. The man that was paddling would watch to see how you were doing.

(*So the flying set got your line out pretty fast.*) Oh, yes. Sometimes they'd only use the foresail to take them along. You see, the schooner'd go across the wind, broadside to the wind. Well, you'll set right before the wind when you start setting. So they'll slack the mainsheet right out—the mainsail's not taking wind at all. Probably just the foresail or the jumbo. They'd lower the jib down. Sometimes they'd not be going fast enough and sometimes they're going too damn fast. Depends on how much wind there is. I've been in the dory when you couldn't see for spray water between the two sets of dories, towing on the stern of those vessels going like the devil. Blowing up a gale of wind. (*Then when you'd release, you'd slow up.*) Oh, sure. And you'd swing your dory right before the wind and start setting your gear. One man would row, and if there was a little draft of wind, he wouldn't want to row very hard. Just keeping the dory straight, that's all, with the compass. All the dories would be going down, going the same course.

(*And when you'd get to the end of your set?*) The schooner'd come down and pick you up again, pick up the dory—take the dories aboard. Then beat up the windward side again, to the first end you dropped. Well, then you'd stay there probably for a couple hours, let your gear fish. You'd probably get in the bunk and have a little nap. Something or other. You had no fish on deck yet. You only just set. So then, same thing would happen again. He'd put you on a long painter and when he gets to your buoy, you let go. (*And then you go along the line, taking the fish.*) Well, underrunning, you don't take the gear in. One fellow hauls and the other fellow baits the gear. Take turns at it. You had your bait in tubs, what they

88

call "bait jacks." And the gear goes right back in the water. You just haul the fish in. If you have a big one, you just give them a shake. There's a knot above the hook and you just take that in your nippers—you know, you wear a thick rubber band that'll nip the gear—and that sets, and you give him a shake and the fish will drop off in the dory. (*And if it wouldn't come out?*) Oh God, you'd straighten the hook. Shake it that hard. Then you'd shape it again on the gunwale of the dory. When you get aboard the schooner, when you're shacking your gear, you had your hookset—for shaping the hooks back in the right shape. Put them in that and give them a little twist. Then you'd take your file and you'd sharpen them. You had to sharpen your hooks, too, if you're a good fisherman. Some of them don't, but they don't catch much fish. And if the hook got down their throat, you'd shove down the "gob stick"—flat on one end and a little V onto it—catch the hook in that V and push down, haul it out.

You put your fish in the "middle place," between bulkheads. Then if you get more than you can put in with the bulkheads, you stick up the thwarts (seats across the dory)—turn your thwarts up on edge. Then you could take a lot more fish in the middle place. When you got a middle load that's level with the gunwales—then you've got enough fish to go aboard with. Plenty. What they call a doryload. You've got 4 or 5 quintals of fish in the big dories. Some days, the fish is all around you—good days you'll fill them right full—but any lop or anything, you've got to be careful you don't sink your dory.

Back to the schooner, you fork your fish onto the deck. Then you have something to eat. Always have something to eat. Never forget that. You make your first run in the morning; when you come aboard, you have your breakfast. Then you'll go again, you might make another trip, you'll come aboard at dinnertime. Well, next time you might make two runs. If you've got plenty of fish, you can get a load pretty fast—you might make two hauls, two runs, before you eat.

And now, the dress gang is splitting all the time. When the first fish goes on deck, he's put right in the gurry-kid right off the bat, start to split. The header will cut the head and throw him in and the gutter will take the gut out and break the head off, throw it overboard. The sound bone is taken out, and the fish is flat. Then when they get 6 or 7 quintal split and washed in tubs full with water, you fork it down the hold. The salter takes it then. You'd carry 30 to 40 tons of salt in the schooners. The salter has a little scoop and he spreads a layer of fish, then salts it, spreads another layer—the fishside up, not the skin.

Meanwhile, you'd go and the third time you'd come back, you'd have your supper. Then you'd go again. But the last time you'd come aboard, you'd get nothing. The deck might be half-full of fish. Well, everybody

90

starts splitting. There might be four tables then rigged up, four splitting tables. Then more salters. Then there's flunkies—that's fellows washing the fish, putting it in the hold. And then when the last fish is down at night, the table is laid just the same as for dinner—that's aboard the Lunenburg vessels—and the very best of food, too, and good cooks. And the deck is washed off—oh, every night. The Lunenburg schooners, oh yes. Every bit of gurry and everything is washed off the deck. But the Newfoundland schooners, there's trawl tubs bottom up and there's blood and there's codheads—because they've got no dress gang, you see. The crew does everything, and they don't care too much about that—they're good and tired. But Lunenburg fellows, they keep those vessels just like yachts.

You go to bed. You take off your oilskins before you go to bed—but you don't take off your pants. A lot of people sleep even with their rubber boots on. They're clean enough—they're washed clean—but they won't take them off. Never took your main clothes off—because next you know, probably somebody would run into you—some other schooner or some ship. You'd go to the bottom with the vessel if you had to wait and get dressed. That's the reason. To be ready to go. If the watch would hear a horn blowing, a ship's whistle or something—call everybody to be ready. If she'd get too close, dories overboard and out. It has happened, to other boats. It could be the finest kind of a night—see a steamer, for cripe's sakes, 20 mile—some people, they won't take off their rubber boots. So unless it's your watch—it might be your watch the very minute you're through fishing—you go to bed.

(*And what time will you be called in the morning?*) Four, half past three. Summertime—I've seen it on the Grand Banks down the east of the Virgin Rocks, we were splitting fish aboard a Newfoundland schooner—and before daylight was gone out of the sky in the west, you could see it coming back in the east, starting to get bright. Hardly any dark at all. A week at a time you'd hardly see the bedclothes. (*Hard work.*) I don't know. It never killed anybody. (*Did you like that work?*) Oh, yeah. I mean, everybody was doing it, anyway. (*But did you like it?*) No. I never did anything yet that I liked. No, that's a fact. I didn't see anything to like about it—if you've got to work for a living. But still, it's all right.

(*And Wishie worked for a living. For a couple of seasons he was skipper of a Banks schooner, but he didn't like that—"Didn't like to fish the weather that I could see some of them were fishing—bad weather—I was scared of losing men." Then he took a spell at rumrunning, for awhile on a big American schooner, but mostly on the Canadian coast, "on a small running-in boat. We did all right. But I didn't like the rumrunning on the boats. You're always waiting, nothing to eat half the time. You'd smashed the windows out, you know, be cold and wet and everything else. You're always wet. I didn't like that. The skipper, from out of St. Pierre—hell of a fine man. The poor fellow, he got drowned afterwards. He said to me one day, 'I don't think this is for me—I don't mind rumrunning on the big boats, but not this.' So he quit, and I quit too."*

(Wishie went for a little while collecting swordfish for an American outfit, and worked 8 years for the Bras d'Or Coal Company, taking coal to Newfoundland, up the St. Lawrence River, Madeleines, P.E.I., along the Nova Scotia shore, and down to Labrador. He was on a water boat in Sydney Harbour before the War—taking fresh water to ships. And he was in the Navy for two years, on re-fit jobs in Halifax—"That's another thing you didn't need qualifications for. They'd damm well skin you if you knew anything about an engine." Then he went with W. N. MacDonald, the Margaree Steamship Company. This brought him to Baddeck as engineer on the ferries in the Bras d'Or Lake. "We had a spree, anyway. It wasn't a bad job." In among all that, he worked on herring seiners and tow-off boats—"keeping the seiners off the rocks"—the cable boat patrolling the transatlantic cable, pleasure boats, and then 8 years as variously engineer, mate, and skipper on smaller Irving oil tankers. And he did coastal work on his own vessel, officially called the Mudalhapladu. *The word means "carrier of heavy loads." But the vessel was always called* Muddy.)

Wishie Rose: I had the *Muddy* 18 years—that was all coastal work. I got that from the Margaree Steamship Company— (W.N.) MacDonald of Sydney. I was on the ferry down here then, the old Shenacadie from Baddeck to Iona. I saw this thing advertised, and I went down to see him. "I see you've got the old *Muddy* for sale." "Yes," he said, "want her?" He was going to sell her up here in Baddeck, anyway. I said, "I wouldn't mind having her." I said, "Having her and getting her is two different things, Mr. MacDonald." He said, "She's no good to us—I don't know what good she is to you, she hasn't got enough power, what she has is broke down now." He said, "You can have her, but I don't see what good she is. Pay for her when you like or how you like." He said, "Let me put a bigger engine into her, a new one." I said, "It's gonna put the price of the boat up something awful. I might not make enough to pay her insurance." He said, "Take her as she is—as far as that's concerned, she's yours—I don't want her, she's no good to us—I don't see what good she is to you like that, but you can still have her." I said, "I've got no money to give you." He said, "I know, I don't want any money, take her out of my sight—you need a new crankshaft for her—take her." So that's all right, then. No money involved at all, not a cent.

So I did coastal work. We used to haul coal, wood, whatever the devil we'd get to haul, anything there was money in. I had three men with me. You had to give them as good a wage as you possibly could, and then your food, and your oil. Anyway, in the last few years, you couldn't make it. If you're hauling coal, you'd have so much a ton. You'd pick it up in Sydney and take it to Newfoundland or wherever the devil they wanted it, the North Shore there somewhere, all over the place, the Madeleine Islands. When the gypsum people were in Dingwall, we used to haul a lot of coal down there. Haul coal to Canso. So much a ton—the further you had to go, the more you'd get for a ton.

(What would you pick up to bring back?) Nothing. Nothing to pick up. Unless you'd go to Halifax with a load of fish, sometimes you'd get a load of salt back to Cornerbrook or Bonne Bay. You might—then it'd be a paying trip all the way. But if you couldn't do that, you wouldn't make anything, you know. You'd pay expenses, all right, but when you had a house and a family to keep, you want more than expenses paid.

It was some bad weather on that thing, but she was a good sea boat. We were out in Hurricane Hazel. We were taking up coal to the Madeleines a Friday, I guess. A fellow came down, said, "What about going to Caraquet for me—we got a truckload of fish boxes." I said, "We got 50 ton of coal in the boat yet." He said, "That's all right—good ballast. And the man who owns the coal, he's satisfied if you go, if you want to." He said, "A few dollars in it." I said, "That's all right. Tomorrow morning, we'll leave." So Saturday morning we left and went to Caraquet; we got over there Saturday night. Sunday afternoon we had everything aboard. We had 250 empty fish boxes, lengths of 3-inch galvanized pipe on the back deck. We left. We got the forecast—they wanted sou'west 15 that night, sou'east 25-30 the next day, and then we'd be over on the Madeleines by that time, anyway. We left at 4 o'clock that Sunday evening.

About 10 o'clock I was in the bunk—by God, I heard the water going back over, you know—rain—spray water going back over the boat. I got out and the mate was at the wheel. I asked what was wrong. You couldn't see anything, the blinding rain then. He said, "Storm and wind." I said, "I know." I said, "Slow around a bit, it's only a bloody squall, probably only 15 or 20, something like that ." He said, "It's a good 50 now, not 20." So we hove her in to for awhile, slow, but it got worse. I said, "Swing her stern to it." We run it up nordeast, and when it start to come daylight, start hauling more to the west. Blow—God, didn't it blow. Like a fog, you know—wind.

Couldn't keep her broadside—too much sea, shallow water, too. So we got something to eat, we got a bit of breakfast. Just after breakfast—we had a liferaft up on top, well-lashed to her—the sea struck her, and she parted lashings on the liferaft. And it tore the insulator up through the set, the telephone, tore her up through the roof of the house. Couldn't get ahold of anybody. I could hear Grindstone calling for a little while before the set got wet. I got the heel of a rubber boot, and I got out and drove it back, and got the wire down through, hooked on to the telephone again. By God, the red light came on. I called Grindstone—that was the middle of the day then. "Well," they said, "we've been calling you and calling you, where are you?" I said, "Well, we're out here somewhere."

I said, "What have you got for weather tonight in Grindstone?" He says, "We don't like to discourage you, we got 78 mile of wind." I said, "You're not discouraging anybody, old boy, we got just as much." He said, "Where are you?" I said, "I don't know." The sea used to break. If she'd strike her, you'd think she'd be like a matchbox. But the waves didn't hit her. They'd break before they'd get to her and they'd break after they'd pass her. We were just running slow with two engines, just to keep a serious way on her. I said, "I don't know—we should be 20 miles in back of the Madeleine Islands—we should be. But 'should be' and 'is,' I don't know." I said, "We're going down for Brion Island, somewhere down in that direction."

At two o'clock I said to the mate, "If you can get up on top of the house—if you can't, I'll try to get up—you might see some land. We got to be getting close in back of the Madeleines somewhere—I know we are." The sounder wouldn't sound; too much froth under the boat. I said, "If we don't see something pretty soon, I'm going to run her before us—we'll strike something before dark. It's easier to save your life in the daylight than it is in the dark."

Well, everybody was satisfied. He got up on top of the wheelhouse, and he wasn't up there long, tied onto the spar. "Skipper," he said, "I can see land—you might know where it was if you were up here." He got down and got in through the wheelhouse window. I got up, and the minute I saw it, I knew it—just exactly where we wanted to be—top of Brion

Island—I knew it so well, I worked around there so much. I said, "You get to the wheel and open her wide open and get her going." I saw her scoop the water up over her head, trying to get through between Brion Island and the Bird Rock before dark. Only 10 fathom water at the most going through there, only 60 feet of water in that storm of wind.

Well, we went right through in the right place—it looked like she was breaking everywhere. But when we got through there, an hour from that we were up on the east point of the Madeleine Islands. We were all right. 12 o'clock that night we were in Grindstone, tied onto the wharf. We had had 152 fish boxes on deck—you couldn't lash empty fish boxes—and we took off 150. We lost 2 overboard in that wind. That's how good she was.

Oh God, that boat was good. If you keep her clear of the rocks, she'd kill you before she'd drown you. She was that good. You won't believe this, but it's true. We had a little one of those ship-mate stoves in the fo'c's'le for cooking on, and it never was lashed. There were holes in the four legs of the stove on the block it was on, and there were just three-inch nails put down and bent over—that's all that was there—it never was lashed—and she never knocked a cover off all the time I had her. But you'd get her broadside on a roll, and she'd roll the milk out of your tea. But head on, you wouldn't know she'd ever blow. If she could steam, you could steam, she wouldn't hurt anything. She was a good old boat. They told me there at Grindstone, you couldn't see Entry Island all day for wind, and that's only 10 miles across to Entry Island from Grindstone.

We did all right on the *Muddy*. I mean to say, on the end of it, it was getting that a coaster was no good. See, the place didn't increase anything. And when the roads got through, the trucks were taking everything. But the first 4 or 5 years I had her—if I had let W. N. MacDonald put a bigger engine in her, oh my God, I'd've cleaned up. Because she was just about the right size. Then they got it so you had to go way the hell down to Labrador, pick up a load of fish in the fall of the year. You'd be two weeks probably getting a load. And you'd beat your way up to Halifax or the Bay of Fundy—time you'd get back you'd be in debt. You may pick up a load of salt in Halifax—you come back to Newfoundland, you're in debt. And you had to try to give your men half enough to live on. So you couldn't make anything. Ships were too long and the freights were too little. But we did all right first. We paid for the old boat. Then we bought a house and we lost that to fire, and we built this, and we don't owe anybody anything. And we had a big family, a fair big family. So we didn't do too bad. I got no kick coming, anyway.

And the *Muddy*, she's finished now. Worms got her all eaten. Hardly anything to see now, the wheelhouse is gone and all, almost all gone out of her. But I was through with her. But what I intended to do—I guess in

June I put her in there, and I was going to take her out in the fall or the next spring, take her somewhere, take the propellers and shafts out of her, and burn her or do something with her. And by God, I couldn't get her out of it—the worms ate her just in that time. I had four 4-inch pumps on her, and couldn't move her at all. Ralph Pinaud there, he had the power from the winch on her, trying to move her, never moved her, she was stuck fast in the mud that much. The *Muddy* stuck in the mud.

Wishie Rose and the remains of the *Muddy* in Baddeck

The photographs of dory fishing are by Frederick William Wallace, taken with a Brownie box camera, about 1911-14. They are part of the collection of the Maritime Museum of the Atlantic, Halifax.

Mary MacMillan's People Come to East Bay

They came from Scotland, the MacDougalls. And my great-great-grandfather was Ian Allan MacDougall. And he settled in P.E.I. for a period of time, him and another brother. Then they moved over to Ben Eoin, and he granted 200 acres of land—that's where I'm at today—MacDougall Hill—always will be.

The other side, my mother's side—MacIsaacs. They came from Uist as well. And they landed out on the rear of East Bay. My grandmother was 5 years old—and you can imagine how long ago is that!—and I am an old woman. And they walked. They had friends out on the back of East Bay. So, it was a hot,

hot day in July. It was 5 children, and the father and the mother. So I guess the children were just going crazy. They were thirsty, and I suppose, hungry. So—I cannot tell it to you, this in Gaelic, you don't know what I'll be saying—the father, he says, "I am going to stop at this house at Sydney Forks." Which he did. And he said, "Could I get a drink of water," he said, "for my children?" Hot day in July—and we had heat. This is 200 years ago—honest, it is, dear.

She said, "You wait." And she was a coloured lady. And I remember, we had one here—I'm old—a place called a "dairy." No fridge. And milk and what-have-you was kept there. She said, "You just wait." And she went out, and she got a thing called a "keeler." I saw a keeler—great big thing, full of—not the milk that we get today—it's poison. Great big keeler. It was a big, big, big dish, full of the best of milk. And she said, "Just wait." And she had all kinds of strawberries—you know, wild strawberries? And she poured all the strawberries in the milk, and that milk was rich then, my dear. She walked up to the road. And when the children saw the dark woman, they started to bawl and cry. They came from Scotland, and they never saw dark people before. She said, "Sit down. I'm not going to hurt you." God love her heart. She put them sitting down on the side of the road, and gave them the strawberries and this beautiful milk—rich—better than the cream that we buy today. So. And she said, "Don't be a-scared, I'm not going to hurt you." The father and mother were there, and 5 kids. She gave them the whole business that was in this great big keeler—strawberries and the best of milk!

They started. They had walked from Sydney Forks. You know the fire hall at East Bay—you know. They walked out there 3 more miles. Didn't know where they were going. But they had friends there. Everybody was so good to each other then. They were really good. They built a log cabin for them. They were sleeping outside, of course. They had a bit to eat of corn meal, bread, and what-have-you. So. Oh, this is true. It's a true story, dear.

So they built a place. They knocked the woods down, and built a log cabin. And there was another nice person. She had two cows. And she came over, and she brought one of the cows over to Mom's grandfather. And she said, "Look. You've got nothing here. Here is a cow with milk." So, they lived there. But they were really poor. They were very, very poor.

So anyway. But they were good workers. And in the spring, they planted potatoes. Not a bite in the house. And he went to North Sydney—Ian—Mum's grandfather—he says, "I'm going looking for flour." The children were so hungry that she went out and dug up the seed from the ground. This is the Almighty God's truth. They were starving with hunger. And he came back from North Sydney with a bag of flour on his back. He walked from North Sydney to the rear of East Bay. He said, "Put that down." They had milk, and she made pancakes. You know, fast as they could get. Poor kids were starving. He said, "You put that seed back in the ground." Listen, you cannot believe, but it's true. They were poor. They had nothing. Not a thing. Only they were great workers. I was told this when I was this high. (*When you were a little girl.*) That was not yesterday, dear! So, I'll put the teapot on before I'll tell you any more.

.   .   .

The rear of East Bay, where my mother's people came—nothing there but tall timber. They had to make a living. Anyway, they got along. They had sheep, cows, horses, and what-have-you. The only problem they had—the bears were there—it was all tall timber out there. This is on the rear, between East Bay and Ben Eoin. So they were losing their sheep, which they could not afford—the bear was taking them. So anyway, all the good people got together out there. They had no guns—they were too poor at this time—lucky to have a bite to eat. So there was a Ronald MacDonald fellow that said, in a group of them one day, he said, "I'm going to walk to Grand River, and I know a man that has a muzzleloader out there"—that's a double-barreled gun. "And if you fellows, now," he said, "will make a corral for the sheep, right here, and put all the sheep into it, I'll be home at dark from Grand River."

He was back at dusk, and he had the muzzle-loader. And anyway, all they had then was log cabins. They had moss, which they had put between the logs to keep the cold out. So this MacDonald man, "Okay," he said— the house was full of all the neighbours, and the sheep were out in the corral. There was a beautiful moon came over the sky. And Mr. Bear came, as the moon came out, and he was looking in. Looking for the pack of sheep, to go in and kill. Well, I guess the sheep got scared. And he said, "Everybody keep quiet." And he had the gun between the logs. And Mr. Bear was looking for the fattest one. So when he was about ready to jump in, this MacDonald fellow shot him. He knocked him down, and he told everybody, "Be careful, perhaps he's not dead. And if he's not dead, he'll jump and he'll kill us all." So they all went out. He was still breathing. And he had to put two more bullets in him before he killed him. Four bullets he put in the bear—a monster of a thing.

So—well, I call him my grandfather, MacIsaac out there—he had a double team of horses and a "sloven." It's an old sleigh that they used to haul wood and what-have-you. It took 7 men to haul that bear on the sloven—they were going to bury him somewheres in a swamp—7 men. And the poor horses had a hard time to haul him. He was terrible—no wonder—he had all the sheep.

So anyway, there was a man out there, he was a composer, a bard, as I call him—and he composed a song. And it was the bear that was supposed to have composed the song. I have a few verses of it. And that will be the end of her.

Oran a Mhathain

1. Gur e mis tha fo eiginn
Seo nam shìneadh 'san lon
Mi cho teann air tigh Mhìcheal
'G eisdeachd pìoban Mhic Leoid
Tha na fearáibh nan deannaibh
Tighinn 'gam fheannadh 's mi beo
Ma thug mi bhuaithe-san gamhainn
Cha robh e reamhar gu leoir.

The Bear Song

1. I am in sore straits, lying here in the mire, so close to Michael's house listening to MacLeod's pipes: the men are rushing out to skin me alive. If I stole a yearling from him, it wasn't that far.

2. 'Se Raghnall Og leis na caran
Rinn mo mhealladh rón am
Nuair a dh'fhalbh e 'sa mhadainn
Bu mhor aisling mu'm chall;
Cha bu chòir dha bhi gearain
Nach tug mi bhean bhuaith' 'sa
  chlann
Ach ma chaidh mi dha'n bhathaich
'S daor a phaigh mi 'ga chionn.

2. It was young Ronald with guile who deceived me before my time. When he left in the morning, great was his dream of my destruction. He shouldn't complain since I didn't deprive him of wife or children, and if I made a trip to the byre, I paid dearly for it.

3. Truagh nach mise bha dluth duit
Nuair chaidh am fùdar na cheo
Fhir oig gur ni duilich
B'e do dhùrachd mo leon:
Gun tugainn ort leis na dubhain
Mhora dhubha nam spòig
Gun gearrainn dhìotsa na lamhan
Eadar chnamhan is fheoil.

3. Pity that I wasn't close to you when the powder ignited—young man, it is a sad thing that you desired to harm me: I would attack you with the great black claws in my paw, I'd cut your hands off, both flesh and bones.

4. Gur e mis tha fo eiginn
'S bochd Mìcheal ri sheinn
'S truagh nach robh mi 3 mìle bhuat
Mu'n do dhìrich thu bheinn
Le'd ghunna dùbailt 's le'd chrios
Mharbh thu mise le foill
'S ann le solus na gealaich
Thilg thu fairis mi'n raoir.

4. I am in distress, what a pity that Michael sings of it. I wish I were 3 miles from you before you ascended the mountain. With your double musket and belt, you treacherously slew me—by the light of the moon, you knocked me over last night.

I wish you knew what that meant.... (*You're remembering very well.*) Oh, not too good, dear, not too good. I know another verse, if I could think of it. And those are songs that had been composed here, right around this neighbourhood. And nobody knows them but old Mary Ann.

See, I don't know what's the matter with the people here, if they lost their Gaelic, or they don't want to hear it. They don't remember. But I do. But I lost a lot of it. (*Well, if you don't use it that often....*) No, dear, I see or hear not a word of Gaelic. Not a word. Not a word of Gaelic.

Mary MacMillan was interviewed by Pam Newton, Point Edward.
The Gaelic song was transcribed and translated by
Effie MacCorquodale Rankin, Mabou.

Dr. Austin MacDonald, Down North

I got married the day after I found out I was going to graduate in medicine. See, Marie was a public health nurse, and she had already been working for two years in Hants and Colchester Counties. We had intended for some years, whenever I graduated and knew what I was going to do, to get married. And I knew in March of 1942 what I was going to do, because the Nova Scotia Minister of Health called me into his office one day, along with the M.L.A. from Victoria County here, who was John Sam Campbell, and a doctor from Whycocomagh who was a native of Neil's Harbour, Dr. M. G. MacLeod.

Anyhow, we all went down to see the Minister of Health, and he laid it on the line. He said, "These fish plants down there are having increasing difficulty getting Newfoundland fish cutters and workers and canners over because there's no doctor in the area." Although they had a nurse, but the nurse could only do limited repair work, if they cut themselves badly or broke a limb, things like that. (*These are fish plants north of Smokey?*) Really, from Bay St. Lawrence to Smokey.

(The people in charge of these fish plants)—with all these Newfoundlanders to look after—they were driving (them) right up the wall. They came from fishing villages along the south coast of Newfoundland. They were brought over in groups to the various fish plants and installed in groups. They had to leave their girl friends at home, usually. And after they were here two months, they went nuts. The local girls didn't want to have too much to do with them, you see, there were too many of them. And these young fellows, they simply didn't know what to do. They used to get all kinds of psychosomatic illnesses. And at first, I was as fooled as the people in charge of these plants. After a month or two, I realized that these fellows were in, for them, a very abnormal situation. They left Newfoundland. They'd never seen a car in their lives, for instance. And everything was changed.

And they wanted a doctor. They wanted a doctor to talk to. They'd fake every kind of illness just to see a doctor. But there was no doctor. And this was what put the political pressure on Johnny Sam Campbell, who was the M.L.A., and threw him to the Minister of Health, who was at that time the man from Liverpool in Queens County—F. R. Davis—he was a surgeon himself, a very good one, too. And he's the man that called me into his office along with Johnny Sam and Dr. MacLeod from Whycocomagh. And they didn't have any kid gloves that day at all!

They said, "You're going north, and you're going to work there for one year. You'll have the people who are native there, and you'll have perhaps another 500 or more who are import Newfoundlanders. You'll have whatever other people happen to get off the road and break a leg while they're down there. You have no hospital. In the winter-time you have no open roads. You'll have to have horses, and all the equipment to go with them." This didn't bother me, because I had been brought up in a village (Whycocomagh) where that was the way of life, too. And they knew this.

And I said, "I want to go in the army." "No," they said, "this is where you go. But next year you can go in the army. We'll release you at the end of a year." I said I had no money to buy the instruments. "I have no money to buy drugs." "We'll fix that. We'll give you an honorarium of a thousand dollars for one year to go down there." Since there was no argument available anyhow, that's where we went.

So I told Marie—this was in March. We got married on the 8th of May. And I finished out my exams and everything by June. And on the 9th of June, 1942, we went down to Neil's Harbour. Marie had a car for her work in the public health. I didn't even know how to drive a car at that time. (*And in 1942, you could drive over Smokey?*) Yes. In the summertime. In the winter-time you couldn't drive anywhere there. It wasn't paved until the mid-1950s.

102

So, I remember we got to the top of Smokey that night, and Marie stopped. She said, "We'd better see how much money we have left." I had none, and she had exactly $5 when she added up all the pennies and nickels and dimes. She said, "What's the best thing to do with this?" We had found that we could rent a house that belonged to the Buchanans in Neil's Harbour—$25 a month. They didn't ask, fortunately, for any rent in advance. "Well," I said, "you'd better put half off it in gas in the car, and the rest of it, we'll buy food."

Now, my mother had given us several loaves of bread in Whycocomagh, and some jam and some butter and stuff like that, so we weren't too badly off. And a bag of oatmeal for my porridge. So, we thought we were adequately prepared, and we drove to Neil's Harbour.

It was dark when we got there. The last doctor that had been there was a year and a half before. And he didn't like the winters there, so he left. And that's what happened to most of the doctors during the 1930s, most of them only stayed a year. They couldn't take the winter where you'd have to travel all the time from house to house.

Okay, we got there. We went to bed. And we thought nobody knew we were there, because in the dark, you didn't see anybody. Actually, there were about 500 pairs of eyes in Neil's Harbour, so they all knew we were there. In the morning when we got up after daylight and looked out—there was a man with a cane walking back and forth back of the house. I said to Marie, "We'd better get something to eat, and I'll go out and see if this man is looking for me." So we did. And I went out after awhile; he was still walking back and forth. "Are you the doctor?" I said, "Yes." Told him who I was. He said, "My wife is sick, and I just wanted to be here in time, before you got called somewhere else, so you'd come see her." It turned out she was a blind lady, and that was my first medical visit there. From then on, I had no lack of work at any time. The people flocked in.

Now, before I left Halifax, I got this Dr. MacLeod from Whycocomagh to draw up a list of drugs that I absolutely had to have for any kind of medical practice, and the necessary dressings, and the things to do up a fractured arm or leg, stuff like that. And there was a little coastal motor vessel, called the *Josephine K.* She used to run from Halifax with freight for all the little outports. And these big boxes of medicines were loaded aboard of her. They would have been down there the day after we got to Neil's Harbour. Except that the next day a fog set in, and for two bloody weeks that fog never let up. That was the worst fog I've ever seen in Cape Breton! So, the *Josephine K.* was tied up in some of these little ports around the west end of the island, and didn't show up until two weeks later.

By that time I had lists of patients that long written down, and what they needed in the way of medications. Finally I got a telegram—there were no telephones there, but there were telegraph operators in every village—and I got a telegram from Dingwall saying the *Josephine K.* was in. So we hurried down and we loaded up the car with all these packages and came back. By that time the telegraph operator in Neil's Harbour

The old Buchanan home, Neil's Harbour, the first cottage hospital north of Smokey

spread the word, "The doctor got his medicines." I got back. This long line of people were at the office door waiting. So I told them they'd have to come back later, it was going to take me all the rest of the day to just put their medicines in bottles and label them.

Anyway, that was that. That was the big event, then. And from then on, it was pretty standard medical practice—until the end of June. The last week of June, we got a summons from the local clergyman one afternoon to come to a meeting in the Orange Hall in Neil's Harbour that night. It had to do with trying to establish a hospital. A 12-year boy from Dingwall had developed appendicitis in the winter, and the drift ice was on the coast, so they couldn't get any ship in to get him out. And they did send a plane down, and that crashed on the ice. By the time they did get him out, he was *in extremis*, and he died about the time they got to North Sydney. So this really shook everybody up, because this boy had a lot of relatives and friends. They decided there's no reason why they shouldn't have a hospital. And by 1942 the fishermen were making far better incomes than they had made for 15 or 20 years before, during the depression years. And they thought they were pretty well-heeled. And they'd put up the money and they'd have a hospital.

Oh, I remember the meeting well enough. I just sat there dumbfounded at the gall these people had. And no fooling, they were going to have a hospital. They didn't know what it would cost to establish a cottage hospital. They didn't know how many beds we'd need, or anything like that. I knew we could find out all that from the Department of Public Health in Halifax based on the population. And I knew what we would require in the way of instruments, dressings, food, bedding, beds, nursing care, and all the rest of it. They wanted to call another meeting, and they wanted me to get down on paper what these things would cost. So Marie and I went to

Janet MacDonald Dowling, Euphemia MacKinnon, Marie and Dr. Austin MacDonald

work on them. We came up with a figure. We'd need about 2000 dollars worth of instruments and—things were cheaper then. This included a 32-volt lighting plant. That would run lights and a fridge. (**Marie:** 1951 the first power came down.) You had to have some electric light. And a water pump.

And in the meantime, the women, and a lot of the men, had turned out. This was in June. They went from house to house, and asked people for donations towards the new hospital, and they came back with $3200, I think it was. And $3200 would finance the thing, as far as bringing it to opening day. It was a tremendous amount of money, then.

Okay. Next thing they had to think about was staff. Now, Marie was a public health nurse, and had quite a lot of experience in various branches of nursing. So she offered—if they got one other nurse and a couple of good maids, or maid-cook, who could take instruction like that—that she would help train them to be sort of nurse's aides. And this is the staff we had at first. Marie was matron for the next 6 years. There was just no other nurse available down there. Euphemia MacKinnon from Whycocomagh, we persuaded her to come down the first winter. She was a trained nurse. And we had Janet MacDonald, Janet Dowling, as a housekeeper and a cook the first year. And Janet was a very capable girl. She would, you know, help with patients, or do anything. We could see that she had a great deal of natural ability that could be used, both in nursing and everything else. So we persuaded her to go away to the Grace Maternity Hospital in Halifax for a year and a half, trained obstetrical nurses at that time. She graduated, and she was a very, very valuable nurse with us for all the years we were there, till her retirement. She had a native sound common sense and ability that most of the young ones didn't have.

But who looked after the laundry? (**Marie:** Sadie Warren.) Mrs. Matthew Warren—she was a very good laundress. (**Marie:** With a gasoline washer.) In her kitchen. The hospital people had to buy the washer, you see, and install it in her kitchen—so it would be as safe as a gasoline washer in your kitchen would be, which wasn't very safe. But it worked, anyway. And she never lost her house! (**Marie:** Cecil Rideout was the janitor.) And looked after my horses.

Then, for women who were going to have babies—you know, they might live 10, 20, 30 miles away. Well, they couldn't come there with horses once they were in labour. So we had to persuade a couple of women in Neil's Harbour who had good homes, you know, to take these women in as boarders, say, a week before they were due to have their babies. So they would be close to the hospital when their time came. And that worked out. Mrs. Organ was one. (**Marie:** And Mrs. Henry Ingraham.)

(*Before the hospital, were you ever keeping any of your patients there?*) No. In their own homes. Now some of them—there was a little hotel there at that time run by Ann and Donald Daye. And they had 3 or 4 rooms. And sometimes somebody who had, well, a bad wound, that you wanted to keep an eye on every day. See, infection was a big problem then. Penicillin didn't show up in the world, that is for medical use, until almost two years after we started in practice. And it was after the war was over that the next of the antibiotics showed up. (*Like streptomycin?*) Yeah. And that works on tuberculosis. And that's the first effective treatment we had for tuberculosis. Now, we had effective treatments before. We had lung collapse, which I did right in their homes....

(*What other procedures were you doing in the home?*) Well, setting fractures. You carried a little bottle of chloroform. In the winter-time I had a driver who came with me—Murdock E. MacLeod of Cape North. Murdock got so good at giving a chloroform anaesthetic, that all I had to do was count: 1... 2... 3... and he dropped the chloroform on the mask at exactly that rate. And we never ran into difficulty. We set numerous broken arms and broken legs, dislocated jaws. Murdock would put them to sleep like a master. And as soon as he took the bottle off, when I stopped counting, up they'd pop.

I sewed lots of wounds up, and things like that. (*But you wouldn't operate?*) No. I didn't do any of that. In fact, the first patient we had in the cottage hospital—she had appendicitis, that was obvious. I was hoping and praying that it would subside because we weren't quite ready to open the hospital. Her husband came back one evening, "She's getting worse. What are you going to do about it?" This was in February. During the summer and fall, she would have gone to Cheticamp or North Sydney. I said, "We'll just have to bring her in, then." So, we got everything arranged. She was the first in the hospital. Okay. So we got along all right, got her appendix out okay. It wasn't the first time I'd been into an abdomen or removed an appendix, or repaired it afterwards. (*Had you been in a lot of times?*) No. Two or three. I was very thankful to the Almighty when we got her all sewed up and she was doing fine.

Look, you wouldn't believe how lucky we were in the wintertime there. We only had 3 or 4 people that we had to go into abdomens in— when did they start opening roads? 1949—7 years. In those 7 winters, I think we only had 4 abdominal operations. The roads weren't opened. People didn't get sick. The *Aspy* (the coastal steamer) usually stopped in December or early January. And from then until sometime the end of April, we were sealed off pretty well. (*And people didn't bother getting sick?*) That's right. And you know, in the hospitals in those days, we were terrified of infection, post-operative infections. We had no antibiotics—it was before that time. I said to Dr. MacLeod in Whycocomagh, "What should I do for the infections after surgery, and repairs of wounds?" "Forget about them," he said, "they don't get sick from their own germs!" And he was right—they don't. In their own homes, they don't get sick. He said, "In the hospitals, they have no resistance to somebody else's bugs."

(*Before there was a doctor down there, I take it that there were midwives.*) There was a doctor there in the 1920s, Dr. H. A. Grant. And he was an old-time country practitioner, a very sound one. He didn't know perhaps as much as we did later on, but his principles were sound. (And) in Smelt Brook, in Cape North, in Bay St. Lawrence, in Black Point and Capstick and Meat Cove, and in Ingonish and in South Ingonish, and in Neil's Harbour—he trained women. The lady in South Ingonish was a registered nurse, but some of those women couldn't read or write. But the simple rules he gave them, for midwifery, they couldn't do any harm. And they could save lives in a lot of acute episodes that would happen, like acute hemorrhage and stuff like that. It's amazing what you can do from outside the body.

They knew exactly how to do everything so that there was no infection, and no difficulty. They could look after the newborn baby. They knew exactly how to produce a sterile dressing for the baby's cord. On a white cotton, like that, they'd lay the string out—those were sterilized in the oven until they turned brown like toast—the string to tie the baby's umbilical cord, and the cotton that it laid on. That was the sign there were no bugs left on that. But they didn't practise on their own, mind you, unless they got caught and couldn't get a doctor. That he taught them, too—get the doctor if you can. But if you can't, these are the things to do.

.   .   .

The first summer we were down there, very few people came to get teeth pulled, that is, very few of the fishermen from Neil's Harbour. And the few that did come, they'd all been down to a lady at the Cove. I was told she had magic powers. And she could make spells on people that had toothache, and she could charm the toothache away. So they all went there first. And if her charms failed, then they came to me and got the tooth pulled out. But a lot of them, well, toothaches, you know, get better quite often. (*Any idea what kind of a charm she had?*) She said certain words— she wouldn't tell me. She said she got it from her mother, and she got it from her mother, and it went a long ways back, probably. They were very potent women, these. She could charm warts off, too. And as far back as she knew about it, they had this power to charm warts and toothache. And it wasn't till after she died that all the people that got toothaches started coming to me to get them pulled.

(*In their homes, or in the hospital?*) Oh, whatever. Sit them on the running board of their car and take them out and throw them in the ditch. I always carried lots of local anaesthetic, you know, the carpels of novacaine— that's what we used then. And then procaine, which was a little less toxic. I used to get them from Pollett's Drug Store in Sydney. And they would send me fresh supplies all the time. You never knew how many you were going to need. You needed about two carpels per tooth, on the average.

We got down there in June. Well, the next spring. The Newfoundlanders used to come over and fish off our coast in what they called "hookers"—they were the two-masted schooners. And they carried usually from 10 to 14 dories, with two men to a dory, and the skipper. So they would come off our shore, and at night they would be anchored in a long line right off Neil's Harbour. There'd probably be 20, 30, 40 of these schooners. Quite a sight. And every evening the boats would row in from the schooners. And they'd have 1 or 2 or 3 or 4 men in them. It'd be usually the skipper and some of the crew. And he'd be bringing them up to the office to get "teeth hauled"—pull teeth, you see. I'd pull them, whatever they had. And my reputation down along the south coast of Newfoundland became tremendous. They heard from word of mouth, from one to the other, about this doctor over in Neil's Harbour, where they fished every spring— sometimes they came back in the fall. And he pulled teeth without hurting you! "He'd freeze an old son and he'd take 'n out, 'n you don't feel at all!"

And the second spring we were there, I couldn't believe it. I had sent up to Harry Pollett for a thousand carpels of procaine, you know, for pulling teeth. In a week, I didn't have one! I had to send a telegram to send me 2000 more, because 3/4 of these hookers were still off the shore, full of bad teeth. And I didn't want to start pulling any without anaesthetic because my reputation would be ruined. And every spring from then on, I used to get 10,000 carpels in. And by the time the Newfoundlanders sailed back to Newfoundland about the first of July, I'd have all the bad teeth pulled out.

But Marie and I were down in a little place in the south coast of Newfoundland one afternoon. It was one of these September afternoons with sunshine for awhile, and then a big cloud would come over and a little burst of rain, and then a rainbow would be over, and the high hills on the other side of the bay—it was a beautiful sight. And Marie was down near the shore trying to get pictures of some of these phenomena, and I was lying up on the hillside in the grass, just enjoying life. And there were 4 houses above me, every one with what they call a bridge across the front, that's a verandah. One door opened, and this big fellow walked out. When I looked up at him, I knew I'd seen him somewhere before, but I couldn't recall when or where. And after awhile he called down to me, he said, "I know you." I said, "I know you, too, but I can't name you." He said, "You're a doctor." I said, "That's right. How do you know?" He said, "You live over to Cape Breton, Neil's Harbour." "Right," I said. He said, "1943, we were fishing off there in a hooker. And," he said, "our skipper got sick. We took him ashore in a dory. You kept him ashore and you looked after him that night. He was dead the next morning!" (Marie) was down at the shore. Laughing! "That fixed you, boy!"

(*You thought it was going to be praise!*) The skipper, he was in his 70s, and he had had a stroke aboard, and he just fell on the deck, see, but still breathing. So they took him ashore. And there was a lady lived next door to us, who was an old retired nurse, and she offered to keep him in her house overnight. And she looked after him all night, and it was about daylight he died. There was nothing you could do. He was going to die, and that was it. But the way this fellow put it. "You looked after him," he said. "He was dead next morning!"

. . .

Called one winter day to Smokey, or the foot of Smokey, at Ingonish Ferry. And this girl, about 14 years old, was very sick with lumbar pneumonia. Her fever was up near 104 or 105. And I went all over her, you know, looking for side effects of the pneumonia. But her feet were all wrinkled up, the soles of her feet, they were just ridged, the skin on them. I said to her mother. "What happened to her feet?" "Oh," she said, "that's where we had the salt herring tied to her feet to take the fever out." And there were two places. They used to split a salt herring, you know, tie half on each, the soles of the feet, supposed to take the fever down. Or they put them on both sides of their neck and tied them around with a collar. And that was supposed to take the fever out. I don't know whether it cures it or not—I doubt it . But it was an old, old cure. And a lot of people used it.

Anyway, the girl got better. By that time we had sulfapyradine. I gave her that. And I stayed for some hours with her, until she began to show signs of breathing better. The house was hotter than hell, and full of cigarette smoke. I put all the smokers outdoors, told them to go somewhere else and do their smoking. Opened all the windows. She had lots of clothes on, so she wasn't cold. And we got her fresh air and stuff, and told her mother to do likewise, and keep the smokers out of there. She got better.

(*Did people ever feel that their medicine was better than yours?*) When I went there first, Dr. MacLeod told me, "I'm not going to order too many pills." He said, "They're expensive. And you can order your own after you get a little money ahead. We'll order all liquid medicine. If they don't get something out of a bottle, it's no damn good." Well, he knew them better than I did; he grew up among them. But liquid medicine—the more horrible it tasted, the better it did them. So there was a lot of psychosomatic effect there. (*Of course, they were used to things like sulphur and molasses.*) Yeah, but that was very bland. They all used that every spring. I had it every spring I was growing up, too. The school used to stink of sulphur so bad, hard to walk in. For a week or so, when every kid was getting sulphur and molasses at home.

Oh yes, another thing they used Down North a lot was dulse—seaweed. They just ate it. Washed it off with fresh water. They didn't bother drying it. (*As a food, or as a medicinal?*) Medicinal. They claimed it was good to get rid of pin-worms. I don't think they ate it for food, although it was good food. (*Did you think it was effective for pin-worms?*) Well, I had to go by what the mothers said, and they said that the pin-worms would disappear from the stools when they gave them a few days on dulse. So I have to assume that it worked.

At that time, legally, you couldn't go into school unless you had smallpox vaccination. A lot of them got away with it, because nobody looked on their arm. And the government of Nova Scotia thought in the 1930s that

110

most of the population in Halifax were immunized and safe from smallpox. A ship came in one day with a man in full-blown smallpox. They took him to Camp Hill Hospital. He was very ill there. They appointed an orderly and a male nurse to look after him. The male nurse developed smallpox and died. The orderly developed smallpox and didn't die. And they discovered that neither of those men had ever been vaccinated, although both went through the school system. So they set up clinics and they used all the interns in the area, and all the public health nurses. And free vaccination for everybody. They figured there might be quite a few people, maybe 1000 among the 100,000 in the city, that hadn't got protection. Inside of a week, they vaccinated 44,000 people out of that population who had never been vaccinated. So that's how lax the system was that forced them to be vaccinated before they came to school.

Down North, there was practically no immunization at all. There was none except for smallpox vaccinations Dr. MacMillan did. He was county health officer. And he didn't get nearly all of them, because a lot of them didn't go to school the day he was going to come. So, Marie being a public health nurse, we decided the first year we were there that we'd better immunize these kids for diphtheria—that was the big problem at the time. So she got some help from a public health nurse and they organized all the schools. And nobody turned up—they wouldn't come to get the injections —nobody. Out of the 1200 kids that we knew were registered in the schools north of Smokey, we got 11. Eleven kids.

We didn't know how to approach the thing, because it meant educating the people. They were just afraid to bring the kids for these inoculations.

Anyway,...a man who was working on one of the Navy construction jobs in Sydney came home for Christmas. And he wasn't sick or anything like that. And about 10 days after he came home, two little girls in the house came down with diphtheria. They sent for me that one evening. Of course when we went in the door, we both smelled diphtheria—there's a characteristic rotten smell to the damn disease that gives you the diagnosis before you see the patient. And we went in. And these two little girls were in horrible shape. One of them obviously wasn't going to make it; the other one might. We had no antitoxin or anything like that to treat them with. I had to send to Sydney and they did send down antitoxin.

But when we went into the thing, we found out that the night before, they had had a community card game in that house, and 43 people were at the card game, and every one of them had gone in to talk to these two little girls, so every one of them was exposed to diphtheria. And the chances of any of them being immunized were almost nil. So we spent all the next day and late that night, going from house to house to find out what went on. The next day we went down, and we got a blanket quarantine put on that community—nobody could go out of it, and nobody could come in. We invoked the full force of the law on that—we didn't want it spreading to other communities. The next day, the little girl died, the one that I thought was going to die. The other one began to get better. And by that time we had some antitoxin to help her along, and she did get well.

Fortunately, there were no kids at this card game. They were all adults. And two adults came down with it. I suppose all the others would have the bugs in their throat. But they didn't get sick. You see, a lot of adults would have been exposed in their younger years, probably, because an epidemic at the turn of the century wiped out 60 kids in that community. And that gives you an idea of what diphtheria could do in a community then.

As soon as Marie could get over the roads in the spring, she went down and organized the clinics again. And by the time we had 3 clinics 33 weeks apart, we had 1100 kids inoculated. One didn't get inoculated—his people were conscientious objectors—which was a bad loophole. So they didn't get their kid inoculated. At Christmas time, the grandmother came back from being in North Sydney, and 10 days later, this young fellow came down with diphtheria, and so did she. So we had lots of antitoxin—I wasn't going to be caught without antitoxin that year. We had plenty of it, and we loaded them, and they got better. But that kid was the only one north of Smokey that winter that wasn't inoculated against diphtheria. And he was the only one that got diphtheria.

After that, we had no more trouble. They were lined up waiting for us every year after that when we came with the clinic. But it had to be some tragedy like that little girl dying, you see, to really break down this hostility towards getting needles. You see, there were clergy in those days that were devils incarnate. They used to preach over the radio about the evils of doctors injecting poison through needles into kids. They were broadcast from a side-track Presbyterian sect, but every Catholic in the country listened to them as religiously as the Presbyterians did. So, that fellow really frightened people away from this sort of thing. (*Was it local clergy?*) No, no. The local clergy were kind of neutral. I don't know if they believed in it or not. They didn't show up with their kids for inoculation, I know that, until after this kid died of diphtheria. From then on, they did. So I suspect they were influenced by that kind of propaganda, too.

.   .   .

(*You were Down North from....*) '42 to '60. I was there in full-time practice from '42 to '55. And being alone—seeing Dr. MacMillan maybe every month or two or something like that—that's the only other contact I had with doctors, see. We didn't even have telephones. I couldn't make a telephone call to somebody in Halifax to ask a question, because we had no

112

phone service outside of there, just a local. So if you wanted to send a message away, you had to send a telegram. So there were no conversations with other people, unless I went somewhere. I used to go over to Cheticamp occasionally to have a conversation with the doctors there, you know. Ask them questions, and they'd ask me questions. Because you're always trading information back and forth....We were isolated. You couldn't get somebody else's advice. So you had to go to the books and see if you could nail it down that way. There wasn't any other way if you didn't know.

(*Did you have things like x-ray?*) No. You had to depend on physical signs. Which everybody depended on up until x-rays became generally available, during the First World War. And you went by what you learned with your eyes and your ears and your stethoscope and your fingers. You could percuss out tumours. I can still do that better than any of the fellows that have been brought up on x-rays.... All you know is there's a mass there. You can't tell whether it's a cancer or it's an abscess. But you know something's wrong. And young fellows coming out today, I don't think can do that.

Fractures. You didn't need x-rays. After all, like I said, for a hundred thousand years, the medical men set bones without x-rays. No reason why I couldn't.... Any country practitioner before the days of x-rays had to do it that way. And you relied on the physical signs. When you examined a leg that was broken, you knew exactly where it was broken, and you knew where there was any shortening. You knew what had to be done to set it up in plaster so that it maintained its shape. And we got very good results. If you took a hundred patients with fractures, and you had x-rays for all those hundred patients, I would assume your results on the whole would be better, than doing them the way we did them. But we didn't have outright failures.

·   ·   ·

I used to get called occasionally to Pleasant Bay, but that wasn't part of my practice. That belonged to the Cheticamp practice. One winter, though, an epidemic of flu over the whole country, and a very bad variety of flu. A lot of people were sick enough to have pneumonia and pleurisy and stuff along with it. And I got called out, because the 3 doctors in Cheticamp were sick all at the same time, with the flu. They couldn't get out of bed. I happened to be well, or fairly well, at the time—I had been in bed with the flu for a week, got out and went to Pleasant Bay.

At that time you drove with a horse to Big Intervale, which is 7 miles above Cape North. And then the roads weren't open, of course, over the mountain. The Pleasant Bay fellows had the dog team that they used for hauling their mail from Cheticamp to Pleasant Bay, twice a week I think it was. They would come over the mountain from Pleasant Bay, meet me at daylight at Big Intervale where the park warden lives now. A man named MacGregor lived there at that time. And I'd have breakfast at MacGregors', leave my horse there and he'd look after it, go with the fellows with the dog sleigh. We'd have to walk across the mountain—dogs can't pull you up that kind of grade. But they can pull you along the level, or down grade. But they could carry the bags, and I carried three big satchels. 'Cause you never knew what you were going to have before you. You had to have lots of stuff you didn't need. But you could deal fairly well with whatever you met. The dogs carried those over.

Between 7 or 8 o'clock in the morning we got to Pleasant Bay after walking over the mountain. And a fellow with a horse and sleigh drove me around. (**Marie:** A total of 32 flu patients.) So you were just from house to house. And two of those had massive pleural effusions, so I had to tap them, take the fluid off their chests. And the rest were not too badly off. I had a lot of sulfa drug with me. Because if it didn't do anything for the flu, it would likely prevent pneumonia and pleurisy from occurring. And long before I finished the last calls, I had used up the last of the sulfa drugs.

At 10 o'clock that night, we came to a house—MacIntoshes'—and they had supper ready. We ate a big supper and then started back over the mountain. MacIntosh drove me up to—do you know where the Lone Shieling is?—that's as far as a horse could go. And the fellows with the dogs were there and ready, the same team that came after me in the morning. Went back over the mountain that night. Mrs. MacGregor was up and had a meal waiting. And when I ate, I hitched up my own horse and started back for Neil's Harbour.

We had done an appendectomy the day before, and I just didn't dare stay away any longer because you didn't know what might take place. I wasn't all that experienced an abdominal surgeon, you see. So I kept going till I got home. I got home around daylight the next morning. I had been 33 hours, I think, from the time I left home till I got back home. I never stopped at all, except to eat here and there, and for all these calls. Even on the way back from big Intervale down to Cape North, two people had the lanterns on the gate. And that meant someone was sick in the house. (*Everybody would know that you had gone to Pleasant Bay?*) Oh, sure. Everybody knew every move you made, from the time you woke in the morning till you went to bed at night! But that's the way you had to live.

You might be all night answering these calls. Gone for a day and a half or two days lots of times. You know, when a lot of people were ill and spread out from village to village. Nobody liked paying the doctor to come 30 miles for something like that. So they waited for somebody else to call him, and then they all called him in off the road. So it worked fairly well, because if one fellow had to pay the doctor to come to Bay St. Lawrence or Cape North or something like that, the next time somebody else would have to pay that. And the ones that hung the lantern on the gate or stopped you otherwise, they just paid your house call. So nobody in the long run was out much more than anybody else. But it was time-consuming.

(When you'd leave home....) I'd only know the one that called me. But after the first winter of experience, I knew there'd be

Mailman and horse, Pleasant Bay to Cheticamp

a lot more than that. The telegraph service, it used to drive me nuts sometimes, because, you wouldn't have any idea who was sick at the house that you were going to, what was wrong. Might be anybody from an infant to an aged grandmother. So you didn't know what you had to take with you, so you had to take a little of everything.

The first summer we were here, we had a call to somebody, but as we were coming up a hill, a man was out in the road waving his arms. And a little boy was sitting on a big rock beside the road, maybe 6, 7 years old. I asked the man what he wanted. And he said it was his little boy—broke his arm. And I went to look at the little fellow. His arm came out like this and down like this. And it was solid. I said, "When did he break it?" "Oh, three weeks ago," he said. And they didn't put anything on it, they didn't do anything to it, and so the bone had begun to heal in that position. In children those bones heal very rapidly.

Anyway. Couldn't leave the little fellow like that. We had no hospital at that time. I sent the man up to the barn to get some shingles. And he pulled 2 or 3 shingles off the side of the barn and brought them back. Marie was with me. We made splints. I had to take that little fellow's arm across my knee, and break the healing bone apart, straighten it out, splint it together, and set it up and put it in a sling. I told him to bring the boy out in a

115

week's time till I'd see how things were going. And I never saw him again. I never saw that boy again for 20 years. And when I saw him again, he showed me the arm that I set when he was a little boy. You couldn't tell it had ever been broken. It was as straight and as useful as the other one. But I think there was a good deal of luck in that!

(*Did you use chloroform?*) No. That kid never batted an eye. You could hear the bone break again. And believe me, a breaking bone is not a pleasant thing. That kid never batted an eye, he never changed expression. This was almost a religion among that particular group of people. They regarded themselves as being tough, and they were tough. And even the young children, they wouldn't admit to pain.

Marie and I were inoculating them in the little school there one day, and there were 17 kids. And she had set up the syringes and needles with the right amount of antitoxin and stuff that we had to give them. And I ran out of stuff. They were coming in this direction, and each one would come with a big smile, and his arm out like that, and I'd inject him, and he'd keep going. Ran out of stuff. And I said, "Marie, I'll have to fill another syringe." "No," she said, "I have enough for 20." "Well," I said, "it's all gone." Here they were coming around for another shot! They didn't get outside people paying that much attention to them ever before. So they weren't going to miss the chance. And these little kids, coming around for a second shot. To me that's far-fetched. But it's not. That's what happened. That's a true thing. That's the only time I ever saw kids come back for a second shot.

There were two little kids there who were well-known around the communities for being very good at the Scottish step-dances. And the teacher asked them if they would dance for us before we'd leave. And the little boy said he couldn't, he didn't have his shoes. This was mid-May, and they were in bare feet. But anyway, the teacher sent a bigger kid home to this fellow's house to get his shoes. When he came back with the shoes and a fiddler, the fiddler sat down at one of the desks, and the little fellow put his shoes on. The little girl already had shoes on. And they put on quite an entertainment for us before we left. But there was no crying in that school when they got inoculated.

. . .

(One) night, coming from Pleasant Bay with the dogs—it was a bright moonlight night. And coming down the north side of the North Mountain into Cape North—the road winds down around these bluffs like that. Well, the road at that time was narrow, compared to today. And in the wintertime, with frost and thaws, the rocks would fall out of the cliffs and they'd fall down right on the road. So we were coming down. We got to

116

the top of the mountain and we were getting pretty tired, anyway. And the driver, he was standing on the runners of the dog sleigh behind. He said, "You get on there." And the third fellow, he was just running alongside. They were used to running. They were the mail couriers from Cheticamp to Pleasant Bay in the winter, and I don't think they ever tired out, those birds. (*On snowshoes?*) Sometimes. They didn't have snowshoes that night—there was crust that you could walk on.

Anyway, we came around one of these bluffs. And here were two deer came up from below, crossed the road, and started up a little ravine on the other side. And the dogs went nuts. See, these dogs hadn't been fed, then, for over 40 hours. You can't feed dogs if you're going to work them— they won't work then. They've got to wait and sleep till they digest their food. So dogs are always worked hungry. And these fellows were getting ravenous. So they went for the deer. And they came down, they didn't pay any attention to the driver, who had a long line on the lead dog, and he just couldn't stop him at all.

This sharp rock came up out of the crust like that in the middle of the road. And I came up when I saw we were going to hit it—I got my rear off the sleigh. But the sleigh hit, and it went in a thousand pieces. These sleighs were built very small and light, see. And the driver and I just went head over heels down over the side, and away down the ravine below, bumping off the little birch trees as we went. And my three bags of equipment, they were scattered hell west and crooked all over the side of that hill. But you could see everything with the (moon).

Well, we examined each other when we got to the bottom. We had a lot of bruises but no broken bones. Which was a very fortunate thing, because we got some rough handling going down that hill. And the other fellow, I thought was worse off than me, 'cause he seemed to me to be hitting the trees in a worse way than I. He was perhaps 50 feet up the ravine from me. Anyway—gathered up all the stuff. It took us a long time to get it up this mountainside to the road again. By that time the other fellow had captured the dogs. But we had no sleigh. They tied the dogs. And we went on down to MacGregor's, which was about two more miles, I suppose. And it was the longest two miles of my life. I was getting dead tired.

Got into Murdock's, anyway, and we got a big breakfast, started for home. They started back over the mountain for Pleasant Bay. But you know, a fellow should have got killed in an accident like that, but we didn't.

Another night, Murdock MacLeod was the driver, who got very expert, as I said, with the chloroform bottle. And Murdock was a brave, tough man—nothing ever bothered him very much. But have you ever been down into White Point? You know, how you come off a ridge and you go down a steep crooked hill to the bottom. Well, in the middle of the night one time, we had to go down there. And I was at Cape North when I got the call. Murdock had a big red mare—she was fairly fast and reliable. And my horse was getting tired. So Murdock said, "We'll take my mare." And that was 8 or 9 miles to get there, and 8 or 9 miles back.

Anyway, we got along great. We had a thaw, and the road was icy, so it was good traveling. We got to the top of this hill. And the britching came loose. You know, that's the breech part of the harness that goes around and fastens to the shaft to keep the sleigh from bumping the animal. We had already come over the top when this thing came loose and the sleigh hit the mare in the heels. She went down the hill as tight as she could gallop. And Murdock dropped out on the right side of the sleigh and I on the left, and we just held on, you see, to slow her down—just let our bodies drag out on the ice. And we thought she'd probably get killed when she hit the turn at the bottom, because it was a square turn. But she didn't. She landed in the snow-bank. That stopped her—she couldn't move a leg. And here we were—our clothes were torn, and we were full of bruises—but no broken bones. Mare didn't have any broken bones. So we got her out of the snow-bank and back on the road, and went down to White Point. About daylight in the morning when we got back home to Cape North.

Marie kept track of my mileage during the winters, you know, with the horses, from the time I'd leave home till I'd get back. In the 5 winters that I had to travel all winter with horses, the one winter the mileage was about 3500 miles, and the others were between that and 5000 miles. And that, if you add it up, brings you almost once around the earth at the equator. Within a thousand miles.

We used to cross the ice from what they called Courtney's Shore, where the Courtney family used to live at Cape North. Crossed the ice and came ashore down in Sugar Loaf, down near where the Wilkies live in Sugar Loaf. And when the ice was good, it was a good shortcut, it was a good way to go. And in the beginning of the winter, the county used to pay a fellow to take some little spruce trees, you know, chop a hole down in the ice, and put the trees there for markers. Oh, about a hundred feet apart, so even in a storm you could follow from tree to tree, as a rule. What they called "bushing the ice."

But this was getting on late in the winter, in March. And we'd had some warm days, and the ice was good. I had a big gray road horse—Harry. Anyway, Harry was making great progress down the ice, and we were enjoying the whole ride, and this was about 8 or 9 o'clock at night, I suppose. I was going on a call to Bay St. Lawrence. And all of a sudden, we go in the drink. The ice simply went down, and Harry disappeared in the water.

We were in the sleigh behind, but we got out in a hurry and scrambled up onto the ice. And about a mile back was the Courtney home. There were 7 men in that house, and we knew if we could get them, we could get Harry out of the ice. He tried to get out, but more ice would break and he'd go down. So he gave up then. So Murdock started back for Courtneys, and I stayed with the horse. And just his head above the water.

Anyway, I got the traces loose, a rope that we carried in the sleigh for emergencies, and the reins. And I stripped off—it was a bright moonlight night—I went down beside him in the water, and got the reins and rope around under 3 of his 4 legs, and got back up and got my clothes on again, and—jumped around awhile. And I heard them coming half a mile or so away. When they got there, we were all ready to go to work, 'cause I had the lines on the horse and everything.

And the 9 of us, we got on these, and we pulled it. That horse weighed 1400 pounds, so it took some pull, you know. And we got him out on his side on the ice. But a horse gets paralysed with the cold very quickly in that icy water. Most horses that ever got in—even if they got out, they died on the ice afterwards, because they couldn't get on their feet. Once they get on their feet, they can warm up in a few minutes. And Murdock said, "My God, he's gone, and I haven't got a knife." I said, "I've got a knife." I took it out, and I just took the back of the blade, and I ripped him up the leg in here, you know—not right through his skin. And he let a scream out of him, and jumped to his feet. So, we're all right.

Once he got to his feet, we hitched him up. We came back to Cape North, got dry clothes on, and we went to Bay St. Lawrence and back that night with the same horse. He never even got a cold. Neither did I!

A Visit with
Mary & Clarence Lashley

Clarence Lashley, Sydney: I was born in Barbados in Under Britain's Hill, St. Michael. I was born in 1898. I remember the Barbados, oh yes, I'll never forget that. I lived in a town. My father was a coachman. He'd drive out his employers, just like a taxi-man—but it was carriages rather than cars. My mother was a cook. I came from a family of 9. Only myself came to Canada—in 1923. I would have gone out sooner if I could.

When I was in Barbados, I had lots of opportunities to go to the States but my mother didn't want me to go. I'll tell you why. If a foreigner come to Barbados and want to take away a kid from there, the parent wouldn't let you go. Don't care how you may like the kid. Because one time a guy came from Brazil and he took a boy away and killed him, to take his heart out to make some kind of witchcraft or other—that's what I heard. After that no parent would let the children go. That kept a lot of kids from getting out.

Mary Lashley: It was the same in Cape Breton. Wouldn't let you go anywhere. See, I was living with my aunt down Margaree. She had 9 children. And a family from America used to come down to fish salmon in the river. So my uncle used to cook for them at their camp on the riverside—there a month or two they had a house too, and I was working for them. The woman wanted to take me with her, to the States, just to be her friend, to go around with her. That would be good for me. I was 14 or 15. But my aunt wouldn't let me go. "First thing," she said, "they're Protestants." Anyhow, I wasn't able to go. She had to give consent to cross the border. So then I figured I'd go and be a nun. People talked to my aunt. You can't let her go to the convent, so far from home, what if she gets sick? I was going to school at the convent. And I was so tired, working and working, I was only a kid—and the Sister asked me if I wanted to be a nun. I wanted to be a Sister or a nurse and it took money to be a nurse. So I was supposed to go in June but my aunt said, "No, it's too far from home"—but I found out what she missed was the work I would do. So I can't be a Sister. I can't go away to the States. What can I do? I had no school. All I could do was housework, housework—and I was sick and tired of it. And I said to myself, if I had a child maybe I'd get married and I'd have my own home. That time was just like today—the men were no different. A promise and that was it. Promise they were going to marry you. I admit he would have, only for his mother. But that time the parents would stop you. And I wanted to get away.

Clarence: I had many offers to go to the States, rich people. Then an American woman did carry me to Demerara—and she was very nice to me, kind. I had my own bicycle, good clothes, and she used to give me a pound a month for money—but then I got malaria fever and had to go back home.

So I grew up in the Barbados. Not much school. I had to leave school and work after my father died. I was cooking on a ship and the ship was in Barbados 6 months—all winter you might say, waiting for sugar and molasses. I went aboard this ship and asked the captain if he wanted any help. He hired me as a cook. I cooked the 6 months he was there. So he was leaving and asked me if I would come to Canada. Nova Scotia. I said yes. Only too glad to get out. So I came. There was myself and he had 8 passengers—but he said he would smuggle them in. They paid him $50 and they had to feed themselves, bring their own food. I used to cook it for them. And they ran short of food. It wouldn't have taken so long to get there, but the captain didn't seem to know how to land these passengers. He lingered and lingered. He wanted, it turned out, for these men to go on his son's boat to work—for Barbados wages, not Canadian wages. They wouldn't go, so they jumped.

I was on watch this night, in Sydney here. So I see these 8 guys jumping the boat. I didn't say nothing. The poor fellows were damn glad to get out of Barbados, make a decent living, you know? So I went in the engine house. But the captain's son saw these men jumping and told the captain and the captain called for me. He said, "You saw those men jumping and never reported to me." I said, "No, I saw nobody jumping." He said, "When we go back to sea you'll pay for this." Well, that's a cinch. Because any time

of the night he might call me on the deck and he may throw me over and who would know?

So I jumped the ship too. I had two hard-boiled eggs in my pocket and I left the ship in Sydney. I met a fellow who said he'd try to hide me. So he sent me to Glace Bay. Streetcar was running then. He gave me 50 cents. Said, "You go to Maple Street or the Hub"—because that's where the coloured settlement was. I went to Maple Street. Those 8 passengers who jumped were there, but they were all against me—because they had paid their way and I had worked my way across. So I went to Glace Bay. A fellow took me in. He was working in Number 2. He said, "I'll go to work and you cook for me till I come home." So when he came home I was sleeping. I didn't know shifts were 8 hours. It was 12 in Barbados, and I didn't have food ready. Anyhow, he cursed me and put me out. All the clothes I had was pants and a shirt in a paper bag, and I didn't know anyone.

I came down Maple Street. And I ran into a fellow named Charlie Blackman; he's living in Glace Bay yet. I told him my story and he said, "Come home and stay with me." He was working Number 2. I used to keep the house, wash his clothes and everything. He said, "You stay with me as long as you want to." But I wanted a job. I had a girl home in Barbados, she had a kid—and I left home to get a better living, you know? I used to scrub floors, wash clothes for different guys, whatever I could get. And if I happened to accumulate 2 or 3 dollars I'd send it home to this girl. This girl was staying with my mother.

Charlie kept me 9 months, for nothing, free food and a piece of clothes now and again—overall and a shirt. But no money. Things got so tough I wasn't able to send money to the girl in the Barbados. I wrote and I told her all about it. I said, "I don't know, girl, I got no money to come back home." I got to use whatever I could get here till things got better—and then she died since I was here. And my mother too.

I met Mary in Waterford. The boys that jumped the ship with me went to Waterford and I heard they had got jobs in the mines. So I went over from Glace Bay and I went to the priest, Father Nicholson, in Waterford and he gave me a job around his house—he helped me out quite a bit—and then he got me a job in the mines, Number 15 colliery. I worked there a good while but I didn't like the mines, didn't agree with me. So I wouldn't work steady. I was scared of the mines, underground. I must have worked in all 10 or 15 years, different collieries. One closed and I'd go to another. Then they fired because I wasn't a steady worker. So I came back to the priest and he gave me a job stumping the graveyard in New Waterford. Up on Chapel Hill. Cut down the trees, take up the stumps, stones, clean it up for a graveyard. He kept me when I was out of a job, the handyman around the glebe house. Anyway, I met Mary. She was living in 14 Yard.

Mary: He knew my child before he knew me. My aunt used to sell a little bit of wine and play cards—and that's how he came to go there. He fell in love with my baby before he even saw me.

Clarence: That's the truth. Mary had had a kid. So I love kids, you know. I went boarding with her aunt. I told her aunt, "Is it a boy or a girl?" If it was a girl I wouldn't take it, because when you raise a girl child, then you get to like them so much you hate to see them go—I don't care who they're married to. So I said, "I'll give you some money to go and get this kid." I didn't know Mary. "I'll pay you for it, for minding him." I had goats then. I said, "Feed him on goat's milk and barley water—make him good and strong. Bring him up." So she kept Percy. His name was Joseph Francis. I used to call him Percy. So I used to go and visit this kid often.

(That's a beautiful story.)

Mary: Yeah? If you've got to live it through, it's not so beautiful. It's beautiful to hear about it but it's not so beautiful to live it. Living it is not beautiful.

123

See, when I first came in the Yard, there was 7 of them married to black men—7 white women. They were all from France. I was the only Canadian that married a black man. So that made a little difference because France never was against the black man. They were always very friendly among the black and white in France—but the Canadians weren't the same thing. So all my people were against it. But you see I had a white child and the father left me on the road—because of his mother. His father was dead and the mother had these boys, so they were all supposed to get part of the farm. But they had to marry  like the mother wanted, and she didn't want to part with him—she'd have to hire somebody to put in his place—and she knew I'd never live with her. And that's where the cut-off came.

So I had this child. My people didn't want me because I had this child. In 1928 it wasn't popular for a girl to have a baby. Aw, well, I'm talking straight. They would not give you a job; they would not talk to you. My child was born on Easter Sunday. My uncle took me two weeks after to make my Easter duties—and the women in the church took their long skirts like this and turned away. **Clarence:** They scorned her.

Mary: And they thought I'd catch hell from the priest because he was a tough customer, but he already knew and didn't say anything but pray to the blessed Virgin it don't happen again.

Well, I had to leave down there. People wouldn't speak to me, wouldn't give me any work, and my aunt already had 9 children. She couldn't keep me.

Then I came to Waterford, to my aunt there. She took the child and I went working in Glace Bay. I worked for Jewish people there. Three-

124

story house. My child only three weeks old. I had no place to stay anyhow. I had to sleep on a verandah. I worked there till I almost dropped dead. My aunt wanted me home to mind the child. So I left my job and came there and she went out and she'd take in all the coloured fellows' washing and I'd do the washing, and the ironing, and she wouldn't give me a cent of the money.

Clarence: I was supporting the baby.

Mary: Like I say, if you have to live it, it's not beautiful. But if you just hear it, well, it's okay. One day my aunt had me working so hard I passed out on the floor. Dr. Poirier said, "This child has nobody and she's working to death and she just had a child." He said, "She's got one cup of blood in her body." And I'm sick in bed. And that's when Clarence asked my father if he could marry me. And my father said, "Yes"—till his people, my people, got after him. He came back and tried to change it to no. So we had a heck of a time. But the priest, Father Nicholson, was for Clarence because Clarence had worked for him. He was willing to marry us. Clarence told him, if you don't marry us we'll live together. So hah. And we're married 48 years, you know.

Clarence: And we were happy as that.

Mary: After we were married a few years, my family got to love him as much as their son.

Clarence: All that was against me came back to me because they saw I was a different person than they thought.

Mary: Some down Cheticamp, around Margaree, they had never seen a black man. He went down and the children used to get under the table when they'd see him coming in, but before he'd leave they were all climbing all over him. He said, "Everywhere you'd look you could see a pair of eyes."

(When you decided to marry Mary, what was the reaction in 14 Yard?)

Clarence: There was no discrimination at all there. People got along fine.
Mary: That time your neighbours would run. Say a fire catch you, they'd run and take your clothes out and if you're sick they'd come and bring things. In 14 Yard everybody had a big garden. Vegetables and potatoes. Oh, lovely gardens around there, and what you didn't have in your garden the other had—and they would trade. We had two goats and pigs and

chickens and ducks. We were allowed with that then. You're not allowed today. And pretty near all the houses had their own. And we had little house parties each weekend.

Clarence: In 14 Yard we lived like one family.

Mary: Of course, if there were any jobs, it seemed the white had it first. I looked at it this way. I believe there was prejudice. See, 14 Yard was mostly coloured and Italians and what you would call foreigners. There was only a few of us Canadians. In 1928 when I came there to meet my husband—I found people prejudiced. If we went up town and we had a complaint, say about your taxes or the roads—we were all right till we mentioned we lived in 14 Yard—then we were the last ones to get taken care of. (*It wasn't just because some of the people there were black?*) Oh no. They were foreigners. They weren't Scotch. It was not colour, it was foreigners.

Clarence: But in the pit we all worked together. The same you get I could get, the same place you worked I could work. No discrimination in the pit. There was in the line of one district people didn't like the other district people, but in 14 Yard we were all like one family. The Italians, the Germans, everybody used to live together. Didn't care black, white, yellow or green. Each would go to the other's house. Everybody would join together. Then we'd all go to the hall—Italian, Jewish, everybody.

It was the capital of enjoyment. Fourteen is the best district in Waterford when it comes to friendly. If you're an outsider and interfere with anybody up there, the whole crowd'll jump you. You look after one another like brother and sister. If you belonged to 14 Yard you were as safe as in God's pocket. You white or black—it's the same thing, makes no difference. But if you were a stranger coming here looking for trouble, you'd get it.

Mary: Police used to say, "I hate to come up to the Yard to ask questions. I never get any answers. 'I don't know. I don't know'—that's all I hear."

Clarence: Everybody—even the chief of police—used to come to my place. I used to sell a little drop at that time too. Everybody used to come to my place—I don't care what society you're in. I always use everybody right, as I can. One tell the other—one friend bringing the next, have a good time.

Mary: It was really a good life. All the years I had there I don't regret one. With the neighbours, with the law, with everybody you know—and

126

Clarence, he could sing and dance like I don't know what. (*Did you sing songs from the Barbados?*)

Clarence: Oh yes. "Sly Mongoose"—ever hear tell of that?

> Sly mongoose,
> Sly enough but the dog knows your ways,
> Sly mongoose,
> Sly enough but the cat is on your track
>
> The mongoose went in the Mrs.' kitchen,
> Took up two of her fattest chickens,
> Passed them into his vestcoat pocket,
> Sly mongoose
>
> You look to me like a mile and a quarter,
> You look to me like you require some water,
> You look to me like your blood's out or order,
> Drink bush tea
>
> Drink bush tea, drink-y bush tea,
> Sure to do you good,
> Drink bush tea, oh my belly, drink bush tea
>
> The mongoose went to the Mrs.' kitchen,
> And he took up two of her fattest chickens,
> Passed them into his vestcoat pocket,
> Sly mongoose.

The mongoose kills snakes. They're in Barbados. They used to take them from Barbados and carry them to Trinidad and Demerara and different places to kill snakes. I caught them myself and sold them. Ten cents apiece.

Back home, everybody was so lively. Everybody used to sing and dance and we had a good time. And in 14 Yard, Waterford, we'd dance to those songs many a time. That's calypso. We'd dance probably every other night, for God's sake. Dance in the houses, dance in the street, dance in every open spot you'd get.

> Millie gone to Brazil,
> Oho, poor Millie.
> Millie gone to Brazil,
> Oh poor Millie

127

With a wire wrapped round her waist
And a razor cut up her face,
A big rock to keep her down, boy,
But Millie belongs to me.

You know what happened? A fellow killed a woman and he carried her to the sea and put a rock on her to sink her. He said Millie gone to Brazil, but no, he killed her. This song came up after that. They are strange songs to what you hear, because they originated in Barbados. This one's a fisherman's song. A magistrate, he had this case. A barber is a fish. He asked this person to sing this song—and after every line the magistrate would sing, "14 days."

Mrs. see the barber—14 days
If the grocer want him—14 days
If the boiler want him—14 days
Take him up and give me—14 days
Offer Mary dinner—14 days
I want my barber—14 days
My big blue barber—14 days
I caught him in the harbour—14 days
If you also want him—14 days
If you two want him—14 days
If the boiler want him—14 days
Take him off and give me—14 days
Offer Mary dinner—14 days

(*Did your mother sing songs?*) No. She used to sing hymns. She was a very religious person. If you tried to sing a song in the house she'd chase you out. And my grandmother was the same. She was too much a Christian-minded person for any of that rough stuff. She'd sing like this:

Oh, come let us hark unto the Lord/ let us hark and rejoice in the strength of his salvation/ let us stand before his presence with thanksgiving/ and show ourselves joyful and be glad/ for he's the Lord, he is God/ and we are the people who pasture the sheep of his hand/ when your father tempted me/ proved me and saw my works/ 40 days were we living in misery and sin/ from the heart, for they hath not known my ways/ and whom I swear in My wrath/ should not enter into my breast/ glory be to the Father and to the Son/ and to the Holy Ghost/ as it was in the beginning, it is now and ever shall be/ world without end/Amen.

Mary: He couldn't play any instrument, but he could sing and dance and was very good. Now he has to be quiet. That just about kills him. Sometimes I watch him, you know, I remember him so lively—and it hurts. He was a hi-jacker. Now he's got stay quiet.

Clarence: I had a heart attack.

Mary: Like I say, we had our days.

We worked for years in Montreal. We couldn't get anything to do here. What are you going to do? We had a home. All right. You can't eat the shingles off the wall. I said, "It looks like it's easier for a woman to get a job in Montreal than a man." So I got housework with a Jewish family, from the train. I had never left Cape Breton. I got a newspaper in the station and I read the want ads, and this Jewish woman wanted to go to the country for the summer. They got these wood stoves and these coal stoves and they didn't know how to handle them—so they wanted a Cape Bretoner or a Nova Scotian girl. Well, that was just for me, because I was scared to get in a rooming house alone. Work in a family home; I'll have my room and board right there. I phoned her. Said, "Come right up, I'll pay the taxi." So from the station I went right to the job. And I found a cooking job for him.

Clarence: I worked in Montreal in a hospital till my time was up—I was 64—they lay you off. Then I came home. We were living in a rooming house. This is Montreal. I used to do odd jobs now and again, if I could get it. But while we were working, me and the wife, we'd take it easy—used to smoke but didn't drink. And we managed to save $2000. It took us about 7 years to raise this money. Then I said, "Mary, would you like to go to Barbados?" and she said, "Yes." Okay, we'll take a trip if nothing else.

So we took a plane and we went. We stayed a month. My mother was gone. My father had died long before her. Barbados was all built up now, a million per cent different. (*Did you think you would have liked to have spent your whole life there?*) Oh yes, if it was possible. I had to get out. The wages was so small. You could only get 4 dollars a month and sometimes you didn't get it. Here was better because wages was better. All they were getting was 40 cents a ton for coal—but that was better than Barbados.

Mary: You know, Clarence and I tried to have a child and lost that—only lived 10 days. Then through sickness the doctor told me I wasn't to have any more. I was only in my twenties. Then my first child, Percy, died—8 years old. That's the year the diphtheria was so bad—1935. That's why I pick up everybody else's children, people who had too many.

You know, you'd really like to forget. But I can't. Like I hear some people today say, "You should not live in the past." But you're a young man now, tell us, try to tell us, what is in the future for us? If we don't think about the past and enjoy the fun we had in the past—what is there in the future for us? So I think it's silly to tell the people not to live in the past. That's all we've got to remember, the nice things in the life we've had.

Neil A. MacKinnon:
Rear Beaver Cove

Of course I left there—The Rear—in 1912. That's about 72 years ago. And I got work in Sydney. I was 15 then. I got work at the steel plant. That was two years before the War started.

The reason that this sort of migration started from The Rear: when the railroad went through to Sydney, and the steelworks started there, there was a lot of work going on. They had to have extra mines to supply the steel plant, and there was a lot of activity. And those people in the country, the most of them started drifting into Sydney and the mining area.

The way it happened—when the railroad went through, there was a certain number of the farmers along the railroad line that could work on the railroad. And some of them that had political clout, they got permanent jobs. They were like senators? Because if you got a permanent job at the time, well you had a steady income. Which was never known before by the farmer. And of course, that meant that those people in The Rear area where I was, and beyond, were only a sort of hewers of wood and drawers of water for the front people. Because they didn't come in on this activity along the railroad. And they had to work the farms for those that got steady work on the railroad.

So the people—there was so much work going on in the mines and the steel plant—they started drifting from The Rear—one or two families a year, until we were the last family leaving there. When I came back from the War, the First War, there were only two old families and our family. Well, our family, my father was gone years before that, and we were fairly active. But those two families that were there a mile from us, in two directions, they were all old. And they never married.

So my brother made arrangements to get a place at Beaver Cove. That meant that there'd be nobody there, you know, to break the roads, and those people were too old to maintain them. At this time of the year there might be maybe 3 feet of snow out there, maybe more. And they'd be stranded. But they had a lot of relatives around Boisdale and Barachois and that. And they came out and took them away. That was around 1921, The Rear was totally abandoned.

My father died in 1901. He was only 46 years old. That was a kind of disaster. Because we were all small, 7 of us, you know, to do the farm work and the plowing. The oldest was a girl—I think she was 13 or 14. The oldest boy was around 13. The next one was around 12, a little less than 12. And they had to do all the work as far as the outside work is concerned. Our uncles were gone to the States—that was my father's brothers. I was too small. I was only 4 at the time.

It was a disaster when you lost your father. Those kind of farms out there were only a pile of rocks. And my god, you know, it was no place to farm. When we got big enough, we were picking those rocks and making piles of them. Couldn't take them too far. They used to make line fences with that rock too.

That was our biggest handicap. (*The death of your father*.) You see, he used to get an odd shift on the railroad. Didn't get steady. But he wasn't keeping too much cattle. He might have a couple of cows and a horse, and about 28 sheep. And then, when he died, my mother used to keep extra cattle. We'd survive by selling butter and the likes of that in the summertime. And eggs, and a few lambs, and so on. The trouble was, she didn't provide for the extra feed for the cattle. And then we'd run out of feed in the middle of the winter.

And that's the time, the winter of the big snow—we (did) run out of feed. After getting a ton of hay from Sydney. They used to drop it off at the train, at Beaver Cove. And the snow started. There was a nice sleigh road, about a foot of snow, good sleighing. And we hauled that hay home. Then the snow started in earnest. And it'd snow today. And then possibly into the next day. And it'd kind of clear up, and the wind would shift. And then the next day it started snowing again. It kept on, like about 3 weeks.

Nicholson was leaving The Rear the next spring, and he sold all his cattle. He said, "There's a barnful of hay there." And to get the hay, you know—there was about 6 feet of snow on the level. In some places there was as high as 12 feet, in the gullies and that. They didn't have too much in the form of snowshoes or anything. I remember my older brothers left one day for this Nicholson's. And they weren't organized for a frolic at that time. They went about 2 o'clock. And 2 o'clock the next morning they got back with 2 bags each slung over their shoulder — 2 bags tied together, stuffed with as much hay as you could get in them. That didn't last long.

So they organized a group the next day. And they took a light sleigh, one

Neil A. MacKinnon and his mother

of those riding sleighs, and they put standers in it. They put a big rope on it. And some of them had snowshoes, too. There were 6 or 8 of them. They put about 5 or 6 hundred pounds of hay on. And they hauled it. Well, that lasted most of that week. And then shortly after that, they broke the road from Beaver Cove out, you know, with a group of horses. They put the best horse ahead, and they came out light, and they broke the road. And then we got another ton from North Sydney. That's how we survived during the winter.

I think that was in 1905. That would be over in March, the crisis was. But the big snow started from late in December to early February—the big snow, that blocked us in.

We could get out to feed the animals. Our greatest crisis was the water. The water was in a brook. It would be about 500 yards (away), or something like that. And it was going downhill, running at the edge of the woods. In the summertime they used to have a fire there, and wash the clothes and everything—you know, a nice area just on this side of where the brook was. And then when this (big snow) came, you couldn't get the cattle out to where we used to water them. The cattle couldn't travel through that.

We had to water them in the barn. And the older boys, they dug down where the brook was. And when they got (down), there was nothing but gravel—it was as dry as a bone. The sheep, they'd eat the snow, you know; we weren't worrying about the sheep. The cattle, they wouldn't eat the snow. The same with a horse. We had to start keeping the kitchen stove going day and night, melting the snow. My god, it takes a lot of snow to make a bucket of water!

I'd be 8 at that time. I used to go out on top of the snow—the crust would hold me up because I was light—and I used to cut the tops off the small trees. I'd take a bunch of them home and pile it in with the sheep. Sheep were under the barn—that was their home, like. And they'd come out. They would just get a small batch of hay with that. And they'd eat this little spruce that I was throwing in, along with the hay. And we brought them through the winter, with very little as far as hay feed and that.

The weather wasn't very cold at all. A little blustery at times. But it wasn't a real cold winter. But it was the darn snow.

(*What about your firewood that winter?*) Firewood—you see, young people like that, they don't look ahead. We used to just work some in the woods, used to make pit timber and that. And we'd haul a load of wood home as we needed it. You know, with the horse. We only had about a week's wood when that big snow came. And we couldn't get the horse out. We had to haul the wood out on our backs—yokes that'd be big enough to put on our shoulders. That was on account of not providing wood ahead. Possibly if my father was living, he'd look after that part.

When the spring came, my mother was going down to North Sydney. She was talking to the (train) conductor. And the conductor said, "How'd you get along?" The winter was pretty well over, you know. She said, "We saved all the cattle. We had a hard time on account of running out of feed for them." "Well," he said, "you did better than people around Mira. They lost cattle—and they were only about 12 miles from Sydney—on account of they couldn't get the feed to them." She said that she considered that we did all right—"We saved the cattle...."

Then as we grew bigger and could handle the farm business, people started leaving The Rear. And we used to do the hay on their place, and

134

store it in some of the barns, and haul it home. We fared off all right. But we were getting bigger and stronger, and we could handle it.

We had lots of disasters.

There was a time they were working on the road—there were about 20 or 30 of them working. The snow off the mountain was making big ditches in it, and they were in with carts there. And this morning, it started to cloud up. My mother told one of the older boys, "Go and tell the men (on the road) to come to the house"—they weren't so far away—"to get out of the downpour." And she darkened up, you know. So they got to the house and they filled up the kitchen—they had awful big kitchens at that time. And it started to thunder and lightning. And of course that lasted maybe an hour or so.

And where they used to milk the cows (was) a big clump of big tall trees. When you'd take the cows home for milk, they'd get in amongst those trees and they'd milk them. When the boys came in off the road, they left a little gate open. The cows were in this clump of trees, and they went in, in the hay field. And my mother told one of the older boys, "Go out and close the gate." Because they'd ruin the hay field—that time of the year. He went out, drove them out. And they went in the clump of trees.

The downpour of rain, that was pretty strong. There was a bunch of (men) at the house. I guess there weren't enough seats for all of them. I know Roddy Nicholson told me he was standing near the door. And he said, "This clap of thunder come, and the lightning at the same time—just flash, and the blast at the same time, you know." That would be possibly overhead. And he said when it did stop, in a half hour or so—it calmed off and the rain stopped—they went outside. And here, I don't know if it was 4 or 5 cows, that were in the clump of trees—they were all dead. The whole bunch. All that was saved was a little heifer, a 2-year-old. The reason he was saved, you know, the cows resented him, and they used to shun him, and chase him. And he got outside the trees for a little bit, and he was saved. He was the only one left.

That was a real disaster.

Mother had a serious ailment before the First War. I think I was around 9 or 10. We used to make hay on those places that they were after leaving The Rear. Stephen MacInnis's farm—there was a lot of good hay. And my mother used to help, you know. She'd go out. It was all small hand-rakes that time. Just little scythes. There was no horse machine or anything. And the two older boys, they'd have a scythe each. Then my mother and Rachel—they'd go out and start to raking that in rows. And she was after doing this.

And she was after making a big wash that morning, I guess, with the clothes out. That MacInnis's place was about a mile and a quarter from us.

And we started walking. And she took the rakes and went out. She used to make lunch for us, too, out there.

She took this pain and she was hollering all night, you know. We didn't know what to do. Of course, the older ones, they were big—but they didn't know what to do for her. Didn't know what the pain was like. And Hughie took off for Boisdale. There was a telegraph at Boisdale Station. There used to be a train leaving Sydney, they called the way freight. And I think it left around 9 or 10 o'clock. Just a passenger car on it. He called Dr. Kendall in Sydney. This fellow used to go around the country. You know, if something happened to people, get a bad cut or somebody break a leg or something—he'd go and he'd fix them up. And he got ahold of him. And he was early enough that he could get this freight.

Then they met him at the train with the horse and wagon, and they took him out. My mother was still suffering with the pain. I don't know what they were giving her—hot drinks or what. But he diagnosed right away that it was appendix. Of course, appendix was a very new thing at the time. "Now," he said, "you've got to be very careful, if we can get her to the hospital without that appendix breaking. If it ruptures, she won't have much chance.

So by God, they went in and they got Big Mick's express wagon, a wagon with two seats in it. They took the back seat out, and they took it out to our place with the horse. They fastened the mattress on the wagon, the spring under the mattress. And then put her on there. And they had to tie that pretty well, because you know that mountain was pretty rough. So they had left in lots of time.

They took their time going in, and they got her in. They notified the train to stop at Beaver Cove for a patient. They backed up until they got the baggage car right in front of the little station there. And they put the whole thing in there—the mattress that she was on, and the spring—just took the whole thing and put it in the baggage car, with the mail and that. And the older two boys went on the train, too.

And she was operated on, I guess, the next day. She got in there all right without any rupture. According to reports, the operation was successful.

So in the meantime, when she was starting to recuperate, they had her all strapped, you know. And they used to take and put her in the chair alongside the bed, until they fixed up the bed. That was being done by a nurse. And she was called somewhere, emergency—she was called away, anyway. And she forgot to strap my mother with this bandage, to hold this thing in place. What happened was, in the meantime, one or two of those stitches gave way. There was what they call "proud flesh" started to form in this where the stitches broke. And the proud flesh—it's dead flesh—

there's no circulation. And she never healed. The rest of it healed, but where the stitches broke, that never healed.

So she went home. And they gave her a belt, you know, to put on her. She lived 12 years after that, but never healed up. I think eventually what took her, was this turned into cancer, because it never healed properly. She never was really well after that. That's how she went. She was only 59 when she died. She was working too hard, you know, working the field and working home. Got too much for her.

(*But didn't you have neighbours come and just move in and help your mother through that winter?*) Oh no, no. They just had their own problems. Because everybody was, you know—it was a hard-pressed area anyways.

The nearest family was MacLean's. They had no children. They were middle-aged at that time. He was active enough. Of course, if you went for him, you see, for any emergency—which my mother did. She used to do the washing outside in big pots, in the summertime. And the house was shingled with wooden shingles. The heat of the sun, probably, on the shingles, and a spark from the fire that she had under the big pot lit in the centre of the roof. She was washing quilts. And she told the oldest boy to jump up on the horse and run for Neil MacLean, a mile away. And there was an upstairs. The roof wasn't sealed inside, just the rafters. She put the ladder up. She took the quilt—she'd soaked the quilt—and she crawled up the ladder, got on the roof. And she fired the quilt over where the fire was. Then she took a bucket, and she went upstairs and she started firing the water. She put the fire out. MacLean came right away—he came as fast as he could, but the fire was out when he got there. She saved the house at that time, anyway.

(*I'm just trying to think of how much was on your mother and how much was on small children—not just the winter of the big snow, but any winter—just to get all the work done.*) Well, it was just—she had to depend on the neighbours if there was any work that the children couldn't do, she'd ask a neighbour to do a day's work, and they wouldn't charge anything. In the old days there was no such thing as welfare, only what the neighbours would give you. The neighbours had to do that because they didn't know when their own turn would come, and somebody would have to help them. And that's the way it was. But today, there's no such thing as getting a neighbour. The government has to do it....

But my God, you know, we had a hard time in the old days. It was terrific. And of course, that stood me good in the War (World War One). Because I really appreciated what we went through. And I often told them there, "Now, we have it tough over here, but we had it tougher in The Rear where I come from."

I worked hard when I was 9 and 10 years old. you know, when Sydney Mines was going strong, they used to take timber for the pits, carloads of it. My mother'd go down, she'd get an order for a car-load of pit timbers. She'd take that home. And the older boys, they'd go out cutting. I was only about 10. I'd be hauling this stuff out, the trees, out to the road. And then we'd fix up that lumber—double sleighs, you know—we'd haul it in to where the train was. When we would get enough there for a car-load, we'd load a car-load and ship it off to Sydney Mines. A lot of work in that. But still, it was the only source we'd have for to get supplies.

When you'd make a car—it would take about 160 dozen 6-footers and 6-foot-8's, hewed on two opposite sides. Two flat sides. You'd get a little more, couple of cents more, for that than the round ones. If we got a box-car, we'd be lucky. But very often they'd only give us a flatcar. We'd have to put about 36 hardwood standers, about 10 feet high—that would hold the timber in place. We wouldn't get anything for that—all those standers we put in. Oh, somebody was using them. But they wouldn't pay us for that. That was going with the car. And then we had to pay half of the cost of the freight, to Sydney Mines from Beaver Cove. And you had to have the car loaded within 48 hours, or they'd charge you for standing. So you had to load it pretty fast.

(*How long would it take you to cut enough to make a box-car?*)

It'd take about a month. Sometimes a month and a half if the weather was bad. When we'd be through planting we'd cut possibly 50 or 100 dozen, pile them. Then after hay-making we'd start hauling them out. And then we'd cut more, till we'd get the car-load. We'd have to haul it in that mile and a quarter. Order a car, load the car, and ship it. And after all this work was done, you'd possibly get—if it was only for ourselves, we'd get about $120 for that. That's it. That's as much as we'd get, if we were lucky. And if they were condemning too much, we wouldn't get that much. If there wasn't 3 inches in the small end, they could condemn it. Very seldom they'd condemn it.

Sometimes we'd make a car-load, and we used to sell them to the stores. He'd give you groceries in trade.

So anyway, that's the story of the days before the Great War. When the Great War came, it changed everything. And then of course, the older people got old, we got big, and decided to leave that place. That's the last that I lived in there, when I left in 1912. I only used to visit after that.

It wasn't so bad till the railroad came through. And when people along the railroad got work on the section—they were farmers—they used to get the Rear people, where I lived and way beyond, to come in and do the farm work for them. And of course, some of them were only paid in— maybe if you were short of potatoes or something like that, they'd pay you in (that)—not in cash. That's the way, you see, the people in The Rear were set up to serve those people that had the railroad work.

(Why didn't people from The Rear work on the railroad?)
They'd just give them the spare time. If they were short, you know, they'd give The Rear people a shift.

(Why did they not usually give it to them?) Because they wanted them to work for themselves—the farmers.

When the railroad came through, The Rear end was doomed. They had to leave because there was no solution for them.

(None of the houses are standing, are they?) No, no, there's none of the houses, I don't think. Our house is gone. I planted a tree there, Balm of Gilead tree. It was a little sprig, about up as far as the lights there (about 4 or 5 feet), little striped thing. I planted that, I think it was 1910 or something. And that grew and grew and grew. And the last time that I saw that tree, it was after decaying. The top of it, a piece of it after dropping off. It was after growing up about 30 or 40 feet. And I planted it just below the front door there a little bit, in line with the other trees. I was often looking at that. Now, my God, it's after going—an old dead tree now.

This article is taken from interviews by Pam Newton and Ronald Caplan

Neil A. MacKinnon at Loon Lake, on the road to Rear Beaver Cove

A Visit with Wilfred Prosper, Eskasoni

In 1955 we had just gotten a new truck, and we were up in Judique, picking blueberries, way up in the backwoods there, in the fields. As a matter of fact, I was with the chief, Donald Marshall. Dinner break. We were lying down between a bunch of trees. Donald had his hat like this, over his face, to save himself from the sun—we were lying down—and I didn't. I was just lying there like this, looking up at the sky. And all of a sudden I saw something. I'd heard about them, but I never believed it. This flying saucer thing.

And I said, "Donald, look!" Before he could remove his hat, it was gone. Just flying over between the trees. It looked like a saucer, a big saucer. That was the first sighting I saw. I saw this as clear as anything sitting there. It was quite a bit up the sky. It was moving. I didn't know if it was rotating—I didn't see it long enough. I just saw it come out from this tree on this side, and I said to Donald, "Look! Look at the saucer!" Donald didn't see it. Before he could look up, it was gone beyond the other trees. 1955. I told people, and I knew what the reaction was going to be. "Oh, baloney!"—that would be the first reaction. I said, "To hell with it, what's the sense? Nobody would believe it anyway."

Then I saw—we were coming from Mass here on Sunday. It was just after Mass. There was myself, and this fellow who stayed with us, and my nephew. We were just going into the house when I looked out and I saw what looked like a balloon. But it was a clear—you know, like water colour—what would you call it?—it wasn't coloured—a clear balloon. It was like a bubble, a big bubble, falling from the sky (into the Bras d'Or). And I said, "Look!" And they looked up, and they both saw it. And I'm telling you, boy, we didn't spend long before we decided we'd go up and check what it was. We headed down the shore, we took a couple of oars. And we'd seen where it landed. And we rowed around that spot for a half hour. Never saw a glimpse of anything. (*Or anything on the water?*) No.

But there was a stranger sight than that. This one particular night—it was a moonlit night. Oh, a beautiful night. Beautiful, clear skies—not a cloud in the sky. Except two. And the moon was just across there, above Big Pond. And those two clouds—one was below the moon to the left, one was to the right—both of them were just below the moon. I didn't think anything of it. I looked out and I saw those clouds, and I walked away. And it dawned on me. "Isn't that awfully strange?" I said to myself, "Those two clouds could be the same shape." So I looked out again. And sure enough, they were both oval-shaped clouds, exactly the same size, exactly the same shape.

Then I said to the kids—to the bunch of kids and the wife—I said, "Look out there. Look at those clouds. Don't they look strange? They look exactly the same. Look at them." They went out—all of them—some of them went out to the platform there, some of them were up on the window, looking out. They looked at them. And I walked away. And before I walked away, one just disappeared. It just disintegrated, like. And the other one started to move where the other one was. Now, I walked away. But as I walked away, the kids saw—and I believe this, the wife—lights formed around this other, the second cloud. And then it just disappeared. But I never saw it, 'cause I walked away. But the funny thing was that the two clouds were of exact same—both oval.

I don't know. Being an Indian, boy, you hear all kinds of weird stories. A lot of people say it's mythology; I suppose a lot of it is. Oh, you hear all kinds of queer stories, about ghosts and goblins and what-not. I've never seen people so immersed in things like that, as Indians. (*The Scottish people seem to have their share.*) Yeah, the Scottish people have. (*I sometimes think it's Cape Breton Island.*) I don't know. I've heard some weird stories.

My father had a couple of them. He used to tell about this particular place between Barra Head and St. Peters. He said that he and the other fellow were coming home, coming off the train. And they had no way of transportation but walk home in those days—that was a long time ago. He was a young man then. And this fellow happened to be drunk. And he had a few of them, I guess, himself, but he wasn't near as plastered as the other fellow. And he said the other fellow was an awful man for hollering. Some Indians are like that, you know. Holler at the top of their voice, kind

141

of a camouflage—is it fear, or what? Trying to scare people or—I don't know—psychologists would know that. Anyway, they were walking. It would be about 6 or 7 miles to Barra Head, plus another 2 miles walking down to where he was going.

So, he said, "We were walking along, and all of a sudden I heard footsteps. And I had all to do, to keep this fellow from hollering and screaming and that, to try to keep him calm—as they were approaching us," he said.

"There were 6 men carrying a log about this big around," he said, "maybe 90 or 100 feet long. Six men carrying it. And they headed for the ditch as we were meeting them. They took to the ditch, or the other side of the road, over the bank. Never said anything. They just kept on going with this log. I thought to myself, 'No human being—even 100 men couldn't lift that thing.' And they went, they kept going. We kept on going. And all of a sudden there's a fellow walking across the road in front of us. He never stopped, he never said anything, and this fellow (with me) hollered at that time. Oh, God," he said, "I just about lost my pants. And this fellow kept on going. I glanced over. When I looked," he said, "there was a fire coming from his heels. Every step of that, he was dragging a chain, and it glittered. Every step, there were sparks coming from his heels. Like he was dragging a chain. He kept on walking, right down to the shore. That's when I took off. I never came to it till I got home." And my uncle told me he landed at the house pale as snow. I don't know what happened to the other fellow. I suppose he just put him on his shoulder and he carried him, I guess. And he dropped him off home, and he kept on running. He said he never stopped till he got home, till he landed at the house. Oh, I don't know about crazy things like that. What is it? What are they?

Oh, the Indians are loaded with that. I don't know if you can call it mythology. I suppose it is, I don't know. Who's the operator behind all those weird things? Is it good or bad? Is it bad omen or good? What the hell is it? I don't know. (*But you think it has a meaning.*) It must have a meaning. I don't get a very good feeling out of it, myself, anyway. If you're a Christian, eh? That's opposed to Christian belief.

(A fellow told me,) coming home from Maine, all by himself in a car. So he said, "I saw this fellow walking up the road, hitchhiking. So I picked him up. A little further on, he said, 'This is where I'm getting off.' I stopped, pulled up, and he got off. I kept on going, and I was doing about 60, 70 miles an hour. All of a sudden, there's the same guy. Picked him up again. He got on, we went a little further, he got off again. My God, I suppose we got up around Grande Anse somewhere—the same son-of-a-gun is on the road, hitchhiking again. Holy God," he said, "my hair stood on end. I put my foot down!" I guess he picked him up 2 or 3 different times before he realized.

And the same thing happened to these guys in Barra Head. Coming from Nyanza after an outing, you know, fooling around all night. They picked up the same fellow 3 times before they got to Barra Head. And the third time, he said, the fellow lost control of the car—driving over stumps and everything, but, he said, "We were just lucky—we got back on the road." And they were scared to death. Queer stories, eh?

(*Do the Indians ever talk about little people, what the Scottish call fairies?*) Well now, I've got one here, a dandy, a real dandy. This Noel, he lived alone. He was quite a man for making bull beer, you know, seed beer, yeast cake beer and that. And there was always a bunch of young fellows or older people, drunks, there, they'd take advantage of him. 'Cause he was a very good-natured fellow. A very good singer, oh my God, he had a lot of hymns. I used to go up and see him. You know, we'd get together and sing a bunch of hymns. 'Cause he learned from his old man, you know, his father.

So anyway, one day he told me this story of these people. He said there were 6 of them came in. And he told me exactly where they sat—one sat there and one sat there, one on the table. Some sat on the bed, some sat on the stool, window stool or somewhere. "Little people," he said. "And they were talking, and I couldn't make out what they were saying. I'd heard if you were confronted with these little people, to give them something. All I had was cookies. And I gave them cookies. So," he said, "it wasn't too long after that, they went, they went their merry way." (*They never talked to him?*) No. "But my God," he said, "I was scared. I was scared to death. And someone came in, to deliver oil or something, and I was so damn glad. And I told him about them. He just laughed at me."

After he told me about that story, you know, back around 1975 I guess it was, we decided to go to see this old fellow in Restigouche. He was supposed to be a man full of Indian hymns. And there was another old fellow there, and he was about 91 at the time, and he'd sung in the church for 71 years. So I was mainly interested in this old fellow. We were kind of heavy on hymns at that particular time, trying to gather up as much as we could before it was lost completely.

But anyway, we landed there. And dinner was ready; his wife cooked dinner for us. As we sat at the table, he said, "Now as soon as we're through eating, we're going to go visit another Indian community called Maria"—that would be in the Gaspé Peninsula somewhere. We had just sat at table to eat—I was sitting there, and he was sitting on the end, Noel was sitting next to me, and another fellow was sitting on the other side. And he said, "We'll come to a place"—called it by the Indian name—"and there's a very interesting story about this place. It's a story about fairies."

Well, Noel sat around like this. "Fairies!" "Yeah." "Tell us about it!"

143

So the old man started—and Noel wouldn't eat his dinner. He just sat there; he was just mesmerized. And I watched him, you know. So I said to myself, Now, there must be some truth, because he's so interested, you know.

So the old man said, "In this particular place you'll see tracks coming down the mountain. And you'll see a cross around the edge of the mountain, you know, just at the corner of the mountain. It's a fairly steep mountain. Next to that, another mile or so, is a mission, they call Mission St. Luke. We'll go up there too." But Noel wasn't interested in this mission—he was more interested in the fairies. He said, "Tell us about this fairy business." So the old man said, "This is farming country. And some very big farms there, and they have horses and cattle. And these fairies used to harrass the animals to the point where some of them died. Some of the horses had died. And in the morning the farmers go and tend to the animals, and they find them full of sweat, they're just frothing with sweat. And some of them had died. Mostly horses. And their tails would be all braided. And their manes and everything. They'd be running wild, and right nervous and everything. So they contacted the bishop or the priests or—the bishop, I guess, of the diocese there. And there was a bunch of"—I don't know if it was a bunch or a priest—"came down with this cross. You'll see that, you'll see that cross up there. And they took the cross up there and planted it there."

Sure enough, after dinner—I don't know if Noel ate his dinner. But anyway, we went—it wasn't too far from there, maybe 20 miles, I guess. So he said, "Stop here." I stopped. "Now," he said, "pull ahead a little bit further, you'll see it better." So I pulled ahead a little bit further, and we stopped again. He said, "Look. And you see those marks coming down, like little brooks. Those are the marks put there by the fairies where they used to slide down, slide down." And my God, Noel was taken in by that, was he ever. So he said, "Drive up a little further, now." So I drove up a little further and stopped again. "Now, look up," he said. "There's a cross there that the priests had put up. After they put that cross up there, that put an end to it. No more fairies. No more harrassment, no more nothing." Well, my God, was Noel ever interested. Then it dawned on me, you know, now there must be something to what he said about what he had seen, eh? Because the other fellow couldn't care less; he wasn't a bit interested; he was eating away. And I ate all my dinner. But Noel—my God!

.   .   .

Noel Francis told me a story; he was there with his father. His father was one of the primary prayer leaders in Barra Head—he had a lot of hymns and prayers, Indian prayers. "So," he said, "this woman was dy-

144

ing. But she couldn't die. For some reason or other, she couldn't die. So," he said, "my father was saying the prayers out of his hieroglyphic book. And all of a sudden"—he had the book on either the chair or the table—"all of a sudden, the leaves started to turn by themselves. They came to this one particular hymn. When it stopped, he knew the hymn, and he started singing it. Just as he was finished, the woman died." That seems strange. I don't know what to make of that.

I know the hymn. Psalm 20: "The Lord answer you in time of distress. The name of the God of Jacob defend you. May he send you help from the sanctuary, from Zion may He sustain you. May He remember all your offerings, and graciously accept your holocaust. May he grant you what is in your heart, and fulfill your every plan. May we shout for joy at your victory, and raise the standards at the name of our God. The Lord grant all your requests. Now I know that the Lord has given victory to his anointed, that He has answered him from His holy Heaven, with the strength of his victorious right hand. Some are strong in chariots, some in horses, but we are strong in the name of the Lord our God. Though they bow down and fall, yet we stand erect and firm. Oh Lord, grant victory to the king, and answer us when we call upon you."

That is sung by the Indians. (*In Micmac?*) Yes, it's in the hieroglyphic book. It's the very last hymn, or psalm—the very last one.

So, I don't know. He said that this woman couldn't die till those leaves turned, till they came to stop there, the very last one. He said, "And my father sang that to her. And just when he was through, she died."

(*Is it common for someone to sing at the bedside of someone who's dying?*) Oh, it was years ago. And I often wondered about that. My God Almighty, I said, what's going on here—why would people do that? (*How do you mean?*) Well, it sounded so crass, somehow—a person is dying, and you're singing away at the top of your voice. But this was the faith they had. Which we haven't got. They'd be singing before a dying person. And they'd administer to him, you know. Now all these things are done at the hospital—they administer to the dying. The Indians did that in the old days. And they knew—how was it they knew that a person was going to die? Because of their experience, I guess. They knew just when a person was dying. And they'd gather, and they'd sing, and say a prayer.

(*When a person dies, the Indians—do they have a wake?*) They had a wake, yeah. In the old days, they'd clean up the remains, you know. They'd put the remains in a cot or bed or somewhere. Clean them up and put clothes on them. And sometimes make clothes for that person that died. And then the men would get to work and make a coffin. They'd be hammering away all night. No such thing as (a funeral home) in those days. They were there, I guess, but these people weren't, you know, rich enough. So they'd get boards and lumber—the cloth. And they put the remains in there. And then there'd be a wake for maybe 3 days.

And they had a custom. And there's a little bit of comedy effect, anyway. Charlie Gould told me this story—because I brought it out—otherwise he wouldn't have told it, you know. I only said this as a joke. I said, "The Indians—if one person came in, a stranger from some other community, they'd all gather around the coffin and they'd sing. Say their prayers, their beads, and singing, and everything. When they were through, the person, you know, the stranger, is welcomed then. Now he was welcome, all right, but it was—what would you call it?—the proper thing was done, the custom had been fulfilled. So, 15 minutes later, another stranger comes in—all over again—the same thing all over again." And I said, "I guess maybe there was a little bit of competition there. Because let's say somebody died in Barra Head, and there was a group coming from Whycocomagh or Bayfield, they made damn sure that they had a singer with them—somebody that could recite the beads, the rosary and that. And I very seldom saw a group of people coming without a prayer leader. And," I said, "I wonder if there isn't a bit of competition involved there, or a little bit of showmanship.

My God, Charlie Gould opened up then. He said, "There is. There was. I can attest to that. Because I was with a bunch one time. And Simon Morrison was there. And," he said, "Simon was the driver. So there was old Stephen Gould, my father, and there was Johnny Gould, and there was Noel Moore, and there was somebody else, another singer, and I was only a young fellow," he said. "And we came to this house in Barra Head where—I don't know who happened to be waked at the time. Anyway, we

Wilfred Prosper in the choir at the annual St. Ann's Day Mission,
at Chapel Island

arrived by the house there, at the road. They asked me to get out. I was
only young, I didn't know what it was all about. 'You go to the door,
Charlie, and see if they're not singing, if they're not saying prayers.' So I
went to the door, and sure enough, they were blasting away. They were
singing and praying and all of that. I went back and I told them. So, all
right. Told the driver to drive on. Because...the spell would be broken,
you know. As they'd walk in, they'd walk right up to the remains and
kneel down and pray and sing. But if they were already singing, you
know, this couldn't happen.

"So anyway, they asked the driver to keep going. So he drove up to the
little schoolhouse. When we got there they filled up their pipes. They lit
up. And," he said, "every one of them had a smoke, or they were chewing
or smoking. When they were finished—'All right, let's go back now.' So
we went back. We parked at the same spot, and I had to do it all over
again. I went to the door and checked again, looked out—it was all quiet.
So I went back and I told them. We marched in. We went right up to the
remains and just started singing and saying the hymns and that."

This was the custom. But there was a little—what would you call it?—
a little showmanship involved in it? Competition? Whatever.

(*Didn't they also used to have a kind of auction?*) Oh, they still do. Oh,
they wouldn't do away with that. That's one of the greatest things, one of
the old traditions that we have left. One of the best. If they do away with
that, boy, that'll be the end of us, I guess. (*What is the auction?*)

Well, after the burial, we just go up to the hall or whatever. And they
auction off the person's belongings. And a lot of the time, the people take
donations. I remember I took a shaving outfit here, to be auctioned off.
Same day. We go right from the cemetery to the hall, and there's a meal.
And either during the meal or after the meal, the auction takes place. My

147

God, there's times they realized—what?—$1500, $1000. (*The auction is of things that belonged to the person who has died?*) A lot of them, yeah. (*And things that people donate?*) Sometimes. A lot of the time, people donate things. And they can buy them back if they want to, or buy something else. (*And who does the money go to?*) Well, to pay the expenses—the undertaker, the coffin, the digging, all those things. And if there's any money left over, usually they turn it over to the church, or the mission fund at Chapel Island, whatever they want to do.

(*And you think this is an important part of Micmac tradition.*) I think so, yes. I think there's a little bit of brotherly feeling connected with it. (*Oh, more than a little. I think that's true. And you say if this would go, if they'd stop doing that....*) Well, we've lost so much already, that's one of the last, one of the few things we still have left. And I wouldn't like to see that go. It brings people together, you know, makes a lot of them feel good, that they donated something, or contributed.

The statue of St. Ann is carried in the procession at Chapel Island Mission.

Cape Bretoners in World War One

H. L. Livingstone • Howard Reid
Dan E. MacQuarrie • Thomas R. Langley
Bill Daye • John Angus MacNeil
Fr. Leo Sears • Thomas Gillard
Kristopher Mayich

H. L. Livingstone, Marble Mountain: It was just all that men could stand in the way of hardships. If it was a little bit more, of course they would have died. Lousy, hungry, cold—so cold that your feet began to rot, lack of circulation. They issued us "gum boots," rubber boots, one time, shortly after I joined the battalion. They were no good at all, because you were always getting over them, getting mud inside them, and they'd be worse than nothing. But the winter of 1917 was one of the coldest in history, in France. We'd be up on what they called the firing step, little step up where you peered over at night. In the daytime of course, you couldn't—too many snipers. And we'd step down off when a machine gun would open up, just flop down, in water up to the waist. And then crawl up again dripping wet, with

that water freezing you. That's exactly what it was: the edge of what man could stand. And man can stand more than would kill a dog or a horse in the mud. He can stand so much. That is, if he's young and in good physical condition. It's almost incredible what a man will stand.

Howard Reid, Sydney: (*Why did you join up?*) Well, that's a conundrum. I suppose it was born through my school days. When I was about 12 years of age, I read in a boys' magazine all about the "Invasion of Britain," "Britain at Bay," and "Britain's Revenge." I can remember all the different stories—it was quite a story. I think it was two boy scouts that held up the Germans on London Bridge. The pictures of the planes that I saw were very good—there was a plane in it, I remember—like one of our modern planes. I read those stories, and they did something. And I was always a marcher, I guess. Went off. The soldiers were parading past the end of our street one time, and I followed them all the way to the barracks. I think I was about 6 years of age.

Dan E. MacQuarrie, Middle River: (*When did you go to the military?*) 1907, I suppose. The militia. (*Why?*) Well, crazy to go to camp. Aldershot. Used to go up to Nova Scotia—Kentville, you know—camp out

Iona Soldiers in the militia leaving for World War One

for two weeks—it was great. There was a company from Middle River—well, the companies were small, probably 50 men and officers. There was another company in Big Baddeck, Baddeck, Margaree, Inverness, and Iona. (*All separate companies in the militia?*) Yes. And they'd have the camp every year, around September. People would be through with their hay then. I went about 6 or 7 years to that camp.

We'd drill at camp. Rifles. Uniforms. We had the red coats, same as the Mounties. We had tents. Go from here on the boat, the *Blue Hill*—and we'd get the train in Iona. Then we'd go to Truro and they'd shift up through the Valley. It was quite a trip for us young fellows. And everybody

Dan E. MacQuarrie

was crazy to go. They didn't have to coax them. Stay for two weeks. Drilling. Learn how to shoot. They had the old Ross rifles then. And when the war came, we took those Ross rifles overseas with us.

I was away five years. We went overseas from Halifax on the old *Olympic*. She was a big one—there were 7 decks on her. Went from Halifax to Liverpool. We were on the ocean about 5 days, made it in 5 days. They had them stacked, boy, and it was wonderful the way they had it arranged. Every 7th man was appointed to feed, to draw the grub for 6 other men. There was no confusion. There were so many appointed every day. And we slept in hammocks. On deck. There were 7000 numbered, 7000 men on that ship.

(*What did you think you were going to?*) We were going to our deaths, that's where we were going. Sixty thousand of them stayed over there, in the First World War.

H. L. Livingstone: I joined the 106th Battalion because my older brother was an officer in that outfit. I joined up in a recruiting meeting in the schoolhouse at Big Bras d'Or—a town meeting with a colonel talking to it. A lot of it, I think, was showing off. I became an important person—I was only a boy, 18—before the community meeting, joining up. This feeling—

feeling created by propaganda—permeated the whole of society, even to the country districts. I can remember somebody coming to our house, and my mother posting up a picture of a soldier, with quotations from Robert Burns: "For gold, the merchant plows the main, / The farmer tills the manor./ Glory is the soldier's price,/ The soldier's wealth is honour." That was clever propaganda. It became an emotional thing. Patriotic, emotional. And everybody was very well brainwashed, I would say. Oh, Cape Breton was completely. And everybody went in the army, and about half of them were killed. See, they all joined infantry battalions, from Cape Breton, unlike Halifax and other cities in Canada, where they joined the artillery or army service corps or medical corps or something else. And the infantry was almost sure suicide. Your only chance to escape being killed was to be wounded.

The only thing I ever did in my life that I'm thoroughly ashamed of was going away to war and leaving my mother alone on the farm at Big Bras d'Or.

(*I often wonder whether I would have the stomach to do the things that I might be called on to do.*) Well, you probably would. I can remember catching a German patrol when the fog lifted in the early morning, right in the open field, not more than 300 yards away, and shooting them with as much gusto and as much fun as I would shoot rabbits. Now, I can't understand that myself at this point. Why? Why?

John Angus MacNeil, Inverness: The only thing that I know, that the majority of us knew, was that we were so proud of the Maple Leaf. The Maple Leaf was on our crest, that was our motto. That's the only thing that we were so proud of, that we were fighting for the Maple Leaf. Now if you asked me, was I fighting for Canada, was I fighting for Europe, was I fighting for the King—I believe in the Queen, yes, sure I believed in the King. But beyond that, it was that emblem we had on our breast, that Maple Leaf—that was Canada's emblem, you know.

(*Was war what you thought it was going to be?*) I never thought of such a thing as war. No, no, never. (*What did you think you were going to?*) Really and truly, if God Almighty struck me dead, I didn't know. Only, I was there.

There's nobody in the God Almighty world—I'm telling you God's truth—that can understand the idea of seeing a poor soul dying. I remember we went up—shells came and struck—we were going through the Ypres, the moat line, you know—and that was all concrete. And when shells drop on concrete, she scatters. A fellow got shrapnel shell through the head, in his temple—pierced right through. I was on my way up the line. "Sergeant"—I was a sergeant; I was made a King's sergeant on the battlefield—

"Sergeant, do away with me, do away with me." "Darling, no, I couldn't do that. I can't do that." "Why?" And you could see the blood coming up, blood coming up out of his eyes, as the heart was going, and then the heart was easing up, the blood was easing, and away he went. It's the saddest and the horriblest thing that ever you see in your life. Oh, many other times, you know, I'd be in the trenches, a shell would come, I'd be lucky enough to escape it. Somebody else would get it. I'd have to go to work and try and do my best to comfort him, knowing that he was dying.

And I saw another thing, too: I saw Germans dying. I saw Germans dying on the Hindenburg line. There were 21 machine guns there, and not one bullet fired out of them, with 15 poor dear soldiers dying below on the ground, 15 feet underground in a dug-out, that they dare not come out. I saw them dying. My God.

There was nobody to tell you. Who knew? Nobody knew, at the time, you know. There was such a thing as a war.

Listen, darling, do you think that I intended to kill anybody? Never. Never. But I was fighting for John Angus, yeah, I was going to save myself. There was Hill 70. It was bayonet fighting—we had 15 minutes of it. Now, you'd ask me, was I there? I was in it. You'd ask me, did you kill anybody? I wouldn't know. I was there, as a daze. I was just helping John Angus, saving his life. Who I did, who I didn't, I don't know. And I don't think anybody else would know, if he told the honest truth. Because, when you were in that, you just lost control of yourself and your memory and everything else. If I hurt anybody, I don't know. God forgive me if I did. See, I didn't intend to. I didn't want to kill anybody. I never intended to kill anybody.

The big push came to Amiens, a city comparable to Saint John, New Brunswick. It was on the side of the hill, and the river flowed around.

There was a Catholic church up at the top. There was a machine gunner there, and he played on that river until the river was red with blood, with all he killed. But anyhow, when the battle was over, and he surrendered, we didn't do anything to him. We just passed him over as a prisoner-of-war.

But the funniest part about the war, that I was never lonesome, I don't know why. It appears that God Almighty was doing something for me, that I wouldn't be lonesome for my mother, for my father.

Fr. Leo Sears, Mabou: (*You were anxious to be in the artillery?*) Very anxious. To be honest, I wasn't sure that I could take a rifle and a bayonet and kill anybody. But the artillery was useful enough, and sufficiently combative, to satisfy my feeling that there was a job to be done. I could kill what I couldn't see. Because the other person was trying to kill us. We were doing a great deal of counter-battery work, trying to protect the infantry. I felt that if I saw someone my own age, drafted into the army, perhaps serving against his will—if I had to shoot him or bayonet him, I just don't know what the effect on me would be. I would do it, but I don't know what the effect would be. And I had the greatest sympathy and admiration for the infantry, but I felt in the artillery I would be helping them and protecting them. It was a chore that had to be done, and I could be happy doing it.

We didn't see enemy at all, only prisoners coming back. We didn't see at all. We had observers within observing distance of the target. He was equipped with a telephone. He would telephone back the corrections for our fire, whether we were on the target or not, to our own signal there at the battery, at the gun. That went on steadily during the shoot, during the attack.

Howard Reid: We generally used to shoot on them at night. Generally on the barbed wire, you see. The entanglements in front of their trenches. They would try to fix them up at night. We'd maybe shoot, oh, say at 6 o'clock perhaps. Then you'd shoot maybe at quarter past 6. Then we'd maybe go to half past 6. And we wouldn't shoot maybe for half an hour. And we'd shoot again, and catch those fellows trying to fix it, you see. And also break any wire that was being fixed. (*Were you able to see what you were shooting at?*) Oh no, no, nothing. I never saw anything at all in all the time I was there.

Most of it—unless there was an attack by the enemy—most of our work was cutting the barbed wire, keeping the Germans off the wire as much as possible. Sometimes it's quite easy. Like if we were going to make an attack, like in the Somme, we'd put up a barrage. We'd have a list of what we had to do, you see—so many, so long a time at this, and then we'd have to raise it, because the infantry would be already going for-

154

ward. We'd have to guess on that somewhat. As the infantry went ahead, we'd try to keep our artillery shells going a little further ahead of them again. Sometimes they went right through our artillery shells.

At Vimy Ridge, the Germans had the high ground, until we wiped them out of it. (*How did you manage to do that?*) Just heavy gun-fire, nothing else. Shell-fire. It was just terrible. For them. We didn't feel it so much. Thousands and thousands of tons of stuff. We could tell what it was like when we got moving up. We moved three times—the artillery—and we never got stopped once, only by mud and holes, shell-holes. (*Your own shell-holes?*) You have to watch the shell-holes. At Harvest Woods everyone was stuck. And it was dark. I went in there to see how they were get-

Howard Reid

ting along, if I could help. And I went to walk towards them. By jove, I went down a 115-inch shell-hole. Right to the bottom. I crawled out, up to the top—it's a good thing there wasn't much mud that time. Clean to the bottom. Deeper than this room. Oh yes, it'd be twice as deep as this, I guess. Great big 15-inch shell, tear the earth right to.

H. L. Livingstone: The Germans hit upon a plan just before the war ended, to try to break us down. The artillery would put a barrage about 300 or 400 yards behind us. And then in front of us, in No Man's Land, and then keep stepping in closer and closer, till they got the range on the front line, and then they just smashed the trenches to pieces. And you begin wondering then—if I move into the next bay—see, the trenches are not in a straight line—if I do move, one might hit in the next bay, and I'd be safe staying here. See, you keep debating with yourself all through the bombardment. Now what should I do? Should I move 10 feet over that way, or stay where I am? And they just smashed the thing to pieces. You'd wonder how anyone could live in a trench after they were through with it.

We were bringing water up to the front line, when what we called a "rum jar," a big German trench mortar, weigh about 100 pounds or so, landed right in the middle of the party. And I just turned like that—this would be the line, see—in a zigzag. One landed on a chap in my platoon, apparently a direct hit right in the back. Right beside me. I had just turned the corner. He was turned into a red patch on the wall of the trench, with splinters of white bone sticking out of the mud.

Thomas R. Langley, Port Hawkesbury: I went into battle the first day I was over there. Full blast, full blast, alright. Just used to take off days to bury the dead.

There wasn't much of a trench then. There were about 3 or 4 feet—then a couple of sandbags up on top of that. And mats—we called them mats—to keep you out of the water. It rained all the time. We were only there about three days and we were full of lice. Nearly eat you up.

Oh, it was wicked. You couldn't tell what was in the ground—mines and bombs and everything else. I know, there we were, playing ball—we were out on rest. We had a whole ball team there. Batter was up, waiting for a ball, and he was hitting, hitting the plate—and she exploded. Killed 4 or 5. Oh, a lot of duds—wouldn't go off. They were dangerous, could go off any time at all.

There were no winters. It was cool, but no snow, nothing like over here. Nothing like that. It would rain—drizzle—no heavy rains. Very seldom heavy rains. (*Were you ever dry?*) Oh God, no. Never. Your feet were the worst. They gave you whale oil for your feet, to keep them from peeling. (*Were you ever comfortable?*) No. I fell asleep standing up. I don't know if it's called sleep or not—a shell would bust or something, alongside of you, wake you up. (*What about a roof?*) Oh, we used to have a piece of corrugated iron, put over the trench, just enough to cover you, keep the dampness off you.

(*How often would you change your clothes?*) Oh, they were pretty good about that. Change about every two weeks. You'd get clear of the lice—awful, awful bad. The longest I remember going was 54 days without a change of clothes—it was pretty thick. Lice as big as bed-bugs. We used to take the cordites out of the shells—they were about that long—and we'd string them along. Then we'd get the lice and put them on. We'd set fire to one end, see them going.

A little round loaf of bread and a bit of cheese—that'd be a day's ration. Perhaps you wouldn't get that. It was nothing to go two or three days without anything to eat. You get a drink of water, you'd be all right. (*Aren't you surprised you survived?*) It makes you think. (*I'm surprised men were able to fight.*) That's what made them fight. That put fight into you. They can tell you what you like, but if you're hungry and starved to death, you would kill a man easy enough.

156

She was kind of stiff. One fellow'd take a part, then the next day he'd lose it. Then seize it all back. We had dug-outs, like a cellar, here and there—when he wouldn't blow them up. A lot of them were ones we had taken from him. And he knew where they were, and he would fire on them all the time, keep you busy. You'd dig trenches—find arms, and legs, and heads, and everything. Used creoline—used a lot of that. It helped—the smell would kill you.

(*Do you really remember those days well?*) No, not in a way. When they're brought to memory, I kind of remember different things. Tried to forget it—you can't get to sleep.

Bill Daye, Sydney: (*Did you feel you wanted to fight?*) No, Jesus, no, no idea we were going to fight. In the engineers, you don't do any fighting. You're a working party. You go ahead—we'd be in towns in the night, two days before the infantry would go in there. We had guys used to take us in, in the night—work in the dark, putting up barbed wire and stuff like that—entanglements, you know. Then we'd be building pontoon bridges at night. We put them across the rivers. And digging out mines. They'd be buried in the streets. We had detections to find out where the mines were. We'd dig them out in the night, too. We were a working party.

I remember one fellow though—they were flooding this bloody place—the Germans had let go a dam or something. It was morning. "I want one man to come with me," he said, "I'm going to go down and check a certain place to see if the water's rising or falling." I'll never forget it. He said, "You, boy, you come." "All right." "Take your rifle," he said, "never mind the rest of your stuff." So we climbed down and we were creeping round the corners, looking here and there, watching. Across the canal, there was a fellow getting out of his boat. He was a sniper who was over all night. "Now," he said, "that's your job." He said, "I mean it. He might get you tomorrow night." So he was just getting out of the boat. I nailed him. I saw him falling in the water. Jeez, I felt queer, you know. I felt queer as hell. But your heart was hardened from seeing what you saw.

Thomas Gillard, North Sydney: I was in the working battalion, you know. I wasn't in the front lines. There are different working battalions. It takes three men to keep one man on the front line, you know. We were in the forestry, had sawmills, different things like that.

But I didn't know what we were into when I volunteered. All they said was they wanted people to go overseas right away. They wanted this lumber for trenches and houses and huts and things like that, you know. There were 5 or 6 companies like that. A lot of fellows were taken out of the army and put in there, who knew about the woods. We were cutting up from 75,000 to 100,000 lumber a day. Going in the woods and cutting them out and bringing them out and sawing them up. That was in Scotland. Then we went to France. Eighteen men and three horses in a box-car went right across France. Right down to Marseille, pretty near down to Marseille, around the Bay of Biscay. And did some more work.

We had the big crosscut saws. The timber was big. Two men to a saw, saw them down. And then we had railroads, and little diesels, had them on trams, you know, just a little small tram, like a little railroad hooked up together. We loaded the timber on that and hooked them on the little diesel. She'd go out with a train-load of this wood, to the mill.

(*Some people might say you weren't really in the war because you weren't in the trenches.*) They say that, yeah. I never mind that. (*Would you think it was true, that you didn't serve?*) Oh no, I was in the army. They could send me where they liked. We trained with rifles. We always had rifles, even there at the mill. We had rifles always in the quartermaster's store. When you were out on guard, and things like that, you had your rifle. (*So it was very military?*) Oh yeah, sure, very military, yes. You'd do guard duty and things like that, you know. We were down in Marseille. But one of our companies was up close to the front, and Germans came over and took it. Took the works. And when we took it back again, they had all the wood and timber sawed up, ready to go.

Oh, we lost a lot of men in the lumber woods. The flu hit down there. I saw a big man could hold me out straight-armed—he'd be in the bunk next to me—next day he'd be gone, dead. It was hot up there, you know. It was 110 in the shade, day in and day out, where we were working, near Marseille. We used to wear a cork hat, with 9 yards of linen around the top of it, so you wouldn't get sunstroke. We'd try to take the horses and put them in the shade in the heat of the day. But we had to stay out and take it.

John Angus MacNeil: We tunneled under Hill 60. In this country, you wouldn't say it was much of a hill, you know. But over there, it's so flat, and it was quite a little hill. But the engineers, they tunneled under Hill 60. The Germans held 60. They went under them. There were the Canadians and Australians and New Zealanders—tunnellers, you know. (*Did that tunneling take weeks or months?*) Oh yes—years. They started way back—a tunnel about 3 feet wide, about 4 feet high—and they loaded her up with TNT. And you couldn't use a shovel. And you couldn't use a pick. The Germans were listening. When you'd loosen the dirt, you were using the bayonet. You'd push the bayonet in, push it down, and that dropped. And you had a canvas bag underneath it so it wouldn't make any noise. And that's the way you advanced in. (*They were mining this for years?*) Oh yeah, yeah. I worked there before I got my stripes. And listening, you'd have to—when there was no mining going on, you'd have to be listening. You had earphones, you could hear the Germans working. The Germans were tunneling, too. And sometimes you could hear them talking, plain.

When the Russians gave up, you know, all the German troops that were on that Eastern Front were taken back to the Western Front. And they were changing, relieving the Germans that were on Hill 60, replacing them with the new people that came from the Eastern Front—giving the fellows that were on Hill 60 a rest. That morning that they were doing the changing, the button was pushed. And (Hill) 60 went up in the air, with all those

Germans with it—the fellows that were relieving, and the ones that were there before them.

We were in the trenches to the left, towards the ocean. And when the bomb went up, the ground went like that, you know—just like waves. What we used to have as a hill, it was a big shell-hole. We could look down it. That finished 60.

Dan E. MacQuarrie: The first thing the Germans knew, the front line all blew up. And they were coming out with their hands up, hundreds of them. They knew the jig was up. Just tell them, "Here, there's the road, and you follow it down there." There might be one or two fellows following them with rifles. No trouble at all with them. I suppose a lot of them were glad to get out, and get something to eat.

John Angus MacNeil: The Germans had to retreat and build their trenches back further. (*Did you move forward into that?*) Yeah. In fact, the whole front then moved ahead, moved towards the Germans—new positions, new trenches, and so on. (*It wasn't really a battle?*) Oh no, it wasn't. It was just a few, maybe 25 or 50 feet or so, like that. It wasn't like a battle would have been, what you gained. It was just that you just moved your front, because they had to move back, they had to straighten their line because of Hill 60 being out.

Passchendaele was a hard place to take. You know, the English tried it, the Australians tried it, and the French tried it. and they failed. But the Canadians tried it—they took it. But the downpour of rain—it wasn't raining—it was pouring down, the rain. And there were more people drowned in the shell-holes than were killed by the bullets. On account of the bombardment that the Canadians put on at the time.

It was so dark; you couldn't use any light—it was as dark as the hounds of hell. You see, there were duckboards around the shell-holes, but you couldn't see them. You just went off the duckboards and into a shell-hole. You'd be drowned. (**H. L. Livingstone:** Couldn't get up with their heavy marching order—that is, carrying a full pack, about 70 pounds.)

You couldn't get out, the shell-hole was so deep. It was the shells, those big army shells, makes the holes. They filled with water, with that rain that night. They claim more (were) lost in the shell-holes. In fact, the Germans didn't put up any battle at all, they retreated. And the funny part of it: before they could gain a secure ground, they had to retreat half a mile. There was a ravine, a gully. And they had to go down that gully and across, and then they had a wonderful opportunity against us, on the banks there. The Germans had pillboxes, you know, all made of concrete, right at the head of the hill, the Passchendaele hill.

Dan E. MacQuarrie: A bloody slaughter, that's what it was. And a lot of it was—they never should have sent them in to Passchendaele, because it wasn't fit for human beings. Just a mud-hole. There were places there you could fall off the track and be up to there. I saw fellows in to their hips, and it'd take 3 or 4 men to haul them out of it. It's hard to believe that, but it's true.

You saw death, mostly. Barbed wire. And mud. And probably fellows lying there, dead. I saw them when we'd be coming out, when we were in Passchendaele—and you'd see the stretcher-bearers coming out with the wounded fellows—and the wounded fellows were dead and the stretcher-bearers were dead, lying in the mud. We couldn't touch them. Somebody else would go in and do it. Well, I can tell you right now, it was just the same as if it was a pure hell, that's what it was. I don't know how anybody ever came out of there alive. We had over 700 casualties there, in 7 days. There were only about, probably a hundred, could answer roll call when we came out—killed, wounded, and missing. Of course, a lot of them were taken off to the hospital and we never saw them any more.

(*What would they do with someone who died there?*) I'll tell you what they did with them—they were rolled up in a blanket and buried, with their shoes on. Be all they got. (*Cemetery?*) Oh yes, they had nice cemeteries—still there, and still looked after. Just women that I saw put in a box. Two officers—the boys thought so much of them that they went to an old house and ripped the ceiling out and made a rough casket for them. No, none came home. The Americans sent their dead home.

Fr. Leo Sears: We got orders to return to Vimy, to the Ridge, to prepare for the Germans' last effort, which was very nearly successful. On the way out, we spent our Christmas—oh Lord, I've forgotten the name of the place—but we were billeted in a hay mow with chickens over our head, on the side of a canal. But our Christmas parcels had all come through, and we had a marvellous Christmas dinner, with lots of refreshments. (*Would you have clergy with you?*) No, we went to the church in the French village, half-ruined church, with daylight showing through the rafters. One of the Christmases I'll always remember. It was an old French priest, not a young one, who had the midnight Mass. Only old people there, and girls, and children. Christmas Day, in the evening, we were on the side of a canal—some way or other, some of the lads found bicycles in the village, and very happy, they started riding up and down the canal.

(*Religion had not left you?*) It was very important. While we were waiting to get ready to go into our final position for the attack on Passchendaele, it was brought to our attention that there would be a Catholic chaplain at Ypres on a certain day. We got permission to go into Ypres this day, to get

to confession. And we went there in the morning. We stayed there all day. There were crowds of Canadian soldiers, Canadian Catholics, waiting their turn to go to confession. And late that evening, the chaplain came out, and he said, "I'm sorry. I've been hearing all day, and I can hardly hear any longer. I'm dead beat." He gave us general absolution, which was a comfort, going into the line. You've often heard that expression that there are no atheists in a shell-hole. It's perfectly true. It makes a difference. Anybody who had ever had any faith, experienced a revival of faith.

(*I would think of war as such a hardener.*) It hardened, and it softened. It hardened to the experience of violence. It softened you to the extent of wondering how God could allow this violence to occur, and that the reason must be rebellion of man against God—that God would leave mankind to find his way out of the situation for which he was responsible himself. And of course, the sense of camaraderie and loyalty to one's friends was out of this world.

(*Had you decided yet to become a priest?*) I had thought of it before I graduated. And I just put it out of my mind for the time being, the war. I said, I'll think of it if God spares me. I probably more or less reached a decision: if I came back safe.

H. L. Livingstone: They started to march up to Vimy—I could almost draw a picture, still. We had a goat for a mascot. The goat was ahead of the column. And when we came around a turn, we could see the front of the column. And there was the colonel on his horse, behind the goat, and the pipe band, and the whole brigade. There was a column of fours that I marched in. And behind us, there was another column. A sergeant in the military police, and two guards in the military police, and a young man from Cape Breton. He had left the front line, went back to see a French

162

girl that he was sweet on, put on civilian clothes to make his stay a little longer, and was picked up by the military police. Now he was under escort, behind me. And when we were up at Vimy for about a week, I was detailed for guard behind the lines. When I got back there, I found that we were guarding him.

The old A.P.M., head of the military police, came and read a sentence to him at 9 o'clock at night: "You are to be shot at daylight." And that fellow went to sleep at 10 o'clock, and slept like a carefree child till morning, when we woke him up. They pinned a piece of white paper over his heart, blindfolded him, lashed him to a chair, lashed the chair to a tree—and riddled him with bullets. And here's the joker: the firing squad was picked from his own platoon—men who knew him as well as I know you, or better. Now that wasn't necessary at all. And I only missed the firing squad by getting on the guard. He was in my platoon. Now, he was just reported as died, so if he has any relatives still living, they probably think that he died in action. Nineteen years old, and he'd been in the line then for two years. So that's war, as the generals run it.

The second time I was wounded, I was over in one of those raids. We had laid down, waiting for the barrage. And when the barrage came, we were right behind an old hedge that had been a part of a farm before the Germans broke through. And I found a gap in the hedge, and I got ahead of our people. I could run pretty fast then, anyway. I got round an old gun-pit. It was just sloping down one side, to get the guns down—it was about the size of this house. And there were little holes where the Germans slept all round it. And I was shooting them as they ran out. And this little fellow, he couldn't have been any more than 16, came out. And I didn't have the heart to shoot him. So I took him prisoner, with his hands in the air. And just at that moment, either a German bomb, mortar, or grenade—or one of ours. Our people landed after me, see, and they were throwing them down in the gun-pit; thought I was German, I suppose. One instant it's bright as day—a flare—and the next instant it's pitch dark. And it threw me right back on my heels. It's a wonder that I wasn't killed. I guess I was lucky. And I got a piece of shrapnel in the upper part of my arm, in my left arm.

It was time then to leave, and get out quick. So I took the little German with me. We stopped in No Man's Land, in a shallow trench that the British had dug, had started to dig—it was only about two feet deep.

So the two us lay there, myself and the little German. And in the light of a flare, he saw blood dripping from my fingers. He must have been a stretcher-bearer, because he found somewhere in his tunic a little pair of scissors about that long, and slitting my sleeve from wrist to shoulder, he bandaged up my wounded arm. And every time a shell would burst close enough to us—they put a barrage in this trench, you see, as well as in the front-line—every time a shell would burst close, he'd put his arm around me for protection. I often wish I could have seen him afterwards. He may have been killed in Hitler's war.

I was there about 20 minutes, this little German and I, then we sprinted back to our lines. Soon as we got into the front line, I stumbled over the body of the captain who had been in charge of the raid. He was killed by the shelling that occurred afterward. I turned the German over to battalion headquarters. He went his way to peace in a prisoner-of-war camp; I went my way to all the delights of an English spring in a hospital in Kent. Just an immense garden. Just like going from hell into heaven. Bunch of nurses fussing over me.

Bill Daye, Sydney: (*Bill, were there towns right near the battle-grounds?*) Yeah, yeah. It wasn't all really smashed to pieces like you'd figure. Some places it was like a desert—there wasn't a bloody thing left. But other places there were streets and villages. But they were all—holes in them and the roof off them and everything—you know, smashed up.

You'd see a dirty, rainy, miserable, stinking cold night. And the roads were nothing but mud—there was no pavement or anything—real mud, halfway to your knees, from so much traffic on it. The frost coming out and everything like that. You'd see men, women, and kids—dark at night,

when we'd be traveling to another town—coming through that in the night in the rain and cold without a god-damn thing with them to eat or anything else. Maybe a woman carrying a baby. You might come across 50 or 60 of them, plowing through there in the night. Getting the hell away from what they could get away from, and getting wherever they could get. My God, it used to make your heart sick, you know.

(*How did you know the war was turning?*) Well, the Germans were on the run steady, going back to Germany. You could have all you could do to keep following them. They were on the run, everything pulling out, pulling out. Of course, an awful lot they didn't pull out was smashed and no damn good to them. We were supposed to follow them, whatever work to be done. We didn't have a hell of a lot to do then, when they were pulling out. I don't know how many days' march we had to be to Germany, to the Rhine River. And just two days before we got there, we were ordered to come back. The war was over. Well, we didn't believe it. We didn't believe it. That firing was going on for 3 or 4 days, more than a week, after the war was over. But the war was officially over.

Eleventh of November. I'll never forget it. We didn't believe it was over. We were told there's no need of us going all the way to Germany. To turn round and go back, and they'd billet us. We kept all the company, what was left, together. There was no more fighting or anything like that. There were a lot of fellows stayed over there to bury an awful lot of the dead after. They could sign up and stay there and do that if they wanted to. I remember one of my buddies that went in the army when I did, he stayed over for a whole year doing that, burying people. A lot of them had to be dug up and their remains sent to a certain graveyard. We all had a tag on so you'd know who we were.

(*What was the greeting in Halifax?*) Oh, the people were there by the millions, you know. Lot of them had boys that were in the army. They were everywhere, blowing horns on cars. And the bands playing and the people cheering, and God knows what. The train was waiting to take you home to Cape Breton; there were a couple of strings of cars to take us home.

(*How did Bill Daye feel about all that?*) I didn't mind it. You didn't feel like—I don't know how to express it—it was just them that was doing it. You weren't interested in it one bloody bit. They were—we weren't. You wanted to get the hell home, and that was it. You weren't having any part of it. But you were there sitting in a car with God knows how many, you know. And other fellows in other cars.

And then we struck Sydney. Oh my God, the people that were over there. They drove us all over the place, too, blowing whistles and all kinds of bloody stuff like that. We were there, but we weren't taking any part in it. You know, not interested in it.

H. L. Livingstone: My brother was reported missing about 12 o'clock at night. The sergeant major came and told me he was missing. And I paraded before the colonel, asked for permission to go out and look for him. And the colonel refused permission. I never forgave him for that. Because I think that my brother Dan lived for perhaps two days. (*What happened to him?*) He was hit—he was out on patrol—he was scout officer, in charge of a battalion of scouts. He was out on patrol with another officer, Fraser.

165

I don't know why the two of them went out, because it's usually the scouts that did any patrolling in No Man's Land. The next day, a sergeant in A Company saw movement in No Man's Land—somebody raising his hand. And he rushed out and brought Fraser in under fire. But Fraser was killed on the way in, so we never found out exactly what happened.

And my brother was found about a week later by the 24th Battalion scouts. He had crawled almost to our lines. He had taken off his Sam Brown belt and put a tourniquet on his leg—he was shot through the thigh. But he was shot again through the neck. But whether that was that particular day or two or three days later, we don't know. I suspect it was later. So, my platoon commander came to me about 3 o'clock in the morning and said, "Report at once to Whaley Orchard Cemetery—light marching order"—that's a rifle and gas mask only. I knew then that Dan had been found. "Report to cemetery"—I knew it was for him.

I started out. We could see Whaley in the distance, from the front line. Instead of taking the long way around the communication trenches out there, I went overland. I'd been about halfway to Whaley when daylight overtook me, and they started sniping at me with everything they had. They even threw gas shells at me. Gas shells—German artillery. I put on my gas mask and plodded on. At that stage, I didn't care two hoots whether they hit me or not. Dan and I'd been very close. We had found together the first Mayflower and Blue Violet in the spring, and we knew the location for every bird's nest on the farm at Big Bras d'Or. But he was an officer and I was a private at the time. So, I couldn't even talk to him when I met him in the trenches. I couldn't speak to him.

I found the cemetery quite easily. When I got there, there was just the body wrapped up in burlap by the empty grave. In half an hour or so, the chaplain came, with two or three of his fellow officers. They buried him, and that was it.

Dan E. MacQuarrie: We were in a place called Bethune. A little town. There's where we were when we got the word that she was gone, ended.

(*Were you fighting the day before?*) Yeah, and there were 11 of our boys killed that day. And that was the sad part of it. One day, and they'd be safe. (*How were you told?*) The officers got the message. They signed in an old railway car. You might have heard that. It came over the wire; they had telephones, you know. Told us the war was over. And of course, the Germans were pulling out, for home. We started following them. Followed them right into Germany, across the Rhine Bridge. Oh Jesus, their horses were dying everyplace. When we were on the way to Germany, they were trying to pull some of their guns back, and you could see where the horses would give up, dead alongside the road. The guns were still there. And I saw a couple times there was a big piece cut out of the rump of the horse—they must have been getting hungry. I guess we took about two weeks following them. Till we got to Germany. They didn't keep us there, though. None of us were allowed in Berlin. It was out of bounds.

(*What did you do to celebrate?*) Came back, and this is where we found the wine cellar—in a castle in Belgium. And we stayed there over 6 months. (*Drinking?*) Yes, there was quite a bit of drinking. I know, myself and another fellow from Glace Bay, we were pals. He died last fall. And I went to bed—you just think of the luxury of getting into clean sheets, a good mattress, after sleeping on the ground. We were put there, you see, there was room for so many men there; I forget how many. It was a big castle. But every man had a bed. My friend came up and he shook me by the shoulder. He said, "Get up!" He was drunk, you know. "What the hell is going on?" I said. He said, "We found a wine cellar."

Well, of course, I got up too, and went down; and we started helping ourselves to the wine. It was in shelves there, in the basement. It was fellows from Glace Bay found it, too. Started exploring, you know, and they saw this door, and wondered what was behind the door. Well, the door didn't last long with those fellows, it was broken in. Here was this big wine cellar, and quite a bit of brandy there, too. They called it cognac over there. Well, we started lugging it out—we got feed bags—and hiding it—we were putting it into the hedges. And the room I was in, there was a flue going through it. There was no fire in it, of course. We started shoving it up the flue as far as we could reach. We had it there for months. They never bothered us.

Oh, they found out, all right; a lot of them were drunk the next day. The colonel raised hell, said, "You fellows will have to pay for that." And they boarded the door up. They put a guard on the door. Had a guard on it day and night. And this fellow was on, I guess, in the evening. A person waited for him to leave for a little while, the devils, and they broke in again. And I guess they practically cleaned her the second time. Well, anyway, Col. Ralston said, "We'll have to pay for it." But he went to see the fellow that owned it, or got into communication with him, and he said, "No. Give it to the boys. Only for them, I wouldn't have a castle left." He was a rich Belgian. I don't know what business he was in, but he must have been damn rich, because it was beautiful. There were glass doors and everything in that place.

(*When did you come back to Canada then?*) We landed back, I think the 13th of June, 1919. We landed in Quebec, the bunch I came with. We came up on the *Empress of Berlin* to Quebec, and we came down to Halifax by special train. We got our discharges there. We were only in Quebec one day. We had a parade through the town—you know the hilly city it is, cliffs up and the houses on top. And of course, we paraded to the train. And a special train came down to Halifax.

(*How were you greeted in Halifax?*) Well, I'd say it was rotten. We couldn't get a drink there—Prohibition was on, you see. The only way you could get a drink there was to go to the vendor. Had all the saloons closed down. Some of the fellows said, "To hell with it—let's go back to Britain!" Well, I went to a house, a fellow I knew, he was a MacDonald. And we used to visit him—he was a Cape Bretoner—and I told him my story, that I couldn't get a bottle of beer. He said, "I'll get you a beer. I'll get you a whiskey, too," he said.

(*Didn't Halifax get out and greet you?*) Oh yes, they did, they met us at the boat, a lot of them, and a pipe band marched us up. (*How'd you get home to Middle River?*) Came down by train. And when I got into Baddeck, do you know how many cars were in Baddeck? Landed at Iona and got over on the boat. The *Blue Hill* was running then, twice a day; it met every train. And there were just two cars in Baddeck, and I came home in one of them. And I went to work in a few days, hay making.

Kristopher Mayich, Whitney Pier, who served in the Austro-Hungarian Army: I came home (to Croatia). And I was a couple of years up there. Then I got married. No place for me up there. Somehow the agent was in Dubrovnik in Dalmatia, picking out men to come to Canada. And I went up there, to Dubrovnik, and I made application. By golly, two weeks after, my application was passed. I got a ticket—I went to travel, get out of the country, 1926. I left a wife and four kids home. I boarded the ship in Antwerpen in Belgium. I was seasick when I came across. Took me 11 days from Antwerpen to Saint John, New Brunswick.

(*Kris Mayich fought on the Eastern Front. After the war, he came to Cape Breton. He finally got miners' papers.*) **Kris Mayich:** In New Waterford, we got a job in 16 mine. Next day we went to work, 3 o'clock. I'm not a superstitious man. I don't believe in those things that they talk about—witches and all that. But when I went to 16 mine up there, when I looked in the shaft there—a mountain in Italy came in front of my eyes. A hill where I was buried in, in a cell, with the gas. We were in underground, all the battalion. We had a hole alongside the road. In times they were shelling the road; people ran into those holes. We were buried there. A gas shell exploded on the door. That blocked the door. Some gas went in; we got our gas masks on. And we were working on that, one after the other, with little shovels, trying to get some fresh air in. We were trapped in 11 o'clock in the evening; 9 o'clock in morning, we got fresh air in it. All the time, gas

masks on. (*You were digging all that time?*) All the time, one after the other. You couldn't stay too long up there. Little while, see, and you turn around, and the other fellow came behind you. That door was plugged. (*Did you have light?*) No, no light, no. (*How many people?*) Thousand. A full battalion.

Well, that came in front of my eyes. I went back outside—New Waterford, all right. I looked back in there, that mine again—I see the place in northern Tyrol, where we were buried underneath a hill. And I said to myself, "I'm not going to work in the mine. I was buried alive one time. I don't want to be buried again." The other fellows jumped on me. "Why are you doing that for? Why don't you go to work?" "No, no good." "Are you scared to go in the mines?" "I'm not scared of anything. But I don't want to work up there." But I didn't tell them what I saw. I went to the lamp-house, I blew the lamp out. "What's the matter, boy? No work?" "No, no work." I went home.

(*Tell me, what was the war for?*) For nothing. I told you yesterday: I was fighting some Italian fellow; he was wounded that night. Second of August, 1915. In the Italian line. He was my enemy. He was in the Italian army, I was in the Austro-Hungarian army. We were about, probably, 100 feet one from the other. If I had seen him, I'd shoot him. If he saw me, he'd shoot me. And we met in 1946 here in Sydney, in the coal wash plant. Our foreman said, "They were fighting together in the night in war-

169

time, and they came to Canada, make the peace between brothers." Joking, you know.

(*Do you ever think about the war any more?*) What do you mean? (*Well, do you dream about the war?*) Oh well, when I first came home, every night, I was getting up, even after I was married—get up, go open doors, and get the broom, shooting. After I got married. I used to get out. My wife came after me in the yard—I woke up. So I woke up like this, and I saw her, and I was in the yard. I had the broom in my hands. That was the last time.

John Angus MacNeil: I was through a whole lot of it. I enlisted in '14. I landed in Halifax May 1st, 1919. You see, the war was over in 1918. Okay. We were marching on toward Germany. I only got to the Rhine. I didn't get into Germany. The Nova Scotia government called all the miners back. So we were up just to the Rhine. We started back, got into Etapes. And we were there for God knows how long, because our documents were lost. And we didn't get back to Canada till May, 1919.

(*How was the greeting when you got home?*) Oh, God bless you, wonderful, because my mother and father, brothers and sisters—all very glad to see me. (*Did Inverness put on a parade?*) Oh well, of course, yes. When we landed at the station down there—trains were still coming in then—well, the place was just black with people. I remember on my way home from Hawkesbury, there was a certain gentleman there, he said, "We're having a dance tomorrow night in memory of the returned soldiers, and here's my invitation to you." So I went to the dance that night, had my uniform on. So from there on, we just worked along. Far as I'm concerned, I never thought very much of as far as being a hero or anything else, I thought I was just doing what I should have done.

I came back and went in the coal mine. First of all, when I came back, I couldn't get a job here. The manager said to me, "What are you looking for?" I said, "I'm looking for a job." "Where are you from?" I told him. Said, "I left a job here, and I was told when I came back I'd get it." "Oh, there's no jobs here." "Can't stay here," I said. We were getting a few cheques, you know, but they weren't going to last forever. The lumber camps down in St. Ann's were working then. So I went down there. That was in July. And the flies near had us. Just worked one day there. I came back home. I said to my mother, "I'm going to Boston. I'm going to look for a job."

My sister was in Boston. So I went down next evening and I bought a ticket for Boston—$15 to Boston—just imagine! So I landed in Boston, at my sister's. I was talking to her husband. He didn't know if he could help, but he'd do everything he could. I told my sister, "I'm going to take a walk down Washington Street."

So I had my button on, you know, return button. So I was walking down, and I met a fellow. He said, "Hello, Canada." I said, "Hello. Do I know you?" "No, but I know your button. I'm one of them. When did you come up?" I said, "Day before yesterday." "Looking for a job?" I said, "Yeah." "Take that button off you." I said, "What?" "If you want a job, take that button off you." I said, "You mean to say that they won't hire you if you have that?" "No, no." I had to do it. I was ashamed to do it, but I had to do it, because I was hungry. That's as true as I'm telling you, God's truth.

But the happiest day of our life, when General Foch (Commander-in-Chief of all the Allied armies in France) took it over. General Foch took the matter over on the 18th of July, 1918. We started that advance, and we never stopped until she ended, under General Foch, God bless him.

So I went back to the coal mine. I started working the coal mine. And then I got married. I married a very happy woman. And the first son I had, I called him after General Foch. And poor dear soul, he went to the Second World War and was killed. So that's my history.

*This chapter was edited from a much longer article
in Issues 30 and 31 of* Cape Breton's Magazine. *That article included
nursing sisters, and men who served in Canada and Russia.*

Rose Grant Young, Crane Operator

I grew up right here (in Whitney Pier). My mother was a MacDonald from Irish Cove. Now, they came to Sydney before the plant was built. And the old house that we lived in on Henry Street was taken down from Irish Cove on a scow. It was drifted right up, and they pulled it up over Henry Street hill with horses, and they put it where it's today still, on an angle from the Royal Bank. Then they built the front on it and they built a back on it and a side on it; and in the end, it's an enormous house. But that's the way it started.

Now, my Grandfather Grant, his name was Jim. And when I was on the plant, the older men told me that he was the best rigger they had. Of course, he was dead and gone years before I was born. A rigger is the man that does the knots and holds the swings and everything, gets everything ready for the lifts. All the knots and everything to hold all that heavy equipment. Of course, they're a climber, too, they have to climb. And of course, the Newfoundlanders were fishermen and they were good riggers, so there was an influx of Newfoundlanders after the plant was built. He came from St. John's. They rented or bought a house on the top of Henry Street, and my mother lived at the bottom of Henry Street. This is how they got together.

I was only born in '21. And we lived on the street where the gate to the steel plant was. It was a mainstream for everything there at the Pier. Because the bank was on the corner, all the shops were along, and the gate to the plant was right at the foot of the hill. In fact, when we were kids, I had a bobsled. And we used to take the men down over the hill on the bobsled to work in the winter-time—those that were brave enough to come with us!

(*Did you ever really have a desire to work on the plant?*) No. This was 1942, that I went on the plant. At that time, my mother was in financial difficulties. And I asked for a raise at the place where I was working, and I didn't get too much satisfaction. So when I heard that they were taking names on the plant—there were two of us, another girl whose father was dead, too, came with me. In fact, there were four of us out of this store. We went over and put our names in. But we didn't have a clue as to what we were going to do or anything. We really didn't think it over. As I say, we were only kids, really. Two of us were called, and the other two weren't. And I often thought afterwards, it was because we were the children of widows that we got the jobs ahead of the others. At least, that's the way it appeared. Or any women whose husband had worked on the plant and for some reason, through sickness or something like that, weren't working, they got the jobs, too.

Of course, towards the end, they were taking all the applications. Everybody was crying for steel, of course, during the war. Everything was swinging. We were working double shifts, triple shifts, everything to get the steel out. It was totally different. The rail mill was on two shifts practically all during the war. And then they rolled tie plate and the different type rails—the different poundage, you know—and mine arches—where today they only have rail. Of course, they had markets for it. The mines were crying for the mine arches, and now they don't even use them any more, they tell me. Every section of the plant was working, working, working, all the time.

The superintendent in the department that I landed at—it was the plate mill—he told me, "They tell me a woman will never run the rail mill crane." And he said, "You and I are going to prove them wrong!" He was quite a psychologist. And of course, that's all I needed to hear, was that the men were against the women; in other words, that made me try that much harder. (*He felt that the men were not going to accept the women on the plant?*) Especially in the jobs overhead, where their lives were at stake, see. I carried an awful lot of tonnage above their heads. And they didn't have faith in the women.

173

I didn't have sense enough to realize what they were putting me into, to tell you the truth. First, they broke me in on the pipe mill cranes, which were wide open bays—in other words, there was no interference. They taught me how to use the magnet and the shifts and all the different things. But they were really getting me ready for the rail mill, without telling me that, see. I thought it was always going to be the long open bays, but it wasn't. (*By "a long open bay," that means...?*) That it's all open. It would be like the length of this street.

And perhaps they were the scarfing the steel. Do you know what scarfing is? They take the flaws out of the steel, big chunks of steel; and I'd have to turn them over so they could take the flaws out of them. Things like that.

But then they took me to the rail mill. And he told me, "Now, this is what we've been getting you ready for." He said, "This is the one mill that we always make a dollar on." That was the way he described it to me. But he took me to the foot of the ladder, and he said, "You'll have to go the rest of the way yourself." He was an electrical engineer, and he was scared of height. (*You didn't operate this from the ground?*) Oh heavens, no, I was overhead. Twelve feet, I suppose. All the workings of the crane were on top of the crane. We had to oil them every day and get ready for the shift. Which meant that I'd have to go to perhaps 15 feet. (*You not only operated*

A view in the rail mill where Rose Grant Young worked as crane operator. The crane can be seen near the top, from one wall across to the other. It runs on tracks, one along each wall. The crane hook is at the right side; the crane operator sits in a booth behind that hook. Across the centre of the photo are the housings containing the rollers. A red hot rail is passing through the rollers on one of the several passes toward forming a rail.

the crane, then, you were responsible for maintaining it.) Oh, yes, for oiling it and seeing that it worked. Now, if anything went wrong with the crane, like the fingers—we had the old-fashioned boxes. I suppose you wouldn't even remember the old tram cars, they had the box-type levers. And it's like a finger that makes the connection.

But anyhow, as I said, he was scared of heights, so I had to go the rest of the way by myself. But this man, Maynard, they gave me to him to break me in—he was a fantastic operator. He had been there for 35 years. He taught me how to pick up the boxes with the scrap in, take it down, dump it, bring it back. Of course, they were all old men, remember that— all the young fellows were gone. And this old crane-chaser that I had—he must have been 85 then—I think he lived till he was 100! But anyhow, to save him walking the whole length of the mill, this is what Maynard used to do: he use to dump the boxes, and he taught me how to catch them back up again and bring them back so that that poor old fellow didn't have to walk all that distance. Well, I thought it was part of the job.

He also taught me so many things about the lifts; you know, when you get the lift up, to keep it from swaying, and things like that. Another thing he taught: this great big enormous screw on top of the housing—they had to tighten that to hold all the things in the housing for the rails to come through, so they wouldn't move, so there wouldn't be any bumps in the rail. But Maynard used to take the big hook—a great big enormous thing—we had two hooks on our crane—and he used to sway that hook, and he could tighten with those hooks so the men didn't have to hammer that screw down. Save the men the work. When the men were standing on the top of the housing, they could almost touch the cab of the crane, they were that high up. But he would use that, and he would pound it. Well, he taught me that. And I thought it was part of the job. I never realized that he was making a show-off of me.

Because later, I discovered, everybody used to stand and just watch, and they were in awe of the things I could do, with the straps. Now, we'd take hot steel—and the steel things were about the same length as this room—I could take the straps and put them on the end, lift them over, drop them on the pile, and then take the straps off and come back again. I didn't know that the others couldn't do that, see, 'cause I only worked with Maynard. (*What would the others do?*) Well, they would have to have a crane-chaser take the straps off for them. They would have to follow the crane. They had great big long hooks, and they would unhook the straps off the hot steel But see, he taught me all this, and I didn't know but what it was part of the job.

He was proud that they'd picked him to break me in in the first place. He was so proud. And he was crazy as the birds, and he and I clicked right from the Day One. Now his son, Roy, was on the other shift. They also later gave him a girl to break in, and of course, the race was on. There was only one job, right? So it was whoever was going to make the best crane-man was going to get the job. There were other cranes for this other girl to get. You know, she wasn't going to be out of a job. But the rail mill crane was the piece of cake. So, the race was on. He was determined that I was going to be the one. There seemed to be rivalry.

(*He not only made you a good crane operator, he made you a better one.*) Well, a show-off-y one. I wouldn't say I was better, because I wasn't as fast. I was too careful to take any chances that they would do, for saving time. In other words, both him and Roy would come through the mill, they'd drop their chain on their way in so that the chain was right at the spot. Where I would wait till I got there, and then drop the chain. Because there was too much in between. You know, I wasn't as fast as they were. And I was always scared of hooking the end of the chain into the housing or—you could do a heck of a lot of damage.

I went on the plant on October the 19th of '42, and I went over to the rail mill the last week of November. And then I was with Maynard—I guess till January, they left me with him to get the training. Perhaps even longer. But then his son, Roy, on the other shift, he went into the army in April—and this is what they were grooming me for. By that time I had taken over the crane.

The interesting part of that is that Maynard became my father-in-law and Roy became my husband. Roy came back in June, and we were married. We met through his father, really. It was unusual. I could see how much like his father he was. And I thought his father—the sun and the stars shone out of his father—and he was very, very much like him. (*And they were both crane operators.*) Yes. (*And so were you.*) Yeah.

(*It wasn't enough that you pulled the levers. They wanted you to know the mechanics of the crane as well.*) Nobody wanted me to do it, only Maynard. Now, there was a trouble-man. If there were trouble on different shifts, all we had to do was call a trouble-man. If we had trouble with the electric, we called a fellow from the electric department. And one time a man came up. He said, "I'm from the electric department." And I said, "Okay." "What do you do," he said, "if the fingers on your board jam?" I looked at him and I said, "I change them." He said, "You what?" I said, "I change them." He said, "Show me." He didn't believe me. So I took the skirt off the box, and I took one that was kind of frayed, and I put a new finger on it, and I put the thing back on. He said, "Do you know what you're doing? You're taking my job." He said, "I often wondered how come we don't get a call on your shift." And he said, "Now, I know." He said, "Maynard." They never got any calls off Maynard's shift, but they

176

knew him so long, and they knew that he knew as much about the crane as the fellows that had to come to fix it. And what he knew, he taught me, see. But I never realized that there was a certain man for a certain job. I had never worked under that system before.

(*Would being a crane operator be considered a dangerous job?*) Not in most areas. The only place that I figure would be, would be the rail mill and the open hearth. Both of those. The open hearth has great big pots full of hot lead, and they have to tip that into casts and form blocks. Now, that was a dangerous job. (*How was it dangerous in the rail mill?*) Well, you were working so close to the men. Especially when they were changing rolls to make different sizes—the rolls that steel would have to go through to form rails. When they came up, they were just a square block, about 10 by 10. Then they would pass through these, and they'd get smaller. There'd be about three sets. Now, the crane wasn't that far up above the housing. The housings are solid. So the men stood on top of them, and there was an opening that they could go in, to see that the ends of the rolls fitted. So when that turned, as the steel came through the pass, it'd start changing shape. It passed through, and it got skinnier and longer. Then they'd turn, and they'd come through—begin to take shape. They'd get narrow in the centre. You know the way a rail is formed. It's long like that, and then it gets narrow, and then it's flat on the top again. So that would start coming through—it would take another shape. Then it would go back and take another shape. Well, by this time, see, your rail is formed. Now, this is yellow heat. It still had to be hot or they couldn't shape the rails.

(*So you've moving overhead....*) While all this is going on. Now, I had to lift the rolls, and put the rolls in between those two housings. Those men were all working there. This is why I say it was dangerous. You had to be so careful. And you only had a certain period of time to change the rolls—about 4 hours, it took me, to change the rolls. Well, perhaps Maynard and Roy could do it in 3 1/2; it would take me almost 4 hours to change that, a complete change. (*And you're setting up for different widths and thicknesses of steel?*) Yeah, the poundage. See, the 135-pound rails or 150-pound rails, or, if it was mine arches, you stripped it right down from the bottom. It was a different set of rolls altogether that went in for mine arches.

It wasn't really till almost a year that I began to realize how responsible the job was. Because the novelty was so different to anything I had ever done. I had been a clerk in a store. And it gradually sank in.

I found men more careless than women, while I was on the plant. They have steps for you to go up, especially in the plate mill—you'd go up the steps and then go down, like that. The men wouldn't bother about the

177

steps. They'd jump on the plates with the rollers moving and the plates moving, and they would jump off. You never saw a woman do it. She's too careful of her limbs to take any chances, stupid things that some of the men used to do. Another thing: I used to carry steel on a magnet. Well, a magnet—you can't depend on it any time because it's only on an electric wire. And some of the fellows used to walk underneath that, no matter how much I banged that bell, the smart alecks would run underneath the loads. And if that electricity had ever given way, they'd have been killed. But you never saw a woman. If you rang the bell, a woman stayed where she was supposed to stay till you passed with the load.

I had no trouble. Never. I was just one of the men. There was a Frenchman there—he was foreman on the shift—he had been there for years. He was like Maynard, he was there for about 35 years. He used to give me the signals. And he'd say to me, "Take it up." Well, that meant just touch the lever. And he'd holler, "Blue hair." Well, that meant you just blew on the lever, because that's how much difference it would make in the steel. But he used to swear and curse at the men all the time. Oh, and he'd get vicious if you took it up a little bit too much, and you'd have to put it back down again. So anyhow, this day, the superintendent came. And he said to me, "How are you two getting along?" I said, "Well, I'll

Four women who worked in the steel plant during World War Two.
Left to right: Selina Haddad Hollohan, Minnie Paruch, Bernadette, and Lil, with two co-workers.

tell you the truth. He curses and swears at me the same as he does the men." "Well," he said, "don't let it worry you, because if he couldn't swear, he couldn't talk." After that, I didn't mind him swearing at me. Half of the time it was in French, I didn't understand it anyway.

(*Not only were you well trained, you felt like you were one of the men, you really had a position there. Weren't you angry about losing your job?*) Well, I knew it was only temporary, we all knew that when we went to the plant. Only till the boys came back. It was only a temporary measure. (*Did you desire to stay on?*) Well, not really. No, I was willing enough for Roy to come back and for him to do the work. No, I didn't feel bad about it. I went on in October of '42, and it was January of '45. (*No regrets?*) None. I never felt any resentment or anything like that, because we all knew when we went there, we were only taking the places of the men till the men came back. And they were starting to come back by then.

(*In your heart, though, did anything change about the kind of jobs that women should do?*) No. I don't think it's a place for a woman, really. I really don't. It's so dirty. Everybody there, their lungs are full of the smoke and the oil. All that, you get it right in the face all the time when you're working. When my husband died, they did an autopsy on him, and his heart was encrusted. And it was nothing else but all the oil. Of course he used to drink, too, and he smoked—so between it all.... And Maynard was never without a cough, never. Of course, he used to smoke, too. But all that had to get into your lungs. (*And you feel it was too dirty for a woman?*) Yeah. Well, it's too dirty for a man, too, physically. But it had to be done.

(*So you didn't have regrets when it was over?*) No. Perhaps it was because Roy was going to take back his job, perhaps that was the reason why I had no regrets. I don't know. (*Did you love him already?*) Oh, yeah. He went in April, he went into the army, and he came back in June, and we were married.

(*So you had already kind of got that started before he went into the army.*) That's right. I remember when he went to get the marriage slip. He went to a man to look for the license. And the fellow said to him, "What do you do? What's your occupation?" He said, "I'm a crane-man." He said, "And your bride-to-be?" He said, "Crane-man." He said, "I mean your bride-to-be." "Well," he said, "crane-man!" He said, "My God, man, I can't put that on the certificate. I'll have to put 'crane-woman.'" So he put "crane-woman" on the slip. We used to laugh about that.

Archie Neil Chisholm, Margaree Forks

This story that I'm go-
ing to tell has a slight
background. It's a sto-
ry that I will tell con-
cerning myself. Part
of it is not maybe as
good as it should be.
But it starts back
when I was about 11
or 12 years of age—I
learned to play the
fiddle. My brother
(Angus Chisholm)
and I started playing
dances when we were
about 14. I was badly
crippled, polio in both
legs. But I still man-
aged to get to all the
local dances. And we
were, to say the least,
quite popular as
young fellows. We'd
go and we'd play.
There was no money
involved, but we had
a lot of good times.

But the one habit I
did acquire, which I
wish I hadn't, was the
fact that I was able to drink quite freely, and it sort of acted as an equaliz-
er for me. The result was that I grew up with that very great appetite for a
good time, for dancing, and for drink. Much to my father and mother's
worry. Because the other boys were very physical, all my brothers, but I
wasn't. And for me to walk out, or to be out alone in a snowstorm, possibly with a horse and sleigh or something like that—they were very, very
much worried. So it got to the point where I used to come home in pretty
bad shape at times. Now this is actually as it happened.

180

But one particular night a friend of mine and I were driving home, and he dropped me off at my own house. And I managed to get into the house all right. But the next day I met him, and he asked me a rather strange question. He asked me, "Who was the chap who walked in from the gate to the front door of your house last night?" I laughed at him, because I figured that he was putting me on. And he described a man—tall, and dressed in a certain way—which immediately struck me as being the identical image of my father, who was then dead, had passed away. I figured that possibly he was just making this up.

But on three different occasions other people had told me that they were seeing this particular man walking with me whenever I would leave a car. And it was particularly in the wintertime. So one night I came into my own house, and my two brothers were in the living room. One of my brothers opened the door for me, and looked over my shoulder, and didn't say anything. But the next morning he told me that my father had followed me in to the door, that he was positive that he recognized him. This I again assumed to be just a ploy to try to scare me into not drinking any more.

But time went on, a year or so after that. I was at a dance, a place called Cheticamp. And we left Cheticamp in a very bad snowstorm. And I got home to my own driveway. I got out of the car. I started in to the house, home. My last recollection was of sort of falling down in the snow. And I made no attempt whatsoever to get up. But somehow during the night my brother woke up, and he woke his wife up, and he said, "Archie Neil is someplace out there." And he came out, and he picked me up. And without his assistance I would have died that night.

I didn't speak very much about it for a couple of days afterwards, and then I asked him, I said, "Rod, how is it that you were able to come out and find me at 3 o'clock in the morning in a snowstorm when you were supposedly sound asleep?" And he looked at me for a moment and then he said, "Well, if I tell you, you won't believe me." I said, "Yes, I will." He said, "My father appeared at the side of my bed and told me that you were out there, and I went out." And he said, "Otherwise, you would have been dead."

So, a few things happening like that made me decide that I was through with drinking.

(*Now is that really what made you decide to stop drinking?*) No, actually, it wasn't. What made me decide to drop it was the fact that I was on an Easter safari with a group of people, and I came home to my boarding house. I was boarding at St. Joseph du Moine. I left school on Easter Thursday evening. And that was in the days when they had a full week. I hadn't taken a drink for quite a few weeks. And I decided, I've just got to have it—no more school for 7 or 8 days. So I went on a bad one. And I

Archie Neil's mother, Isabel MacLennan, and father, Archie A. ("Archie the Teacher"), with the late Fr. Daniel Doyle.

was traveling around with the same guy all the time. We weren't sleeping. We were just going from house to house, bootlegger to bootlegger, liquor store or anything. And I came home and I was broke. I didn't come home—I went to my boarding house—and the man with whom I was boarding said, "Archie Neil, come on in the house. You're in pretty bad shape." And I said, "I know, Thomas," I said, "I won't. I don't want your wife, Adele, to see me like this." And Thomas said, "Adele—you have her worried worse than your mother. She sees you going by, and she likes you. And she said you've never done anything in the house, or said anything that was out of the way. You've always managed to get to your room. Come on in. I'll tell you what I'll do. If you will stay home, I'll get you two quarts."

I went up to the house, and I said hello to Adele, and I walked—I was able, navigating okay with a cane, just a cane. I had dispensed with the crutches in 1927 and started using a cane. And I got that I could walk very well with it. And the idea was to get me off the road. By gosh, he brought the two quarts up to my room. And I said, "I'm broke, Thomas," I said, "I'll pay you when I come out of this." And I started to drink alone.

I had the couple of bottles of rum, and I was drinking alone in my bedroom. All of a sudden I put my hand in my pocket—they had a little store downstairs, and I was going to get some cigarettes. And I didn't have a cent, not one penny in my pocket. And I thought to myself, Here I'm 43 years old, and I've worked since I was 19, and I didn't have the price of a package of cigarettes. And the strangest thing about it was—you may think this is crazy—but I had drunk myself sober rather than drunk. I was drinking, drinking, just all alone, straight out of the bottle. And then all of sudden this hit me, and I said to myself, "This is it. I'm going to quit."

There was a full one and a half a one there. And I took the half a quart. The window was up, and I threw it out the window, smashed it on the rocks. And Thomas heard the smash, and he made for upstairs. He said, "What in the name of God is wrong with you?" I said, "I will never take another drink, Thomas." And Thomas laughed and he said, "I've heard that one before. Well, if you're never going to take another drink, I'm going to take that quart." I said, "No. Leave it there. That's going to be the fight between that quart and me—between us," I said.

And that night—of all the sickness and pain and everything else I went through, that night was the worst I ever went through. You're going to laugh at me and say, "He's making it up." But I'll tell you that that bottle had arms on it. It seemed to reach out to me. And I said to myself, for the first time in my life, I'd say, Archie Neil, you have D.T.'s now—when you see things and all of that. And I was able to rationalize. And I'd do that. I'd just pinch myself—yeah, I'm awake. As there's a Saviour above, I'm telling you the truth.

I'd see snakes. As there's a God above me. There were snakes and everything, and they were coming through the keyhole, and they were getting larger as they were coming through. And I was seeing all sorts of ugly faces around me. Nothing pleasant. The most horrible looking faces. Then when I'd sit up in bed and get my bearings, they seemed to disappear. Then I'd just relax and go back to sleep, and as soon as I would be just dozing asleep, back they'd come again. So I knew it was a figment of the imagination.

I was alone in the room, alone all the time. (*Nobody came to you.*) No. They would have come up if I had called them. But I was alone in the room. And Mrs. Deveau would come up now and again to see if I wanted a cup of tea or something. She was a lady I'll never forget. I was in this shape that when she brought me a cup of tea I wouldn't take the tea in front of her. I asked her to put it on the chair. When I went to take the tea I couldn't—my hands were shaking that badly I couldn't.

And I stayed in bed for two days. I wouldn't come down—I was ashamed. And then I came down. And when the following Monday came, I was ready to go back to teach. It was right on the hill above them. It was a two-room school then. I went to teach.

And about two weeks or three weeks afterwards, I came downstairs one day with the quart. I had broken the half quart out the window, but I left the full one. I came down and I put it on the table. And I said, "Thomas, I've gotten a cheque, and I'm going to pay you." So I paid him for the quart that I drank. And I said, "There's the other one, or I'll pay you for that. What'll you do with it, break it?" "No," he said, "I'll keep it." He looked at me straight in the eyes. "For the first time in my life," he said, "I'm believing you."

And so, from that day on I never looked back. (*You never took another drink?*) No, never. That will be 36 years (last) March.

. . .

(*When were you born?*) In May 25, 1907. I had polio when I was just about 5 years old, and it affected both legs. I was 4 years before I could stand. Four years after I took polio, I crawled. That was the only way I could get around. And then gradually I began to be able to stand up by a chair. Then my godfather, whose name was Peter Pat Coady, made me a little set of crutches. And I learned to slide along with the crutches. I was 9 years old when I could walk. And I went to school at Margaree Forks. There are dozens of people around here still living who went to school with me, and who can remember.

I went to school on horseback. We had a little brown mare by the name of Ida. One of my brothers would put me on Ida's back and take me to school. And then I would slide off with the crutches and go to school. The mare would find her way home. I'd let her go at the school, she'd go right home. But at 3:30 when the school got out, one of the boys would come home and take the mare up, and I would get on her back and come home.

Now this was great in the fall and the spring. But in the wintertime in those days there was no such thing as a snowplow. And you would have 5 feet in certain areas between here and Margaree Forks, and just a horse track. Sometimes she'd plunge. I got several tumbles off her back, but I managed to crawl back on. And that was for 5 years. I went till I got my Grade 11, like that, on a horse's back.

(*You were born and you were fine. Did you learn to walk as a little boy?*) Oh, yes. In fact the day before I took polio, my brother Angus and I were out playing in the brook. Oh yes, I was walking when I was about 10 or 11 months old. I was 4, going on 5, and we were out playing in a brook that was right back of our house. There were 3 or 4 in that summer who took polio. See, it started in our spine. It's supposed to have started with spinal meningitis, and then developed into polio too.

Playing one day in a brook, and then the next day I woke up, and my head was going back. The back of my head was almost touching my spine. And I was in terrible pain. My mother didn't know—she thought I was dying. And there happened to be a nurse living next door to us—Belle MacDo-

184

nald was her name. My mother sent for her. In the meantime, they sent for the doctor. But the doctor would have to come by horse and buggy from Margaree Harbour, and that was 8 miles. But she no sooner looked at me, this nurse, when she told the folks that I had spinal meningitis, and to get ice.

Now nobody had ice around Margaree at that time, with the exception of those who were running hotels. They would have big ice houses and they'd store ice in the winter, cover it and store it in sawdust, and then they would have ice all summer, because the ice wouldn't melt if they kept the doors closed. And they went to what is now the Margaree Lodge. It was owned then by a fellow by the name of Dougald Campbell. And Dougald sent down what ice they wanted, and they kept me in icepacks for I don't know how long.

And how they discovered that I was paralysed was the fact that I attempted to get out of bed to get a glass of water that was on a little stand. And my mother was sound asleep. She had been up day and night with me, taking turns with my father. And when I went to stand up, they buckled. And that was when the real pain started. So I was in bed for probably a year. At home, all home treatment, there was nothing they could do about it. They would lift me—I wasn't very heavy—they would lift me and carry me out to the kitchen or carry me to the window to see something or anything like that. I could sit on a chair. My hands were unaffected. From the waist down, pretty bad.

And somehow I learned to crawl. One morning I got out of bed, and I would say it was with the strength of my arms, I dragged myself out to the kitchen. Gradually I learned to stand with a chair, by a chair. I'd be pretty wobbly. They'd encourage me all the time. Otherwise I would probably never have come through it. Didn't embarrass them one bit. And it seems that it didn't embarrass me. Even if people were in, I'd crawl out.

But it was just the fact that I couldn't do anything but be in somebody's way up to that. There were 9 of us in the family, you know. Mother wasn't needing the help from me, or anything like that. Also, my father away from home. My father was a school teacher at that time, teaching for $200 a year. And 9 children. He would have to move from anywhere from Scotsville to Bay St. Lawrence. He'd go alone; the family would be home. Couldn't afford to move them. But my mother was a great big strong woman, and she was the boss. We kept a few cattle and sheep and two horses—she had to do all that with the aid of the boys, and see that it was done. They were able to do enough farming to get our own vegetables and meat and stuff like that. But there were times when things were pretty rough, but we managed to come through it okay.

So she didn't have too much time. But every minute she could, she would devote it to me, to try and rub, massage the legs, and all that sort of thing. But even at that, she was working like a slave to do that. And after I started to school, then I used crutches. Until I was 18 years old, and they got enough money together to send me for one year to St. F.X. But I couldn't continue, we didn't have enough money. And a fellow from Newfoundland had broken his leg. His leg cured, and he had a cane. He was rooming next to me at St. F.X. And he got trying me with a cane. The first thing I knew, I could walk with a cane. And I dropped the crutches. And from that until 1954, I never used anything but a cane.

And in 1954 I fell and dislocated my hip. So there's only one thing to do, is put a brace—a caliper, they called it—on that, and try it with that. So that's how I got along since 1954. But I drove a car since I was 17.

(I'm interested in how you did it. I want to know how Archie Neil put his life together. Literally, you were cut off at the legs quite early, and you were dragging yourself around your own home. I take it you were not just the little baby—everybody taking good care of you—they all were busy.) They were busy people. I read an awful lot. I read an awful lot. I think I'll tell you something I never told anybody else before. I realized that I was crippled. And I realized that there must be something I could do that was not going to leave me dependent on anybody. I wanted to make my own way somehow. The fiddle started it—I was picking up a few dollars. And once I got to school and got my Grade 11, I decided I was going to cut the strings from home. In those days you could get a "permissive licence." They were looking for teachers—South River Lake was one of the places. And with only Grade 11 and going on 19, I went, took my first trip away from home. I went to South River Lake and I got the school, and I taught there.

Apparently I must have had a fairly good reputation as a teacher, in spite of my shortcomings, because the next year, just before that school term was out, there were three fellows—total strangers—arrived at my boarding house one night, and they asked me if I would take over the principalship of a school down at St. Andrews, rural St. Andrews. And this gave me a terrific boost in my own ego, as it were, to think that I was going to be principal, even if it's only a two-room school. But there were three rooms in this one. So I became principal there.

And in spite of the fact that I was drinking—not so much then, but drinking some, and all of that—I wanted to work up and try to—but the salaries were awfully bad. I taught 5 years, and I still couldn't accumulate enough money to go to Teachers College. Finally my sister helped me, and I went to Teachers College.

I don't know how—some sort of an innate sense of pride—I didn't want to be dependent on anybody else, just making an existence, not a living. I was learning all the time, and reading, and learning a lot of poetry, and doing a lot of work, you know, whatever I could to help somebody

186

else out, as far as—if there was a person having difficulty in school or anything like that. But I think the turning point came about 1950. 1950 was when I began to get my life together. 1950 I stopped drinking. And about three months after I stopped drinking, I bought my first old car. I was as proud of that as if it had been a Cadillac. An old '35 Plymouth—15 years old when I bought it—I bought it from a fellow from Nyanza. And it had a rumble seat, and I was the big guy then, driving my own car. Then I started to, oh, in 1952, I started to go with the girl to whom I'm married now. I was 4 years sober before I ever would risk asking anybody to marry me. I wanted to know. I was 47 when I got married. I would never put anybody else in misery. I was intelligent enough for that. I knew that I was an alcoholic. And I wasn't going to make anybody else suffer with that. And in 1954 we were married.

And always the idea was that I could, that I was going to try to do better. Then in '56, two years after I got married, the Conservative Party came after to run an election. They couldn't get another soul to run Tory. And I ran against J. Clyde Nunn. His majority was 1750. And I took it down to 725. I didn't have a cent of money hardly—just enough gas to get around—they'd give me enough gas to move from one meeting to another. Then I ran the second election, and I took them down to 56—56 of a majority. That was the only difference. And then they wanted me to run a third time, and I wouldn't. Thank God I didn't. Dr. Jim MacLean came in then, and he ran. I had the door open for him and he went right in with a big majority.

I started then getting better schools. And I was trying to make a reputation for myself as a teacher. It was the only thing I could do. Just working as hard as I could. And I started doing a lot of emceeing at concerts. This was exposing me to more and more people all the time. Then I got the idea that I was going to go back to college. And my wife used to have a job in Halifax, where she used to go—political pie—where she used to go once a month. It gave us a little extra money. And she worked all the time. I'd be teaching school all week. I'd go up on Saturday to Antigonish (for classes at St. F.X., then) come back to Margaree and play (fiddle) Saturday night. And then all during the summer, when I would be up in Antigonish, I'd get home. I'd see myself playing, in the wintertime, when I didn't have the money to put gas in the car hardly. I would go and play at a dance and I'd get 10 bucks. And then play till 2 o'clock in the morning, and come home, and leave at 5 for Antigonish. And that was Saturday after Saturday. Because there was a dance at East Margaree every Friday night, and I played for it, see. I'd play, and then leave about 5 o'clock, in the stormiest weather. I was driving my own car all the time. And finally I got my degrees.

Then through some exposure, they came after me from Sydney to see if I would do a radio program ("Archie Neil's Cape Breton," CBI). And that

187

gave me a little more exposure. Than my friend Allan J. (MacEachen), who was Liberal cabinet minister at the time, knew I was Conservative and all of that—but he appointed me to this Canadian Consultative Commission for Multiculturalism. And it just worked out like that. Gradually I was getting a little bit more exposure, and getting little paying jobs. Then I spent 10 summers at Acadia University. In the old days when they wrote provincial examinations, I was on the correcting board, the marking board, for English. And you'd be given one question, each paper, and it got so monotonous. But the money was good. In those days, now, you'd get $25 a day, it was big, big money. And your board free. I'd come home every Friday night—leave Annapolis Valley at 5 o'clock and get down here between 9 and 9:30—and keep straight to Northeast Margaree and play. And come back, and do the same thing Saturday night, and then head back for the Valley Sunday. You had to be kind of half iron to do it, but I managed it, as long as I wasn't drinking. And I wasn't drinking.

(*You kept on being a fiddler for dances for many years.*) Up until three years ago. Tendonitis. That's why I stopped. I was never a real good player at all. And I was never satisfied with what I played, myself. I was just what you'd call a fair fiddler for a square set or for playing a Scottish strathspey or something like that. But the finer art of playing, I couldn't do. I was considered fairly good.

(*Was there a lot of music in your home?*) There was not so much music in our home until lately. But there was always singing, and there were always these old tunes and old Scottish ballads and Gaelic ballads. My mother would sing Gaelic by the hour. I could quote you dozens of Gaelic songs that are played now as music, that she'd know verses to them. Fiddle tunes. That's what we play now. (Whistles tune.) " 'S iomadh ceum crubach a chum air deireadh mi"—"It was my lame foot that kept me behind the rest." That was commonly known. It's called "Miss Drummond of Perth" in the music books, and everybody calls it now, but the older people down the North Shore, you ask them, and they'd call it "Calum Crubach"—"Lame Malcolm." And there were verses to that. And that famous piece, "Tulloch Gorm"—one of the original stanzas to that is in mockery of the classical fiddlers. And it's, "Fiddlers pins in tempers fix, and rosin well your fiddle-sticks,/ And banish all Italian tricks from out your variorum./ They're duff and doy at their best, duff and doy, duff and doy./ They cannot please the Scottish taste, along with 'Tulloch Gorm.' " Now that's one of the verses to that "Tulloch Gorm."

And we would learn from listening to her; it unconsciously became part of us, this music. She sang when she was washing the dishes. She sang when she'd be churning. The old-fashioned churn. She'd be singing a song, and the foot would be going, and the churn would be going. Her uncle was a violin player, her brother was a violin player, Angus MacLennan. I had three sisters, and there were lots of the younger people used to come to visit. And quite often there'd be what they'd call a kitchen racket, a party, and there'd be a fiddler there. We used to just eat up that sort of stuff, by sitting around and watching the fiddler play. We weren't interested in the dancing when we were small, just watching the fiddler play. And when we started to learn, we learned fairly quickly ourselves.

So we learned a few tunes. And we started in country places. Our neighbours would have a party and they'd say, "We'll get the Chisholm boys." All right, this was fine.

I remember my first drink as well as if it were today. Playing at a dance. And Angus wouldn't take it, he was a year younger. (*He wasn't drinking*.) Not then. But I took mine. An old man—man of the house—called me in. It was what they called a kitchen party, just everybody dancing in the kitchen. We were playing in sort of a doorway like that, and they were dancing in two rooms in this house. Called me into the pantry. And I was too big-feeling or something, or I was bound to fall. He passed me this and he said, "Try that." It was about half a water glass full of moonshine. He didn't mean anything bad. He probably thought I'd taken it before. And I took my first one.

That was all I took that night. I was offered it again, but I wouldn't. But the glow—the glow you got from it. Angus couldn't understand it. And Angus was scared then. My father was very strict. Although he would take a drink himself, but he was very strict. And coming home, horse and wagon, Angus said, "I'll put the horse in the barn, and you get in the house and get to bed." He said, "I can still smell that." He knew that I had a drink. I was scared for months afterwards that they'd find out. You never forget certain things like that.

And I began to realize that after I got a few drinks in that I felt that I was—these were the equalizers—these made a fellow who was lame equal to anybody. I couldn't dance, I didn't go for girl friends at the time. I had a bit of an inferiority complex, on account of being crippled. And I played and played and played at dances with my brother Angus, who was a big, fine-looking fellow. Angus would go for the girl friends all the time, and have them by the dozen. And I never had quite the courage to do very much of that. Because I was always afraid of being turned down on account of being crippled. Now I'm telling you the truth there. But once I had a few in, I felt as good as anybody then.

(*Did you feel there was any competition between you as fiddlers?*) No. There was no competition because I realized that he was far, far ahead of me. There was no competition. We'll say that for the first three years of our playing there was a plateau, we were about equal. And then he began to

189

learn music and go for it, and I was—I couldn't be bothered with it, by the way. And I couldn't perform anyway, as he could. He could do anything with the violin and I couldn't. I was just a straight country player, that was all. I could do a fairly good square set—that was about the limit of my playing. But handling anything intricate, I could not. And he could. But I wasn't a bit jealous of him, it didn't bother me at all. I was kind of proud of him.

When we were playing, there was one type of music that—how will I say it?—

Angus Chisholm

that I was considered to be rather good at. That was the music for a square set. And when we were playing, Angus could have just blinded me with selections that he knew. But he would always say, "Archie Neil, now you take the lead." So I had quite a number of selections that I played. And I'd take the lead. For a square set, we'd play two in 6/8 time, and then what they called a reel—fast music. And I wasn't a noteplayer at all—everything was by ear. Angus used to tell me, "You should learn the notes," he said, "you have a keen ear just as good or better than mine. Because," he said, "we play together, and you play exactly as I do." But I knew I couldn't play exactly as he. He could do pretty near anything with a fiddle. And I always felt, you know, a little bit behind.

And I used to use this—and I realize it now—as a crutch—a mental crutch that would sort of free my conscience—the liquor. I'd say, I drink because it makes me feel good, and I'm equal to the next fellow when I have quite a few drinks in me. But it wasn't that. I was trying to psyche myself. This is in retrospect. I was thinking then that, well, I can be excused because I'm crippled and they'll say to themselves, poor devil, he's got to have some fun in all of that. But it wasn't. It was because I wanted it. I know what an alcoholic is, as well as anybody. And I look back on it now, as you say, in retrospect, and I feel that I was just making this excuse.

But then we got—what started as a one-drink dance became two, and three. And then everybody wanted to treat the fiddlers, later on, as we

190

were growing a little older. So that we got to the fact, or place, where we began to buy it for ourselves, see. (*You and Angus.*) Oh, yes. And it would be nothing to land in with a pint of rum by the neck of the fiddle in the violin case. When you'd go to a dance, nobody would see it. And then you'd get your chance and have your drinks. and it gradually, like any other drug, as you became addicted to it, you wanted more and more of it. (*Were you getting drunk?*) No, just having a few drinks. But gradually it was coming to the point where we were getting drunk. I had around here the reputation of playing when I was very full, and they couldn't tell the difference. But Angus could not do that. He was more of an artist and was more sensitive, and after a few drinks, it got so that it was affecting his playing. But unless I was extremely drunk, I could still play for a square set and get away with it, too.

(*But I don't quite understand. What did it do for you, supposing you couldn't dance? It wasn't going to give you legs to dance.*) No. But that feeling of good fellowship. That feeling of being able to communicate. I was using it as a crutch at the time. Now I realize that I was thinking to myself, Now I'm just as good as anybody, even if I am crippled.

I was asked by Fr. Webb to go down to Talbot House (a rehabilitation centre at Frenchvale) and tell my story. I went down. And the Sunday that I got down there, he told me, "I have quite a crowd in," he said, "and you're not going to probably enjoy talking to them, because a lot of them are badly hung over and in bad shape." I figured that my subject, at my age, could be: You can always make a come-back. Because I was almost 60 when I graduated from college. 1967. I went every Saturday for 5 years. I drove from here to Antigonish. And I spent all my summers there, all summer. And I got both degrees the same day—B.Ed., Bachelor of Education, and B.A. They made quite a fuss about it at the time. I was the oldest one that graduated and all that sort of thing. Even Time magazine had an article about it.

So this was the subject that I was supposed to tell them at Talbot House. They were just sitting down, very dour, and all this sort of thing. I told them. "You people figure that you're feeling very miserable. And you are. I know it. I went through it all. There's not one of you any sicker than I was the day I quit. But," I said, "none of you were arrested for riding in a wheelbarrow, or very nearly arrested." And I could see their heads coming up as much as to say, This is Cape Breton's outstanding liar.

And I told them a true story. I said, "This is true, whether you believe it or not." I said, "When they used to sell these jugs of wine, Catawba wine, for $2 a gallon. There were a couple of sets of boxing gloves in each jug. I went to Inverness and I had $4. And I got two jugs of wine. I came back on the truck that takes the mail down to Margaree. I got off at Margaree Forks about 10 o'clock at night, and put the two jugs on the side of the road. And I figured to myself, I'm a mile from home. I was sitting there wondering. I said, Somebody will come along. And I heard this fellow walking down the road, and I spoke to him. It turned out to be a young fellow quite a bit my junior. And he said, 'I'll tell you what we'll do.' He had a couple of drinks. It was like Bobby Burns and Souter Johnny. We had a few drinks. And he was becoming more active. He said, 'I'll tell you, I'll take the jugs and we'll walk the mile down to your place, and we can rest every now and again, if your legs are tired.'

"We only went about 100 yards and he decided we'll have another drink. We did. All of a sudden he was inspired. There was a group of nuns at Margaree Forks and they had a little barn and a farm, and we were right across from the barn. He said, 'I got it. I'm going to steal the wheelbarrow on the nuns.' He stole the wheelbarrow and he came down, and we put the two jugs of wine in the wheelbarrow, and we were walking like this. We came down to the bridge at Margaree Forks. As the wine was taking hold, he was getting stronger. He became a potential MacAskill suddenly. And he said, 'You can get in the wheelbarrow, and we'll come home like that.'

"We started down, and we were meeting cars. I'm not exaggerating or anything like that. I met one particular car. And when they saw the wheel-

barrow, and me sitting in it, and this fellow hauling me home like that, they just ditched her! Went right into the ditch on the other side.

"Everything was going good. Cars were meeting us, were giving us a wide coverage. Until suddenly this car, a fellow slammed on his brakes, and I felt a flashlight right in my face. And here was the constable from Cheticamp. He recognized me. And he said, 'What are you doing there?' and the wine was right there. I said, 'I'm taking these home.' And he started to laugh. He couldn't stop. He said, 'Look, I'm giving you 5 minutes and I'll be back. And if you're on the road, I'm going to arrest the two of you.' Never touched the wine.

"The fellow ran all the rest of the way home, with me, and I wasn't too light at the time. And we made the gate there at our place just as the constable went down!"

But I embellished it quite a bit when I was telling them. And the first thing, they were just roaring and laughing. And Fr. Webb said he didn't know how in blazes I had done it, but he said, "I laughed myself till I was sick when I heard the story." And it was true. Actually true.

.   .   .

It was a fight, in a way. But the funny part of it is that, even now, I don't consider myself crippled. Well, yes, handicapped, and I know I'm crippled and all of that. But it never bothers me. I challenge the world to find out if anybody ever heard me whining or saying, "Why should I be crippled?" It was my lot, and that was it, and I took it that way.

You may think that I'm trying to be—I don't know what word to use— trying to be impressive when I say this. But I owe everything—as far as I'm concerned—I owe everything to God. And I often thank God, when I say my prayers—if it was a cross, and I use that term—for giving me this cross to bear. As He's my witness, I'm telling you that, that there's not a night that I don't thank Him for giving me this. Because I might have been in the penitentiary if I wasn't crippled. God knows what would have happened. If it was a cross to bear, well, I thank Him for giving me the strength to carry it and not to worry about it, see. And I'm talking frankly.

A Visit with Dave Epstein

Dave Epstein, Sydney merchant: I was born in Russian Poland, White Russia, in the province of Minsk. In 1890. I was born in a small place. My father had what you'd call a flour mill, worked by water power. He also had all kinds of lumber, woods, farming, fields that we used to hire out. He never used to what you'd call farm himself, but hire out, and get a third. If you hired a piece of land, and you planted it and you harvested it yourself—my father was getting a third out of that. In those days, Jews weren't allowed to own their own land. Under the Tsar Nicholas. But under the tsar before, they were all allowed. So, the reason my father had all this land is because his grandfather had it. And then they made ghettoes, in those years after.

We lived in a small place, just in a hamlet. Nor far from us, 4 miles, there was a little town. So that's where I started going to school. The Jews weren't allowed the regular school. You had to finance yourself. The *cheder* was private. Private teachers, had about 15 or 20 kids. Some of them would board, some didn't. Hebrew, you know, *torah*—writing, you know, Jewish. I was there till I became about 10, 11 years of age.

When I was 13 years of age, I went to the province of Grodno to learn a trade—typesetting, printing. The first year I had to pay $50 to learn it.

Second year, I didn't. And on the third year I would *get* $60 a year. (*Doing the work?*) Yeah. In the meantime I involved myself with a gang, what you'd call the Jewish working class—the Labouring Class of Zion, of Palestine. It was not Israel then. An organization—socialist labour. And that wasn't allowed in Russia. So, we used to hold meetings in the woods, and all that kind of stuff, you see. And then in 1905, the tsar proclaimed freedom of speech. That was a trap for catching the revolutionaries. So, when they got freedom of speech, everybody used to go into halls, and preach. And that was a trick to catch all the leftists, you see, all the revolutionaries. That's how they got me. They came in the hall where we were having meetings, and they took away my passport. You couldn't go without a passport from here to North Sydney. Without a passport, what can I do? So, when they took the passports away, I came home.

I spent the summer at home, visiting different places here and there. And in the fall my aunt's husband said that she should come to America. He was there. I borrowed a passport and I came with her. We had a little money. We had pocket money. And I came under an assumed name to get over the border. There were agents used to take you over. You paid for it; everything was paid, paid, paid.

My uncle, Lubchansky, had arranged with the agent in Halifax to meet us on the boat. And we stayed there overnight in Halifax, in the station. And they sent us on to Sydney. We got in here on a Monday night, I remember it. Sydney had about 12,000 people at that time, 1907. The steel plant opened up in 1900. The mines were working. Things were going pretty good. But they were only paying 9 1/2¢ an hour. That's all they were getting. They were working 11 hours by day and 13 hours at night. And they raised families. Nine and a half cents an hour. But things were so cheap. Eggs 3¢ a dozen. Butter was 10¢ a pound. Fish, meat, everything. Meat was 10¢ a pound. Unbelievable.

I always wanted to go to America. (*Did all the Jews want to leave?*) No, no. Some did and some didn't. But I wasn't responsible for anybody but myself. I went, just myself. I saw what goes on there in Europe. There's nothing for a young man, no future, and I decided. I was supposed to go to a family that lived in Philadelphia. And my uncle, Lubchansky, the fellow I finally came to—he heard from my father that I was going to America. So he wrote back and he said, "Let him come here." That's how I came to Sydney.

(*How did your uncle get to be in Sydney?*) My uncle came to New York in 1895, and he struggled there for awhile, couldn't get any work. He was working, making 2 or 3 dollars a week. And he had a friend who also came to New York—a Nathanson. And Nathanson had a cousin living in Sydney—Dr. Harold Davidson's father—he had a store here on Charlotte Street. He used to go to New York to do the buying. And he saw them struggling a-round down there, so he brought Nathanson here, to Sydney. Davidson brought Nathanson; and a few months later Nathanson sent for Lubchansky. They came here in 1898 or something like that. At first, Lubchansky peddled in Victoria County, carried the pack, like I did later. And then he settled and he got a store in the Pier. A general men's store.

(*How did Davidson get to be in Sydney before them?*) Davidson had an uncle up here. He was one of the first settlers in Glace Bay. Brodie was his name. He came here, and he was an aggressive man, and he put up a nice business. He got

Standing, l. to r.: Perlin (came to Canada in 1914), Dave Epstein, Celia Lubchansky Epstein, Saul Epstein (1910). Seated, Bella & Morris Lubchansky, Max Epstein (1910). **Dave Epstein:** "When (Celia and I) got married in 1918, my father-in-law (Lubchansky) was well-known here. He says, 'The only daughter I have.' So we invited the whole town. There were 75? people at the wedding. The table was set for 250—three time. Cooks cooked for a week."

along very nicely. (*How did the first Jews, like Brodie, locate Cape Breton as a place to go?*) Well, because they were just opening up the mines. They were opening up the steel plant. They were peddlers, they came through the States. In the States, they heard about this place. One brought the other. One brought the other. That's how I got here.

I stayed with Lubchansky, worked in the store, from March till May. I didn't have a cent of money to hire a tutor or anything like that. And Lubchansky had nothing but a foreign trade. So he decided that I couldn't learn to speak English down there. And I wasn't a good scholar. I must say that I didn't have that. I was a dreamer, you know. Aggressive. I loved the life, you know. So they sent me down to Victoria County. A nice husky boy, 15 years old—they decided to make a pack, send me to the country peddling.

(*And you had never been down there?*) No, no, no. (*What did they put in your pack?*) There was all kind of dry goods, you know, little notions, towels, soap, hairpins, and all that. Mostly for ladies: wrappers, dresses, petticoats, and all kinds of stuff. By the time they made up the pack, it was 125 pounds.

I was 4 days on the *Aspy* 'cause the *Aspy* couldn't get over in the ice. Four days to get to Ingonish. And I didn't have a word of English. So the mate of the boat bought me a can of biscuits and I lived on that boat, slept on the boat, and everything. And I was kind of shy, too, depressed, that I had to do that, you know? That was against my will, but they thought that would be the best way for me to learn the language.

A cousin of mine peddled in Victoria County a year before me. He had a horse already. His name was Marcus, and he was a grandfather to the judge, Nathanson. So he met me in Ingonish when I got there. Then later, they put the pack on me and I started walking in Ingonish, from house to house. Made the first day, I think, a couple of miles—the Intervale. Family by name MacKinnons. I stayed there overnight. They were very friendly; you know, good to me and everything—and I had no money to pay them with. I used to pay with a towel, a piece of soap. They wouldn't take any money. Only barter. So it went on like this for a few weeks. I'd go around the bay. Then take the boat from North Bay. I went to Neil's Harbour; I spent a few days. From Neil's Harbour I went to Dingwall, and I stayed in Dingwall a couple days. And then from Dingwall I started walking around the Cape, down as far as Sugarloaf. In Sugarloaf there—on a Friday, it was, and it was raining like hell. So I went in where people were living down below, in the valley. So, I asked her if I could stay there. "Sure." So I stayed there from Friday till Tuesday. In order to make myself at home, I started making *tzimmis* (traditionally cooked carrots, sweet potatoes, short ribs of beef, and prunes, mixed together). A Jewish feast I used to make. They thought it was wonderful. And then I came in another house; a woman was giving birth to a child. I acted as a doctor. I was only 16 years old! I came in another house, a boy had had a paralytic stroke. I tried to cure him with different things, massages a lot. My late mother was very good at home remedies. Medicine is only what's in your mind—90% of medicine is of the mind.

There were about 7 or 8 houses, that's all I used to stay. Probably I repeated that 2 or 3 times in the 7 months, you see. Nobody will ever starve in Cape Breton. First thing I used to come in a house, "Did you have breakfast?" Or, "Did you have lunch?" I used to ask, "Can I get a drink of water?" "No"—buttermilk, they used to give me, buttermilk or milk or cream. You know, they were poor people themselves, but they shared. Hospitality galore, this kind of people.

197

Farm to farm, carrying. And I began to learn the language. But I said to myself, Where am I? And I cursed my uncles for sending me down there. And I was debating with myself whether I should commit suicide or what. I hated the pack. The first couple of weeks, till I got adapted to it. After that, I didn't mind. But I hated it at first and at last. When they called me "peddler," that was degrading me. "Oh, Mr. Peddler"—that was degrading to me. They saw me coming in with a pack. I used to leave the pack outside by the road, and come in. Then I asked them if they needed anything. Some of them would say, "Yes, come in." And then they were very kind, very kind. I got accustomed, I was just at home with them. (*But at first you didn't like it.*) No, no.

One time I went around the bay in Ingonish, and I met—I was 15 years old—there were some nice girls down there. They asked me to have lunch. And I was trying to take off the pack. The pack went over me, and I got pinned down in the bag, and I got embarrassed. and I went to the shore. And right by the shore, I started to write a note. And I was going to throw myself into the water.

There was a friend of mine came with a horse and wagon; Sherman was his name. And he saw me sitting there, crying and writing. So, I told him the story of what had happened. So, he took me on his horse and wagon. He also peddled. He carried me around for a week, till I got acquainted with other people. I was already a citizen. I could converse with them, and the people were very nice to me.

I was there 7 months, and I made $312 saved—$312, I remember it. And when I came back, I owed $200—I was behind! They used to send me the refills by boat. I used to write to my uncle. He used to send me whatever I needed. (*So after 7 months' work....*) I was out $200. I came back.

I started working with him in the store. I still owed $200. And I was just 15, 16 years old, coming. But I took like a duck to water. I liked the store. Oh, it was my life. (*What did you like about it?*) I liked to sell, to talk to people selling. Oh, 'cause they're interesting. It was interesting to me. And I was with him for, oh, about a year, maybe a year or so. We used to go to the sample room to buy merchandise. Travellers used to come from Montreal and sell goods. My uncle used to take me along. And suits—we used to buy stuff that sold for $12, $13, in that time, $15. So I picked out a suit that had to sell for about $30, $28. Uncle said, "You buy that? You'll never be able to sell it." I said, "Uncle, just let me buy one." I bought it. The one suit came in a few weeks after. And a fellow walked in, a nice young man. I looked him over. I said, "I've got something nice for you." A Newfoundlander. I sold that suit for $28.50.

And business at that time—he used to take in about $100 a week,

$150, and that was kind of good. What I used to do later, before break-fast, see, he used to take in in a week. So he came out and saw the sale of $28.50. So I told him. He grabbed me and kissed me. And whoever came in, whoever came in contact with him, he told what a wonderful salesman I am, what a wonderful salesman. And that built me up.

.　　　.　　　.

There were only about 15 or 20 Jewish families in the Pier. About 20 Jewish families, 25 then. (*In all of Sydney.*) Yeah. At that time Glace Bay had over a hundred. Eventually we had 300 families between Sydney, Glace Bay, and Waterford. (*How were all those Jews making a living?*) Some of them were peddling and some of them were in business. (*Were any of them just at regular trades?*) None. No. And everybody was bringing their own people in with them. I brought my brother Benny in 1921, him and his wife and a boy and a girl. (*When you say, "Brought them," what does that mean?*) I paid for them, brought them in, and set them up. I didn't send others peddling, like me. Set them up to work with my horse, did a little peddling with the horse—but not carrying the pack. The worst thing you can do. My brother Max, with a little pack, little suitcase—but didn't do what they did to me. Not a word of English, and just go. The hardest way. But it's the greatest thing that ever happened.

I raised four sons and a daughter. I adopted one boy. In 1921 Canada brought in 260 orphans from the Ukraine; their parents were killed by the hooligans, by the Cossacks. Mrs. A. J. Freeman of Ottawa, she sponsored them. She went all over Canada placing the kids. They came first to Quebec. There were some children routed for Sydney, some routed for Saint John. And there's a family came here—a boy, 9, and the girl, 7, a boy, 5. Celia and I went to the station to see when they brought the children in. We were married three years already, we had no children. My wife looks at them, she says, "Wouldn't I like to have that little boy!" And the fellow that brought them in, in charge of them—he happens to be the father of Dr. Nathanson—Joe Nathanson was his name. He said, "You can have it." So, we adopted our boy. He was 5 years old. And exactly a year after we got him, our own boy was born—Nathan.

I built the Epstein Block on Charlotte Street in 1929. I bought the lot in 1928, and in 1929 we built it. And after I moved into the store, the Crash came. Jack Yazer worked for me in the store. William Sherman worked for me in the store. Harry Jacobson worked for me in the store. I was the father of all this.

Glace Bay built a *shul* (synagogue) about 1902. And we built a *shul* in the Pier in 1911. And then, in 1914 or '15 we bought an old church, where the present *shul* is there now (Whitney Avenue). It belonged to the

Epstein's 5-Mile Harbour Swim, 1928. The winners, left to right: 2nd, Geddes; 4th, Neville; 3rd, Rowke; 1st, Anderson; and promoter Dave Epstein.

Baptists. So the Jews bought it. And then the people from the Pier used to move to Charlotte Street. (*The stores moved?*) Yeah. And their homes.

Then we had what you call our YMHA (Young Men's Hebrew Association). There were 10 of us boys, single fellows, we gathered up and made like a library for us, you know, gathered up a few books and this, made some gatherings. And we started building a club. We built one room, then a second room. With our own help. Everybody contributed the work. We built a beautiful auditorium—the YMHA of Sydney. That was the only one east of Montreal. It was beautiful. And then, all affairs used to take place in that, *bar mitzvahs* and weddings and everything. Two story. A big basement underneath, finished, and a floor. There was everything going on. We used to have all kinds of gatherings. That's the only one in the Maritimes, boy. It burned down about 25 years ago. So, the money we got for the insurance, we sent it to Israel. And we have in Israel the Sydney YMHA. In that money, there's a YMHA there in our name.

(*What interests me is that this was important to you, but you did not feel yourself terribly religious.*) No, I was never religious. I am a Jew at heart, but I am not a fanatic. Not *shukeling* and *dovening* (prayer with rhythmic motions)—not for me. I'm a freethinker. But I'm a good *Yid* at heart. In *shul*, I contribute. My hand is always open. And I contribute to everything else.

When I got into Charlotte Street, I joined up in an athletic club. And I started promoting. I promoted a 3-mile race—walking race, running race—5-mile, 10-mile, and 15-mile. All those years. And then later on, I promoted a swimming race from North Sydney to Sydney—5 miles—from 1927 to 1935. Johnny Jessome worked for the *Post*. We had that swim 6 or 7 years. I used to have a real holiday for Cape Breton. They used to race the first Wednesday in August. And the steel company used to give us a big boat. Then, I had baseball. And I had my own team, the Dave Epstein Tigers. (*You yourself, you were playing sports?*) Oh no. I was promoting—Dave Epstein, Dave Epstein, Dave Epstein Tigers, Dave Epstein Tigers. (*Because when you say promoting, it's not only promoting the sport, it was advertising.*) No, no, no. I was interested in the young people. My mind is always involved with people, I love people—that was my policy, always was. I didn't care so much for the business, but that's how I built myself up. Johnny Miles—he ran for me once. Michaelson, Hannigan, Demar—all stars, stars, stars.

I promoted a walkathon, walking 21 miles. Mrs. Corbett, she was 76 years old. She walked. She had a farm. And she milked 16 cows. And then she walked. That was in 1929. And she finished the race. Then I followed up with other sports up till about 1940. (*Apart from sports, you had new methods in advertising.*) Yeah. My mind was always—I used to go to bed—what shall I do? I used to advertise quarter of pages, half of pages, 3 or 4 times a week, in the *Post* and in the *Record*. "Meet me face to face." and I was the first one that had my picture in the paper. My picture was always in the paper. And I used to put, "Meet the old boy—Dave Epstein—the old boy himself." That was my slogan. "Meet me face to face."

Then, I had road signs. I put up 350 signs. I used to say the mileage from the car. Had a fellow that worked with me in the store. He was a genius, he could do anything. We used to get in and go and drive away, and put signs in different places. In those days there were no road signs. (*What would these signs say?*) "So many miles to Dave Epstein." "Dave Epstein wants to see you." And an arrow pointing the way. Used to come to a nice corner and say, "That's a good corner." 20 miles, 15 miles.

Now, there was a boat came in—you know where the City Hall is now—that was a wharf. A boat came in, the *S.S. Beothuk*. She was taking provisions to the Eskimos. They had a fellow from Canadian Press on board the boat. And they went from Sydney to North Sydney. They saw a couple of my signs, took the signs with them to Baffin Island. And in Baffin Island: "So many miles to Dave Epstein's." They sent me a picture of this, and they sent a copy to the *Toronto Star*. The *Toronto Star* used to

supply pictures for other papers, you know, Europe, whatever. I got letters from Africa, got letters from different places. "The Sydney tailor," they called me. And write-ups, all kinds of write-ups. Piles and piles.

(*Did someone teach you how to sell?*) No, no, it came to me. One thing brings another, you see. Like you read the paper. You're interested in the paper. You find ways and means how to produce a paper. That's the same way with me. I knew how to sell, in that little way of mine—some salesman. I always believed in quality. Never fooled the public. I discovered it, that Cape Breton has got a lot of men that cannot be fitted. Tall like you, short, stout. And I was the agent at that time, had an exclusive line of Fashion Craft clothes. And I was with them, and the designer—I could do anything with him. So we designed for a short man, for a tall man, for a stout man. Suits up to 66.

There was a circus came in once in Sydney, on a Saturday. And there was a fellow that was with the circus, he was in a year before and I sold him some stuff. He happens to be a musician, and he joined up with the Barnum and Bailey show. Coming to Sydney, he said while they were coming, "Boys, we're going to Sydney, don't buy"—they were in Saint John, they were in Moncton, they were in Halifax. He said, "I'll take you to a place in Sydney, a friend of mine." They came in. About 9 o'clock, this fellow walked in. Did I remember him? Even though I didn't remember, I would say, "Yes." "Don't close up the store tonight." And I had a promotion they gave me from the Fashion Craft: a suit—4 piece suit—1,2,3, and a pair of plus fours that we wore in those days. And we stayed open. We sold 34 suits from 12 o'clock to 4 o'clock in the morning. That's the kind of promotion I used to do.

I used to go in for big promotions. What I didn't do, my God! And how they worked. Once a circus came that had a little midget. They came to my store. I said, "I can fit you with a suit." I put it on him, went. That helped. All these things helped. It gives you ammunition. So, there it is.

Old Tales of Sorcery Remembered

J. J. Chiasson • Marie Deveau
Marguerite Gallant • Jean Phillip Larade
J. J. and Denise Deveaux

J. J. Chiasson: I had a brother that was servant boy at Arichat to Fr. Gallant, and there was a strange priest came that landed at Fr. Gallant's. Fr. Gallant was getting almost blind, so he got this. So one night he was called on a sick call, and my brother— it was in the winter— he got the horse and the sleigh and he went with the new priest. On the way, my brother asked him about this sorcery. The new priest said, "Yes, there are two kinds of sorcery. One, they use it in a meeting of some kind—for to make the people laugh. Probably work on a young man, you know. They had one one night. Said, 'What did you do with the 50 cents that you stole from me?' He said, 'I didn't steal it.'

'Look in the side pocket of your coat.' Look. Sure enough—50 cents was there. Well, that's for entertainment." So he said, "The next one, they use it with the intercession of the devil." (*So one kind of sorcery is for entertainment....*) And one's with the help of the devil.

(*Did you ever know anyone who could do sorcery?*) Well, some people from Cheticamp, they used it. I don't know if they had the help of the dev-

203

il or not but anyway, people were scared of them because they were supposed to be able to perform that sorcery. (*Did you know any of these people?*) Yes, I did know some of them. And there were beggars that go to a home and beg for something—money or something else—and if you didn't receive them well, they'd say, "You'll be sorry for that." So there were people there, when they'd come to churn the cream that they had to make butter—the whole thing turned like water. Then they had other people who could clear them, someone who could get them out of this trance. Well, it seems that maybe they didn't have much to do any more than the people that were bothered believed that this person could clear them. And apparently they did. When they believed in that person more than they would the person that was keeping them in that trance. (*Do you feel then that it was a trance? More in their mind than in the butter?*) Oh yes, yes. Oh, no—it happened to the butter.

There was one fellow there who used to go around mending, like churns and strainers and coffeepots—he was supposed to be one of them. There was a man there at our place—he wouldn't mind talking to the devil himself. When that fellow came to our place, he said, "What are doing here?" Said, "They tell me that you're a sorcerer." "Ah, tut, tut, tut, tut." He talked to him, said, "Put the wish on me, go ahead." (J.J. grumbled as the sorcerer did.) He wouldn't try, because it seems that you have to have, what will I call it?—an easy mind—that they can work on you. If you have a strong will power, they can't touch you. (*Were you ever afraid of them?*) Not me. Oh no, no. I'd tell them to go to hell. They never tried on me. I wasn't scared of them and they never tried on me. I felt that I could send them away well dissatisfied.

Marie Deveau: In the old times, when the Jersey firm were here at first—there were some people here who could throw what in French we call that a *sort*. When you throw something on a person. (*Like a spell?*) Well...yes. If you're scared of them, it could easily take on you. But if you're not scared of them, they can never touch you. (*Were there any sorcerers among the Acadians before the Jerseymen came to Cheticamp?*) No, because the Jersey were some of the first people that came at The Point there, at Cheticamp Island. There were old, old people but, no, I don't think there was anything like that. (*Before the dispersion of the Acadians—when they were sent from their lands—were there sorcerers among them then?*) No, I don't think. (*Would a sorcerer be the same as a witch?*) Oh yes, something like that. (*Could it be a man or a woman?*) It could be both, it wouldn't matter. There was a family—the whole family could. From one to the other, they were passing it. The woman could, then the man could, then some of the children could. When they were grown up, they were learning from one to the other. They couldn't have it of themselves. They learned it from somebody else. (*And were they Jersey people?*) No—they were not Jersey. He was a French fellow who came here. I don't know where his wife was from. But they weren't Acadians.

They could put a *sort* on you. That was to bother you. For example, when the Jersey came to the Island there, there was a man named Charlie Romeril. Fr. Fiset was here than. Fr. Fiset was one of the first priests, and he built the church down here. He had a servant boy at the glebe house with him—his name was Jeffrey Crispou, I think. A woman was bothered by the sorcerer and Fr. Fiset had done something to make her better. Where she was working, she was working for a family, and the man had some words with Charlie Romeril. And then one day, he had put some fresh hay in the cows' manger, and they say that Charlie Romeril went there and put a *sort* on the hay. Then the girl, in the evening, after they were all through with their work—she went and she cleaned the manger. And then right away she was out of her mind. They couldn't do anything with her. They didn't know what she had. And then the man went over to Fr. Fiset, and Fr. Fiset cured the girl. (*Do we have any idea what Fr. Fiset did to cure the girl?*) No. He cured the girl and the girl became well. Well, Charlie Romeril had a grudge against Fr. Fiset. When he knew that it was Fr. Fiset, he was bothering them at the glebe house.

There at the glebe house they used to hear some chains banging together, and they'd see some fire here and there, and then noise—just to intimidate them. Just to intimidate Fr. Fiset, because he had gone to try and save the girl, see? And then sometimes in the nighttime, they'd hear something in the corner, and then in another—and they couldn't sleep. And then after a few times, the servant, Jeffrey Crispou, he said to Fr. Fiset, "Are you not going to do something about that?" He said, "You were able to get the girl away. Couldn't you scold him?" Fr. Fiset said, "I could. But," he said, "I'm not going to lose a soul." He said, "I didn't come to Cheticamp to lose souls. I came here to save them." Because he was the priest. Because maybe he thought to himself, if she was meant to die—well, then maybe the sorcerer would die, whoever he was. "Well," Jeffrey said, "if he comes bothering us another time—me, I'll do something." "Well," Fr. Fiset said, "I don't care what you do—but me, I won't do anything." (*He didn't want to kill the sorcerer.*) No, give another chance—perhaps he'll change.

Anyway, the same noise was there. Jeffrey Crispou—in his room he woke up. It was all afire. He woke up Fr. Fiset. Said, "The house was on fire, but," he said, "the fire doesn't burn." So it was in the wintertime—I think it was maybe in Lent—I don't know—it was in the winter, anyway. There was snow. Jeffrey went outside and he made a snowman and he took his gun. And he was walking three steps, and backing two. You know? He went at a distance with his gun. Then he was walking forward on, two, three. Then back one, two. Then he was always walking a step ahead each time—walking toward the snowman. And he had his gun. And when he came to a certain distance, the distance he was wanting—well, he shot him in the side.

J. J. Chiasson added: He built a man with snow. He wrote the initials of Charlie Romeril. Then he fired the shot of a gun in this statue of snow. And by gosh, it was after that they heard that Charlie Romeril was sick. And he was sick, sick, getting weaker, and the doctor couldn't do anything with him, didn't know what was wrong with him. So it went on.

J. J. Deveaux told us: The handyman told Fr. Fiset, "At night, when I wake up, a team of horses was coming," would go on his bed, big horses. He said, "You better do something!" The handyman made a snowman and he named it. He named the snowman. He gave it a name. Then he took a shotgun and he shot him. And Sunday morning, my grandmother told me, he was there, "Don't touch that man. Don't touch anything on that. Let him melt there." And about a week after, two weeks after—the man died. He was getting weak and weak and weak, and when it melted, the man who he named the snowman from—he was not sick but was getting weak, weak, weak—and he died when the snowman was all melted. I don't tell you that's the truth, but I heard it from my grandmother....

Marie: I don't know how many times he shot him. Then he went home. The noise ceased. No more noise. And the girl, of course, was well—Fr. Fiset had made her well. But little Charlie Romeril, he got sick. He was sick all the rest of the winter. And when the snowman was melting, as the snowman was melting, little Charlie was getting worse. They heard he was getting worse and getting worse—and he couldn't go over to see the snowman. He

206

was very sick. And melt, and melt—finally, when it melted to the ground, little Charlie died. And that's the real truth—because my grandfather told me—that was his time. He was not a part of this, but he remembered.

Marguerite Gallant: And that Charlie Romeril is buried on the Island (Cheticamp Island, in the graveyard near where the Jersey firm was once located). He was a wealthy, wealthy man. He had a beautiful tombstone. (*I visited his grave today.*) Did you? Is that big black sheet of marble still there? (*No, no. All that's left now is a piece of white marble.*)

The foot of Charlie Romeril's was a piece of marble about 5 feet square. Let me tell you what Charlie Romeril's monument was like. It was a big slab of black marble. And then there was a nice great square of white marble. And then there was another smaller. And all those letters that were on it— they were all solid gold. You hear me? They were all gold. (*The top of the stone is gone. There's part of the word "remember." Then it reads, "Charles William Romeril, Native of Jersey, Born 4th January 1846 and Died at Cheticamp 21st February 1877, Aged 31 Years." On another side it has, "Not gone from memory nor yet from love but to his Father's home above." If there was a black slab it must be further under the ground.*) Or it's been removed.

You wouldn't see a piece of the cross, would you? There was a beautiful white cross on that monument. It was a big monument. It would stand about 5 or 6 feet high. (*Oh no, nothing like that, dear. But it looks like it could have been.*) But it is. I've seen it a thousand times. He was a very young man. And he was a very wealthy man, also. They dug that grave there 5 or 6 years ago. He's supposed to have been buried with a lot of money, lots of jewellery, gold watch and I don't know what else. He was one after the head man at The Point. (*There are only 2 or 3 graves to be seen there now.*) There must have been about 50 people buried there. You should have seen that beautiful graveyard. What vandals can do. It was beautiful.

That story about Charlie Romeril—it's supposed to be true. But you know, the lady he had—she wasn't big then. She was only 16 years old or 17. When I knew her, she was married, and she would always wear a red ribbon with three knots in it. Then when it would get worn out, the priest would bless another ribbon and put it on her neck. (*Was that her protection?*) Yes, supposed to be. Whenever it would get worn out, he would give her another one. If you would tell her that there is no *sorcier*, you'd get it. She knew better.

Jean Philip Larade: But he didn't die in the spring, he died in February. The grave is still there and I can show you the date he died. I remember when the book (Father Chiasson's *History of Cheticamp*) came out, old George (LeBrun) was always telling me about Charlie Romeril. I had it in my mind to go to that grave. I had to dig a foot deep to read what date he died. And after that I covered it back so nobody would see. Except me, I knew. (*The gravestone did in fact state that Charlie Romeril died 21 February, 1877.*)

Those Jersey people, when they came on the Island—there wasn't anything for them to do. They had to let go somewhere, those young people. Take young boys 15, 16 years old, that came out from Jersey—and here on an island—there was nothing for them to do. Except play dirty tricks. And they were doing it. (*Did they have girl friends?*) I guess some of them had. (*Were they girls from Jersey?*) No, no, there were no girls that came out from Jersey, I don't think. (*So these boys would be seeing Acadian girls.*) Yes. (*Do you think the community would like that?*) No, I don't think so, at the time. They were not the same religion. That's the first thing.

(*Were the LeBruns different from the other Jerseymen?*) They were not different, but they mixed more with the people, I guess. All the bad things that were said, were about young people. The young people that came here as clerks—they had a little devil in them. They were young fellows and they wanted to have some fun. (*I guess we forget how young they were.*)

I remember old George was telling me about Charlie Romeril one time—he nearly put The Point on fire. He had a little barrel of coal tar—I don't know what they called it at that time—something they were putting on the boat. He put the barrel on fire and he was rolling it between the old fishermen's shacks—and he nearly started a fire. At that time he was nearly sent back to Jersey for doing that. So the old people thought it was sorcery.

208

(*And back to Charlie Romeril's grave....*) At that time the spring was a lot later than it is now. Now, we don't have any weather. But at that time we had some winters. It started in November. I remember the old people used to haul all their wood in November. Sometimes it was in June before the ice was gone. So you can figure, the winter was a lot longer than it is now. And they didn't put something that wasn't true on his grave. What they put on his grave, you can go by that.

(And you can go by that: February 21, 1877. But Marie Deveau told us that thaws came often, in January and in February. And Mary Fraser, then head of the Cape Breton Regional Library, Sydney, found evidence of an extraordinary change of weather, two days before Charlie Romeril died. She found it in the diary of Robert Elmsley. He was Postmaster in Baddeck. He had received the gift of a thermometer, and delighted in taking the temperature. In his diary for 1877, we see that the weather had been cool all along. And then on the 19th of February, a south wind comes up after 10:00 a.m. It was 45 degrees F. at 2 p.m. on the 19th. On the 20th, at 8 a.m. it is cold again—30 degrees. By 2 p.m., 20. At 9 p.m., 16. And on the 21st, at midnight, it is -10 degrees. It stayed cold from then on.)

Marie Deveau: And then there were some others, another man who would put a *sort* on the cattle. Like with my father-in-law, it was on a cow. That man, he was a tinsmith. We used to call him "The Canadian." He was not Acadian. He came to Cheticamp, him and his wife, and he had a couple of sons, I think—and he was going from one house to the other. He was asking them if they had any pans that needed mending—he was fixing them. He was a good man for that.

And here, my father-in-law, he wasn't scared of the sorcerers—he wasn't scared at all. He used to tell them, "If you put a *sort* on me, if ever I can open my eyes, I'll kill you." He wasn't scared of it, not at all. "Well," he said, "Lubin"—my father-in-law's name was Lubin—"Lubin, I can put a spell in a cow's footprint." Lubin said, "If you do, if I ever find out— you're going to get it."

So, some time went by. One morning, my father-in-law went to the barn, went to milk the cow. The cow—its tongue out of its mouth. She was kicking and she was in her manger, but she was going on the floor. They couldn't make her get up. Then when she was up, she wasn't a bit steady at all—she couldn't keep still. And she wasn't eating any hay. And she wouldn't drink. They tried to milk her but they couldn't milk her. And they couldn't put the milk with the other cows' milk. There was maybe something in it. It wasn't good milk.

So my father-in-law said to my mother-in-law, he said, "Maybe it's some kind of sorcery. I'm going down in Cheticamp and see." There was a George LeBrun here. He was a Jersey. Some Jersey were good to throw a *sort*, but some Jersey didn't do that—but they would make the cattle well, they could break that.

George LeBrun, of course, he was a good man. He had a little store, selling like thread and needles and all knickknacks. He said, "Buy a package of new needles and go home, and go to the barn and get some of the cow's urine and," he said, "you put it in a bottle with some needles in it and then put a stopper on the bottle, tight, and put it in a place where there isn't much space, make it tight—put it in a place where the stopper cannot come out easily." He wanted to make the fellow—the sorcerer—dance. So my father-in-law came home. My mother-in-law said, "He came home. He was going upstairs. He had a bottle. He didn't tell me what he was going to do." They were saying that it wasn't nice to tell. You had to keep that a secret, what you were doing. If you told—it might work and it might not.

So Grandpa—I call him Grandpa—was going to the barn. He was trying to get some urine from the cow. And then the cow wasn't doing it. He'd be going to the barn and she'd be just starting and he'd go with the bottle—she'd stop. He said he had to wait the whole day at the barn, until the cow was so full of it she had to let go. She was bound to let go sometime. But she was trying her best. It took her almost a day. And he stayed there. And as soon as she—he got the bottle there. So he came in the house and he made his remedy—I don't know how he made that—and he went upstairs. He went and put it under some kind of rafter—tight. Grandma said she could hear him—but she would not talk to him.

So my father-in-law, he was making sail for the boats, for the fishermen. He used to work at that sometimes up to 12 o'clock at night. He was doing his work in the daytime—it was in the wintertime and he was going to the woods—and then in the evening he used to work at the sail. So one night, my mother-in-law was in bed and he was working. And then they didn't have the bathroom in the house, and Grandpa went outside—and gosh, he saw a big dog. He said he didn't know what colour the dog was. The moon was up, but he couldn't tell whether he was black or brown—but a dog bigger than he ever saw in his life. But it wasn't quite the winter, because there were still boats that were coming—and he thought perhaps it was a stray dog from a boat. So he came back in. He ate a bite, lit his pipe, and he started sewing again.

And by 10 o'clock or half past 11, something like that—my mother-in-law was in bed—all of a sudden, bang, bang, bang on the dor. "Lubin, let me in, let me in, Lubin. Awww, awww.... Let me in." And he went and opened the door—and The Canadian walked in. He said, "I'm in pain. I suppose it's my supper." He said, "I was over to that house"—that house is not there today—"I was over there. I used to take soda and water, but they don't have any. I hope you have some." And Grandpa went in the pantry and got the drink for The Canadian. And he said, "Aw, thank you, Lubin, thank you, thank you. I'll go back over there because they are waiting for me." So he went.

The next morning, Grandpa went to the barn and the cow was all right. He came back to the house. "I know now what it was—it was The Canadian. The cow was almost dying last night, and now she's well. But," he said, "I'll find out." He went to the mail, at the little store then—and the guy who was living in that house was at the mail then. He said, "The Canadian was over to your place last night, huh?" "Never saw The Canadian." "Didn't he come from your place, his stomach hurting, because you didn't have soda?" "We never saw The Canadian." See, The Canadian made that up. The Canadian used to go to that house overnight, and this time Grandpa believed him. He gave him the drink.

(*Let me understand: The Canadian came back because they were curing the cow?*) Yes, maybe he went in the barn, to see the cow, before he came into the house. (*He was forced to...?*) He was forced to walk or run. (*To look at the cow?*) Yes. He was in pain. Or perhaps he went to see the cow after he drank his drink.

It was so aggravating, having that in the barn. When she was eating well, when they were going to milk her, she would kick. And some other time, she was just lying down with the tongue out of her mouth, making some noise like as if she was dying. And Grandpa took his axe to go and kill her—but the minute that he'd get in the barn with the axe, the cow was all right. But if he had gone there and killed the cow—maybe The Canadian would have died. I don't know. But he didn't give Grandpa the chance to kill the cow. It was so aggravating.

And if he had've known that it was The Canadian, gosh, Grandpa, he was a man like that—he would have kept The Canadian on the step maybe an hour or two. Let him suffer bad enough—*then* he would have given him the drink. But your memory doesn't recall. The Canadian had said, "I won't be able to put a *sort* on you because you're not scared. But I can do it on your animals." And when they do something like that—you don't think it's them.

The sorcerer had to run. And if he couldn't get there in time, he would have died. The one who was throwing a *sort* on another person—if there was one working for her, like to make her well, well the one who had thrown the *sort* on her would have to go and see her, for her to get well. The one who had put the *sort* on her—if the saver was saving a girl, well, for her to be saved, the sorcerer had (to be made) to go back to her and see her. And if he couldn't get there in time—if the girl had a *sort* that was meant to die, he would die. He would die if he wasn't there in time. He had to go.

(*Let me be sure I understand. If I put a* sort *on you, and another person wants to save you....*) He'd do something to me. And you'd be so...you would feel so bad you would have to seek me, the one you have put the *sort* on. (*Because he was trying to cure you, I would feel that I would have to get to you?*) Yes. (*And see you?*) And see me. But sometimes they would get to you in a different person, they could change. (*To another person?*) Yes. (*So I would have to be part of your cure even though I was the one who put the spell on you.*) Yeah. Yeah. Yeah. (*I could come in other forms?*) Yes.

(*What was the dog?*) The dog—it must have been the sorcerer. Grandpa knew there was no dog like that, and at that time of the night. (*Did your grandfather think it was the sorcerer?*) Well, he said it was a warning or something. Because right after, that man came in.

J. J. Deveaux: I heard my grandmother one time, she had 5 cows, milking 5 cows—can't make enough butter for the table. She went to see somebody—I think it was George Lebrun, but I'm not sure—told him she didn't know what to do. He told her to go and get a scissor, heat it up, make the fire and get it red and put it in the butter drum and start to make her butter. She said she had to put a 20-cent piece with that. He told her to put that and put the scissor red in the butter drum. He said, "The person that is stopping you from making butter will walk out to your house—but he'll never get to your house." But she didn't heat the scissor. She just took the scissor cold and put it in the butter drum like a cross, and put in the 20 cents, and started to make butter. Said she saw a woman come on the road. She said when she got to the gate she sat down. Then after awhile she got up again and walked to the house and asked her for a piece of bread with cream. She gave that to her. She ate that. And she went. After that, she was making lots of butter—enough butter she was *selling* butter. That was the *sorcier*.

gave that to her. She ate that. And she went. After that, she was making lots of butter—enough butter she was *selling* butter. That was the *sorcier*.

(*Was the woman coming on the road the sorcerer?*) She didn't know if that was the right one. Because those people went as different persons. One time there was a guy, his wife got sick, and he had a colt—they both got sick. And he went to see George LeBrun, and George LeBrun told him that one has to die. He said, "If you don't want your wife to die, let the colt die." And he said, "About 2, 3 days after, the man, the *sorcier*, is going to go to your house, tell you the horse is dead."

So he was treating his wife the best he could, and he let the horse go. He didn't give anything to the horse. The horse died 3 days after. And his neighbour came to tell him his horse was dead. But George LeBrun told him the guy that was on his wife was going to tell him. The guy who put this on his wife and horse, he didn't go on his own. He went *like* the man's neighbour. If he went there (as himself), that man would want to kill him. He went looking like the neighbour. (*But he was really....*) He was really a *sorcier*. But he went looking like his neighbour. (*And this woman on the road....*) It may have been the *sorcier*. He didn't want the people to know who he was. He'd go as another person. (*So if I would come to your door, you would never really know whether it was me or the sorcerer.*) Because the guy whose wife was sick, he never thought it was his neighbour. He knew him right well, that was a nice man, that was an Acadian. That's the way my grandmother always told me.

Denise Deveaux: There was an Englishwomen, lived on the mountain.

would sit one in each doorway, and you weren't supposed to talk or anything—and that woman was going to come if they boiled the needles—but they couldn't boil them too hard because she'd be dead before she got there. (*Now take me back. What had happened here?*) That was the same as for the milk, they couldn't make any butter. (*But it was a different time?*) Yeah. They'd be milking the cows and the milk would be all sour. They couldn't make butter or anything with the milk. And at last somebody told them—I guess it was that same guy, that George LeBrun—told them to put some needles, I don't know how many, on the stove and boil them. (*In what?*) **J. J.:** Milk. **Denise:** Milk? **J. J.:** Take some milk and put it in a container on the stove, put needles in and boil it. **Denise:** I thought it was water. Anyway, boil that. But they weren't supposed to boil it too hard. They had to give time for that woman to get to the house. She was living on the mountain somewhere.

She had to come to the house and she had to go down the well where the milk was—whatever she did there, I don't know what it was. (*Where did your father and your uncle have to sit?*) One on each door—one at the back door, one at the front door. (*Looking out?*) Yeah. And they couldn't talk. If they did talk, that wouldn't work. And she came. She came in one door and she went out the other one—that's all. And down to the well. And then after that, the milk was all right.

But that woman, I remember my father saying, she went there for something one time—I don't know if it was for a churn, the things they made the butter in—and he refused it. And she put the spell on it. That's the way they were. If they wanted something and you didn't give it to them, they'd put a spell on you. Wasn't that funny?

Marguerite Gallant: There was this fellow, Pierre, he was working at The Point. And this fellow—I think it was the head clerk in the store—says, "Don't go home tonight, because you'll be afraid." "Oh," he said, "I'm afraid of nothing." "Well," he said, "you're going to be afraid tonight." He said, "If I'm afraid, it won't be of you, anyway, because I'm not afraid of you." And he said, "You're going to be afraid." And then the old man started to come home, and when he got to the cliff here—there was something that rolled down the cliff and it almost knocked him down. And it was an iron pot. And it was rolling and it was almost knocking him down. And this old fellow had made himself what you call a flambeau— with bark. And, you know, it was burning. He says, "You better not let me get you because I'll burn you." And all of the sudden he caught him by the ear—he came too near and he caught him by the handle of the pot. (*He caught the pot by the handle?*) Yes. It was one of those iron pots that had little legs, you know. He rubbed the flambeau between his legs and beat

214

around his ears and here and there. And the next day.... (*He rubbed it around the handles of the pot?*) Yeah. (And between the legs of the pot?) Yeah. And then he let it go. And he said he didn't see the pot afterward. But the next day the clerk at the store was very, very sick, and he had sores behind his ears and his legs were sore—and no wonder. Yours would've been sore, don't you think so? (*So the story was that he had made himself into the pot?*) Yes. He turned himself into a pot and came to chase old Pierre. But Pierre wasn't afraid of him. He said, "I never enjoyed myself so much. You can go home and go to bed now."

J. J. Deveaux: They take any kind of shape, to scare you. But they cannot hurt you like that. If he takes the shape of an animal, he can't hurt you. Or the shape of anybody. But he can scare you. What Marguerite told you, about taking the shape of a pot—the pot cannot hurt him, but can try to scare him. That's just like the one where the little horse died—he took the shape of another man, to go and tell him. He didn't want that man to know who he was.

Marie Deveau: And then after that there was one man—and he was from Cheticamp. (*We'll call him The Acadian.*) He was going from one house to another—he was going on a Sunday when the man would be at church—if the wife would have stayed with the children. There was always somebody home. I remember one time he came here after everybody was gone to church. And he wanted to know if my first husband, Charlie, wanted some baskets—he was making potato baskets—and I told him I didn't know if he needed some baskets. "But even if I *knew* that we need some, I wouldn't give you the order. It's Sunday, it's God's day. And we don't make any sale on Sunday." It was worse than now. People didn't want to work at all on Sunday. Less making orders. I said, "If you want to see if my husband wants something, you'll come during the week, he'll be home." But he didn't come.

But me, I wasn't scared. I wasn't scared at all. One day he came here on a weekday. I was all alone—I was giving my oldest boy—he's 56 now—a bath in a little tub. He was a baby. And it was a northeast wind, not very windy. It was windy enough. He came here. And he always had his prayer beads—you know, making believe. He let the door go, and the door banged and all the cold got in the house. And the baby was in the little bathtub. I said to him, "Go shut your door. Don't you see the child is freezing there?" "Yes," he said, "yes, and yes, and yes"—and he went and shut the door. He said, "I'd like to have some bread." I said, "Just a minute, you see I'm bathing the boy. Now, I'm going to make you some tea, and I'm going to give you some bread and butter if you want some. And

I'll give you some flour to make some." "Oh," he said, "flour—that's too dirty. I'd like a big bread." But I didn't have a big bread. I said, "I'll give you flour." "Aw, no." I said, "If you don't want it like that, then go home." So he didn't stay here.

But they were saying that if you were talking about them, if it was on a Friday—they hear what you say about them. I was wishing he would come here. Maybe it was on a Friday. He was going next door here—and he was making the woman give him all the fat pork, you know. (*Just say, "Give me"?*) "I'd like to have a piece of fat pork." Then she'd go in the barrel and she'd get the fat pork and she'd give it to him. (*Why?*) She was scared that he would do something. Me, I wasn't afraid, not at all. So I said, I wish he'd come here and ask for fat pork. I wouldn't give him fat pork. I would give him salt herring. He didn't like herring, he didn't *want* herring—he wanted fat pork. If he came here, I decided I'd tell him we have some nice herring—I believe that he heard me. I believe it.

One day we were at the table here, having our dinner—and he knocked on that door. We said, "Come in." He came in. I still see him. He said, "Good day, madame. I suppose you wouldn't have some nice herring?" He had me fooled, huh? I said, "Yes, we have some nice fat herring." "Well," he said, "that would be nice." So my husband went and got him four big herring. "Thank you, thank you, madame"—and he didn't thank the others, because it was me that had said that. He didn't ask for fat pork. I guess he was just wanting to make a mockery of me. He heard it and thought to himself that he would come and ask me for some herring instead of meat. He'd rather meat. Me, I wouldn't give him any meat. Funny, huh?(*Well, it is funny—but what does it mean?*) I don't know. He always lived like that and he never got any money for it.

(*Did he ever put a spell on anyone?*) Not over here—but he was bothering the cattle. Like, the woman couldn't make the butter. He went in a place. He went to a woman. He wanted something. I think it was a blanket. She had a crowd of kids and she wouldn't give him the blanket. I'm not too sure. But it was something that he wanted. And the next day she couldn't make the butter...she could churn and churn and churn and no butter, no butter. So when she was tired of it, she took an old-fashioned clothes iron. She put it on the stove . She got it right hot. And she passed it around the top of the churn. And a couple of weeks later they heard that that man had his neck full of—it was all raw. (*Like a boil?*) Almost like that, but flatter. There were scabs all over. He was wearing a handkerchief tied on his neck every day—and then they found out. It was like a burn. That's how they found out it might have been that. (*And after that, would the churn work?*) Oh, yes. It worked the next time—as soon as she did that (with the iron). Maybe he went at night, when the cow was at pasture—he saw the cow. He was bound to go. He *had* to go. He had to see the one who he was bothering.

J. J. Deveaux: That fellow—(The Acadian)—a fellow killed him. There was a guy, he had a bunch of hens. He had some words with (The Acadian), and he told him he's going to be sorry, he's going to lose his hens. "You're going to be sorry. You're going to lose all your hens." I think he went there for eggs and he didn't want to give him some. "You're going to be sorry. You're going to lose all your hens." Almost every morning he went to the barn—a couple of hens dead. One morning he went to the barn, there was one that was not dead, but he was pretty bad. He just took the hen and put it in the oven and closed the door, tied up the door. Made a big fire in it. Cooked the hen alive. Cooked the hen alive. A week after, (The Acadian) was in his bed. All one of his sides all burned. He died from that. (**Mrs. Deveaux, laughing:** He didn't turn the hen over. He only burned one side.) **J. J. Deveaux:** He was burned on one side and it was getting bigger and bigger—and he died from that. That's what I heard from the people. I never saw it myself.

.   .   .

(*So you say the Jersey used the sorcery on the Acadians.*) **J. J. Chiasson:** Yes. If they found anyone they thought was weak-minded so they could work on you. They didn't want to tackle one that wasn't scared of them. (*But why did they do it?*) Well, I don't know, as far as the Jerseymen—unless to put it in their mind to go to their store instead of going to other stores. Might have used it for that purpose. (**J. J. Deveaux:** They wanted to try to get control. Of everything that was going on in Cheticamp—that's what they were trying to do.)

(*But were only Jerseymen sorcerers? Were there French people, too?*) **J. J. Chiasson:** Not any more than what I told you already—that some of them believed that the ways of the Jerseymen were all right. And they may have been in with the devil, too. That's the French people, some of them, a few of them—yes. Oh, 3 or 4 families that were.

(*Marie, tell me this, when you were small, when you were growing up, was the devil that real?*) **Marie Deveau:** Well, not in a sense, but in a way, you know. (*In what way was he real?*) Well, he wasn't real among us because I think it was a better time then than it is now. Because I think we were more, maybe, more religious. I don't know. (*Would the priests or your parents say the devil wants you, will try to get you?*) Well, some priests.... Still, before they'd finish their retreat, they'd always say that God is all, surpasses the devil, you know? That if we want to confess our sins, we'll be all right. (*And the devil himself, was it ever said that he was* *seen in Cheticamp?*) No, no. The devil wasn't seen. But they were saying that the ones that were doing that, they must have given themselves to the devil. But maybe it wasn't that. It was some kind of magic. I don't know. But some of them were bad. If they would have a word with you and you can't convince them, or if you would have the best of them—well, they'd turn to that.

I remember when we were small we all had each a Saint Benedict. It was a medal. It was saying on (it) that it was meant for sorcery. I don't know if it was, but we had faith, just the same. And there was a lot of that sorcery indeed, but there weren't many of us in it—because people were so scared—everything that they'd see. And they'd do a lot of things. (*To break a spell?*) Yes.

They say if you put a knife—if there is a sorcerer after you—and if there is a fence, if there is a post—if you open your knife and put it on the top of the post, the knife half-open. (*And that would stop the sorcerer from getting to you?*) Yes. And they said that they cannot pass over a bridge. And that's how people would manage to get away from them. When they'd come to a bridge, they were safe—because they said they weren't crossing a bridge. They can't pass over water.

One of them, his wife—she was going to homes to help when they had babies. She came to help my grandmother. And then she stayed there for 15 days, until my grandmother would be all right to take care of the kid. And then my great-grandfather was living with my grandfather. And they were saying that every afternoon she was going upstairs to take a nap. And while she was taking a nap, they were saying that she was with her mouth open—they were saying that is what they were doing, those sorcerers—they were opening their mouths and they were sleeping like as if they had been dead. And all of a sudden a fly—a big fly—was coming, hmmmmm— and right inside.

My great-grandfather said he didn't know that when that lady came to take care of my grandmother. He said, "If I had known that it was that"— she was going upstairs, every afternoon, to take a nap—he said, "I would have gone upstairs and taken a handkerchief and covered her mouth so that the fly wouldn't have been able to get in, to see what would have happened." But he didn't know. You would have to see it to know it. But someone told the sorceress that story, that my great-grandfather said that. She said, "I don't believe that at all. But," she said, "if I was sure of that, that he said that, I'd put them in a *sort*, that Lubin"—that was my grandfather—"would not sleep with Judith any more." You know, Judith was his wife. She would bother him so much, he wouldn't be able to sleep with my grandmother any more. But they were nice to her, she wouldn't believe that he said that. He *had* said it, but she wouldn't believe.

218

The Jerseys and The Canadian and the others—when they were dead there was no more of that. The generation was gone. I don't know where the Jerseys got it. But it wasn't only the Jersey people after that. That Canadian was French. And there was the man that I was telling—he was from Cheticamp. And the old Jersey people that were here weren't any worse than the French sorcerers. (*And today?*) We never hear of anyone being bothered. It was almost going too far. The least little bother that people had—they thought of the sorcerer right away. If one was sick or if one was bothered with something—some of them were so scared. Maybe they were making a sickness out of it.

An Editor's Statement, Halfway Through

This note is not meant as an "explanation" of the stories about sorcery. It should serve as both an afterword to those stories and a foreword to Herbert LeBoutillier's short talk about his grandfather, George LeBrun, a man who came to Cape Breton from the Channel Island of Jersey.

Jersey is one of the islands in the English Channel. It is off the coast of France but it is English territory—so the Jerseymen are English. But before they became English, they were French—just as before they emerged as Acadian, the people we know as Acadians were mostly French. The French who became Jerseymen were French Catholics who became Protestants and are known as Huguenots. They eventually made up about ten per cent of the population of France. But they were a prominent, visible and economically powerful minority. Out of a variety of attempts to destroy them, convert them, or work out a compromise, came eight religious wars, including the St. Bartholomew's Day Massacre in 1572—an apparently localized attack that was taken as a signal to kill Protestants first throughout Paris, and then across France.

Adversity apparently strengthened the Huguenots, and their numbers grew. In 1598, Henry IV (a Protestant who chose Catholicism for the nation's peace) signed the Edict of Nantes, guaranteeing among other things the rights of freedom of conscience, public worship, to hold public office, to attend universities, and even to maintain armed forces to defend specified Protestant cities. Essentially, this resulted in nearly 100 years of internal peace.

Details aside for now, the edict was revoked by Louis XIV in 1685, and intolerance, demands for Protestant-held lands, cries of heresy and so forth, resurfaced. It led to the high point in Huguenot emigration from France.

To back up: it was six years after the Edict of Nantes, and unrelated to that edict, that in 1604 the first French settlement in Acadia was attempted on an island at the mouth of the St. Croix River. A disastrous winter was passed. In 1605 they crossed the Bay of Fundy and established permanent settlement at Port Royal in what would become Nova Scotia. We tend to think of the Acadians as French

Catholic, but they included Scotch, Basque, and Irish, both Protestants and Catholics. Again, we will not try to detail here the history of the Acadians, except to say that they emerged in the 18th Century as a distinct people holding enviable farm land and carrying on trade with both England and France, while England and France were in varying stages of aggression. With a mixture of conscience and pragmatism, the Acadians tried to hold themselves apart. They tried to give their loyalty to neither, awaiting the outcome of English-French hostilities. As we know, time ran out on them and they were dispersed by the English beginning in 1755.

To return to the Huguenots: in 1685 Louis XIV revoked the Edict of Nantes, and with it the rights and protections assured the Protestants. Even before the revocation, Huguenots had been leaving France, emigrating to countries that welcomed them: principally Ireland, Holland, England, Germany, and Switzerland. After the revocation, some who remained converted, some continued to live as Protestants—and actually, it was only ten per cent of the Huguenots (one percent of the population of France) that left.

While it was a dispersion and disruption of their lives, it is not to be too easily equated with the dispersion of the Acadians. In the first place, the Huguenots were wanted in France: Louis XIV tried every means to keep them there—short of granting religious freedom. While parallels of religious bigotry, coveting of lands and mercantile connections, and general distrust, exist—most of the emigrating Huguenots have to been seen as a people with portable wealth and trades, whose lives were not thoroughly bound up with land they had cleared, as were the Acadians'. Moreover, they had welcoming places to go where their faith was shared or tolerated. The Acadians carried away little for their future support. Members of individual families were often separated. Still, Huguenots often left under cover and threat of punishment if captured; they left behind property and unrecoverable debts; some sailed away in hidden compartments built into foreign-made ships—but often with gold and jewels hidden in barrels shipped with them. Among the several places to which they emigrated were the Channel Islands (Jersey and Guernsey), England.

Though the Acadians were actively dispersed beginning in 1755, there is evidence of their being driven from Acadia earlier. People described as "refugées de la Cadie" arrived in Isle Madame, Cape Breton, in 1749. An idea of their wanderings can be had from this record of one Jeanne Dugast: "Chose remarquable, dit Monseigneur, j'ai rencontré à Chétican, isle du Cap-Breton, au mois de juillet 1812, Jeanne Dugast, agée de 80 ans, veuve de Pierre Bois, laquelle m'a dit être née à Louisbourg, avoir été de là à l'Acadie, au lieu nommé le Grand Pré (Horton), puis être revenue au Cap-Breton, puis avoir demeurée à l'île Saint-Jean, ensuite à Remshic en Acadie, puis encore au Cap-Breton, de là encore à Remshic, puis à l'isle Saint-Jean pour la seconde fois, puis une troisième fois à Remshic, de là à Restigouche, de Restigouche à Halifax, de là à Arichat, puis aux isles de la Madeleine, puis à Cascapédia, et de Cascapédia à Chétican, et ne s'être jamais couchée sans souper."

The Acadians lacked both homeland, world connections, and other people of like ideas. They were sent to Louisiana, the Carolinas, St. Pierre. The English were determined to send them anywhere but to France. A remnant went to Arichat in Cape Breton.

The expulsion of Acadians ends technically with the Peace between England and France, 1763. England possesses Cape Breton. By 1766—just three years later—a French-speaking Englishman, born on the island of Jersey of Huguenot parents, arrives in Cape Breton representing the firm of Robin, Pipon & Co. His name is Charles Robin. He winters at Arichat. He is 23 years old. He establishes a fishing station at Arichat, and at first takes some fishermen from there to work each season at The Point, Cheticamp Island. The boats are returned to Arichat at the end of the season. The Jerseymen go back to Jersey each winter. Finally, a fishing station is established at Cheticamp Island. Whether a significant number of Acadians come to reside in Cheticamp because they know there is a buyer and supplier there, or whether Robin actually recruited them to establish there—this is to be learned.

What is known is this: a kind of circle came round, when two peoples, each once French—one Catholic and one Protestant—engaged in a merchant/fisherman relationship on the shores of Cape Breton. The systems of work, social associations, the villages themselves, and even the legends—are rooted in these backgrounds.

About the Jerseyman, George LeBrun

Herbert LeBoutillier, Cheticamp: George Le-Brun (of the Channel Island of Jersey) was my grandfather. He was just a general handyman who was well-educated. And people used to come to him to write letters and to get things straightened out, maybe about land and taxes or roads or something like that. He had studied by himself, and he could do veterinarian work. A lot of people would have trouble with their cattle. They'd come to him and he'd help them out, solve the problem. They accepted him on equal terms. He was a kind old fellow—very charming old fellow—and he'd help anybody. But all during those years, there was always a big division between the communities, because of religion. The community was French Catholic. And the priest didn't want the Protestants to fraternize with the Catholics. We were considered the English Protestant, though we spoke Jersey French quite fluently.

And there was a dislike generally against the Robins or the Jersey firm—whatever name you want. They looked at them—and you'll hear and read stories on this given by the French Acadians—they pictured them as the villains who took advantage, exploited them. You have to understand the fishing business the way it was set up—the Acadians here were basically farmers at first. So this meant that a company that was going to do business in fishing had to advance them for the equipment. This made big debts. So, the firm would advance the necessary means. They'd even build the boats, equip the boats, sails and oars and trawls and that kind of thing. And the fishermen would come down in the spring, get in the boat. There was bait, hook and line and food—everything was there—they just had to get in the boat and sail out. Of course, things like food were booked against them. And this overhead had to be paid for by the fish.

So there was a case in question which I always remember my father saying. He used to go down when the boats would come in, see what their catch was like—he was manager of Robin, Jones & Whitman at the time—and he'd say, "How are you doing?" And this one day a bit of a breeze had come up and they'd come in early. So he was wanting to know why they came in early. They said, oh, they couldn't do anything with the trawls, blowing too much. And he asked the fishermen, "Well, I hope you picked up all your trawls." "Oh no, no," he said, "it was blowing too hard—we just cut the lines and let them go." He said, "Oh, my gosh, that's expensive." "Oh," he said, "that's all right. We'll go and get another set from the company." I don't know how they figured it. They seemed to think because it didn't cost them any money, all they had to do was go and pick it up. So he said, "You must realize that every time that you increase the cost by doing things like this, it's going to lessen the price of the fish." And then, of course, I would hate to tell you in French what would pass in the language used, but it would be pretty rough, and they'd swear at the company and call them thieves, robbing from the poor. Somehow they thought the company should pay for this equipment, but not take it out of the fish, which business-wise was impossible. And this is part of where the attitude was fostered toward the Robins. Also, Fr. Fiset was quite a businessman as well as being head of the parish here. And he ran the store and the post office.

In those days—you don't hear so much about it now—but there was a lot of talk about sorcery and witches and things like that. And the Jerseys had the name of being *les sorciers* or witches. And that came about for various reasons. One thing, the way I see it, was that a lot of them (the Jerseys) were young fellows, full of devilment—and I often heard my father talking about some came from the city, used to call them "townies" as compared to country people—and they were full of hellery, they'd do anything for a joke—and the people being naturally superstitious—by naturally, I don't know where it came from, but it seemed to develop in the Acadians themselves—things they couldn't explain, there had to be a sorcerer somewhere. This is the way they explained it. Somebody was sick or something strange happened, if they didn't know how to explain it—so they played on this. They weren't averse to build up stories.

And generally it was involving things like this that they would come and see George LeBrun. He was—what would you call it? (*Able to take a spell away?*) Yeah. To withdraw, to send out the bad spirits—that sort of thing. Well, here's how it worked. I'll give you one instance. He had enough psychology in his thinking to know if you told a person, "You're crazy, believing in that," right away they'd turn against you, they wouldn't even speak to him about it. So he encouraged them to speak about their problems. And they'd come, and he listened to them. That was the first thing. The second thing was that in their mind, sorcery was something vile and wicked—and something always bad. So the opposite of bad was good. Which would be for him to come from the Bible. Or in some cases he'd tell them to go to church and say certain prayers or do certain things—and this is where the Bible stories came in. He'd give them Bibles and give them certain passages to read and study.

In one instance that I remember them telling me: there was one fellow came, and I think it was his daughter was reacting a certain way. And he was sure that a spell had been put on her. So there was always the thing that you had to recognize who was putting the spell. And if you recognized this, then you could take defences against this person. So he came to see Grandfather and he asked him about it. And in some cases, by the way, he would also suggest them to take treatment from the doctor. Because in some cases the child could be sick, really sick, and they'd think it was sorcery—and they'd do all kinds of hocus-pocus stuff which was not doing any good for the child. If he thought it was something serious, he'd tell them. But just also to help the person get rid of the spell idea in his mind—in this case he told him to take a 5-gallon lard pail. And this was to find out who was putting the spell. And take a red hot iron. And there's two what they call "ears" where the hoop that supports the pail is fixed into the pail. And right below those ears—around what would be the "neck," you know—make a searing of the pail right around that. And he gave him certain prayers to say. And he did this. And then for the next couple of days, he was to watch who would come out obviously with a burn around his neck. And they came back—"Oh yeah, so-and-so, we saw"—I don't know, he came out with a scarf or something around his neck, he'd hurt his neck. So they found out to their mind or way of thinking who had put the spell on them. Possibly it's not true at all. But it satisfied the person.

This was a sore point in those days—my grandfather giving out these Bibles—because I remember when I went to the convent the nuns used to say that nobody should read the Bible except the priest, because the priest was the authorized person to read the Bible and give out its meaning. And the priest at the time was very much against people having Bibles. But all the Protestants here used the Bible. That was the source of their belief. And I suspect that a lot of these stories of sorcery were put out to keep the people away from the Jerseys. Intermixing. It was a barrier.

(*Did George LeBrun say to these people, "Go away. It's not true"?*) Oh, no. When they came to him and talked to him about sorcery and family problems and things they had in doubt—they came to talk to him because he was a good listener—things they felt they couldn't talk to anybody else. Questions that came up in their minds, legal matters, tax—they came to him because they felt, being an outsider, he had no reason to take advantage of them. He listened to them. He counseled them. Another thing he used to do was pull teeth.

(*But he didn't say, "Go away, there's no such thing as sorcery."*) Some times in discussing, I've heard him say, "You're crazy. What *is* sorcery?" And sometimes in anger, points of contention—he'd send them to go see the priest. "You go to your source of information." (*But if they came to him for help, he wouldn't say....*) Never. You see, when they came with these ideas, they were convinced—like the child in this case had a spell on her. He knew it was useless to deny it. So he went along with their thinking, giving them a means of escape from it. And being a religious man himself, he looked upon sorcery as evil. And he counteracted that by giving them passages in the Bible that generally referred to love and God's power. And he talked to them about that.

(*But do you see what I'm saying? In this way, it seems to me, George LeBrun was encouraging a belief that sorcery was real and could be dealt with.*) What he was trying to do was by reading the Bible, that you would escape from it. (*Oh, there's no question he was trying to help. But he wasn't trying to say it wasn't real.*) Because he thought it was too big for him to put down. Because the source of where they got this information was the source of their beliefs themselves.

And remember, this sorcery was also a belief amongst the Acadians, from the Old Country. Sorcery in the Old Country was a real thing. Joan of Arc was put to death because of it—and there wasn't a religious difference there. The French had roots of it, if you want to go by races. And the Jersey people are French—banished Huguenots from France, banished because of being Protestants. (*What about the attitude of the Acadians toward the Jersey as merchants?*) Well, they always felt that the Jersey were taking advantage of them. They didn't seem to understand how business was being done. And maybe I'm sounding as defending, but as I said, there was another business up here (Father Fiset's), and therefore there was a certain antagonism. And where there's antagonism between one business and another....

When you bring in these prejudices, you're bringing in the lifetime experiences between two groups of people who are very similar in that they're French in origin, different in religion, and different in background. The background being that the Acadians were people that lived in Canada in the colonization period, way back—and they were trying to develop their own community, and now you get the merchants who are coming in, who are seen as opportunists, you might say, who take advantage of these poor people. This is how the whole picture is portrayed. But it's not black and white like that. When you look at the results of these people, the traders who came from Jersey, who came and settled here and became Canadians—over the years, like in the case of my grandfather, none of them made any great wealth—they just survived. From my experience, none seem to have exploited other people more than anybody else in the community then. Because there was a certain amount of exploitation—taking advantage of the community—done in the community by the other business people, among the Acadians themselves, as businesses were run in those days.

I came to my grandfather to discuss things that kids were accusing us of. Just being Catholic meant that you were going to go to heaven. Being Protestant, you were damned right there without even a chance—and this bothered me no end. So I came to my grandfather and he'd chuckle and he'd open the Bible and he'd read, "Those who believe in Me will be saved." This was part of learning. No matter what people said about you when you got the facts, the truth—you could face anything. And of course, the Bible was the truth as far as his religion was concerned.

(*When you asked about sorcery...?*) He'd laugh about it and he'd always give me some off-hand excuse— "They didn't understand." In some cases, as I grew older, he explained to me that superstition and sorcery were in the same class, and it existed because of *not* understanding, especially about things about God. And that really when people could not explain when things did not go the way they wanted, they associated it with something bad which was evil, and that was done by sorcerers. And I suppose people incurring everyday life—it was hard, and people didn't understand why it went that way—it must have been a sorcerer that did it. And therefore his attitude was to try to educate the people, that they should look

225

for truth—and this is why he went to the Bible. His attitude was: he was so sure and confident within himself that good was the only thing that should exist in the world, therefore if everybody understood about good, it *would* exist between people.

The older generation knew him. They accepted him. In fact, they missed him greatly.

The Jerseyman George LeBrun

Our thanks to Elizabeth Beaton for permission to read for background her "Sorcery Beliefs and Oral Tradition in Cheticamp, Cape Breton." Herbert LeBoutillier's talk was edited, with his permission, from a combination of his tape with Ms. Beaton and an interview with Cape Breton's Magazine.

A Visit with Bill Daye, Painter

Look, I was a machinist. I worked 10 years at machine work on the steel plant. I worked 14 years for the highway department, heavy duty construction, repairing all the old equipment on the ferry boats, tearing down locomotives in the steel plant too, build them up from nothing, to refit them all over. Anything'd go wrong. And those big tractor shovels, used (to) tear them down and refit them, build them all up.

I was a farmer for 17 years. I was a trapper and a hunter I don't know how long, and I was a taxidermist years and years. I had a business of taxidermy and fur work. I was a mail carrier in Sydney. And I was in so many things that when I'd go out in the woods, I could pick up a little blue violet and worship that more than the prettiest rose that was ever made. And the way it was created and how it showed up in the spring. I see the beauty in those little things, you see? And praise I'd see in the woods and like that, I didn't get enough of them in here, in my body—I couldn't paint it. Then I'd have it in the house anyway, you see? So that's what I was trying to express.

And you've got to be a draftsman one year before you go in the machine shop to learn your trade as a machinist. You've got to work from blueprints and drawings. So, I had the technique of drawing from that. And I went to night school, learning drawing while I was in the drafting office. You've got to be accurate with no give or take when you're doing machine work for ships and all, that's got to be right. You can't change it.

The Ice Man

City Water Sprinkler

Because somebody'll come back and say, "That didn't work." It won't work if it isn't right. See? And being a taxidermist, I know the posture of the animals and birds in order to paint them. So I learned my painting, what bit I do know, in a different manner than going to school and getting instruction. I learned it the way I lived. That's where I got it.

These old pictures, those old horses and those people who are operating the horses—that was the way those people lived in those years. And that would be lost, because when I was young there was nobody painting like there is today, there were no artists going around painting. I never heard of an artist when I was young, only a photographer. And they couldn't paint the things that were there if they wanted to, because they couldn't paint. Well now, as I grew up and I learned a bit about painting, I wanted to keep that that was going to be lost. I wanted to keep that for the generations that're coming. That's why I paint those things. I can't write and I'm not a good speaker, but painting will tell it in a way that I can do that. That's why I paint—to record history, in the only way I can record it.

(*And what you paint, it's not just what you were told....*) No, no, no, no, no. Those horses, they are painted from memory. I can see them just as plain—and if there was a cracked window in a house, I can remember it.

I was starting to paint when I was about 16. But I let it go for maybe 20 years or so. I didn't do any when I was working machine work and that. I didn't have time. And my daughter sent me a box of paints one time for a Christmas present—my wife asked her to do it—"Get him painting again." And I started, I suppose that would be 25 years ago, and I haven't stopped. I keep painting now and then, a picture some months, some months none. And before I tackle that picture, I can see everything. I'm studying unconscious all the time, all the time—and I get one thing done, I can see the other. I can see the exact colour, the exact figure that's going to come out. Yeah.

(*Do you ever dream about your paintings?*) Yes, often, often. (*Before you paint them?*) When I'm concentrating on them. Sometimes when I get up in the morning I have it half done when I wake up. In my mind. (*You know what the colours are going to be...?*) I know exactly, because it takes a lot of mixing of paints to make colours, you know. Now, I painted a picture of a Dutch ship, an old, old ship that's not in existence any more, and to get the colour of the water that I wanted, I had to mix gray, white, French ultramarine blue, and cobalt blue, and a little speck of gray mixed with white and black—to get the colour of that water that I wanted to get there. And sometimes when I wake up in the morning I've been mixing colours for 2 or 3 hours in the night, while I'm asleep.

(*Do you ever feel that the old people almost want you to do something like that?*) Not that they want it, but I feel responsible, that this thing shouldn't be lost: the way people lived those days, the hardship they went through to live, and the kind of lives. Of course, it was best to them because they didn't know any different or there wasn't any other way to live. That was the circumstances. And I figure if I can put that down so people can remember it, I'm satisfied, I've done it.

I think it matters a whole lot, that people know what was. It may make people feel how easy we're getting by in one sense compared to the hardships they had. We don't have to put up with all that to live today. It would be nice for people to know, the youngsters, what went on and how our parents lived. I think it would be. Because there was nobody that could paint, only me, I know them. They didn't paint before, like I said, and they didn't know that story. I paint it so to preserve it. So it's not perished, not just lost with the wind, like tearing down a beautiful structure hundreds of years old is wasted.

(*Is a photograph the same thing?*) No. I'll tell you. If you take a photograph.... Now let me explain it this way: There's all kinds of music and language and everything going on right here that's being broadcast from broadcasting stations and we don't hear it, isn't there? The house is full of it. But you turn this thing on, the radio, and you'll get it. That's mechanical. Now I can take a photograph that I take with a camera—that's mechanical. Every process of taking that picture is mechanical. It's vibrations, that bring that sound to a sound, it's a thing that you don't feel or see—it's vibrations, and you can make that into a sound with the right equipment, see. That screen on the television shows you what the vibrations look like. They look like a picture. The vibrations from my mind and what I'm thinking, that picture is here—it has come from my mind to the canvas. I make it with the brush as my mind tells me, and that's made with vibrations that went through a human brain, not a machine. It's a different thing.

How would I know what red was if my brain didn't tell me what red was? That red, that comes right through that brush, and that brush makes what that picture is in your mind. Well, that went through a human body, all that paint. The other one's just a camera—a machine made that. They don't look like the same thing, like the thing you're looking at. They haven't got the depth. They haven't got the living thing in them as the painting has got.

What really brought me into painting was the taxidermy work I was doing. If I'd go to mount a sparrow or a fish or something, I had to think of the background in the case that was going to go with it. And that had to be painted pretty darn good. So I used to do that, too. And that old black house that was burnt, every wall in that house had a painting on it that I'd put on the plaster. Right on the walls. I had a big old hound that was half fox and half beagle. And I painted his picture on the plaster wall. And his ears were terrible long. I painted the frame on the wall, and I painted his ears out over the frame. And a fellow came down to get a deer head mounted. "My God," he says, "you mounted the old dog!" And I had a painting of the big falls in North River. And there was a painting on the wall of a hunter. There were three deer leading and one you could see the red where he was struck, and he was collapsing, you know, big deer. And there was another one of a red fox, digging the bones that he had planted, out of the ground. See, it was still nature. (*And what did your wife say about it?*) Well, I didn't hear the remarks she made, personal remarks about it, but she liked it alright. (*I mean, there aren't too many wives that let you paint on the wall.*) No, well, that was my nature. I suppose she wasn't going to kick about it too much.

And when that house burned, we had all new plumbing put in it that year, in the fall, and it burned at Christmas, in such a snowstorm that the fire wagon couldn't even get out.

I never started recording this history till maybe 10 years ago—or something like that—that kind of painting. I got right in earnest. I want to get the history of all those old things that are gone and like horses, the way people do with horses. I drove a grocery wagon for Rod MacNeil one time, delivery groceries, winter and summer. I drove hauling coal. I was a milkman at Blackett's Lake. That painting's down in the college there, when I was a milkman, where I'm coming up with a big 10-gallon can of milk. I was in an awful lot of different things through my life. It all adds up to make a picture now, different things....

And this black house (*next page*), that was my father's house. He built that when they were building the steel plant here. He was a coal miner in Port Morien. That's where I was born. I came to Sydney when I was two years old, we moved in here, see. And he was working at the steel plant. And he built that house from scratch. He carried all the lumber for it on his back over from Chappells to the Pier. It was all woods and swamps going over there. There was no clay road. And he built that house and lived in it. And I remember my mother always had a beautiful little flower garden, you see? And a picket fence. And this old fellow that had this hurdy-gurdy we called it, a little organ that played different old-time little tunes like you'd have for skating in the rink yard, la la la you know, like that, and he had a plug hat on. It was a round hat and it was hard like a beaver hat, and he had it all cut here and showed its white thread, so he looked poor and miserable, you know, and he always had a queer forlorn look on his face, cuts on his clothes, and a little patch here and there. And he used to come occasionally, 2 or 3 times through the summer with his little monkey. He'd play the little organ tunes, and the people would give him a dime, or

whenever the monkey came up to the door they'd give him a few pennies or something. That's the clothes they wore those days. And they had long hair hanging down. And there was never a railing on that front step. That was the way it was made, the way it stayed. It's marked on the back where each house was located and who built them.

This is the Constantine School, up at Ashby Corner. This was where

Jimmy Moore used to drive the Butternut bread wagon. And there was a water trough at the corner, right where that is, and the horses used to stop there to drink. And all the schoolchildren used to have a drink. I often had a horse on one end and me on the other. The horse and the water was clean, circulating and going down all the time, running through. This is going to be destroyed any time now; they're going to tear this down. It isn't safe—there's something wrong, something the matter with it. Maybe not big enough or something. So when I heard that I said, "I've got to go up and paint that." And I went out to see this Jimmy Moore—he lives out by the K-Mart—and I got a photograph of his horse and wagon. And he was getting in the wagon, and you couldn't see the horse, only part of him, the sun was shining, I could hardly see anything, but I got enough of the wheels—and I've seen the wagon so many times—to finish the wagon. But this was on it, this fellow with the bun of bread, the Butternut Boy, and Jimmy there.

Now this one, the horse and coal wagon, the dump cart they called it—you ever see a dump cart? Well, now I couldn't find one, and being's how I hauled coal myself, I said I've got to paint it. And I went down Number 20 mine and I made a painting of the coal mine. There was nobody around with a horse, a wagon like that, so I found out that a man out in Dutch Brook, a MacSween man—I mounted a double-headed calf for him one time, calf born with two heads—and he said, "I had, Billy, one of those dump carts," he says, "and it's years and years," he says, "and it's up at the end of the farm there over the fence." He showed me where. "And it's likely to be buried in moss today," he said. And I found a few sticks of it,

and I raked away all the moss and found the spokes. I counted the number of spokes in the wheels. I had a tape measure and a tablet with me and a pencil, and I got the description of the whole cart right to the inch—from pieces. And that's how I got the picture of the dump cart.

Boats and wharves and lobster pots and all that—I don't care for that. I've got to paint something that really exists and has got something behind it and that's worth painting, you know. (*A lot of people do paint....*) That's *all* they paint; a flower, or some roses, or a lake or some trees or some lobster traps and fishing boats—you see that everywhere. I could paint that all day long. I've got no interest in it.

This is "The Angler's Prayer." **Bill reads:** "This actual-sized trout was caught in Gillis's Lake, East Bay, Cape Breton, April 30th, 1943." I laid the trout on a piece of cardboard, and I cut out the paper the shape and size of the fish. And in years after, when I wanted to paint the fish, I'd go down to the brook and catch a little trout and take him home fresh to get the colour. Every time I wanted to paint, I'd go get a new little trout in the brook. Oh, God knows how many times.

There were two ships, passenger ships, used to sail from Sydney up the St. Lawrence to different ports. One was called the *City of Sydney*. Big white passenger ships. They were repairing some part of this ship and putting in new heavy canvas on the deck and down the galley ways, you know, the inner part of the housing on the boat—not the outer decks. And those big sheets of canvas, when they'd be dirty, they'd destroy them and put new canvas, just like you'd put a carpet in a room. And Capt. John Buffett—he was mate on this boat then—he brought up this big piece of canvas to my mother and said, "Here, Mrs. Daye, this'd just fit your kitchen floor." And she got the canvas, she put it down on the kitchen floor,

and had it painted some sort of blue or bright green. And after that wore on the floor for years and years and years, she threw it out. And this day I wanted to paint a picture. And I said, I'll use it for my trout. Because I was painting on paper they paint signs on, before that, you see, and it wasn't so good, wouldn't stand up. And I took that old piece of canvas out in the back yard, I turned it over and I sized it with sizing. I gave it 2 or 3 coats of good white paint, and I painted the trout on it. And there it is.

("Winter Pork.") I was there when he killed the two pigs. He shot them first with a .22 rifle. And he had an old door or a big piece of heavy 3/4-inch plywood on the saw-horses, and the pigs were laying on there and they shaved them. A big barrel of water and knives—the wet bags to lay on to make the pigs warm, you know. He didn't dip them down in a big container of water. He just laid them there and steeled them and shaved them, and then he hung them in the trees—nice trees there in the scene, too, and the old poles the pen was built out of. And the pig house that they lived in was a house for two dogs that a fellow had given me.

So they lived in that house all the time till they died, till they were killed. And it's got a nice red roof on it, which gives colour to it. And laying on this big board is the liver and the heart, and the two knives stuck in the board, and all the hair on the board, that was shaved, and some on the ground. And a big old water trough is there, too, and the bag there laying on the fence, the big bags he had there steaming them with. Even the rope and the pulleys and the way they're tied—one facing you and the other one, the front facing you, you know, where he's cut and you see the inside.

A woman once asked me about the two pigs. I said, "That's a wonderful pig there." I said, "They're both good because they're fed on buttermilk, cream, curds, yogurt and everything, because the man next door was working for the milk factory—whatever you call it—and he used to bring home all this because one pig was his and one was Jackson's." She said, "I know, Mr. Daye, because that was my husband. I ate most of that pig."

You ever see a mackerel sky? I put a mackerel sky in a picture, and I tried a dozen times, but I could never do it again. That bloody brush just went. I said, "Don't stop that brush, leave it go, boy, you got something you'll never do as long as you live." And I could never do it again. The fashion of the clouds in that sky, that mackerel sky, I've tried and tried and damned if I could ever paint it, and I never saw anybody that ever did paint it. And I got it in there. The brush just started to go, whatever came up with me and that bloody picture, I said, "Jeez, I'm doing something today, don't lay off, keep it going"—and I did. And everybody that's seen that picture, they say, "How did you ever get that sky there?" Isn't that funny? That queer odd shape—that came out perfect.

I read about a painter one time, he had painted a certain thing that he had been a long time practising and practising. At last he did it pretty well, and he went to move around the house and a little dog came over and peed on it. I don't know if it was water paint or oil paint. Well, he came back and said, "Merciful Christ!" he said, "that's one thing I had in my heart all my life to do, and now it's ruined"—so he put it away. A few weeks after, he looked at it, and the water went through and made a picture that nobody in this world could ever paint, and he said, "Jesus, he did something for me this time." It made a picture he could never do, how it blended the colours. I read it in a book.

My father landed in Neil's Harbour. The old merchant down there, he owned the fishermen, what they'd fish. He got the fish, what he gave them was whatever he wanted to give them. They lived in hardship with this man. You know. He looked after the place. Well, without him they wouldn't exist, and just vice versa. So anyway, my father got fed up with it and said, "I'm going to leave here, I'm going to work in the coal mines in Port Morien. I'm going somewheres, I don't know where I'll go." And he left his house standing where it was. And he packed the whole family on a great big two-masted boat that they had. My mother was sitting on the deck like old Granny Clampett in the movies there, in a rocking chair with Tom in her arms. And Rufus said, I remember he said—I wasn't born then, see—he said, "You could see the phosphorus running from the boat in the salt water." Ever notice the phosphorus? And he said he was laying

236

with an oar, holding, watching the phosphorus going. And Jack, the older brother, he was at the wheel, and the old man was telling him which way to go. And it was calm as glass and there were big rolls. He sailed from Neil's Harbour and he landed in North Sydney. And he got into North Sydney and he couldn't find a place to live, a house or anything else.

So he stayed there for a day or so, and then he took off and he landed in Port Morien. And some fellow came down to the wharf, and he said, "Where are you from?" He said, "I'm from Neil's Harbour, and I'm going wherever the fate of God put me right now—I'm through with that place." And he said, "Are you a fisherman?" And he said, "I fished for a good many years." And Jack was old enough to fish. And he said, "When could you go fishing?" "When I get a house." He said, "I'll give you a house, right tonight."

He got a fellow to come down and help them take the furniture to the house, and he said, "When are you going fishing?" "I'm going fishing right this evening, because I passed a place—I know where there's a good place to fish." They have that instinct, they know by the land, the lee of the land, whatever—he said, "I know there's a good place to fish, I found it on my way up." And he went out, and they fished all night, and him and Jack came back with a schooner-load of bloody good fresh fish. And he said, "You're the kind of man I want." And he fished for that fellow for years and years, and lived in that house, and that's where I was born.

Bill Daye and his friend Edna Daye

Serving on the Mine Rescue Team

The words "dragermen" and "mine rescue team" are used here inter-changeably. "Drager" is the older term. It comes from Draeger, which is the German company still making mine rescue breathing and testing apparatus. The photo below is of the first drager crew formed in North America at Numbers 2 and 9 Collieries, Glace Bay, 1909. Other action photos are of a simulated disaster during a Mine Rescue Competition in Glace Bay, 1976.

Allan Atkinson, Glace Bay: Drager crew (the Mine Rescue Team) is called for fire. That's the big thing where you have to wear your drager equipment. Not only a fire, any time when the ventilation is disrupted. Now if you have an explosion big enough that your stoppings dividing your fresh air from your return air were broken down—your gas would mix with your fresh air—and that would be a job for dragermen.

When I got my second class papers, I started loading coal and I started going to night school. I studied for shotfirer's papers. And I remember I got my shotfirer's papers

on a Friday and I started shooting coal on a Monday. And it was just shortly after that that I went on the drager crew in 1940.

(*Was the drager crew something that you always wanted to be on?*) To be honest and truthful, I didn't know what it involved, really. (*I guess I'm sort of asking whether dragermen were your heroes.*) No, not really. We were requested. Managment asked us if we wanted to go on the drager team. What it involved at that time was one Saturday a month. You'd go to the office and you'd either travel Number 20 Colliery—Number 2 Colliery at that time—with your equipment on, or you'd go to the smoke-house with a smoke mask on, and cut logs, build stoppings—to get you used to the heat and smoke and whatever.

On a Sunday night, 1943, somebody found a fire on a belt level. It was about 4 o'clock. And 6 o'clock I was going to go in the mine on day shift, and we got word about it and had to go right to the drager office at Number 2 at that time. And you had to get all your equipment and check it—and then we went over to (New) Waterford. The first day or so, it wasn't too bad. We were using stone dust and water. You could use stone dust and water until it burnt the lagging out—the wood that holds up the roof, where you had your arch booms. And these arch booms hold up the wood. And when it burnt the wood out they allowed falls to come in. And with the intense heat, the arches started to bend. They don't crack—they bend.

You're briefed. "Certain level, 21 East, there's a fire on the coal level and it's out of control right now." And when we went in the mine, a supervisor that was used to that section went in with us so far, to show us where to go. We were green as—you know, as far as that mine was concerned.

The fire was burning ahead of us. It was mostly wood and rubber belting. The stone dust was to smother the fire. But after awhile it got to where you couldn't get into the fire. It was advancing. We had to go down to the wall below and walk up the wall face and come in against all the heat and the smoke that was coming out. When we had to go down below and come in again—before you left, you were given salt tablets. And for each drager team, there were two or three fellows carrying gallon cans of water. And when you'd get in, you'd drink an awful lot of water. But once you get into the heat, your skin would dry up for just an instant. And then the sweat would come out on you.

We had to dig a keyway in the stones on the ribs and on the roof and on the bottom—18 inches deep and 18 inches wide—in order to erect a stopping. We used picks. Had to be dug all the way around, so no air could escape around it, you know. We built this stopping, and then we packed stone dust. The fire was quite a piece away. But the heat coming towards you. It's hard to explain. It was mostly smoke. When we had to

239

go around the other way, we were taking some brattice up—brattice cloth. So instead of having to face this heat and everything, we were running some brattice along and then sealing if off so the smoke and that would go on the outside. We would still have to have our equipment on. We'd come inside that. Working with 4-inch spikes, copper hammers—that's all you're allowed to use so you wouldn't make a spark—I'd hold the spike and he'd tap them in. Then the fellows coming behind would put the boards up. The brattice would take so much of the smoke away, they could see what they were doing. And they also built a stopping on the outside end, to cut the air off. They tried putting water in. But the heat was that great that the air would bring it back as steam.

(*Did your stopping stop the fire?*) It stopped it, yeah. I guess we were there almost three weeks altogether. Fought the fire for quite awhile, trying to extinguish it with water and stone dust and whatever. When we got organized, we were 8 hours at the fire and we were home maybe 12, then you'd go back 8. (*So there'd be 3 shifts of dragermen fighting the fire?*) More than that. It'd take you two hours to go to the fire. And you'd be there two hours fighting it. And it would take you two hours to come out of the mine. Then you'd come up, get washed—and they had a restaurant in Waterford closed. All they were doing was making sandwiches and feeding dragermen. Then they give you transportation home, pick you up. The first three days we stayed over there, slept on the office floor, cold egg sandwiches—but they weren't too long getting organized.

I was a dragerman from 1940 to about 1948. (*And 1943, that was your first big one?*) The only big one. In 1953, I went to 1B Colliery. And I was supervisor on a wall. And 1954—I'd only been there 7 months— when in Number 26 Colliery they had a fire in 3 Deep going into the south side. That fire started around 7:00. At 11:30 I was in the lamphouse and the underground manager said, "Just the man I wanted to see. Get a thousand feet of telephone wire and an electrician and somebody to lower us away into the colliery, and take it in there"—that's how I arrived in there that night.

Dragermen were called. Oh yes, that was a real smokey fire. What they were trying to do was take the water they were pumping out of the mine and pump it into this 3 Deep and flood it. And on the way in there was 1 Deep and 2 Deep. They were changing the air line into a water line. You know, your compressed air runs into the mine to run your different air engines and whatever. They were changing the air line into a water line. Well, they made the changeover on the pit bottom. But they had so many leads off it for air to different parts—and they wanted to direct it right into 3 Deep. To do that, they had to close valves to 2 Deep and 1 Deep, the Arch Deep. The dragermen did that. That's where all your smoke was.

It was in 2 Deep where one man—his machine ran out of oxygen. He was in fresh air when he found out about it. So he just sat there. And his buddy went and shut the valve off to stop the water from coming down 2 Deep. And when he came back, he was dead. The gas was after coming out the lower level and backing down to where this man was. All they could do was take him up, carry him up into the fresh air again—but it was too late. They worked on him about 3 hours—artificial respiration—and the doctor gave him a few needles. Stuff like this, trying to revive him. I worked on him quite a long while myself. I had gone in with this telephone wire.

After this man—we'd sent him to the surface—we went out the Arch Deep. There was coffee and a few sandwiches sent in. And we were sitting in a box, eating, and this fellow, a dragerman, said, "My gosh, you're lucky you haven't got one of these on"—you haven't got the drager gear on, something like that. "Yes," I said, "all I have to do is sit here and look wise."

So while we're in the box, word came to go and shut the valve off in 1 Deep. So it was shortly after that we got word that this fellow I was talking to was down. Still in there. And the other 4 dragermen came out. There was one of them wasn't feeling just right. So they asked me, would I go in, see what we could do about getting the other fellow out. So we got a stick so long and held onto it so we wouldn't lose ourselves in the smoke. Just two of us.

(*You had the drager equipment on then?*) Oh yes. I got it from the regular dragerman that was sick. And it came out at the inquiry that this was the bad equipment.

So we went in to find the man. We got to him, might have pulled him 30 feet or so. He was a big man. My boss, when he was helping me put

In Mine Rescue Competition, each team arrives under guard and is turned over to the judges. The team gets a sealed problem—details of a disaster in a mock mine—studies it, decides what to do, requisitions supplies. They test their breathing apparatus and answer questions, then they are taken to the smokehouse.

the drager equipment on, had said, "Whatever you do, be careful." He said, "We lost one dragerman. Watch yourself." But I guess this equipment was leaking. There was an air line going in. Next thing I knew, I had fallen over the air line. I was bent double, I was looking at my feet. And I was just thinking to myself, Look where I am after being told to be careful. I was lucky enough. This fellow got an arm over his shoulder, got me out to where I could get fresh air. They gave me artificial respiration. (*And the other man?*) Well, they were awhile getting him out. I was in the hospital then. (*And he died, too?*) Oh, yes. Two dragermen died that night.

Gordon Whalen, Glace Bay: A fire in a mine isn't like a fire anywhere else in the world. First of all, a fire in a building, the outside world is probably only through a door or a window to you, if you're caught in that building. Or blow a hole in the wall. But the outside world's maybe 5 or 6 miles away from the guy caught in a mining fire. Different thing altogether. You have very little carbon monoxide from a fire on the surface because you've got all the atmosphere of the earth to dilute the CO. But in the mines, she's loaded with CO when you have a fire, because the fire's in a confined space. It's been known for a guy to die two miles from a fire from carbon monoxide poisoning—two miles away in the mine from a fire. It's a completely different world.

So the fire's got to be handled very differently. You can get very close to a fire in a building or on the surface, and put water on it. You may not get within 1500 feet of a fire in a mine on account of the heat that's generated, because the fire's in it like in a bottle—it's like in a tube. And it's burning—but the heat is what keeps you back, is what poses your worst problem. You can get on the intake side, where it's getting its air from; you can get pretty close to the fire on that side. But on the return side, where the fire is tending, well, you might not get within 2 or 3 thousand feet of that fire on that side. So the only thing you can do with a fire like that is seal it off. You rarely can fight a fire directly in a mine if it's spread, if it's of any dimensions. You can fight small fires. Once a fire gets beyond control, the only thing you can do then is either flood it, flood the area, or seal it off, to cut the oxygen off.

Dragermen have to build fire seals, bulkheads, whatever you call it. They have to build a seal with boards and plaster. On the air return side, only mine rescue teams with breathing apparatus can build that one. Because that's where all the dirt is, on the return side, that's where all the gases are. Coal not only generates carbon monoxide, it generates hydrogen sulfide, sulfur dioxide—very poisonous gases. But on the intake side, you can use ordinary miners—barefaced miners—for that. But there has to be men with breathing apparatus when those ordinary miners start building those seals on the intake side. There has to be a close check kept for carbon monoxide backing up on them. Even though the air is flowing away from them, the carbon monoxide can back up. So the rescue team gets right in past where they're working.

Actually, rescue teams, you could compare them to a volunteer fire department. They're volunteers, certainly volunteers. They're paid a day's pay a month, one day's pay a month, that's all. Now we have those mine

The Mine Rescue Team goes to the smokehouse. Before they enter, nurses take their pulse. The smokehouse tests equipment and the men—reactions to black, heavy smoke from oily wastes. Pulses are taken when they come out. They go on a brisk 2-minutes walk. The captain checks the team again—equipment and emotional stability—before going into the mine.

rescue competitions down at the Forum. Those guys travel, they come here probably 4 times a week for two months before that competition, to train for that. They don't get a penny for that. Nothing. Do it on their own time.

(*Let's put the competitions aside. You know, if you're on a drager crew, and a fire breaks out anywhere, you're liable to be called; and if anybody has to get close to it, if anybody has to deal with it, it's liable to be you. Why would you volunteer to do that?*) I really couldn't answer that question, why. We've never had any trouble getting volunteers. I have a waiting list here all the time of young men. We maintain 6 teams here in Glace Bay, 5 men to a team. Actually, there's 36. We carry one extra man per team, in case a man may be injured or hurt. (*So there are 36 men in Glace Bay alone that are ready, that if the worst thing happens in any mine, they're going to be at the front of it.*) Yeah. (*And you can't tell me why.*) No. It goes back so far. We've always had rescue teams. And I can't tell you why they do it. I don't know.

Rudy Plichie, Sydney: Mostly, I think the biggest thing I was in that gave me a lot of satisfaction, was the fire, the big fire they had in '75 at Number 26. I think the mine rescuers should be credited with the fact that they saved that mine. I was at home at the time. I was called by Gordon Whelan. He told me, "Report to the mine rescue station at Glace Bay." I was in at the kitchen, and I was on my way to work. I was on my way to the foundry. And so immediately, when I get a notice like that, I expect the worst. And when we got there, then we knew it was a fire.

We checked out all our breathing equipment that we can work with in this type of an atmosphere—gases. And before we entered the mine, we were examined—blood pressure, look into our eyes, possibly a quick medical, I'd call it, with the nurses. But the thing they really concentrate on mostly is your blood pressure. I think it's great protection for the people involved. They're making sure that you're up for it. In other words, that you're calm, you're not excitable, and that your endurance is good. You never know what type of work you'll have to be doing there. It might be strenu-

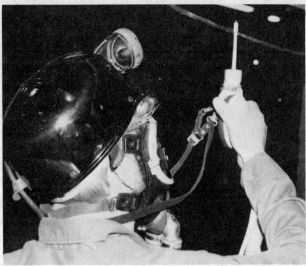

The Mine Rescue Team travels the mine, the captain testing for gases (above) and with a probe—a wood cane tipped with brass or copper—testing the roof and sides. One hand on the stone, he strikes, and vibration tells whether it is solid or loose. When the team stops, the men are ordered to kneel, to rest. Commands are given by a horn. He can't talk. Breathing under oxygen, he has to breathe slow and deep, heavier out than in.

ous. And I don't think you could work under those conditions if you weren't in the condition, if your pressure was up.

Before we entered the mine, they gave us a briefing. Mostly to the captain, and we're standing by. "There's no life involved, at the time, but there's a possibility the fire's out of control. But," he said, "I want you men to know I'd rather lose the whole mine than lose one of you men on this team, or any other team that will enter that mine. So take it with caution and be very careful." Then he went on with the briefing. He told us where about the fire would be, and actually what to look for, testing for gases, how far the fire's out of control, and what area. And what would be the best place possibly to extinguish the fire. So we were to bring back this information.

We go in. We travelled into the mine—in the rake—we had to travel for about 45 minutes to get to our destination, I think. It's a submarine mine, as you know, and I think our destination was maybe 5 miles underground, maybe 5 miles and a half. (*So you're riding a rake, heading toward a fire, and you really don't know what you're....*) No, at that time we don't know what we're going to face. (*What are you talking about?*) Well at that time, we're not actually talking about anything. I talk personally about myself as an individual, the first thing I'm thinking: I checked out my breathing apparatus, made sure mechanical A-1. I was always confident that I was always physically fit. Why I say this, because I always made sure I had two medicals a year when I was on mine rescue. And I always did test my endurance, even before I was on it; because I have a habit, I always work out personally, myself, I keep physically fit. So the big thing at that time is to make sure that all my breathing apparatuses are 100% mechanically. In this way I pretty well—I get a high from that. But at that time, you'd be surprised, things were pretty quiet, nobody's actually saying anything. (*You don't think that this could be your last ride?*) No, you don't—you're trained to a point that you have to discipline yourself or motivate yourself, because I think that if you didn't, I think you'd never get out of the rescue station, because you'd be rejected. Your pressure'd go up, and your nerves would be bad.

I think we got off at 10. We're all hooked up, except we didn't have the oxygen on. The first thing we do, we explore. We're walking. We're all together (both teams) until we hit dense smoke. We hit the heat and smoke when we opened the door on 10 South level. I think it was the return. Our captain gave us the signal—all signals are done by a horn—we hooked up. We're checked out. He checked us out himself personally. And we had a vice-captain, he checked us out. And we check out ourselves, all the gear, make sure that we can proceed in this atmosphere—it's full of toxic gases. We knew what to expect. And during this exploration, we're checked out, I'd say about every 6 minutes. To make sure that everything is working mechanically, and how every man feels.

And we had to determine how long will we be in there. The breathing apparatus is up to two hours, but we had to figure possible 3/4 of an hour to travel in there, 3/4 to get out, so we've got to set our watches. But we don't use up any endurance by talking or walking at a fast pace. I think by going slowly you can observe what's happening, and you absorb the knowledge, and this all helps to help to fight this kind of a situation. Our fresh air base was established outside the doors, on the level. I'd say it was about 500 to 600 feet—the fresh air base. We left the standby team there. Then the gases were checked out—the captain has all the readings, the different apparatus to detect different types of gases—the heat, how far we could travel at the time, the conditions in the level—like the heat at that time had bent the 10-, 12-foot steel booms, most of them. Then we encountered different falls that we had to caution ourselves. We had to go around them. And we had to make sure that everything was safe to travel. We went as far as we could to check. The heat got too severe at the time. And we couldn't see the fire.

So the heat was terrific. And we noticed that possibly there were small explosions, because some of the pump motors seemed to be moved off of their stationary positions. A lot of the pipes were broken, there was a bad

246

water condition. In some areas it was possibly knee high. So we returned at the time with this information and passed it on to the engineer standing by in the fresh air base with telephone communications. We took off our gear at the fresh air base. Management decided which way possibly this fire could be fought. But then it was a long endeavour.

Mostly it was done by barricades to cut the oxygen off to the fire. This became daily routine work. First, we'd stone dust the area. The barricade itself, it's made out of mostly stone dust, well packed in. And they have mortar that will cover the area, cut off most of the air. We had to do some sawing. We're building a wall, it's definitely a wall. Paste over it tight as possible at both ends. And you've got to work with a lot of caution, because if you did start a spark or a fire, it would cause an explosion. At that time I think we built about 5 in different areas.

Colin MacDonald, Glace Bay: What they usually do, when they seal a place off, they put the testing pipes in, and they monitor that on a day-to-

day basis, on a 24-hour basis. The idea of sealing a fire is to get rid of the oxygen content. If you have no oxygen, you have no fire. If the readings that they get from their tests show that a lot of oxygen's going into the area, that means a fire's still there. Then they start tightening up their seals, tightening up their stoppings. They know they haven't got a tight seal. After, they monitor that. These things seem to be right. The oxygen is practically nil, the carbon monoxide is just about gone, and you get a high reading of CH^4, methane—it indicates to them the fire has now been extinguished, hopefully. After doing that, then in order to assess the situation, you must do it with a team of people. They leave travelways in those seals. They build them in a manner where you could allow a team to go in without disrupting the seal.

247

During the disaster, the Mine Rescue Team maintains contact with the mine manager, telling what they've found, requesting materials, receiving instructions. The cloth in the competition symbolizes the boards and plaster of a stopping, a seal.

Rudy Plichie: *(While you were working, did you actually see fire?)* Oh yes, I had seen the fire starting out. Methane burning. The best way to describe it's something like snake-like. You'd see it possibly 30 feet at one side, 20 feet possibly behind you, next thing you know it's in front of you, next thing you know it's in the back of you. A snake of fire, yeah.

(Rudy, you didn't have to do this.) No, I volunteered. *(To my mind, mining itself is a dangerous job. Why would you take on the added danger of being part of the drager crew?)* Well, I'll tell you why. I was quite curious. As far as working in the mine at the time, I worked mostly on the walls, and my mining ability was just limited to that. I was kind of curious. I was wanting to find out more about the ventilation end of it, and more than the basics. And I thought, in order to learn more than the basics of mining, you actually have to be a mine rescue. And I think I absorbed more at mine rescue in one year than the average miner can absorb in 10 years of mining. Because there, you learn all the different gases, what causes explosions, and what the results are. I really feel that the average miner can't visualize this.

From the position I was in, in mining itself, I was just making a living, But I felt I'd like to expand it by being of some help.

You have a compassion toward your fellow miner. There's something there that's deep within you, that you'd have this compassion, that you want to help, you know. And I figured in order to help, I'd have to have training, because it would be disastrous without. But I had a thirst for the knowledge of mining, too, at the time, and I wanted to know more than the basics of mining. You're there, you're a miner, you're making a living—that's its limitations, eh? But I was wondering what's behind it all, how it all came about. And I figured the only way, with

248

my limitations, my educational background, to get a briefing on it—mine rescue was the place.

Gordon Whalen: Maybe you think that work is much more dangerous than I do. Would that be it, I wonder? (*Now that's very good. I do conceive of it as being not only dangerous, but courageous. I'm thinking, for instance, of the fire in 1975.*) The guys, fighting that fire—there was no one ever, ever went through what they went through. They were in heat that burnt the hair off of their necks and off their hands, those dragermen, the mine rescue teams. And their breathing bags melted in the heat. I don't know what the hell—they must have been in 140°. Those fellows sealing that fire—you're talking about 11 South. I don't think there were temperatures ever worked anywhere in the world like those fellows worked under here—to save that pit. It went on for weeks—must have been two months before we finally got that thing under control in the pit. But they were in that heat. And there were lots of ordinary miners that worked just as hard or harder than they did, to save it, too. That was one time that there was 100% cooperation. The ordinary guys, they were terrific, too. They worked—and worked any time. As long as they were asked to work, there were no holds barred, you know. That was probably the toughest conditions that rescue teams ever worked under. I was a team captain in both of the Springhill disasters as a young fellow myself. And they weren't as bad as that one was here. I mean, you weren't in that intense heat. You had a lot of other dirty things to contend with.

(*What happened in 1975?*) It's something can happen in a mine any time. You're mining coal, you're generating a highly explosive gas, methane, CH^4. There's 1 part carbon to 4 parts hydrogen. And hydrogen's the most volatile element you have. When that gas is generated, the slightest spark causes it either to burn or explode. Well, then you have coal dust. If there's coal dust in the area—if there's dust particles hanging in the air, tiny little things that you can't even see, or hardly see—that's more explosive than methane. And where can you mine coal without having them? Usually the methane starts, it's just the trigger, starts the explosion; and then the dust particles propagate it. It's something like an atomic reaction. Now when coal dust explodes—really, an explosion is a fast fire. If you burn coal slow, you get carbon monoxide and you get the other gases. Well, the faster it burns, the more is generated. And an explosion is a great big fast fire.

You get a heavy surge of carbon monoxide that can spread miles through the pit.

I never get into that—what caused it. Because my job is after the fact, not why or how or when. That's our approach here in the rescue corps, we don't worry about what caused it or who was at fault or anything like that. That's somebody else's business. Our job then is to try to contain that fire.

(*How did you find out about the fire in 1975?*) Oh, I just got a call, I always do, from the underground manager, and he told me there was a fire at 11 South. I just call the 5 captains. They call their teams. And in 10 minutes everything is rolling. That night, I'd say in 15 minutes I had 4 teams ready. They come to the station, test their apparatus. And that probably takes 15 minutes—the bench test—they know how to repair, charge, service, and maintain their machines. It's ready for use at all times. And a short time after, they went underground. (*Do they wear special clothes?*) No, no, just regular mine clothes. They put their pit clothes on, put their apparatus on, they get their lamp, and they go. A rescue team is only doing ordinary underground drudgery, but they're wearing a 30-pound pack on their back, and they're breathing pure oxygen.

There's three steps you have to follow. First of all, if there's any men in the mine, the rescue teams must locate them and get them to the surface. That's the first priority. Then the fire—see what can be done with it. Then, when the fire is sealed, they have to travel periodically and test those seals, to try and get an indication if the fire is out. Now when a fire is out, their next duty is to travel the mine and re-ventilate it and make it safe for men to work in. That could be months away. It may be three months before all the oxygen is used up inside the seals and the fire goes out. We speeded it up in 11 South. Along with the seals, we flooded it. That got us in there faster. It's the fastest and best way, but you can't always flood. Maybe the fire is where you just can't get water to. Sealing's your only way, then.

(*And 11 South, in 1975....*) That's spoken of all over North America, that particular one, because that never happened to rescue teams before. That was the hottest I ever knew or ever heard tell of men working in. And they weren't fighting it directly. They fought it from the intake side as far as they could. Then they ran into a cave-in that wouldn't let them get out to the other side of the fire. And they couldn't get near it from this side, it was too hot. And I'd say the seal—I can't be exact on this—it was probably 1500 feet away from the fire, or maybe even farther than that. But that was the heat there, that far away from the fire.

There were no explosions—this fire—I'm talking about 11 South. The one where the mine was threatened. There was no explosion there, just the fire started in gas. The drager crew weren't first at the fire. Some men (barefaced) started to fight the fire with water. Those men stayed and started to fight the fire immediately. Then they had to pull those men out. They said they couldn't fight the fire any more. It was getting dangerous; there was a possibility of an explosion. Then the rescue teams went in and they had to seal it off.

Albert McLean, Glace Bay: At 11 South I was a barefaced man. (*Were you in the mine already when the fire broke out?*) No, I was actually home, and I got a call. I went to the mine, and the manager asked me to go underground with the shift manager. (*You were mine rescue, but you didn't go as mine rescue that day?*) No. (*The fire was on, and you went down barefaced.*) Yes, we did. The drager crew—they were on the return side. But we were on the intake side, and there were men here that were down on the previous shift when the fire started, and they were fighting the fire. Just fighting the fire with a fire hose. Putting it across, and it goes out, and you advance a couple of feet, and all of a sudden the flames would drive you back. There she was, all burning. I guess there was grease and everything burning. She was just like a bonfire. We had the fire hose spraying around, and then we were advancing a few feet, and we'd think we were getting it out, and all of a sudden she'd come back in. We started to build chucks there, trying to make a stopping, but the fire drove us back.

The superintendent at the time, he was there too—he was a barefaced man. He called the manager in the office. Told him, "We have a serious problem here—we have to do something and do it fast." He said, "It's on-

Albert McLean, when he was captain of Team 3 of DEVCO Number 26 Colliery—the team we followed through the Mine Rescue Competition in 1976. Front row, left to right: Chief Judge Herb Zychorta, Albert McLean, Wayne Chiasson. Back row: Jim Proctor, Brian Duhamel, John MacDonald, Sheldon Gouthro, Angus MacLeod, Judge Tommy Baldwin.

ly minutes to do it." The manager told him, "Take the men off the wall face, come down to the bottom level, cut the belt, and build a seal down there." So we did, we left the wall. (*And there you were without any equipment.*) No equipment. Well, you were just willing to help and that was it. If you're there alone, I guess you'd get a little nervous. When you saw the superintendent, he was there—I guess everybody looked at him, and there was no fear. At that time, I think all the men that were there were just anxious to help. They worked tremendous.

When we put up the permanent seal, we only put them up so far, and then we had to get in communication with the fellows up above, and they had to do the same thing we were doing. You couldn't build a seal right to the top without the other one, because you might have an explosion. Different levels. We were down below and somebody'd be up at the top. Same mine, but they are, oh, maybe a thousand feet away—we were on the intake side, and they were on the return side. If you sealed one without sealing the other one, you could have an explosion. So we left about a foot from the top. This was mostly all stone dust, bags of stone dust, just packing them one on top of the other.

Then we got word within two minutes you've got to close the top in. At the same time. When you put the last one on here and the last one up there, everybody left, went out and got in the rake to go to the surface. Leaving the mine, the superintendent stopped the rake. He said, "I want 4 volunteers to come in here with me. It could make or break the mine." Must have been a hundred men got out of the rake. He said, "Hold on now, I only want 4." They went in. And I heard him after that saying, "The men would go to hell with me that night, do anything I wanted," he said. "The best bunch of men I ever saw." I got surprised myself when he asked for volunteers and everybody in the rake jumped out. He got an awful surprise. "My God," he said, "I only want 4, I don't want everybody!" They went in there maybe two minutes or three minutes at the most, came right back out and went up on the rake. I think they were only just checking the stopping for final approval before we could leave the mine for a 24-hour period.

Neil J. MacKinnon, New Aberdeen: I joined the rescue in 1926, I think it was. Number 12 was the first fire I was in on. Number 12 Colliery in New Waterford, which is closed now. Had fire there and they closed the mine, and the mine was closed for the vicinity of three months.... It got too hot and too much—and they decided they'd close it. When they close it, they cut all oxygen off. It should practically go out.

It was closed for a month or so and they shipped what they call dry ice from Montreal, and we were ready. It came special train, and the minute it came, into the boxes and we shipped it down the mine and put it in where

252

the fire was. There was a pipe into that (stopping) that you could put your machine on and measure the heat that was inside. So after about two months they opened the place out and put the dried ice in. We went in. There was no sign of fire there at that time. Everything was burnt black. So we put the dry ice in, piled it in. And then we closed everything off again. And it stood for another month.

Well, that dry ice gives off carbon dioxide. If there is any oxygen in there, that kills it. So we opened it out after a month again, and everything was cool and no sign of fire or anything

Neil J. MacKinnon

else. This carbon dioxide will go anywhere that air or water will go, find its way through. When we opened it up, we had our oxygen on. And the place was as cool...no sign of fire. So they got everything ready and started to work again. And Number 12 Colliery produced a lot of coal after that.

And practically, while I was on the mine rescue, I can say that every fire or explosion, I was the first man that went in it—I took the first team in. Gordon Whalen was on one of my teams. Gordon Whalen was on one of the teams the longest and hardest walk that ever I had—when we opened 26 Colliery. Twenty-six Colliery was closed for fire, and it was closed in the vicinity of two months. There were stoppings. There was no air whatsoever into the mine. And when we opened the mine, we took samples before we went in—there was 95% carbon monoxide and 2% air at the roof. It was solid carbon monoxide gas when we opened that. Well now, we had to travel a good mile with our machines into that solid gas.

I had 4 fellows with me, 4 of a team—and if any one of those fellows had of got in trouble, we were all in trouble. But I had trained them for three days—and I mean trained them. Gave them lots of gas and lots of air and walked them miles down the railroads, hooked up solid with their gear—they couldn't get any outside air. So I was pretty sure of their machines, I was pretty sure of them. I knew I was going in there. I picked my own men. I picked two men from Sydney Mines crew and two men from here. I gave them everything I could possibly give them. They knew what they were going into. So therefore, we had no trouble.

We opened up 26. We broke the stoppings down. Then we had to go a mile to break the other stoppings to let the air start circulating. Then we had to come back. There was no way to come from the other side. The other side, you were three miles under the ocean—that's where 26 is. The shaft is right on the cliff, practically. And if anything would have happened when we were in, they would have had to send another crew in for us—but thank God, we had no trouble. I didn't rush them. I let them do the work, two at a time. Had two standby in case they got in trouble. If anything happened to one of our machines, you get one breath of that, you're out, you're finished.

.   .   .

I was at Springhill in '56. There were two teams from Glace Bay. We got the call, of the explosion in Number 4 Colliery, Springhill. I was in church. It was a holy day. It was All Saints' or All Souls'. And they came looking for me. So when I got home, I went over to the old station. Got everything ready, and just after 3 in the morning, we left. We hit Springhill roughly about 9, and at 20 to 11 I had my crew into the mine. So we went in the mine, not too long—we went in to build stoppings to stop the fresh air going down to feed the fire.

I went in and the first fellow I saw was dead, and it was a friend of mine that had played ball down here in Dominion. I didn't know then who he was, but I covered him up with a brattice so the team that was working wouldn't see it and get a little excited or something. When we were ready to leave, I told them about it. We came back out of the mine. That was the first fellow, and it's funny, too, to think that I could know him. When I came up, I told them what I had found, where he was, and they told me who he was. Then we got settled, got our boarding house and got supper—and the next call was 10 o'clock in the night, our crew was called out again.

(*And what would you do on these trips?*) It was an explosion. Everything was there, full of gas. A lot of the stoppings were blown out and therefore there was no air in lots of places. It was gas. And we'd be travelling through that. We'd come across a body, we'd take the body and lay it aside. And there we went, looking for anybody alive in the mine. There's nothing we could do for those fellows then, they were gone. So just put them where we knew we could get them and take them out later. (*How were these men killed?*) Mostly gas, mostly got in gas after. The fire burnt the oxygen. Most of those men were trying to make it, I guess, to get out, and they got into the gas.

Anyway, Sunday morning, the boarding Mrs. came up. She said, "There's something going on at the mine, you'd better come down and check, see what's going on." Everybody was running. People coming in all directions. Running to the mine. Here the team that had been down, they found in the vicinity of 21, 22 alive in the mine. They were into a pumphouse. It had a door on each end. They had the two doors closed. There were 21 of them sitting around in the pumphouse, and they were taking turns with the hose, sucking on the hose and the compressed air, keeping them going. Well, the compressed air has a dampness of water with it, and that was helping them, too.

There was a gauge on the surface, of the compressed air. Everything was shut off because we were going to close the mine at 11 o'clock. A fellow on the surface noticed a little hand going on the compressed air. Now he was pretty sharp to notice that. Well, he knew there was someone alive in the mine, because somebody was using that air. So, that changed everything.

We had to go back in the mine. They found those fellows. Team went down ahead of us. We went down. We had to build stoppings first, that were knocked down, to get fresh air in before we could start moving them. In the meantime we got down to them, giving them raisins and water and stuff like that. Some of them were crying. So we started moving them. We set up a makeshift engine and a rope and small tram, and we'd take up either a stretcher case or two or three men on the small tram.

We started early in the morning. The last session that my team was in the mine, we were in for 12 or 14 hours. And we took them out. And the place was low. The place was about 4 feet. And there was a foot of gas still lurking at the top. Gas is light, see. And we were taking those fellows out and taking them through, and we had to hold them down so they wouldn't get this gas. Hold them down. Of course, we had on our machines. And when they'd get out to the fresh air base, the doctors were there and they had the oxygen, and as soon as we shoved them there they shoved the oxygen mask on them. And it reacted on them differently. Some of them started to laugh. And some more started to cry. It was really weird.

We had to take them out, and take them slow—and we had about 20 minutes left to take them out to the explosion doors. The explosion doors are double doors with a space between them—and they're steel. And we had to shut the fan off. She was ready to go again. We were taking those men out, and we were just watching. It could snap and we'd have another explosion. Another explosion could happen because we'd cut the air out of the stoppings—the stoppings were ready to blow. It could happen any time. It was getting very ripe to explode again. And the heat was severe. I was the last one to come out behind. My team—I had to have my team ahead of me. We got through the explosion doors. I closed the explosion doors—and that was it. That was the last of Number 4 Colliery. It was never opened again.

This explosion was '56. The bump was in '58. I wasn't up there at the bump. Because after that explosion they cut the age down to 45 (to serve on the Mine Rescue Team), and that left me out. But I was instructor after that. I trained the boys till the last day that I worked. And the last day I worked, in 1965, it was a Friday. And the next day I went over to the rescue station and I took two teams of men to train them, took them down the railroad for a walk with the machines, fully equipped—brought them back. And then I went home, and that was the last.

Gordon Whalen: I'm pretty good at sizing up men. The age limit for service in the rescue corps is 45. What I do, I go to the pit bosses, the underground manager. I tell him I'm short 5, 6 men, whatever I need. Probably I've got 5 guys here going to retire this year. I won't wait till those men are retirement age, I'll take them in before that, so I have replacements. He might give me 8 or 10 names of guys that he knows are reliable and so on. I tell them, Come see me. I don't make any judgments till I talk to him and size him up. Anyhow, I'll have them in here one at a time and chat with them. And maybe out of 7 or 8, I might take 3, or 2. You're looking for a guy that seems composed, not jumpy or neurotic. I'll have a pretty good picture of what they're like when they leave.

Now the training is more important. I mean, I don't think the selection system is important. The training—they're taught a lot of technical mining. They're taught all about the different mine gases, their weights, their flammability, their toxicity. So that's just a practical application of the knowledge of gases. Every miner should know that. Every miner doesn't know it. So we use the rescue corps in a teaching capacity, too, in the pit. They talk about those things, and they tellthe other fellows, you know.

We had a fire in Number 12 Colliery, and we got every man (out). They had to come through a bad atmosphere—that was in '73. Now we got about a hundred-and-some men out of that mine. We had to take them through a bad atmosphere, and take them right alongside of a fire, actually. But there were about 4 or 5 mine rescue trained guys there that got those men out. They told them, "Get on your hands and knees and stay there, and crawl through the smoke." And they all got out. Had they walked normally, they would have all died.

And another thing. The shortest way out of that mine would have been the returns, rather than the intake airway. Well, that's where they all wanted to head for. And those fellows told them, "You'll die if you go that way. You've got to stay here in the intake airway, to get out." And they followed them, and they all got out—oh no, one—we lost one fellow out of a hundred and some. And he had been located—he wandered off. They were travelling through smoke, remember, and crawling. And he was near the end. And a mine rescue fellow stayed at the end. They must have come through a particularly heavy cloud of smoke, and this fellow wandered off. They never knew that the other fellow was missing till they got to the surface.

Those mine rescue trained guys are sort of like apostles for safety, or escape, or what to do when there's a disaster in the mine. They're always talking this stuff any chance they get, and explaining to any group of new men in the pit. They say, "How the hell do I get out of here if they get a fire?" They'll explain to them exactly what they should do. Put on your self-rescuer as soon as you hear of a fire, don't wait for smoke and flame. If there's an accident in the mine, somebody hurt—"Oh, he's a drager-man"—immediately they send for those guys. Out of 36 men, there might be two or three in each section. "Oh, he's mine rescue—get him down here." And they're immediately handed over complete charge, and they take complete charge. They're there, you know.

With Number 26 Colliery behind him, Gordon Whelan stands in the mine rescue training area, posts and boards set up like a room-and-pillar situation. "The army can't start wars to practice. Well, we use competitions—training schemes and exercises. But no matter how many problems you create for them, it'll never be exactly what happens when they get down there. No, never exactly. A lot of preparation gives them good knowledge. But as far as what it's really like when the pit is burning—you can't create that on the surface."

Isabel Bartlett Remembers George

For nearly 20 years, George Bartlett ran a dairy in the village of Baddeck. He stood as a kind of unofficial greeter at a crossroad of Cape Breton. Before that, he worked long years in a gas station, and before that he made the barest of livings from what odd work he could find. Everyone has a story about George—in fact, we would like to gather those stories—the jokes and one-liners that gave laughter and insight to the day. It is to our great shame that we never interviewed George. On the other hand, his personal combination of privacy and bold-ness may not have made taped interviews possible.

George Bartlett died in September, 1984. We have since talked with his wife, Isabel, and we offer here portions of our conversations.

(*Where did you meet George?*) **Isabel Bartlett:** Sydney Mines. I grew up right here in Baddeck, next door. The 5 generations, the 5 houses—you could stand in the middle and throw a stone and hit 5 generations: my daughter's, mine, my mother's, my grandmother's, my great-grandmother's. You could actually throw a stone—they were all around here.

(*How did your people get to Baddeck?*) My Grandfather MacKenzie, he was a carpenter, and he was working here—he came from Boularderie. He was the first caretaker at the old post office, which is the public library now. They lived there, on the third floor and the second floor, when my mother was born. Now my father's father and his father (the Fergusons) came from Scotland. Directly to St. Ann's. He was one of the ones that had a falling-out with Rev. Norman McLeod. Rev. Norman McLeod told them to have nothing to do with this (certain) fellow. He sort of excommunicated him from the church, you know. I can't remember—was it a Munro or something like that—that didn't do things just the way Norman McLeod thought he should. (*How do you know that?*) Oh, just from hearing my father talking, and cousin. Anyhow, they looked out the window, and this man that was in dutch with Rev. Norman was drifting in a boat, something had happened. He'd lost his oars or something went wrong. So the Fergusons went out and got him, and (then) they were in dutch with the minister. He didn't think they should have. At least, that's the story as I was told.

(The Fergusons) lived in what they call Big Hill, St. Ann's. That's where I was born. My mother and father lived there when they were married first. It's all deserted now. I didn't grow up there. We moved to Baddeck when I was quite young. My father worked over with (Alexander Graham) Bell part of the time, with sheep and things like that. And my mother looked after—I guess it was one of Bell's children. And my aunt worked with Bell. She used to do stuff at the switchboard that he had from one building to the other. And she had to have her teeth out. You know, in those days there was no such thing as getting your teeth filled. And she had to have teeth out. So he made her come, and he watched her and made notes on how she spoke before and after she had her teeth removed. And he'd make her read out loud to him, and watch her. (*She was one of Dr. Bell's experiments.*) Yeah. And he'd sort of laugh sometimes.

(*So you grew up right here in Baddeck. Go to school here?*) The old Academy. And there was no money. Actually, we were desperately hard up. I didn't get to go to university or anything. But I had planned to go to be a lawyer—mainly, I suppose, because I liked to talk so much. And in those days we used to have debates, and I loved debating. So that was one thing I thought of. (*That you'd be a lawyer. Did you think you'd stay in Baddeck?*) I don't remember too much. I know my father didn't want me to go away. I remember him saying that—"You wouldn't leave your mother"—and all this sort of stuff. So I didn't. Anyhow, there was no possible way I could have, that I know of, really. 'Cause there was no money whatever. Well, it was in the Dirty Thirties when I finished school.

(*What about working away?*) No. Some were going away then. I didn't go. I wasn't encouraged to; I was encouraged to stay home. My mother wasn't all that wonderfully well, anyhow. I can't remember really wanting very desperately to go. But I remember when I got engaged to George and I was going to get married, my uncle in the States said, if I would put off getting married and go up there, he'd send me to college up there.

(*How does a woman from Baddeck meet George, a man from Sydney Mines?*) Well, his mother and my Aunt Kate were very good friends, and I used to go down and visit Aunt Kate. He used to take my cousin once in awhile to the movies. And when I was down there, he took her and I both to the movies. And after that he just took me to the movies!

He was desperately shy, terribly shy. Nobody ever would believe me, but it's the truth. Ask his brother. He'd go out the upstairs window and shimmy down on the verandah if girls would come in the house to visit his mother and his brothers, he was so shy. But he wasn't shy with me. We talked all night, the first night we went out. I almost got sent home in disgrace, staying out too late. Talking. About things nobody else was interested in.

But I'll tell you what—we were both queer, according to everybody else. My Aunt Kate said, "It's too bad to spoil two houses with you—it's better for both to be in one house." Because she thought I was crazy, the notions I had. And George's parents thought he was nutty.

The first thing we got interested in was the Spanish Civil War. He was the only boy I knew that even knew there was a civil war in Spain. I used to read a lot about that, and so did he. And we really couldn't believe it, that we had met each other. He was wishing that he wasn't lame, so he could go to Spain with the MacKenzie-Papineau Battalion when they went over. That's the first thing we had in common.

He wanted to go, and I was a fearful pacifist. I didn't think they should fight, even though I knew it wasn't right, what was going on. But in those days I never thought you should fight for anything. I knew people, you know, and it was just pitiful, the things that were happening. Refugees then. It's pitiful what happened to the MacKenzie-Papineau Battalion, how ill they were treated by Canada. You know, they were called "godless communists" and all this. And actually, they were upholding the legal government. (*In Spain.*) Yeah.

And we were both sort of socialists. We were both mad as the dickens 'cause they were selling all this scrap iron to Japan—all this sort of stuff, you know—we wouldn't even—when we were so terribly hard up—they'd

260

come around wanting all the old pots and stuff, but we wouldn't. I wouldn't even wear silk stockings, 'cause the silk was made in Japan at that time.

(*Was there no one else but George to talk to about the Spanish Civil War?*) I didn't know anybody. The minister in Baddeck at that time—he was J. Nelson MacDonald—he was the United Church minister out at Big Baddeck. And he had an awful lot to do with starting credit unions and everything around here. And people were mad at him for cooperating with the Catholics—they thought, "Wasn't that terrible!"—he and the people at Antigonish were together. And he and our minister, Allison Fraser, were very good friends. I used to hear him talking, too. And they used to lend me their books.

I'm just trying to think about Mr. Fraser, he's still alive—I wouldn't want to say anything wrong, mistaken about that. But he was very much against fascism early on, before anyone too much was, around here. And he preached a sermon one Sunday night—he's still a marvellous preacher—I wish to goodness they'd have him back for a service. And there was somebody from England, a writer for a paper that published good sermons from here, there and all. And they published his sermon, and he never even knew the people were there. He got quite a bit of people calling about it. Anyhow, when Chamberlain went and gave away Czechoslovakia to Hitler—the Sudetenland, and all that sort of stuff (1938).

We used to have church twice a Sunday then. I remember in the evening service, he said everyone was thanking God for peace, but he prayed God we hadn't purchased our peace at the expense of other people's freedom. Boy, the fat was in the fire! I mean, he had a hard time in Baddeck after that. They were watching him. When the war broke out. Years later he told me that the Mounties were even taking notes on what he was saying.

Allison Fraser and Nelson MacDonald were something in the same mold. Although Allison Fraser was very much milder. I consider it a great thing that I was able to have contact with those two men. I didn't have very much contact with Nelson MacDonald, only through Allison Fraser.

(*Why would they share these things with you?*) Well, I worked at the manse when they had the baby. I was finished with school. So I went and I worked there, looked after the baby, and the second baby. And he let me go in his library and use it, look at his books. And we always had a wonderful library in Baddeck. I always got books out every Saturday night, and had them all read before I went to school Monday. Really good books. We were awfully lucky, living in a little place like this, to have that.

(*And Allison Fraser—was he fired from his position because of his ideas?*) He wasn't fired. But it was made so difficult for him that he left. You know, when ministers get a call, it's always to a place that paid them more. He went to a place that paid him less.

261

(*So you found the town you grew up in a little conservative.*) Yes, in a lot of ways. But in another way, we had contact with the people coming to Beinn Bhreagh (Bell's home). And there would be famous people speaking, and we always had a chance to go. We weren't divided into classes so that I wasn't allowed to go, even though I didn't have a good dress, and all that. So I think we were very fortunate, in lots of ways. And I was very fortunate—my mother and father would let me read any book that ever was in the library. I could take it home.

And yet I was a terrible old maid, I was terribly moral—I missed an awful lot. I'm not so sorry for things I did, but lots of things I didn't do! Don't print that! Actually, I don't care about whether you do or not, because it's the truth. You know, I missed an awful lot by being too careful. (*Although you had ideas about freedom, democracy, and peace....*) I was a terrible moralistic person. I wouldn't take a drink, I wouldn't smoke. The body was the temple of God, and all this sort of stuff. I tried to eat properly—and look at me! I got fat trying to make George fat!

(*And regarding the Spanish Civil War, what was important to you and George about it?*) What was important to me about it was, it was a democratically elected government. The fascists were coming in. I mean, the forces of Mussolini and Hitler. Didn't they try out all their new weapons and everything there? Well, they would get up and speak in the League of Nations, and I used to read all that sort of stuff. I don't know, I thought it was so darn unfair. It was a democratically elected government, and yet they blockaded it, and they didn't let any supplies in to help the Loyalists, as we called them then—I don't know if I'm remembering properly or not. But I can remember the day that the place fell, and feeling so bad, I cried. I felt bad. One person came in—we were living in the jail house then—my father was the jailer. And this person came in and he asked me what was wrong, "You're not laughing like you usually are." And I said, "I feel so awfully bad about what happened." "Oh dear," he said, "they're godless communists—they should have wiped them out."

And I remember at that time, George had met Norman Bethune, you know, Dr. Norman Bethune. He came to Sydney Mines to speak in the union hall. Our minister was very good with young people. He had a Young People's Society, and we were encouraged to talk about all these things. We'd argue back and forth. We were awfully lucky. I'm telling you, who we met when we were young. I never saw Bethune, but George was all excited when he came to visit me, telling me about him. He mentioned about how he had been a quite well-to-do doctor, specializing in treating people with TB, if I remember right. And he mentioned about the blood transfusion stuff. And he mentioned about his disillusionment with the medical establishment. You know, he was supposed to tell people they had to get this medicine, they had to take time off. And he said, "There was no way they could possibly do it. They had to keep going."

I don't remember how Bethune happened to get interested in Spain. But I think there was a fascist group in Quebec or Montreal. And he had seen their leader, it seems, attack a Jewish man, and he started looking into things. I'm kind of hazy about some of it. But I remember George was terribly impressed by Norman Bethune. He had been working in Spain, and he came over to see if he could collect money for them. And he spoke about transfusions, and how that was just new, and how he had transfused (blood) from himself directly into other people. And I remember, the next week, George was up (to Baddeck), and I took him to Young People's Society with me.

The first night I met George—my cousin introduced me to him—he was coming home from being an agent at this Nelson MacDonald's election—Rev. Nelson MacDonald. I don't know if you ever heard of the Reconstruction Party—it just ran that one time. R. B. Bennett was the premier of Canada. That was at the worst of the—that was about the time, I imagine, when they did such terrible things to Rev. Woodsworth, the leader of the CCF. But anyhow, Stevens—I don't know what would be the word—he was in the Conservative party. Anyhow, he broke with R. B. Bennett because of the way he was handling the poor people and the unemployed and all that. And he tried to start a Reconstruction Party. This Nelson MacDonald was the only one that I know of that ran in Nova Scotia. And George went and worked for him at the polls in Sydney Mines that day. And I got quite thrilled that I had met somebody who would do something like that.

He was terribly frail, George, oh, terribly frail then. The doctor had told him if he didn't get out of the mine, in 3 months he'd be dead. He worked in Princess Mine. (*What did he do there?*) Is there such a thing as running a donkey engine? It comes to my mind. That was his job. And he couldn't leave his job because his father had died, and he had to support his mother. There were 6 of them in the family, plus his mother. And at that time, sometimes, all the money he'd get to take home, when the deductions were taken off it, was less than $7 a week. So his one brother went to a farm in Leitches Creek with an uncle. And another brother went to another farm. So George didn't have to feed them. In fact, they helped feed the family, sending them stuff.

Oh, he was desperately, desperately poor when we met, and I was desperately poor. Desperately poor. Really poor. So that when I went to school, I hated to get up to answer a question, 'cause I had the same thing on all week. I only washed it on Friday night. No dryers and things then. Maybe if it was a nice day I could wash it through the week and get it dry

for the next day. Oh, dear.

(*Did you and Geroge marry while he worked in the mine?*) No. Because he had all those to support. His father had died. We were going together. We would have been married about two years earlier, I suppose. I only saw him very occasionally, 'cause it was like going to Florida, to go to Sydney Mines.

The mail went across (the Lake to) Washabuck, and over Washabuck Mountain. I had to walk behind the horse and sleigh, because it was so cold. If I sat in, I'd have frozen. And then down by train to Sydney Mines. It was a journey.

I didn't get down for (his father's) funeral, either. I would like to have known his father, because he was quite a freethinker. He was from Newfoundland, and he wrote letters to the papers about the injustices in the mine, and he was always speaking up in the union. And that's why, when George came to Baddeck, everyone thought he was such a dangerous radical, you know. And he had one heck of a time. I pleaded with him to leave Baddeck, but he said he loved Baddeck. He'd stay here on two meals a day rather than—he wouldn't go. He got stubborn. And that's why, when

I came through the door of the church the day of (George's) funeral, I couldn't believe—people standing in the aisles and everything. George sure made them turn around, turned everything around.

Lovely letters I got, marvellous letters. I got a card from 10 little Indian children, each one signed their name and their nickname. And ended at the bottom, "...and our grandmother." And I was so happy to see Indians at the funeral. And Graham Bell's granddaughters. Everybody like that. I thought, Oh my God, George, you certainly turned everything around—I never saw a funeral with so many people at it, in our church, ever. Up in the gallery, and standing.

He came to Baddeck, and he loved Baddeck. When he couldn't get a job, if we had starved—well, there were very few jobs to get, but he couldn't get one—that dangerous radical. (*Was he really thought as a dangerous radical?*) Oh yes, during the war, yes. Because we were still pacifists when the war broke out, both of us. (*But had he done anything?*) No. Talked. You know how he would say what he thought, no matter what, supposing he was going to get killed. And he said it. (*Where did he say it?*) To anybody—they'd be talking. Anybody would say something about the wonderful victories—oh well, you know, the papers would be full about the marvellous victories and all that. And we might read another paper that had something different, and George would speak up about something. He wasn't patriotic and all that and anything he read, he never forgot. Now, I'd read perhaps 10 books to one of his. But he knew everything he read in that book, and he never forgot it. We never spent any money on liquor, or tobacco, or luxuries. But we always had lots of books and lots of good magazines and lots of nice music.

(*What was George's role in terms of the church?*) Oh, he had nothing whatever to do with the church. His father hadn't been very much of a churchgoer. His father's people were very—oh, what was it?—not Plymouth Brethren—I don't know what it was. They were pacifists, but they were all this about being saved, and don't eat, do this, don't do that. They were desperately fanatical, actually. And George's father rebelled against that. He read a lot, and he knew.

So, the night after his father died suddenly, and when they were arranging for the funeral, one of these—they call themselves Christians— they're not exactly Plymouth Brethren, they're an offshoot—and very good-living people. But very, very intolerant of everybody else's views. And they thought his father was—George overheard somebody saying, "Of course he's in Hell tonight." He came in the kitchen with his mother, and heard somebody saying that. And his mother had hysterics and fainted, and they had to get the doctor. That's the only thing I ever know that George never forgave.

265

You know, people have treated him desperately meanly, have taken advantage of him at times, sometimes 2 or 3 times. And after awhile, he'd forget. He never did anything to harm them back. And you know, he'd still take another chance on them. But he'd never forget—he was desperately anti-religious.

(But) George sang in the men's choir the last few years, just to sing. They went from church to church, you know, singing, on Anniversary Sundays and that—there were 12 of them. And he loved to sing, and he could, too. He didn't mind that at all. But when he'd come home, and I'd say to him something about, "Well, what did the preacher say?" He says, "Heck, I didn't listen!"

The first job that George got (in Baddeck) that actually paid him a salary—he got a few days now and again, cutting wood, cutting the trash—the little trees that come up, bushes —by the side of the road. Or when they'd haul the ferryboat up down here, to fix it, he might get a few day's work at that. I don't know how we lived. We lived on about $10 a month the first year we were married. We couldn't live by ourselves that winter, 'cause there was no way we could heat. We had to move in with my father and mother in the winter. My father had the jail. And he still kept his cows and horses up here. And George used to come up and look after them.

It was Depression, real bad Depression. There was no unemployment insurance. George's brother and his wife and child were on relief. Eighty cents each per week, in Sydney Mines—$2.40 for the three of them. They had to buy at certain places. They were told what kind of dry beans to get. They had to be yellow-eye beans, not pinto beans or navy beans.

I think what got George really sensitive to injustice and everything was, he could remember the strike in 1925, and what suffering they went through. Actual hunger. He was the oldest, and then he had a sister, and then brothers, and all that. And they set up a soup kitchen in Sydney Mines. And he was a queer mixture, you know. He believed in socialism and helping one another, but he was so terrible independent and proud, he would not go. I can remember him telling me one time about the pains in his stomach, smelling the soup as he was going by, coming home from school, and he wouldn't go and get it. And they were selling cookies and crackers and things then in open barrels—you wouldn't remember that. The broken ones they used to put in bags, and people could go, take a paper bag full of that stuff home. And his sister Edith would. And how he'd be just dying to go and get it. And his mother and father would coax him to go and get it. No, sir, he wouldn't. Nobody was going to see him going to get it. A queer guy.

The war came, and the Depression ended. I think it was war work, the first work he got. It was at the naval base at Point Edward. He went

266

down, and he started washing dishes, and he lasted one night. He wrote me a pitiful letter, how he couldn't stand it. I was home alone with our daughter. So he said, "I'm not coming home. I'll get something else. But," he said, "I just can't do dishes again." All night long he had washed dishes for the fellows—they were working right around the clock, you know. So he got a job looking after a boiler, something like that. And then he went with the divers, and he was on the raft, helping the divers.

(*Did George have any problems of conscience, working for the war effort?*) Nope. He didn't seem to. By that time he figured they had to defeat Hitler. He didn't think any war was a good war, but he thought it was the lesser of the two evils then. Once it had started, it had to be finished. I hope I'm getting right, what he thought. But he always, all his life, was very skeptical about anything he read or heard on radio. And anybody that was good at making speeches, he always analyzed them, and looked up both sides. We got different kinds of papers and magazines. And (he) had no education. Actually. Perhaps grade 3 or 4. See, he was ill a lot when he was young. He had polio. He had spinal meningitis. He had typhoid. He had all those things. They told his mother he wouldn't live. My own sister died at the time, when he had polio. But he was a long time—he must have been 10 or 12 before he got rid of the iron brace on his leg and he sold newspapers, going around dragging that brace! He was selling newspapers, walking all around Sydney Mines.

(*A lot of illness.*) Yeah, when he was young. And even up to the time that I met him. Like I said, the doctors said he wouldn't live if he didn't get out of the mine. But he couldn't until he went to the union, so he could transfer his job to his next brother, his oldest brother. and I remember, he got the thing transferred Monday morning. And we got married Monday afternoon at 4 o'clock. And he was a whole hour late for our wedding. I thought he wasn't coming. (*Married in a church?*) No, in the manse, the minister's house. We just had his mother and my parents and the witnesses.

(*Where'd you go for a honeymoon?*) That's really funny. At those days, I used to get car-sick. Of course, he didn't have a car, I didn't have a car. A friend of his brother's drove him up, and they had three flat tires—that's why he was a whole hour late. And the minister had a funeral, and he hurried up and planted the poor corpse, rushing back to marry me. And I thought something happened, George decided not to come. Oh, well—that's a lot of foolishness.

Anyhow, my father said, "Everybody deserves a honeymoon." So he gave George some money to take me to the Isle Royale Hotel (in Sydney)—it was new—take me and the best man and my bridesmaid—go down and have dinner there. We weren't going to stay all night or anything.

267

Well, he often said afterwards, he had to stop at every telephone pole for me to get out and throw up! But we kept going. We got as far as Sydney Mines. I had to go into his mother's place and lie down for awhile. And I thought I was fine again. And I had never in my life—I suppose he hadn't, either—eaten out dinner in a posh place. We got in the car and we drove 3 miles, as far as North Sydney—I couldn't go any further. So we drove from Sydney Mines to North Sydney, and George and I sat in the car outside, and Annabelle and Gordon went to the movies. And afterwards, I had a cup of tea in the restaurant—oh, a little queer hole in the wall—I forget what it was. And coming home, I was sick, sick. It was almost daylight when we finally landed in Baddeck. I never got to Sydney.

Years later, I did see Niagara Falls. I went with somebody else. And I remember writing to a young fellow who was boarding here, a teacher. I said, "Well, I'm having my honeymoon—next year George can come!" So we never had a honeymoon, really. I never had a diamond, nor a honeymoon, or anything like that.

(*Well, obviously, those weren't the things you were looking for. What were you looking for with George?*) He was interesting, he was interesting. We have had some very hard times, but we've had some very interesting ones. And we had a hell of a lot of laughing, really. And every day, we fought. Not the first 2 or 3 years—I don't think we ever fought until after our daughter (Sharon) was born. And then I worried that she'd starve, or she'd do this or that. That's when Geroge went to work at Point Edward. And he was away for so long, he missed seeing her in the crib and everything. She was standing up when he came home. He had to stay away that first Christmas, too. And I remember he was going to come home, I believe it was her first birthday. And the man drove by—he was going out to Middle River, and he was going to pick George up and take him. And he went by and didn't pick him up, whether he forgot or what. George walked to Baddeck, game-legged—got home in daylight. He lay down on a bridge down there somewhere and slept for about a half hour. And then he went back to work at suppertime and worked all that night firing the boiler. So he was so determined.

Another time he came up, I remember, after he had got a car. It was icy. And the lights went out, and he drove all the way with no lights, with his head out. Had a flashlight, and watching the line! Oh, and it was so slippery—oh, lord. When he was going to do something, he was going to do it. And that wasn't easy to live with when I didn't think he should do what he should do, lots of times. It wasn't easy, I'm telling you.

(*So you fought a little bit.*) Not a little bit. Practically every day, you know. And I miss it so much. I really do miss it so much, you know. We never went to bed mad at each other and I fought with him a whole lot more the last few years, 'cause one of the girls down there told me that George kept at me and kept at me till I blew my stack. Then he'd go in the other room with a smile on his face. Then I started to blow my stack right away and get it over with. It's a queer marriage. Forty-six years we had. And he was never one, you know, to be sentimental or anything. But you know, I have a couple of nice cards he gave me the last few years that really were something.

And mean. He would never, you know—I'd say we ought to have a party or something to celebrate. "Why drag the poor people in for something we did," he'd say. Then he'd tell me the story about the wife saying, "Let's kill the rooster and have people in for our anniversary." "Why take it out on the poor rooster?"

(*But his heart was tender*.) Oh, I know. He couldn't say no to anyone except me. And really, I nagged at him too much the last few years. Not the last year. I gave up. But I wish I had nagged more the last year. Then again, he did what he wanted, right to the very end. (*You're not suggesting that you think you could have saved him*.) No. But I do think that he might have lived longer if he had taken a little bit better care of himself, you know, after he found out. He told me, in the hospital, he had the pain all summer, that pain in his chest. And he never stopped. He never went as much as he did last summer. 'Cause he always used to come home at noon, he had his big meal at noon, and a little supper. And then we had a great big feed about midnight, all his life. But he'd sleep all afternoon, from 1 o'clock or so to half past 5 or so, and then he went back to work. But this last summer, it just seemed that he couldn't lie down. He had to get going. He'd go back to see if everything was all right—oh, he'd better check something. And it's so funny. So many strange things happened this summer, it almost seemed as if he knew.

They made him a life member of the Yacht Club this summer. And then the Lions Club made him a life member. He said, "My God, they must know something. I guess this is my last year." Little things like that. And 2 or 3 weeks before he died, I had come from a funeral that Rev. Ian Mac-Leod had conducted for someone that I thought it must have been hard for him to speak for, because the deceased had never gone to church, and he was rather a reprobate. I said to George, "It was a lovely service." And afterwards, several times, he said to Louise and Karen, "Well, if anything happens to me, I want Ian MacLeod." And Ian's Presbyterian, and I'm United Church, you know. But of course, he knew Ian, they both sang in the choir, and they were good friends, like that.

Up in the hospital—it's nothing bad about it, really—but a minister heard George was in. And he had a special nurse on, and she said, "Do you want me to send for the minister, George? We're supposed to ask anyone

that's had a heart attack."
George said, "Hell, no—
he's nothing but a Tory!"
Didn't have the word out
of his mouth when the
minister popped in! I was
scared he'd heard. And
then after the minister
went, George said to the
nurse, "You know, I
don't need anything like
that. If I have to go, I'm
ready to go." George said
there was one time when
somebody asked him,
"Have you made your
peace with God?" "We
never fought," he said.
Was it Paine, first said
that? George said that to
somebody.

Everything about us was odd, you know. We knew that. I knew that
Rev. Ian knew George wasn't a religious person, in one way. But in an-
other way, I don't know, whether you'd say. He was a very good person.
(*Would you say George was not a religious person?*) I guess he was, his
own religion. He had, like that poem the minister quoted, that was one
George thought a lot of. "'That man has no religion,' you often say of
Jack. But I have seen him share his bread when times were hard and
slack." And things like that. I couldn't remember all of it—I just told what
I could remember of it. It comes to my mind it was in *The Steelworker*.

"And I've seen him cross the street with children not his own...with
men like you'd disown. And I've seen him keep his head when most men
went war-mad. And when the savage was let loose, it simply made him
sad...." And it ends up, "That man with no religion, it really seems to me,
resembles more than you and I the Man from Galilee." Something like
that. There's little bits of it I could remember. I know it was in the old
Steelworker, and George cutting it out. And he was referring to his own
father. He said, "Those people saying my father was burning in Hell."
And he said that poem spoke about his father. His father died when he was
only 40-something.

Everybody thought George was so terrible tight, and terrible money-
mad. He was terribly careful. But he actually had suffered hunger. And he

had seen us without things. He's seen me making clothes for our daughter out of old things. Making soakers, panties, out of his old socks, the top part of his socks. Perhaps two different socks together'd make a pair of panties for her. Things like that when she was small. And he was a man, you know, he'd look at something and think about it a long time before he bought it. And put money in the bank, and all that. But a lot of it, it was like Jack Benny, he was making people think he was terrible tight, you know. In other ways, he wasn't. He bought me that organ, and he bought me this nice music thing. And a few years ago—I had never had a car, I'd never driven a car, and I said, "I want to get a car." He thought it was crazy—I should never drive, I'd kill somebody. Anyhow when I went to pay for it, he had paid for it. A little Chevette....

But didn't he have a ball? My God, he laughed every day of his life. And he laughed at his own jokes. When he told them for the tenth time, he got just as much fun out of them.

And Sharon and I have a favourite saying now since years. We're both kind of worrywarts. We worried about this and worried about that. I remember one time we were getting ready to go to Sydney. I had to go down. She was not very confident as a driver, and she was saying, "If it's slippery...." You know. And I said, "I heard it was going to rain." She said, "Yeah. And they said it might turn to snow." And George said, "And it might even be a nice day!" So any time anything's getting us down now, one of us'll say, "It might even be a nice day!"

Last year, the minister before this—he and George were very good friends, and the minister's wife was just like George, full of the Old Nick—terrible woman! When they were getting ready to move, the kids were giving them something, they were having a supper for them, and George couldn't go. And she said to George that the C.G.I.T. girls that afternoon had given her I forget what, but "Wasn't it sweet?" and George said, "Oh my heavens, you're moving!" He says, "Oh heavens, I'll have to give you something." He went over and he got a can of prunes—"This'll help you move!" And didn't she tell them that at the supper that night!

(*Didn't George once work in a gas station?*) Over 20 years he worked at a garage. He was a stock-room clerk and a runaround for everything, and so forth. He went to work at 7 in the morning till 7 in the evening. Until I finally said I was quitting. 'Cause I was keeping overnight tourists then. In here—we were using the whole house then. My sister owned the Inverary Inn then and they'd send us up some overflow. And they'd be coming around 5 and 6, and I'd have to be carrying suitcases. And I said, "I'm not putting my name in the tourist book this year, if you won't ask to get off at least at 6 o'clock!" So he finally did. And he only got one Sunday a month off for I don't know how many years. He worked 7 days.

271

(*Why did he stay at the job for 20 years?*) He loved meeting people. He'd work for nothing if he could be meeting people, and coming home and telling me who he met, and what they said, all this sort of stuff. And he said, where would somebody like himself get a chance to meet people that were significant in the life of the world? He met Dr. Spock, the fellow who wrote the baby books. We both met him. We were up to Sight Point and had an evening up there with him and his first wife. I liked him a lot.

And somebody that I like terrifically—this activist—this Saul Alinsky. He came in our store one night. And I called George, I said, "George, that's Saul Alinsky." "Oh, don't be foolish." He looked at him. I said, "Yeah, I've seen him on television, I'm sure that's Saul Alinsky." So George of course went and asked him, and it was. And he had been down to Keltic Lodge, and they wouldn't serve him because he didn't have a tie on, and all that. And then he wouldn't go to the coffee shop. So we had a lovely talk with him.

(*And why did George leave the gas station?*) Well, George P. Fraser, he used to go to the garage and talk to George a lot, and told him he should be out on his own, working. He should have a store or something like that. And there was somebody had a little dairy where our store is now, but it was separate from the other building, it was just a little narrow place. And it burned. So George P. said to George, "Why don't you start a store there?" So without talking to me or anything, George went and made arrangements to get that store. He told George P., "Ask Isabel how she wants it laid out"—because I was always making plans—I thought another time I'd be an architect. I was always on graph paper. So I did it all out. He never did a darn thing that I wanted! And we rented it, up until we bought our part.

We started because there was no other place open on Sunday, and there was no other place open on Wednesday afternoon, either here or in Whycocomagh. And they had the campground up in Whycocomagh. My father had a little store in his house up here, up on the hill. And the people'd come from Whycocomagh Wednesday afternoon that would be desperate to get something to eat. Everything was closed. They used to open two hours in the afternoon and two in the evening on Sunday.

So, when we opened up, I knew the wholesalers because I had been doing the buying for my father up here. And then when my father died, my mother was there. I used to go up every day and run the store. So the wholesalers knew they could give me credit. But George cashed in his life insurance. And we bought a few things, and they gave us a bit of stock. But we had the shelves only on one side, and one can on the front of each shelf—nothing behind! And we went to work in the morning at 8, and we didn't get home till after 10. Not at all. I'd get up and perhaps make a stew

272

in the pressure cooker and take it to work, and we'd have it down there around noon. That's why George hated to eat there. You know, sometimes he wouldn't be getting home to dinner, I'd say, "I'll take your dinner down." "Oh, I can't stand to eat down there!" He got so sick of it.

Eat in the store. I had a cot in the office, which wasn't as big as it is now—we had just the narrow part then. And when my feet would swell, I'd get there with my feet up on a chair, on the cot, laying down and figuring out the prices. Ten o'clock at night and later. Oh my, my.

George had a nervous breakdown about a month after we started, maybe not that long. Had to go to the hospital. See, they said we could move in in May, and it wasn't ready. So he gave his notice at the garage, and they hired somebody else. So he was all summer long with no money coming in. And worrying and worrying and worrying. And the very first day we were there, something went wrong with the ice cream thing, and we had got stuff in—everything was swimming in green popsicles when we got down in the morning. And we were stupid, we didn't know it was insured. We thought we were out all that. The first milk we got in, a lot of it was sour. It seemed everything went wrong. And George got terribly scared. He couldn't sleep. So he ended up in the hospital for 2 or 3 weeks. Then, after a little while, he was back again, because his blood pressure went up so high. And what he got for it put him in a deep depression, and he was laid up for awhile then.

And a fellow came in one day—a fellow whose buddy wanted the store—and he said that they had just made a bet whether we'd be closed in two weeks or whether we'd last the month. I didn't tell that to George. But it made me so mad. I said, "You go home and tell him that I'll sleep on the floor down here, and I will never give up, and I will never go home, and we'll get through it all right." And we did.

Dan Alex MacLeod:
a Working Life

(*Was Stirling Mines the first time big money was seen around here—cash?*) **Dan Alex MacLeod, Stirling:** I'd say, yeah. Well, the farmers used to make a lot of money here—till the government interfered—you bet they were. My uncle, the first week of September, on Thursday—the week before, he gathered cream and butter and turnips, perhaps a couple of lambs—and he went Thursday, at dark, so that it would be cool, going all night. Into Sydney and Glace Bay. And then he got orders. And every Thursday from there on till the winter came, he went with this load. No problem, just at it, getting fairly good money for it.

Then somebody stepped in—they wanted a license. Okay, that wasn't too bad: they got a license. Then it came that you had to have your cream and your milk and your buttermilk and all this pasteurized. And you couldn't kill a lamb without killing it in a slaughterhouse. There were no slaughterhouses here. You wouldn't go to hauling lambs to Sydney for slaughtering. That put the kibosh on her. (*If we look at Cape Breton and all the farms that are closed....*) That's just government coming in and interfering. If they'd left them alone, there'd still be farms in Cape Breton.

(*So you don't see the mine's coming as a godsend.*) No. The worst thing that ever came here. See, they were working on the farms. They were making, you know, a good living—they weren't living in style or anything, but they had enough to eat and they enjoyed their lives. They had lots of time to go visiting. When you cut wood, there'd be big frolics. In the evening they'd have a quilting party or something. Everybody enjoyed themselves.

Okay. The mine came in here, well, in 1928 it started, and worked till 1930. That was a funny thing. In 1930, election was on the 28th of July. I came up from the mine and voted at 3 o'clock, after shift. See, that was when Bennett got it. Eleven o'clock that night—there wasn't a wheel turning. Just shut her down like that. Tariffs, you know. The Conservatives always went in for heavy tariffs. They were getting their reagents from Belgium and places like that. And for 5 years, 3 months, and 14 days, I think—if I remember right—when a hole came on your pants, you put a patch on it, and when that patch wore out, you put another one on it. And on the 14th of October, 1935, the Liberals got back in. Next day, I went back to work, getting the mine ready to go again.

(*It wasn't just that you lost your job—that mine stopped.*) Oh, everybody lost their job. And see, they had neglected their farms, the farms had gone kaput. They had gone to work in the mine. And they never got back to fixing up their farms any more.

(*Didn't they keep up their farms when they went to the mines?*) Well, a farm is an all-year operation, if you're looking after your farm right. See, in the wintertime they cut timber for the (coal) mine—booms and pit props. Pit props were for Glace Bay. That was part of your farming. Then the pulp came—they cut so much pulp. And at that time, you got 50 cords of pulp, and you cut it and took it alongside of the road, you got your money. (*You're not saying that going to the woods took people away from their farming. You see the pit props and the pulping as part of your farming.*) Oh yeah, in the wintertime....

There's an air vent there (at Stirling Mines) that Savard and I drilled, it came up at 70 degrees. The last we were getting, I think, it was $20 a foot. We paid for own dynamite caps and fuel. The last round we put in, there was 19 feet came out it. Overburden and everything. We got paid $20 a foot for it. He was on one shift and I was on the other—we were working two shifts. (*Was it to put an air hole down?*) No, we came up. (*You were working up from below?*) Yeah. They wouldn't allow you, I don't think, to do that today.

See, what we did was, when we got our round in—we put two holes in this side and two holes in that side—then we had to go down on a rope, after we lit the fuse. I don't think they'd allow you to do that today. After

275

you went up so far, you put a hole in the wall so you could leave your machinery there. And you had ladders. But you had to take the ladders down and then go up on the rope to light your fuse. We took the ladders down—they'd be all smashed. Then we'd put them up again. But then when you blasted your round, you put two steel into those holes—you did that on both sides—and you put plank across them, and that's what you worked on. (*And you were working your way up from...?*) The 100-foot level.

We lived across the lake here, that's where my old home is. And I used to blast at 12 o'clock. I used to go down to the mine when the shift came off at 5 o'clock. I went down. I set up my machine—you

Dan Alex as a young man

only had so much air, you know. I set up my machines. And by the time the other fellows got to work at 7 o'clock and set up their machines, I had my round in. Then at 12 o'clock I blasted, when they came up to eat. And over across the lake, my mother could tell the shots—there's a slip going across here somewhere. And she could tell the amount of shots I put in the round, she could hear them, you know, like "tick,", "tick," "tick," under the house.

See, this was only, like, a prospecting and getting the mine ready, if there was enough ore body there to set up a mill. There was no mill here then. This was in '28 and '27. (*This is the first major mining that they did here?*) Yeah.

(*What equipped you to do work like that? What made you think you could mine?*) Well, when I was born, I thought I could do anything. I tried everything. I never hit a thing that I couldn't do. No doubt in my mind. You make up your mind to do something, you can do it. (*But you had no training as a hard rock miner?*) No, no. Once I started drifting—making a tunnel through—I made bonus every time, every two weeks I made bonus. (*When you say "I" did you do this alone?*) Oh no, you've got a helper. When you're drifting, you pay for your helper and two workers, and you pay for your dynamite, and you pay for your fuse, and you pay for

276

your caps. I believe it was $7.50 we were getting, a foot. And okay, you're getting $7.50 a foot. But when you go over the footage you're supposed to make, you're getting a bonus. See, and if you make so much, you're paying your helper 50¢ and your workers 50¢, bonus. But if you make still better, you're paying them a dollar a day bonus. Over and above their wages. So I generally paid them a dollar.

(*But you were a good miner?*) Oh, I don't know if I was good, but I got along, anyway. (*There's no training for that on the farm.*) No. Well, I think a lot of it is gall. You know, lots of people, well, "I'm afraid to try it," or something. I was never afraid to try anything. To take that step where you make success.

When I started in the lumber business, I had just enough money to pay for 6 pulp sawblades. I and my brother-in-law went to the woods. The first day, we cut 108 logs and yarded them in a pile, where we were going to put the mill. I was cutting them and he was sawing them. That was set then. We cut 108 logs every day we went to work, landed them at the yard. We had pretty near 3000 logs out. Then we went and got a loan and got a mill. Bought a truck, a ton Chev. Wasn't very big. But then after I started on my own, I got a big 3-ton Fargo—$1285. That's all it cost then. They cost about $16,000 now, or more.

(*I'm not surprised to see you cutting wood, or trying to make a go of a lumber business. That was often part of farming in Cape Breton. But mining....*) Well, mining came easy. Well, it's not me, but all the fellows around here, they were drilling, and doing the same thing as I was. See, you went in down there as a helper. I was 3 weeks helping. The fellow that was on the machine, he took a vacation, went to Quebec, and I got his machine. When he came back, they gave him another machine and I stayed. (*That was the training you got.*) I figured at the end of 3 weeks, I could drill a lot better than he could. My impression, you know. So I must have been all right when they left the machine with me: they must have been satisfied.

(*And did a lot of house-moving—you had no experience before?*) No. (*And you raised sheep.*) Well, there were sheep on the farm where I was brought up, all the time. I always had sheep, only the 10 years I was away at Terra Nova. Minute we came back here, we bought sheep. (*I saw your letter to the newspaper. You're really not too happy with the marketing board.*) No sir. (*You don't feel that's going to produce a better product?*) No. Well all right—you've got some drag in the government, eh? You'll be appointed inspector. You're going to come down here and inspect my sheep. I've been raising sheep since I was a kid. What do you know about sheep? Nothing. Or if he inspects my sheep. How is he going to produce a better product than I'm producing? I'm selling lambs for the last years

277

back. Everybody I sell lambs to, they come back and buy them again. Well, if there was something wrong with them, they wouldn't come, would they? This inspection business is for the birds. If somebody is there with a poor class of lambs, he'll come along and—a hundred dollars—his lambs are passed, like a bottle of rum or something. That's how the world is usually run today. Anything the government gets into, it's never run right as far as I'm concerned. Now, this marketing board is for just a few fellows that's got quite a few lambs, and trying to get the little fellow out, kick him out, see. That's what it is.

.　　　　.　　　　.

In 1925 I bought a new truck for $910, brand spanking new. I started hauling from Fourchu. I also had seats—and very few people had cars then. There were few cars even in Sydney at that time, very few. Even the trucks that were there, it would be carbon lights that were on them, and solid tires, chain drive. 1925. That was my first job in the mine, hauling up from Fourchu with a truck. Gas, or anything they needed in the mine. It was coming in to Fourchu by boat. Supplies, eatables, nails, or anything they needed there. There was no mill there then. They were just sinking the shaft, and putting drifts in. *(So you were servicing that operation.)* To a certain extent. They had their own truck, too. If you weren't hauling from Fourchu you were doing something else. You were out after lumber to a mill, or moving stuff in the mine from here to there, stuff like that.

And then it stopped for awhile there, and I went to work in Sydney. It just stopped for a year, I think. And it started, but I was at a job in Sydney. I was working on the coal plant, working for the coal company. Shoveling coal. The boss went in, and a cousin of mine, to see if I'd come back to work (at Stirling Mine). So, "How long will you guarantee me a job?" "Oh, we can't guarantee you a job." "Well, I'd be foolish quitting here and going there, and perhaps be out of a job the next day."

So anyway, we were dumping coal in the coal bank. I worked there all winter. Then out of 175 people, I was one of the 5 that were picked out to work all summer and then that fall, we started dumping coal again. I and another fellow—oh, a great worker—we got a car of screened coal, 16 screen coal—that's long lumps like this—they were jamming in the car. And it had snowed in the morning, soft snow, and we were trying to get this car out. Anyway, the boss used to walk on top of the car. I thought I and the boss were great friends. There was steam coming out of under our oilskins, we were working that hard.

He got snarly, you know. I just fired the shovel as far as it could go and I went in. My time is still there—I never went looking for my time. That was at 3 o'clock, and at 9 o'clock I was over in the old place (at Stirling) with the furniture. So at 4 o'clock in the morning, Murdock Dan woke me up, and they wanted me at the mine next morning, and I went to work. So I worked on the truck, their own truck—I'd sold my truck before that—I worked on their truck till some time in February, till snow. Going to Sydney, or around the thing. When it snowed—I was in an awful snowstorm in February, but I got the truck home. Then I went out of it.

I was 18 months underground, between drilling and all that. I was mucking first, then I was on a machine after that. And then I wrote the manager—you know, he didn't talk to you about any business, you wrote him a letter, and he wrote you a letter. I wrote him a letter and I told him I wanted a job on the surface and I got a letter from him, when I came up from underground. He wanted me to go driving a tractor. Oh God. I called in the office on the way home. I said, "I never even saw a tractor, let alone drive it." "That's all right," he said. "There's a fellow coming from Halifax to teach you." Well, I was on the tractor I don't know how long. I taught 2 or 3 fellows to drive it.

But anyway, he wanted me to go on the service truck then. They were building the mill then. And I'd be moving things here and there, and going to Fourchu.

They had (other) trucks working. And (drivers) used to go to the show (in Sydney) and they wouldn't be here till 10 o'clock at night. I was going by the office one day. And the manager for the construction called me, he said, "Do you know your way around Sydney?" I said, "I should. I was there for quite awhile and I lived there for 3 years." "Well," he said, "tomorrow morning, I'll have orders here for you. And if you can get back here that we can unload before 5 o'clock I'll send for a new truck for you."

Okay, I picked the orders. You may say I wasn't long in Sydney. I went to Sydney and dropped every order I had around. And I came back and loaded. I never waited for dinner. I was back half past two. He said, "What happened?" "Nothing." "Did you get what I sent for?" "Yeah, there's your slip." Just walked over and sent a telegram for a new truck—the best truck that was ever made.

So I was on that. And a new manager had come in, for the mining part. So he warned me, "No passengers—you're not allowed to take any passengers." I used to go to Sydney—there were no snowplows then—and I used to get in every night. Oh, I had all the right equipment you could talk of. Long ropes—there were drums on those wheels. Tie them to a tree or something, and pull yourself through. Chain blocks and shovels and bars—we had everything. Kept her going all winter. See, sometimes there'd be a bunch of miners going home on weekend, and they'd want to get a drive back. And I always had lots of shovels. I'd take them back.

But anyway, I was coming through Loch Lomond one day, and I had two in the cab. And the manager met me. Next morning I was hauled into the office and put on the mat. If anything happened, (the riders) could sue the company. I never said a word. I just let him go. But the next day, he met me with two in the seat, one on each running board!

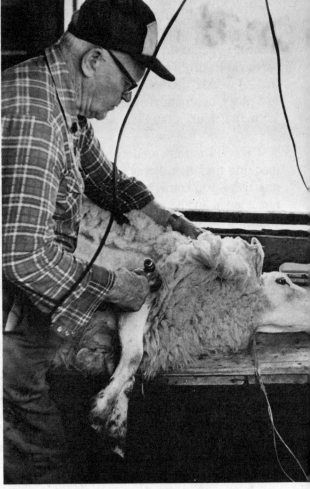

So when I went in— I went in to see Winger, who was boss of the construction company. He was after me all the time to go to work with him. I said, "How about a job?" "Sure," he said. "Well," I said, "I'll be with you tomorrow morning." I was called over to the office. I said, "Before you open your mouth," I said, "I quit last night when I landed your truck in here." I said, "And I'll tell you why. I come in here every night with my load." "Oh yes, good driver." I said, "You know, those fellows you saw with me, they even took their team of horses down to pull me through snow. They shoveled the snowbanks." I said, "When I've got to pass them, the job is yours."

"Oh, wait, wait," he said. "There's no waiting to it," I said. "I'm not going to be coming in here and put on the mat here every day—that's it." So I turned around. "Wait a minute," he said, "we'll give you passes. Get them to sign it, and you can take anybody you want." And he gave me a yearly pass for my girlfriend! He never bothered me after that.

We were in Sydney one time in an awful storm. There were 6 other trucks and a tractor in there. And one of the bosses was with me. I said, "If we can get ahead of those 6 trucks before we get to Big Pond, we'll

Dan Alex MacLeod shearing a sheep (left) and docking a lamb

make Stirling." Well by God, we were getting along pretty good. We got by the tractor and we got by 5 trucks. There was one ahead of us. I said, "That's it. We can't get to Stirling." By God, when we got up on top of the mountain, he was putting water in it. This truck would go 40 miles an hour in second gear. And I always loaded it light when there was a storm. So I drove her in second gear and said, "We'll make Stirling."

So, we went. I knew every (snow) bank the same as I know every chair in my kitchen, and I was back and forth, back and forth. When I'd be coming to a bank I'd put her in second gear and I'd hold the wheel still. And he'd be like this (covering his face), "Jesus, Jesus, you made a post! Slow down!" I wouldn't slow down till I felt her easing up after going through the bank. And we were in here at 9 o'clock. Those trucks never got in. They had to unload in Loch Lomond and go back.

(*You liked doing that.*) Oh yes, it was a challenge. I've come into the mine lots of times, 3 and 4 o'clock in the morning. Going to the cookhouse, and lay down on a bench there. And when the cook got up, got my breakfast in the cook-house and went and loaded the truck, and headed her back again. Perhaps get in that night at 12 o'clock, do the same thing. Till the road would get better, and then you'd be home early.

If I had my life to live over again, I'd be a truck driver, nothing else.

281

You're out in the air, you're meeting different people. I think it's the best job that's going today.

(*Then in the periods when the mine was closed, from the '30s through the '40s, you would hear the mine working.*) Oh, yeah. That house over there—we were sitting one afternoon, and the door was open—you know, the table was right across from the door—you could hear her going as plain as when she was going. We heard it 3 different times, and I was saying there were 3 fellows going to be killed. And there were 3 fellows killed. I think that's what we were hearing, when those fellows were getting killed.

(*And does that trouble you, that you hear things like that?*) No. You wouldn't hear them and see them if they did. If you get scared, you won't see them. All I've got to do is touch your coat. If I'm seeing something, if I touched your coat there, you'd see it. I don't know what in the world is the cause of that.

We went down with a fellow—his wife was dying. And I and my wife went down there, we were down there two months, I think. And oh, maybe two weeks before she died, I was out in the porch just about dusk. And there was a team right at the gate, with a coffin on it. "Well," I figured, "the old skinflint is going to make a homemade coffin"—that's what I thought. And my wife came along, and I went and put my arm around her—I never thought, you know—she went into hysterics—she saw it too, then, the minute I touched her. I said, "It's nothing. The old woman is going to die, and the remains are going to stop at the gate. But the old bugger is going to make a homemade coffin." He had lots of money.

But it wasn't a homemade coffin. It was a boughten one. And the day of the funeral—it was with a horse and wagon they were going to take it to the cemetery—it wasn't far, anyway. It was in the spring and the roads were bad. And Norman Alex MacLeod had a touring car, and he got stuck right in front. Getting the car out of the way, out of the gate, he stopped it there. They had to stop with the remains, too. That's why we saw it. But why should we see an old-fashioned coffin? (*Do you have any idea why?*) No, no idea in the world. (*And when you put your arm around her, she saw it too?*) Oh, yeah. Well, that'll happen to anybody that'll see something, if you touch somebody else, they'll see it. Not the skin, just the clothes. That's the only time I ever touched anybody. I've seen things, and other people with me, and I wouldn't say a word. I'm sure they never saw it, because if they would have, they'd have said.

Oh, I've seen a lot of things. I was working in the mine, and I had a bad cold. Our house wasn't fit to be living in. Dishes were rattling, and doors opening. Dan Patterson used to come to the door and holler, "Whoa!" My mother was wanting me to quit, you know—"You're going to get killed." "No, I'm not. You're hearing all those things—I'm going to get killed, I'm going to get killed—there's nothing."

(*What did it mean that Dan Patterson came to the door and yelled, "Whoa!"?*) Well, he had a horse. Hold your pants on, you'll hear. I had an awful bad cold, and this Johnny MacLeod had come down from Lochaber, he had come home to go to work in the mines. So I said, "Work my shift tonight." We were digging a shaft—the first shaft. So, all right. I stayed home. I don't know what time that night—an 8-by-8 that this blast had loosened came down and hit him right on the back of the neck, killed him. And they just took the body into the compressor house and laid it on a bench there. Sent word to his mother to come down. And we thought it was terrible for her to come down and see the body in the machine shop there. So we took his body over to the house. And Dan Patterson took him over. And when he came to the door, he hollered, "Whoa," stopping the mare, you know. That's what we were hearing, one of the things we were hearing.

Talk. We used to hear talk. I maintain that if a body is above the ground more than three days, that you hear a lot more about it. See, they had an inquest—I think it was maybe 5 days. (*Do you mean you hear a lot more about it before it happens?*) Yeah, that's right. (*How did you feel, realizing that could have been you?*)

It didn't bother me. I guess I didn't have brains enough to bother me. I always figure, when you're born, your life is slated. You're supposed to be sitting there right now. The day you're going to die is there, too. I really believe that.

I'm sure there's an answer to prayers. I'm certain of that. When I was in Terra Nova one time, I took 3 loads of lumber into Sydney, and I had double chains on the truck. To come up the mountain, I had to put the chains on. So I put them on the first two times. And then it was about 9 or 10 o'clock at night and I was getting tired. I started praying up at East Bay that I wouldn't have to put the chains on, that I'd get up the mountain— you know, it was all ice. I came up that mountain the same as if it was July. That's when I was sure there was an answer for prayer.

Another time when I was sure there was an answer for prayers, that's when I moved to Loch Lomond. The winter of '41. It was, oh, terrible snow. And I had got a new truck. I had the boys cutting, and I had 7 loads of wood ready for to send to Sydney. And there was no way I could get out. And there was a bulldozer up on the mountain. I made 5 trips up there, snow up to here, to see if I could get him down. Terrible going up the mountain. And I finally got him, the 5th day, he said he'd come— $5.05 an hour. Can you imagine? Today a bulldozer like that's around $80 an hour. So, I got 7 loads into Sydney right slap bang, as soon as he opened the road. Without drawing any money. Then I got the cheque. I went up and cashed it, and I paid everything. And I came back and paid the boys. I had dinner in Sydney, which would only be maybe a dollar-something at that time. I had $2.60 left, but I could thumb my nose to anybody in Cape Breton as far as my credit was concerned.

(*You had prayed for that?*) Oh yeah. Yeah. I prayed for that bulldozer, to get that road open. Night after night. My wife was saying, "You're crazy. You're killing yourself walking up over the snow, and it won't come." I said, "It's coming, don't you worry." (*And you feel it's your prayers that did it?*) Oh, I'm sure it was. (*When you pray like that, do you do it privately?*) Oh, privately. I think that if you're out in your truck or walking the road or something and you pray, that's a lot more important than praying where somebody else is hearing you. It tells you right in the Bible to pray in private.

(*Was your family always like that, or is it just yourself that has that kind of feeling about prayer?*) My parents before me, oh, definitely. My father died when I was a year old. But my grandfather—oh, I was brought up with my uncles and my grandfather. We were so poor, my mother had to go to the States to work, to send money home. Even if it was a fine hay day, and it was going to rain, my grandfather would have to pray and read the Book at dinner time and at breakfast time and at supper time. This is weekdays, that I'm talking about reading the Bible. On Sunday, you couldn't clean the barn—I think that was a sin. It used to freeze up, and it was terrible to clean it on Monday. You couldn't haul water from the spring, nor you couldn't wash potatoes or herring, or read a paper—oh, that was a terrible thing, to read a paper, if you had one.

Another thing. I used to walk from here to church, you know. When I got married first, I walked every Sunday to church. If you had a cent in the house, you put it in the collection. Monday you'd get it twofold, or Tuesday for sure. It never failed.

(*Did anyone ever come back to you?*) No. But when my Uncle Angus died—my uncle and his wife died on the same day, with the flu in 1918. And my mother and Angus, they were dressed alike, you know, when they were growing up. And Mother came home from the States, you know, when they died. There was only I and my grandfather there. And oh, she was in an awful state, crying every day, crying every day. And when Angus died, he had left a young son. Well, till the day she died, she said Angus came back one night and told her to smarten up and look after his son. We saw a change in her, but she didn't tell us at first what it was. But later she always said that's what it was.

(*You were telling me of a house....*) Oh, that—it was the devil that was there. (*Do you really think so?*) Oh, I don't know what it was. There was a crooked stairs coming down from the attic, around the flue. And this rack-

284

et—oh, loud—started in the attic. You could hear it coming down around the flue. It wasn't orderly walking, it was like this. (*Stamping?*) Yeah. He came down to the upstairs, and then he'd come down this stairs and go into the front room. And that's it. Didn't hear any more. Well, I went in there one night, and I figured it was someone who wanted to buy the place—that he was getting up in the attic some way. And I was sure, if it was something, I'd see it, you know.

So I put the lamp on the table here, and the door was there, and the stairs were coming down here. So sure enough, at 10 o'clock this racket started. Came down to the upper floor, and then started down. When I figured he was—I was right near the door—it was right opposite the light, you know—I pushed the door open. Nothing. Noise stopped and there was nothing. So I don't know what it was. (*Anything else happen besides the noise?*) Oh yes, they had to leave there. A thing would get up off that shelf and go across to that shelf—they'd see it going across. And the clothes that were on your bed like this, used to get up and turn right around—perfect—go on the opposite way. And it was worse in April, every 7 years, it was worse than ever.

There was a fellow came down here—he was supposed to know everything about this. And they came out here to see if I'd go with them, and I said, "Yes. I'll take you up there." (*This is the fellow that used to live in that house.*) I figured he'd have the key. So we drove out, went to the woods where he was. "No," he said, "I left the key at the house." But he told us where the ladder was. "There's a window upstairs," he said, "that's never closed. You could close that window and go downstairs; come up in half an hour, it was open again."

So this fellow (who came down) was all—you know—what wasn't he going to do! He was going to take pictures of the kitchen and all this. We got the ladder for him and put it up, and he went in on the window. It wasn't two minutes he was back out again. I don't know. He never told us what he saw. But anyway, he took pictures outside—toward a window. And there were two women standing in the window. (*Did you see two women?*) Well, there were no women there, but they were in the picture. I saw the picture. (*Did you know the women?*) No. (*Did anybody know the women?*) No.

·   ·   ·

(*Getting back to the mine....*) I think she'll be going again around '90. (The Stirling Mine.) Up this way. (To the west.) Yeah. We've heard her working. Others have heard it too, in the same direction. (*And you expect it in the '90s.*) Well, that's only my guess. Might be longer than that, might be closer than that. Dear knows. (*But it's coming.*) Oh, it's coming, I've got no doubt in my mind. And this hill here, it'll be a city.

When I was 11 years old I was skating on the ice, and this was all full of lights, small lights down below and bigger ones up above. Oh, I took off for home. I didn't know what it was. The next year again, I went into Sydney (for the first time) with my uncle in the horse and wagon. And when we got to Dutch Brook or some place in there, you could see Sydney, you know. I was saying, "That's what I saw." So it'll be here. I don't know, it might be 200 years time, but it'll be here. There's no doubt in my mind....

(After the mine closed,) I had been working up in Guysborough, I was driving a tractor and constructing from Monastery to Guysborough. Working 16 hours a day. They wouldn't pay us when we were there first—I went to start the 24th of May, and in June, the first of June, they didn't have the money. Middle of June, they hadn't got their money from the department. And they gave us so much money. It was the first of July, or the 15th of July, that we got paid. I figured it out—I made 9 1/2 cents an hour. That's all I made. I quit. I figured that's it, I'll never work for a foreman any more, never. Best thing that ever happened.

We were hearing rumours of war, and we figured that we'd get a (saw) mill. We got a mill and started in the woods. Then we moved to Loch Terra Nova. We worked there—we were 10 years gone. My first wife and my kids. There was no farm then. We were running a sawmill. See, all during the war, we could get everything we wanted. We were working for National Defense, you know. If I wanted a pail of lard or bag of sugar, being we were working for National Defense, we were never short of tea or anything like that. We'd get all we want. (*Because National Defense was taking your wood?*) Oh, we wouldn't sell it to you or anybody else. We had to sell to them. (They were) the people that were building the barracks (at Point Edward). And see, they started taking our men away from us, you know, for the army. So they were going and going and going. It was hard to replace men, you know. No need of you taking a man from the city, putting him to work in the woods.

So at last they were all gone but two, I had two good fellows. And they had to be in Halifax on a certain night. So I took them into Sydney and put them on the train. I wrote a night letter to Col. Mingo—that was the guy that was head of it. I told him, "If those men aren't back here tomorrow, I'll shut the mill down and I'll go to work for industry. I can make just as much money there, and shut her down." They were back. Six months' leave, you know. And then they had to apply the next, and got 6 months more. I told them, you know, I wrote a long letter. I said I was getting sick and tired of hiring men that didn't know a crosscut or a bucksaw from a hoe. Oh, I got them back.

Then in 1949 I bought this place. (*Your home here at Stirling.*) And my wife was telling me, "Oh, you're crazy. The mine isn't going." I said,

"The mine is going, I know it's going." So I got this place for a song. I knew the guy that bought it, from the old people that were here. He had bought it through this money from the war. So I figured he was going to sell it. That's how we got this place. I had the mill all set up here, and the first time they wanted lumber for the mine, I had it for them. (*At this time there was no mine or talk of a mine, 1949.*) No. But they started in '50. (*You felt they were going to start again?*) Oh yeah, I was sure. I moved the mill and everything down here to be ready for them. John G. came down when I was building the house and the mill. "Did you buy any shares?" She was after starting. "Did you buy any shares?" "No," I said, "I didn't buy any shares. I've got shares enough right here." I had the mill down here just in time to supply them with the lumber they needed.

(*Why do you think you're able to foretell that sort of thing?*) Oh, I don't know. (*Was that in your family before you?*) The MacDermids and Morrisons, they were full of it.

Now where my daughter is, that house was haunted. People had to leave there. After the power went in, I was telling my daughter, "You'll never hear anything." Oh, they used to see a black dog coming in and going upstairs, and hear noises and things. There were two families had to leave there. But once the power went in there, they never heard anything any more.

You don't see anything where there's electricity—at least I don't. And I don't hear of anybody else seeing things. (*Too busy watching television?*) Well, no. I think there's something in the air that forbids that.... I don't know what it is. When I was growing up, I wouldn't walk in the middle of the road in the night if you'd give me a thousand dollars. You know, you'd meet funerals on the road. Knock you down and, well, pretty near kill you. You'd feel compressed, you know? Like everything was pressing on you. You don't hear that now any more since the power came in. (*You mean funerals that weren't really there.*) There was nothing there. You wouldn't see anything. It was just like compressed, it would knock you down. And I've heard different fellows who rolled off the road. Nobody in this country when I was growing up as a young fellow would walk in the middle of the road in the night-time, no way.

I was coming home up in St. Esprit, or Framboise Intervale, you'd call it. And that happened to me. I was only maybe 19 or 20. So I'd never walk in the middle of the road again. And the funeral that it was, it wasn't too long afterward when it came through. A fellow got killed out west or something and his remains came home, came in a horse and sleigh from St. Peters. This happened to me in the wintertime, and the funeral came before the winter was over.

(*We call this place Stirling—it wasn't the mine gave it that name?*) Nothing to do with the mine. (*That name has been here since when?*) Since the first settlers settled here, nothing to do with the mine. (*You were telling me that the highway department changed the name.*) They spelled it "Sterling." We had a post office right here—"Sterling"—that's sterling silver. But "Stirling," that's Stirling, Scotland—that's what this place originally got its name from. We didn't go looking for it early enough, I guess, to find out who called it Stirling, or how did it happen. (*The highway department tried to put up signs?*) They put up "e" instead of "i." I think about 30 of them. I went up to see the guy. He got kind of saucy to me. "I'll get the dictionary," he said, "and I'll prove it to you." I said, "You get the map of Scotland and see what it's spelled like." They changed all the signs but one that's at the end of Grand River bridge. We lost our post office, but we weren't going to lose our name. People come looking for you today down at Gabarus—you know, it's R. R. 1, Gabarus.

I'll tell you another instance, just to show you the way they used down here. When Danny was going into Grade 9. See, the teacher here taught him till Grade 8, and a very good teacher. When he was going into Grade 9, he was going to St. Peters. And Kenny Angus Ferguson was going up to St. Peters, and I told him, "Pick up Grade 9 books for Danny." This was just a week before the school started. So when he came back, he said, "They haven't got them. Have to wait two weeks till they see if there'll be any left over in Arichat or L'Ardoise or someplace." I jumped in the truck. I went up there, and I said, "I'm here for Grade 9 books for Danny, my son." "Oh," she said, "we haven't got any. We've got to wait a couple of weeks." "Well," I said, "order a set." "Oh, can't do that." "Well," I said, "let me use your phone." I said, "I'll call a fellow in Halifax, and I'll guarantee you there'll be a set of books on that express coming out of Halifax." I have a first cousin in Halifax—oh, he'd tear the damn place apart if he wouldn't get what he wanted. She went into the back room, boy, and came out with a complete set of books. Just holding them there to see if any of the other schools wouldn't need them, and to hell with my son down here. I got the books, anyway. (*So you really feel that this end of the country gets the last of everything.*) Oh, yes. Always has been the case.

．　　　　　．　　　　　．

Oh, I trapped. I bet you I wasn't much bigger than that fellow (Dan Alex's young grandson) when I got an otter. Oh, I could trap, oh yes. I used to trap muskrats and set snares for fox. (*How did you learn?*) My grandfather. (*What would he tell you?*) You wouldn't understand it, it would be Gaelic. It'd be just telling you how to set it, and showing you, and setting one, that's it. That'd be all Gaelic, you know, there'd be no English.

Then it was a good thing he did teach me, because in the Hungry '30s, in 1931 and '32, I worked at McGuire's Ice in Sydney in the summertime—$3 a day. And I used to quit the 15th of October and come home and get my trap-line ready. And then when the season opened, I used to leave as soon as it would be light enough to see in the woods. And I'd go in here and travel all the back country. Twice my wife got people to go looking for me—I wouldn't be back. But I made twice the money in the trapping season that I did all summer in Sydney.

(Did you enjoy trapping?) Oh, did I ever. Any day I'd enjoy it. I used to make sandwiches of beans. You know, to make the bread right juicy. Oh, I loved that. I'd have a sandwich in this hand, and I never stopped to eat it, I just kept walking. I remember one day in the wintertime, I got 5 fox, and I had to skin 2 of them, they were too heavy to carry. And I got some other little furs beside, muskrat or mink or something.

I imagine the biggest thrill of my life was when I got the first fox. I'd say I was only, maybe, 9 or 10 years old. In 1914. I guess the first otter I got, I was only 10 years old—and he was alive. Well, I thought I killed him. It was muskrats I was looking for. But I put him on my back—his head was up here, his tail was on the ground. I was only small. I took him home. I thought he was dead, but he was only stunned. Oh, my grandfather got awful cross. You know, he could have bit my neck or something. But I got $20 for him in 1914. That was a lot of money for a little fellow to get. So I trapped all my life then.

I figured when I stopped trapping on a big scale, I'm sure you could take me out of the house here, blindfolded, take me any which way you want, spin me around in the woods: "Home is there" (pointing), and I

have no doubt in my mind, that's where it was. You seem to get like an animal when you're in the woods all the time. Didn't bother me a bit to go in the woods. Since I got older, I always take a compass, but I never use it. You know, you lose faith, I guess, in yourself, or something.

(When I look at your diaries, it's you worked, worked, worked, went to church, worked, worked, worked. Now, I don't think working like that is something that comes automatically. I mean, I think that people learn to work. Maybe I'm wrong.)

I always liked work. We had to walk a mile and a quarter to school. And the girl that came to school with me walked about a quarter of a mile further. I'll bet you if you got the register for while we were going to school, you'll never find where we missed a day—rain, shine, or storm. And in the spring, you know, there'd be snowbanks along the road. We had a sheep-house down below the house. We used to go in there and take our shoes off and leave them there. We always went to school in the summertime, without shoes.

My grandfather was a good worker. He worked right up till the last. He was 84 years old when he died. My other grandfather was 95 when he died, on my father's side. So there's hopes for me to get a few more years in. I'll be 80 my next birthday. But if you get enough rest and good food to eat, I don't think hard work will ever kill you. I think it's good for you.

Oh, I had a good life, I was never sick. I had an operation about 6, 7 years ago. That's the first time I was in a hospital. That's the first time I got a needle—I wasn't vaccinated when I went to school—I don't know why. And that's the first time I ever wore pyjamas. The first night I went in there, before the operation, at 9 o'clock, I was sound asleep. And I felt something working at my hand, and I woke up, and there was a nurse there. She had two pills—I said, "What's that for?" "Sleeping pills." I said, "Are you crazy? Waking me up to give me sleeping pills!" "Well, doctor's orders." "Well," I said, "you put them in the waste-basket." I said, "I'm not going to take them." Neither did I.

Hector Carmichael & Alex Kerr

In some cases, names have been changed in these stories, both to maintain the intimacy of good friends getting together and to still honour privacy.

Hector Carmichael: I had a visit from another fellow recently. (*Did you tell him stories?*) No, no. He wouldn't pay me. But tonight you took a fellow with you with lots of money.

Alexander Kerr: I hope he'll find it. You know, I'll be 16 the first of June.

Hector: If you had horns on, I'd believe you were 16.

Alex: No, but I'll be 53.

Hector: Now, boy, the first thing you know, you'll be as old as me.

Alex: That fellow with the chains will be looking for me long before that.

Hector: I hope you won't be like that fellow, they wouldn't take him in Heaven for sure, and then they wouldn't take him in Hell—there were too many like him there. And how are you? (*Good. A little greyer.*)

291

Hector: Are you? If you'll be coming here too often, boy, you'll be grey. And if you'll be traveling with Alex, you'll get grey soon enough.

Alex: You'll be liable to be bald-headed if you'll be traveling with me.

Hector: And how's everyone up with you?

Alex: Oh, they're all growling and complaining.

Hector: How's the old man?

Alex: He'll be 79 in February, and he chews about 3 pounds of Club Tobacco a day. He's got it sprayed right from his eyebrows to the toes of his shoes.

Hector: Last time you were here, you were with a minister.

Alex: That's why I was traveling with him. So I'll stay religious.

Hector: Here about 25 or 30 years ago—no, more than that—40 years ago. Fellows used to go around selling bootleg coal from over south there. It was much cheaper than the other coal. So I got a load of coal, and a few mornings after that I got up and put the fire on and I went to the pantry there to wash myself—holy smokes! Away goes the stove. The lights were all over the floor. And I couldn't see anything but smoke and the side of the stove was blown out to smithereens, all in pieces. A dynamite cap, I guess, was in the coal. You, Alex, that's the winter you fellows were cutting lumber.

Alex: It must have been all the cursing I was doing out there that blew that stove. Hector, you were the one who painted Donald's new shoes.

Hector: Yes. We were working over at Murray there, you know. And I was painting the boat—red copper paint—Donald was standing and he couldn't see me at all, but I could see his feet. Poor soul, it was a new pair of shoes. He was showing us the shoes before. So I got the brush under the board—I could get to his feet—and I painted his shoes red.

Alex: Was it you that took the can of linseed oil on a fellow, and put the gallon of waste oil in the can?

Hector: Yes. We were working at Murray over here, you know. There was work over there for years and then they quit, they were closing up, and aw, there was a lot of stuff they had over there—fellows used to swipe it, different ways. But I never swiped a nail. I wouldn't. But there was a gallon of linseed oil there, and one fellow that was over, he says, "By gosh, there's something there that I'm going to have. I'm going to do a lot of painting when I move." So myself and another fellow went to work and we took the linseed oil out of the can and put old motor oil in, used motor oil. Next morning he came up—"Where's that can of linseed oil." "Oh, it's here." "Oh," he said, "that'll be awful handy for me anyway."

Alex: Heading down the road with the gallon of waste oil.

Hector: Yeah. I was wondering if he put it in the paint. I never found out.

Alex: Remember there was a 5-gallon can of brake fluid down there in the garage, and Ian took it for his own truck, and he was telling us about it, he was going to hide it. And Sandy was in there and he took it when Ian wasn't looking. He got it out the garage door and went up the doctor's brook with it and hid it up there. And I told Ian that he'd buried it in the sawdust out back where they used to keep the ice, told him he'd find it there. Well, he shoveled it right to the cement floor trying to find it, and he never found it to this day.

Hector: We used to have a lot of fun out of there.

Alex: Boy, I'm telling you. Well, Hector, Philip's wife was telling me a funny story this winter. About this fellow went to a wake, and I guess he was sitting down talking in Gaelic for awhile, and he said, "Oh, indeed, I think I'll go in the bedroom and cry for awhile. It won't look good unless I cry." And he went in the bedroom and you could hear him roaring all over North Gut. And then he'd come out and talk and laugh for another spell. And then he'd go back again and have another cry.

And Hector, was it you and John J. put snowshoes on the fellow the night of John's wedding?

Hector: Yes. That was early in September, over in Murray there, away up on the hill—there was a wedding there that night and a lot of people there. And there was this fellow, and we were having a few drinks. And I don't know what possessed him, but he went up to the outhouse, and he met me, and he had the snowshoes with him. And I said, "Come on, put them on." So, he started walking around with them on on bare ground, and at last he went over a rock and he tumbled with the snowshoes on—and he couldn't get up.

Another time, I played a trick over at Red Murdoch's one night. There was a milling frolic over at Rory Kerr's, you know. It was in the spring of the year. And the ice was bad, but I could go across from down here. I wasn't married then at all, and living up at the other home. There was nobody went across the ice that wanted to go but myself. Went across. That was all right. They had the milling. Then, shortly when I was getting ready to leave, there were 3 fellows and 3 girls left there, and they came over to Red Murdoch's and they went in there, and I was coming behind them. And they were all sitting down in the kitchen. Well, I thought it'd be a great joke to lock the door from the outside. I went to an outhouse there and I got a rope, you know, and there was a big tree right opposite the door. I tied the rope to the door and tied it tight to the tree. So after awhile, when the boys were ready to go home, they couldn't get out. But the kitchen was low, you know, and they went upstairs and they went out on a roof and they jumped off the roof—probably 6 or 8 feet—and that's how they got home. But that wasn't the funny part of it. This fellow was still on the milling board. And when he was going home, he went right by Red Murdoch's. And they had a great big long platform crossing there, and there was a great big hole down below where they would throw everything, garbage—well, this fellow came along and he never noticed this rope and it tripped him and away he went, down among the garbage. Well, the first time he met me—"Oh well, you're a devil. If I had a gun, I'd shoot you."

Alex: I remember Willy when he was up at the house one time telling us a story of old Peter when he was down at Murray. Somebody came up from Englishtown selling eels one day and old Peter bought some, and Willy watched his chance and he stole the eels on Peter—Peter was going to send a water boy or something for them, so his wife would cook them for supper. Willy watched his chance and took them in and was going to get the water boy himself to take them up, so Peter wouldn't know a thing about them. He took them up to the forge and he was telling the blacksmith what he was going to do with the eels, and in the meantime he happened to look out the door when he was telling the blacksmith about stealing Peter's eels, and who was coming to the forge door but old Peter. So Willy just real quick buried them in the coal. And Peter came in, and he was taking a leak in the coal, telling them about somebody stealing his eels.

Hector: Did he ever tell you the time he sent the lambs over? You know, everybody had sheep then, and they used to have lambs in the spring of the year. And this morning Willy went to the barn and there was two dead lambs there—it was an awful cold morning. So that night he took the two lambs over and put them in Peter's sheep stable. So next morning when Peter went out to the stable, there were two frozen lambs there. Came in and was telling his wife about the frozen lambs, and he couldn't figure out—he was trying to figure out—what sheep had them. He wanted his wife to go over to the barn and try and find out, could she tell what sheep had had them.

(The trouble they would go through to pull a joke.)

Alex: Well, I'm telling you. Spend all night at it to put somebody through misery. Who was it now, Hector, that tightened the sulky wheels on Allister when he was going to Baddeck?

Hector: That was Murdoch Ban and John J. They put a washer on the nuts, you know, and tightened them up, and Allister was going to Baddeck. And my gosh, started off and the wheels wouldn't turn around at all. Used to be a lot of tricks. They played another trick on him one night. He had a little flat-roofed shed with the barn there, and they put this sulky up on the roof of the shed. Well, I don't know which one of them went there early in the morning, start telling them about the gale of wind last night, that he never heard such wind in his life, you know. Then he says, "Look where the wind must have put the sulky, look where your sulky is." And the fellow turned around to his wife, "Aw, look—look where the wind put the sulky last night."

Norman Carmichael: And do you remember the fellow, when his brother died, he went over to North Sydney to get a suit for him. So he went into this place and they asked him what size he wanted, and he said, "Well, about my size." "Well," they said, " I've got a suit here that'll fit you, but the legs are a way too long." "Oh," he said, "that's nothing. He can roll them up."

Hector: That same fellow came into John J.'s and he was looking for boards to make a box for a casket. He came in and he said to John J.—the old fellow was dead two or three days now—he said, "The old fellow wants to know if you would give him any lumber."

Alex: And at wakes. I saw two fellows putting a clothespin on a woman's nose one night—she was asleep in the armchair about 3 o'clock in the morning. It was at a wake, and the noise she let out nearly woke the dead fellow up. She fell asleep and these two fellows went out to the clothesline and got a clothespin and snapped it on her nose.

Hector: I'll tell you about myself. I had a vessel one time and she capsized, a schooner, a sailing vessel. We left Sydney in the morning. There was a big mill up at South Haven, and I was mostly hauling lumber from that fellow all summer. So coming back—this was the first trip in the spring—I had three or four truckloads of stuff we dumped in the hold before we left over there—hay and oats and stuff—most of it for this fellow that had the mill over here.

But coming off Cape Dauphin, you know—nice little sailing breeze—there was something awful happened. And I don't know and I'll never know what it was. I heard an awful queer noise, and I couldn't understand what it was. It was to windward. And the first thing I knew, it tipped the vessel. It hit the foresail first and it went through the foresail, the foresail went in ribbons. And she capsized. She leaned over so fast everything went over on her side and she filled full of water on her beam end. The boat was on the davits and she was head first down in the water and we couldn't get it clear. She floated, but there was so little of her up.

The fishermen came out from the shore with their motor-boat and they took us ashore. I sent for a tow-boat from North Sydney. He came next morning, and she drifted out with the tide pretty near off Breton Cove. It took him two days to take her in. Took her in along side the old plaster pier—it was still up. But when we'd raise her up, she'd go down underwater. But we hauled her in at high tide one morning with tackles and everything we could get on her, as high as we could. Then we straightened her up. When the tide went down, the deck was clear of water. There were about 20 men there that day, and in two hours she was dry—not a drop of water. There were two pumps in her and about 10 men with buckets—didn't take us very long to bail her out at all. And after that, we got her going.

Alex: Now that was a funny thing whatever caused that.

Hector: There was an old fellow at Englishtown. And he happened to be outside about that time, and he heard the same thing that I heard—he heard the noise but couldn't understand what it was—the same thing I heard just a few seconds before it struck. That was strange, you know.

There was a rumpus one time and they were drinking. And there was a fellow when he was going home, whatever possessed him, he tried to go through the river down below the bridge—in place of going over the bridge. He went across the intervale there and the river carried him away and he got drowned. And they were looking for him everywhere for two or three days. But there were two or three fellows in a boat up there one day, and this old Allan MacDonald, he lived down below the river on the Murray side—he told those fellows in the boat a place to go—"Look over there, see if he's there on the bottom"—they went over there and by gosh, they found his body on the bottom. Old Allan said that he was sitting one fine evening, a few years before then, and it was calm—he was sitting at the door, and he saw a man's hand sticking out of the water, waving— right where they found that fellow. Well now, that was pretty funny. That's 1926.

Norman: Didn't John Hector see something down here one day, and he pulled the horse and sleigh off the road into the snow and stopped.

Hector: He claimed he met a horse with a casket, a funeral.

Norman: His mother asked him, "Why did you pull off here?" He said, "Why? I'm letting the funeral by."

Hector: But you know, I used to come round that cove all hours of the night, and I never saw anything. I remember one night how I met the ghost all right. But I found out in a little while it wasn't a ghost at all. I was coming around there one night—12 o'clock or later—but, by gosh, right near the end of the cove there, the fellow was standing right in the middle of the road. And I figured he had a white shirt on him, black suit— and by God, I thought he was a man, you know. So I stooped down and got two or three rocks in the ditch of the road. I said, "Whoever you are, you better move or speak." And I hit this thing and it jumped up, and it was a horse, a mare—and she had a white streak down her nose there. The way she was standing there, you'd think it was a man. And I'm sure there are fellows that run back, they saw that ghost there.

Alex: That would be a real *bochan*. (*But would you say no one ever saw anything?*)

Hector: Oh, I don't know, you know. I don't know. I never saw anything. But my wife's brother, Norman, he lived down near Wreck Cove, and do you know, he was going home one night and there was a man come out on the road from a house, and he was coming behind him. And when he'd stop, this man would stop. And at last he got scared, you know. Started running. And when he'd run, this man would run too. Followed him down to the cemetery. And this fellow that was following went into the cemetery. The two men came alongside each other. The fellow in the cemetery said, "Good thing for you, what you have in your pocket"—that's the only word he said to him when he walked into the cemetery. Norman ran home. He was pretty scared when he got home. Well, what Norman had in his pocket was a testament—I think it was a catechism.

And another time, you know, the night at the wake over on the hill there, where the old fellow died. You know, there were two fellows went over from here, two young fellows—I guess they were 15 or around—and they didn't go over there for anything good, you know. Went to try and have some fun. They were laughing a lot there. And look, boy, after they left there, something happened to them, they got scared by light. Some queer light came around them and scared the living life out of them. They got down to where one of them was living on this side, but the other wouldn't come over home that night alone, unless someone was coming. Those fellows got that scared after they left there. Isn't that funny.

The reason I tell you stories like this is, I want to keep Alex here on the right path.

Alex: Did you ever hear about the time when Gillis was up at North River and Angus was janitor of the church? And you know how Gillis would preach for hours. One Sunday there was a hell of a storm and frosty out in the wintertime. And the janitor went out early to put a fire on for 11 o'clock. And then there was the minister and only two or three more showed up for church. And they were wondering if they'd have church or not. So one of them said to Angus—they were talking in Gaelic, you know—"What do you think about having a church service, Angus?" "Well," he said, "if I went to the barn to feed the cows and there was only one there, I'd feed her."

Then they went into church and Gillis preached the same as if the church was full. And poor Angus was starved to death with how long he was away from home, putting the fire on and all this in the church. Well, lo and behold, they get out and Gillis was shaking hands with them going out the door, asked if he liked the service. "Oh yes," he said. "Service was all right. But if I went to the barn to feed the cows and only one showed up, I wouldn't give her the whole mow."

Hector: They used to chew tobacco in church sometimes. There was a minister in the North River church then, his name was John Fraser, he was pretty stern—he was a real preacher, but he was cross, you know, and cranky. And they used to have to go to church every month and scrub the floor because of tobacco spit. So he turned turk this morning—this day he told them: "Some of you gentlemen," he said, "has got a habit of chewing tobacco in church. It's a dirty habit. Now," he said, "the next day you come to church with a chew of tobacco in your mouth, put it on the gatepost out there—and I'll guarantee you that a crow or a dog won't touch it—and it'll be there when you go out, and you can go with it."

Alex: Was Malcolm ever telling you, Hector, about the time he went working for the undertaker? He went working with this undertaker in Sydney—he was only a young fellow and he was scared to death, but I guess jobs were scarce so he had to take what he could get. So there was this little old man dead upstairs, and the undertaker wanted Malcolm to take the remains—go up and carry it down so they'd get the remains ready. When he was coming down the stairs with him, there was still some wind left in the old fellow and Malcolm got scared to death and he dropped him on the stairs and he kept on coming. The undertaker asked him, "Where's the body?" "Look," he said, "anybody that can blow wind can walk."

Hector: I'll tell you a story. Did you ever hear of the fellow that stole the skates on the Indian? That'd be a long, long time ago, when they were building the railroad through Cape Breton down here to Sydney—they were working up around Orangedale. And this Hector MacLean, they say he was a wonderful skater—there was never a man on the harbour here that could touch him skating. So in the wintertime he took a notion to come home, and he was walking home. And he got down to Nyanza. There was a bunch of Indians out on the ice, skating. Whatever possessed him, he went down and he pretended he never saw anybody on skates before. And they thought, you know, it would be a great joke to put the skates on Hector. Aw, Hector wasn't very fussy. He pretended, you know, and they coaxed him to put the skates on. They put the skates on, tied them on him—Hector got up. And he fell down—and aw, they were laughing to beat sixty. They were gonna have a great time. But Hector got up and away he goes. And the Indians after him. And they couldn't catch him. He skated down to Baddeck Bay, then walked to South Gut, and skated from South Gut. And Hector landed in Goose Cove with the Indian's skates. And that's a true story, you know.

Did you ever hear of Ottawa Angus? He was born, I think, up at Ottawa Brook, about 30 miles above Baddeck, you know—he used to spend most of his time the other side of Boisdale—but he came up and worked at the Quarry and out in the woods there. And oh my God, he was an awful comical man—he'd make a dog laugh, you know. Anyway, he used to be witty as the deuce. He was out in the woods and a fellow was there, claimed he could cure toothache. And they were sitting in the camp one night, and they were telling stories. They asked this fellow how to cure toothache. And he told them, "Well, I have two ways: there's one way, I give the person a verse out of the Bible—write it down and give it to them, and I make a little prayer. But some other times," he says, "if there's a hole in the tooth, I put my tongue in the hole before I pray"—and Ottawa Angus was sitting down there. He was witty. And he said, "By God," he said, "I wonder would that be any good for the piles?"

Ottawa Angus, he was working over at Sydney one time, and every meal was fish, fish, fish—pretty near every meal. This night it was fish again. After supper, Angus came down with his suitcase filled up. "Where are you going," they asked him. "Aw my God, I think I'm going to Margaree to spawn."

Alex: Remember when yourself and Frank were killing the bull?

Hector: It's well I do. The bull was a little cross and Frank was scared of him. I asked him, "Where are you going to hang him up?" "Oh, inside here." "Well, we'll take him in there." "Oh no, no, God," he said, "he's cross. We'll kill him outside." So I hit the bull with the axe that was there and the bull came down and Frank bled him. And Frank's sister hollered to us, "I have tea in here. You fellows better come in and have a cup of tea before you start on that animal." Went in, had our tea. We went out and there was no sign of the bull. Well, that was all right. The door of the outhouse where we were going to hang him up was open. Look around, no sign of the bull. But I noticed a streak of blood on the door. Looked. Here was the bull. He was standing inside, just below the tackle. Wasn't that funny? And we went in and Frank gave him a push and down he went.

Alex: He was just trying to help you fellows along.
Was I ever telling you about the time when we were kids up home—Peter and I had a .22 and we were forever—if we had money—we'd be getting bullets. Firing bullets at every damn thing. And jeez, we got to be pretty good with this .22. But one day Danny MacAskill was over with the old man, gonna kill the pig. Peter and I started wanting them to let us shoot the pig. The old man was telling us to fly the hell out of the barn with that .22. But Danny said, "Let them try shooting her. If they can hit her, fine; if not, I'll catch up with her with the pole axe." The pig was in the sheep place, and the door was boarded up so high. At last the old man said, "All right, shoot her." Peter was the fellow that got the job of shooting the pig. And the pig had a habit of climbing up on her back in the trough. And she was kicking to beat hell. And the old man went in to put the knife in her and his toes caught on the top board and he just went on her. Well, if you ever saw over-

alls coming off a fellow in a hurry. She didn't leave him a thing but the braces. God, it was comical.

Hector: Used to be a lot of fun around here long ago.

Alex: Well, I guess, all kinds of it. (*Well, we'll have to take Alex home and let him get to bed now.*)

Hector: Oh, he doesn't go to bed at all, all night. (*What does he do?*)

Alex: I pray.

Printed in Canada